OX

MW00476166

ELEGIES OF CHU (in Chinese, *CHUCI*) is one of the two surviving collections of ancient Chinese poetry, and a source of inspiration for Chinese culture ever since. In spite of its historical importance, though, the anthology remains relatively unknown in the West. The *Elegies of Chu*, which contains passionate expressions of political protest and also shamanistic themes of magic spells and spirit wandering, has never fitted well within orthodox Confucianism, and as a result has often been excluded from the basic canon of early texts. Even in modern times, the anthology has only been translated once into English in its entirety, and that half a century ago. Precisely because of its unorthodox character, the *Elegies of Chu* is particularly fascinating to read today. To readers accustomed to thinking of traditional Chinese culture as pragmatic, group-oriented, and materialistic, *Elegies of Chu* presents a startling counterpoint of shaman-poets, gods and goddesses, mythological journeys, and solitary protest. Along with a select group of ancient prose texts like the *Zhuangzi* or *Classic of Mountains and Seas*, it presents an alternative face of early Chinese culture, full of the strange, marvellous, and magical.

NICHOLAS MORROW WILLIAMS is Associate Professor of Chinese literature at Arizona State University and Editor of *Tang Studies*. He studies and translates classical Chinese poetry in the contexts of comparative literature, Buddhist studies, Sino-Japanese cultural interactions, translation studies, intellectual history, and other fields. His publications include *The Residue of Dreams: Selected Poems of Jao Tsung-i* and *Imitations of the Self: Jiang Yan and Chinese Poetics*.

OXFORD WORLD'S CLASSICS

*For over 100 years Oxford World's Classics have brought
readers closer to the world's great literature. Now with over 700
titles—from the 4,000-year-old myths of Mesopotamia to the
twentieth century's greatest novels—the series makes available
lesser-known as well as celebrated writing.*

*The pocket-sized hardbacks of the early years contained
introductions by Virginia Woolf, T. S. Eliot, Graham Greene,
and other literary figures which enriched the experience of reading.
Today the series is recognized for its fine scholarship and
reliability in texts that span world literature, drama and poetry,
religion, philosophy, and politics. Each edition includes perceptive
commentary and essential background information to meet the
changing needs of readers.*

OXFORD WORLD'S CLASSICS

CHUCI

Elegies of Chu
An Anthology of Early Chinese Poetry

Translated with an Introduction and Notes by
NICHOLAS MORROW WILLIAMS

OXFORD
UNIVERSITY PRESS

OXFORD

UNIVERSITY PRESS

Great Clarendon Street, Oxford, OX2 6DP,
United Kingdom

Oxford University Press is a department of the University of Oxford.
It furthers the University's objective of excellence in research, scholarship,
and education by publishing worldwide. Oxford is a registered trade mark of
Oxford University Press in the UK and in certain other countries

Translation © Nicholas Morrow Williams 2022

The moral rights of the author have been asserted

First published as an Oxford World's Classics paperback 2022

Impression: 1

Published in the United States of America by Oxford University Press
198 Madison Avenue, New York, NY 10016, United States of America

British Library Cataloguing in Publication Data

Data available

Library of Congress Control Number: 2021950970

ISBN 978–0–19–881831–1

Printed and bound in Great Britain by
Clays Ltd, Elcograf S.p.A.

ACKNOWLEDGEMENTS

PAUL KROLL first suggested that I tackle the anthology and inspired me through his own iridescent translations of Chinese poetry, not to mention his now-indispensable dictionary. David Knechtges has for two decades been my model for rigorous attention to Chinese texts and their entire historical contexts. I would like to thank my many students and friends in Hong Kong for their patient and wise corrections. Above all I am grateful to my late father, who read this volume in draft, and encouraged me at every turn of the meandering journey that has somehow led me into the wilderness of Chu.

CONTENTS

CONTENTS

INTRODUCTION

THE anthology *Elegies of Chu* (*Chuci*) is one of the earliest collections of Chinese poetry, compiled in the second century CE, and a touchstone of Chinese culture ever since. While other ancient Chinese classics are dedicated to achieving political harmony or to recounting historical events, the poems compiled in the *Elegies* offer voices of protest, private frustration, and otherworldly longings. The vivid symbolism of the poems is drawn from the natural landscapes of southern China, while the spiritual journeys and dreams of immortality are inspired by local religious rites as well. The *Elegies of Chu* thus offers an enlightening perspective on ancient China that is often at odds with the orthodox political tradition that later prevailed.

The fundamental background of the anthology is that of the Zhou dynasty (1045–221 BCE), the long period when much of China's culture was established. But the unique literary and spiritual features of the anthology are distinctively tied to the specific cultural milieu of the southern state of Chu, an independent kingdom until the 3rd century BCE, as well as the Han dynasty (206 BCE–220 CE) when the text of the anthology as a whole was established. Indeed, the most remarkable thing about the anthology as a whole may be its synthesis of these various origins, beginning with the inspiring legends and governing models of the Zhou; taking flight from Chu with its reverence for magic and spirits unusual in the orthodox culture of premodern China; and ultimately coalescing under the sophisticated bureaucracy of the Han empire.

The Worlds of Ancient Zhou, Chu, and Han

In approximately the year 1045 BCE, King Wu defeated the ruling dynasty of Shang to establish the Zhou dynasty, with its capital near the modern city of Xi'an in Shaanxi province.[1] Though the historical sources for the early Zhou are limited, its governing institutions and doctrines have been inspirations and models for Chinese culture ever

---

[1] I generally follow the chronology established in the *Cambridge History of Ancient China*, edited by Loewe and Shaughnessy.

since. In particular, the Zhou victory was said to have moral implications, proving the Zhou regime to be vindicated by the mandate of Heaven itself. King Wu and his father, posthumously awarded the title King Wen, were seen not just as effective leaders but also as models of virtue. One of their most prominent virtues was said to be their appreciation of merit even in unlikely candidates, such as the hero Lü Wang, formerly a butcher in the Shang capital, but later a keen minister to both Kings Wen and Wu. Lü Wang is praised by name already in the first poem in the *Elegies*, the 'Li sao', where we read that while he 'was brandishing a butcher's knife—he found his true métier by meeting King Wen of Zhou'.

Though the Zhou remained the nominal authority over central China for some eight centuries, its actual power waned steadily. In 770 BCE, the capital was moved eastward to the site of modern Luoyang in Henan province, initiating the Spring and Autumn period, which lasted till 481 BCE. The tenuous nature of political authority legitimated by an ancient but impotent dynasty, but contested by numerous local states, was the context for the thought of Confucius (551–479 BCE) and his followers, who were closely concerned with the rituals and documents inherited from the early Zhou. Though Confucius and the key texts associated with him, like the *Analects*, are not mentioned frequently in the *Elegies*, the poets of the anthology share his deep concern over how a moral person can serve an imperfect ruler.

While most of the Spring- and Autumn-period states were located in the region around the Yellow River valley, several prominent ones were located to the south near the Yangtze River: Wu and Yue in modern Jiangsu and Zhejiang, and Chu in the area of modern Hunan and Hubei provinces. These diverse cultures included non-Chinese elements from other southern tribes, and their gradual incorporation into the Zhou realm was one of the major developments of this period. Chu in particular maintained an ambiguous identity, asserting its continuity with the Zhou while also possessing many unique beliefs and customs.

By the fifth century CE, the authority of Zhou itself became purely symbolic as China entered the period of rule under Warring States (481–221 BCE). Chu competed with independent states like Qin, based in modern Shaanxi, to its north, and Wu to the east, in an unceasing sequence of military encounters and diplomatic engagements. Though there were seven major states and other minor ones in this period, by the third century Qin was steadily absorbing its competitors, and in 221 completed the unification of the realm under a new dynasty, Qin. Though the Qin unification was pivotal in creating a unified sense of a Chinese culture, the Qin itself soon collapsed and was replaced by the new dynasty of Han in 206 BCE, which would endure for four centuries, a mighty empire on a par with the contemporary civilization of Rome.

It is because of Chu's unique position within Zhou history that the *Elegies* represent features of ancient Chinese culture that are not well described in other early Chinese texts.[2] For instance, another key source for our understanding of Zhou culture is the earliest anthology of Chinese poetry, the *Book of Songs* (*Shijing*). This is a compilation of 305 poems presenting a spectrum of voices from court and society that includes priests and lords, soldiers and farmers, husbands and wives. By contrast, the *Elegies* focus more narrowly on a particular figure, the frustrated courtier writing in critique of the current regime. But the anthology compensates for its narrowness of scope with a depth of interiority and longing, not to mention its depiction of transformative encounters with gods and goddesses having their origins in shamanistic rites barely hinted at in the *Book of Songs*.

Like the other Zhou states, Chu was an aristocratic one whose elite lineage putatively descended from the Yellow Emperor and other remote culture-heroes. Chu paid homage to the Zhou and engaged in diplomatic intrigues and warfare like the other states. Though its language had some dialectical differences it seems to have been more or less consistent with the reigning Zhou koine. But Chu was nevertheless distinctive in early China with regard to religious ritual and associated beliefs. We obtain a particularly vivid sense of Chu's distinctiveness from the vivid colour schemes and fantastic iconography of the paintings and sculptures of Warring States Chu that have been excavated in modern times.[3] The distinctive use of animal totems, in

---

[2] For a balanced overview of perspectives on early Chu, see the volume *Defining Chu*, edited by Constance A. Cook and John S. Major.

[3] Lothar von Falkenhausen has argued convincingly that Chu ritual music was not especially distinctive (in his essay 'Chu Ritual Music'). A survey demonstrating both the innovative and traditional features of Chu art is Jenny F. So, 'Chu Art: Link between the Old and New'.

particular birds and dragons, may reflect Chu's inheritance from the Shang civilization which had preceded the Zhou.

Chu religion was distinguished by its 'shamanistic' tendency in which the border between the human and the divine remained fluid. Instead of merely worshipping deceased ancestors, or spirits located remotely in the heavens, in Chu religion one class of specialized religious practitioners, the shamans (in Chinese *wu*), acted as spirit mediums who could cause the spirits to descend and possess them; or, alternatively, by entering the appropriate trance-like state, could cause their own souls to roam outside of their bodies to meet with the gods above. These shamanistic practices later became widespread throughout Chinese popular religion, though they were diminished in status relative to their role in Chu. In early China, though, they were a distinctive feature of Chu and perhaps other southern Chinese subcultures, but not as widely practised elsewhere.[4]

These religious practices are not described in much detail in the primary historical sources, probably because of the Confucian orientation of the Han scholars who edited and transmitted these texts, but they were fundamental to the art and literature of the Warring States era. Apart from the received textual tradition, the Chu region has been the source of many of the most remarkable archaeological finds of the past century, above all the funerary banner excavated from Mawangdui in Changsha, with its epic vision of an afterlife populated by ancestors, spirits, and animal totems. Though distinctive in ancient China, many of these beliefs would become more prominent in later Chinese religion, such as the 'summons to the soul' ritual. There was a contemporary belief that each person possessed two distinct souls, and that upon dying or on the verge of death one of these would fly outside of the body. A shaman would then perform a ritual summoning it back into the body, either to restore health or to console the departed. This forms the basis for the extraordinary 'Summons to the Soul' and 'Greater Summons' poems in the anthology, as well as the secularized adaptation 'Summons to the Recluse'.

Apart from their regional characteristics, though, the *Elegies* also reflect the broader historical context beyond Chu itself. Throughout the 3rd century BCE, Chu suffered a series of defeats at the hands of

---

[4] For a more thorough discussion of these issues see my article 'Shamans, Souls, and Soma'.

the expanding Qin state, leading up to its ultimate defeat in 223, and the establishment of a unified Qin empire in 221. The First Emperor of Qin (259–210 CE) was an extraordinary leader who standardized the Chinese script and established governing institutions, and whose vision is commemorated in the famous Terracotta Warriors who are entombed with him. His military victories and political reforms decisively ended any hope of Chu autonomy.

Less than two decades later, though, Qin itself was overthrown and replaced by the Han dynasty (202 BCE–220 CE). The Han was one of the golden ages of Chinese power, a vast empire that lasted four centuries, divided neatly by the interregnum of Wang Mang's rule, 9–23 CE, into the Former and Later Han. The founder of the Han, Liu Bang (256–195 BCE), was a native of Chu and elements of Chu culture were perpetuated by the Han aristocracy. The extant version of the *Elegies* is a product of the Han more than any other period, as it was compiled during the Later Han, and the better half of its contents were composed during the Han. There is continuing debate about which pieces actually do originate in pre-Qin Chu, but there can be no simple answer to this question, because even the Han poets were consciously following Chu models.

Under the Han, the legacy of Chu literature and music seems to have been maintained most vigorously at certain regional courts. This was partly the result of the gradual deterioration of the Chu state. By the mid third century BCE, after its old capital had been conquered by Qin in 278, the centre of gravity of the Chu state shifted eastward to the Huai River region, and its final capital was located at Shouchun (in modern Huainan city, Anhui province). Shouchun then became the central court of Liu An (179–122 BCE), Prince of Huainan, who may have compiled one early version of the *Elegies*. Several pieces within the anthology may have been composed at this court, and other poems show numerous parallels with the philosophical treatise *Huainanzi*, also compiled under the auspices of Liu An.

While poetic forms of old Chu were thus preserved and continued to thrive, moreover, they also exerted influence on new cultural forms more fitting to the vast Han empire. The primary literary form of the Han was the long poem known as the *fu* (or in English as the 'rhapsody'), which developed in large part out of the poetic styles in the *Elegies*. At the same time, though, it was during the Han that Confucian thought became the orthodox and ruling ideology. The scholars of the Han established a textual canon used in education and governance, and they consciously excluded the *Elegies* from the highest stratum of this canon, presumably because it contained rebellious and critical sentiments at tension with their ideals of political order.

Indeed, though later readers have sometimes tried to claim the *Elegies* retroactively as a Confucian document, there is not too much evidence for this in the poems themselves. Rather, the *Elegies* frequently borrow from a shared corpus of images, proverbs, and sayings that were widespread in Zhou and Han China. One of the most important sources is the tradition of Daoist philosophy initiated by the classic texts *Laozi* and *Zhuangzi*.[5] These are less oriented to the active methods and rules of governance than other Chinese philosophical classics, advocating instead self-cultivation and harmony with the patterns of nature. These books were also a source of inspiration for the practices and beliefs of religious Daoism, which began to take form during the Han and shares much with the shamanism of the *Elegies*. Other Daoist compilations which contain important references for the *Elegies* are the *Liezi*, attributed to another Warring States sage but apparently compiled later, and the *Huainanzi*, a more syncretistic compilation from the early Han that contains much common lore of the period, such as proverbs and cosmological speculation.[6]

Another key reference point for our understanding of the *Elegies* is the *Classic of Mountains and Seas* (*Shanhai jing*), a deeply mysterious work compiled in the Han but containing earlier material as well. Though it presents itself as documenting curious flora and fauna throughout the known world, it includes much material of mythical or even fictional origins. There is a considerable overlap between this text and the *Elegies*, with a number of deities or myths being mentioned exclusively in these two texts. This probably reflects the fact that most of the early Chinese texts that have survived were written from a rationalizing, Confucianistic perspective that excluded precisely these supernatural legends.[7]

---

[5] For *Zhuangzi*, which contains numerous parallel passages and sources, I have quoted mainly from Victor Mair's translation *Wandering on the Way*. There are innumerable translations of *Laozi* and I have not been able to rely on any single version.

[6] In the notes to this translation I cite the excellent modern translations of these works: A. C. Graham's *Book of Lieh-tzu* and the *Huainanzi* translated by John Major et al.

[7] For this text I have quoted from Anne Birrell's complete English translation, which has the unique feature of translating all the proper names literally into English.

Thus the *Elegies* possess an ambiguous historical role in China's culture, between shamanistic rituals of spiritual dislocation and the ruling institutions of a great bureaucratic empire. It is perhaps for this reason that the individual authorship of the poems has been so deeply contested in modern times, when this original tension has been re-evaluated in terms of modern debates around individualism, secularism, and political orthodoxy. The focal point of these debates has been the principal author of the anthology, a culture-hero who has been celebrated and even worshipped for the past two millennia.

Qu Yuan: Martyr, Sage, and Poet

The epic poem 'Li sao' is placed first in the *Elegies* as the most ambitious work in the anthology.[8] It is attributed to the Chu courtier Qu Yuan (*c*.300 BCE), who would have earned enduring fame for this poem alone; but in fact Qu Yuan has never been viewed simply as an author, as his life story is deeply embedded in broader political, historical, and religious developments—not to mention that many of its details may have been invented or at least embellished by later interpreters.

Qu Yuan's original name was Qu Ping, with 'Yuan' being the style name he adopted on reaching adulthood, and one can even distinguish, to some degree, between a historical 'Qu Ping' and mythologized poet-martyr 'Qu Yuan'. He belonged to one of the three ruling clans of Chu, and hence to a lineage that was traced back to the divine ancestor, the Yellow Emperor. Qu Yuan is the subject of a lengthy biography in the *Grand Scribe's Records*, the vast history by Sima Qian (145–86 BCE) which can be said to have invented the art of biography in China.[9] But the biography has a number of textual irregularities that indicate it was compiled by Sima Qian from sources of uneven quality and reliability, so even though it is our best source for his life, it is not entirely trustworthy.[10]

---

[8] This is true of premodern editions, though some modern editions place the 'Nine Songs' first instead.

[9] The biography has been translated in full in Hawkes, *Songs of the South*, 54–60; Watson, *Records of the Grand Historian: Han Dynasty*, 1:435–43.

[10] One scholar has even argued recently that Sima Qian only had access to poems by Qu Yuan in their written form as standardized in their early Han, but not the original Chu script, so that he read many of these works through a considerable barrier. See Zhang Shuguo, 'Han chu libian Chuci yu *Shi ji: Qu Yuan Jia sheng lie zhuan* de cailiao laiyuan'.

The opening paragraphs of Qu Ping's biography identify him as a talented young advisor to the King of Chu, who was slandered by jealous colleagues and removed from his position of authority. The narrative continues on in considerable detail through the reigns of King Huai (r. 328–299 BCE) and his son Qingxiang (r. 299–263 BCE). The famous strategist of Qin, Zhang Yi (373–310 BCE), employs clever schemes to deceive King Huai, leading to several grave military defeats. This section has much of the flavour of the classic *Stratagems of the Warring States*, a collection of quasi-historical episodes of deception and intrigue from the Warring States period. But Qu Ping's only part in these events, according to his biography, is to voice scepticism and resistance to the Chu leadership.

Ultimately King Huai joins a parley with Qin where he is taken prisoner, and ultimately dies there. His son King Qingxiang continues to ignore Qu Ping's advice and exiles him to the south.[11] Qu Ping engages in an entertaining dialogue with an insouciant fisherman (see 'Fisherman' below), then composes the poem 'Embracing the Sand' (in 'Nine Avowals' below), weighs down his body with sand or rocks, and drowns himself in the Miluo River. The state of Chu soon thereafter suffered a humiliating defeat, having its capital at Ying conquered by Qin in 278, and was subjugated entirely to Qin in 223.

Thus it was only during the earliest period of his life that Qu Ping held any official position at court and was engaged in contemporary politics, so his reputation as a prescient observer of Chu's fortunes, whether true or not, lies outside the bounds of verifiable history. We may trust Sima Qian when he tells us that Chu would have been far better off had Qu Ping's advice been heeded. But according to the biography itself, there was never any likelihood of that happening, because it was only for a brief time in his youth that Qu Ping served as a counsellor to the king at all.

Later readers, though, were irresistibly drawn to Sima Qian's portrait of Qu Yuan's virtue and sagacity, and for two thousand years he has been idolized as a political martyr, first and foremost.[12] He even

---

[11] The term used is 'Jiangnan', literally the area south of the Yangtze River, but probably a specific region on the south side of the Yangtze River from Mount Wu.

[12] The political mythology and religious symbolism of his legend are an important theme of later Chinese culture. See Laurence A. Schneider's classic study *A Madman of Ch'u*.

became an object of religious worship. Sima Qian tells us that Qu Ping drowned himself in despair, and this is indeed implied in the poem 'Embracing the Sand'. At some point not long after his death, and certainly by the Former Han, Qu Yuan's watery death began to be interwoven with the cult of an aquatic deity. Later on he would become the universal object of popular worship at the Duanwu Festival—still celebrated throughout the Chinese world today. Duanwu is celebrated on the Fifth Day of the Fifth Month with dragon boat races and rice dumplings wrapped in bamboo, which are said to be offerings to Qu Yuan's drowned soul.

Though the later tradition attributes this idolization of Qu Yuan to his actual deeds and character, the principal cause may in fact have been the tragic effectiveness of the various poems attributed to him, all of which are included in the *Elegies* and which comprise nearly half the anthology. These are:

1. 'Li sao', long autobiographical poem conveying cryptic political complaint
2. 'Nine Avowals', suite of nine shorter pieces mostly similar to the 'Li sao' in character
3. 'Nine Songs', suite of brief shamanistic pieces
4. 'Summons to the Soul', the text of a religious summons to the soul of a person on the verge of death
5. 'Heavenly Questions', queries about cosmology and history
6. 'Divination', dialogue between Qu Yuan and a diviner
7. 'Fisherman', dialogue between Qu Yuan and a fisherman
8. 'Far Roaming', narrative of Daoist transcendence modelled on the 'Li sao'

The 'Li sao' is first and foremost of all these. The gnomic title of the poem relies on the polysemy of both its constituents to convey a sense of both 'encountering' and 'overcoming' a period of 'strife' and 'sorrow', a complex and paradoxical set of ideas which I translate loosely as 'Sublimating Sorrow'. According to Sima Qian's biography, Qu Yuan wrote it in protest after being dismissed from the court of King Huai, and this poem is autobiographical, in some sense, but at the same time it employs numerous symbolic substitutions which make its literal meaning a matter of speculation. The author—who seems to be but is not explicitly identified within the poem as Qu Yuan—refers to a king—who may or may not be King Huai—by pseudonyms like 'Spirit Paragon'. But the author also employs erotic imagery to represent his relationship with this sovereign, botanical imagery to represent both allies and rivals, and a shamanic flight as a correlative of his own political career. All of these elements seem to contain both real and symbolic elements for the reader to interpret.

A similar set of challenges affects the interpretation of the 'Nine Songs', a set of eleven poems apparently based on a suite of shamanic ritual pieces, mostly describing romantic encounters with deities. But these have traditionally been understood as applying to Qu Yuan's political dilemmas as well, based on the interpretation of the earliest commentary, compiled by a Later Han scholar named Wang Yi (*c*.89–*c*.158).[13] The Han commentary regularly identifies the speakers and images of the poems as referring directly to Qu Yuan and the Chu court. For instance, the 'Mistress of the Xiang' describes the poet-speaker's longing for the goddess:[14]

> The High Lord's child descends – to the northern islet,
> Her gaze glinting in the distance – fills me with sorrow.

The Han commentary explains this couplet of longing for a mystical love object as follows:

Qu Yuan mourns his own situation, that he is not able to meet with a Yao or Shun, but instead has come upon an imperceptive ruler, and so must throw his body into the currents of the Xiang. That is why he is melancholy.

Instead of a tryst with a river goddess, then, Wang Yi's commentary reads the couplet entirely as an allegory of Qu Yuan's political situation.

Though the Han commentary is often criticized for its allegorical readings, in fact there is plenty of evidence for this kind of political allegory within the poems themselves. Another poem in the 'Nine Songs', for instance, praises the deity 'Lesser Controller of Destinies' as follows:

> Holding upright your long sword – you aid the young and fair:
> you, Lord Calamus, alone are worthy – to bring justice to all.

---

[13] Because there is strong evidence that Wang Yi is not the author of the entire commentary, however, and that it was instead compiled from various sources, I normally refer to it as the 'Han commentary'.

[14] Note that the genders of pronouns are not explicit in the original text, but the romantic relationship is indisputable. For more on gender in the anthology and its reception, see Zipki, 'Wanton Goddesses to Unspoken Worthies'.

Here the hymn to the deity has explicit political resonance, not to mention that 'Lord Calamus' is the epithet also used for King Huai of Chu in the 'Li sao'. The Han commentary may be employing the same political allegory as the poems, only reinterpreting the poems to apply to contemporary concerns of political corruption and instability in the Later Han.[15]

The *Elegies* are full of this kind of dual symbolism, with both political and religious referents. The shamanic flight of the hero, in particular, is a political metaphor but also reflects the genesis of the *Elegies* in Chu religious culture. For instance, the 'Li sao' itself refers twice to a shadowy figure named 'Peng Xian', whom Qu Yuan takes as his model. Though the precise referent of this term remains unknown, it most likely relates to two mythical shaman heroes of antiquity, Shamans Peng and Xian, or perhaps to Peng Zu, a minister said to have lived so long that he served all three dynasties of Xia, Shang, and Zhou. Thus the very earliest poems attributed to Qu Yuan already present his quest as being aimed not just at political fulfilment but equally at some kind of personal immortality. Another poem attributed to Qu Yuan, the 'Far Roaming', portrays its hero as achieving a state of Daoist transcendence beyond and apart from society.[16]

The obscure relationship between Qu Yuan's life and these poems has led some modern scholars to attempt to read Qu Yuan out of the 'Li sao' altogether. The reformer and critic Hu Shih (1891–1962) suggested, in a seminal 1922 essay, that much of Qu Yuan's biography had been invented post hoc.[17] A number of modern scholars led by Okamura Shigeru have pointed out how the use of formulaic language in the poems challenges any attempt to read them as responses to specific historical events.[18]

---

[15] On Wang Yi's motives and intellectual context see also Michael Schimmelpfennig, 'The Quest for a Classic: Wang Yi and the Exegetical Prehistory of His Commentary to the *Songs of Chu*', and Chan, 'Wang Yi on Integrity and Loyalty'. But the commentary was only compiled, not composed in full, by Wang Yi alone. On the composite nature of the commentary see Kominami, *Soji to sono chūshakushatachi*, 299–369; Schimmelpfennig, 'Qu Yuans Weg vom wahren "Menschen zum" wirklichen Dichter', 675–751; and Chen Hung-to, 'Lun *Chuci zhangju* yunwen zhu de xingzhi yu shidai'.

[16] The pursuit of Daoist immortality became very popular during the Han, one indication that this poem was composed not by Qu Yuan but by a Han imitator.

[17] Hu Shih, 'Du Chuci'. See James R. Hightower's essay 'Ch'ü Yüan Studies' for a survey of early modern scholarship.

[18] See Okamura's two classic articles, 'Soji to Kutsu Gen—hīrō to sakusha to no bunri ni tsuite' and 'Soji bungaku ni okeru "Shūshi" no ichi'.

On the other hand, there are solid grounds for relating most of the poems mentioned above to Qu Yuan. Sima Qian's biography already praises the 'Li sao' as Qu Yuan's masterwork and quotes the entire text of one of the pieces in the 'Nine Avowals', 'Embracing the Sand', as well as 'Fisherman'. Sima Qian concludes the entire chapter by asserting that he 'laments the aspirations' of Qu Yuan every time he reads four works: 'Li sao', 'Heavenly Questions', 'Summons to the Soul', and 'Lamenting Ying'. 'Summons to the Soul' was later attributed to Song Yu instead (see discussion below), but otherwise this leaves us with a solid traditional corpus of Qu Yuan poems, to which a few more were added in the Han compilation of the *Elegies*: 'Divination', 'Fisherman', 'Far Roaming', perhaps the 'Greater Summons'.

Some of these attributions remain especially dubious. 'Divination' and 'Fisherman' read like fictionalized narratives about a character named Qu Yuan more than works composed by Qu Yuan. The 'Far Roaming' seems to be a later work inspired by the 'Li sao' but also drawing on a new infusion of early religious Daoism. Controversy over the attributions to Qu Yuan began as early as the Song dynasty, and has continued into modern scholarship. There is even a century-old tradition of theorizing that the entire anthology was created during the Han dynasty. Although these debates are inconclusive, they can still shed light on the poems' construction and meaning. For example, the ancient suggestion that Qu Yuan composed the 'Heavenly Questions' while looking at actual mural paintings of the events described, while implausible if taken too literally, may offer valuable avenues of enquiry into the poem's relation to ancient myth. The millennia of debate over the attribution of 'Summons to the Soul' to either Qu Yuan or Song Yu has elucidated much valuable contextual information and also suggested new readings of the poem itself.

Without having resolved these questions, though, the poems attributed to Qu Yuan build up a compelling authorial persona, one that I will call 'Quvian' below for convenience. The author of 'Heavenly Questions' is deeply curious about ancient history and legend, but profoundly indignant at the wickedness of certain rulers from the past. The 'Li sao' also burns with righteous anger, but directs it more specifically at the contemporary sovereign. This attestation of historical references in service of righteous protest also features in several of the 'Nine Avowals'. At the same time, the author of the 'Li sao' employs a vivid body of imagery drawn both from the natural world, using fragrant herbs to represent the clashes of honest and malignant courtiers, and also from spiritual themes, such as the celestial journey to consult with the divine ancestors and spiritual force, which bears a close similarity to the subject matter of the 'Nine Songs'. In other words, we have much to gain from the traditional practice of reading these poems in relation to one another and positing a common origin which we may describe as 'Quvian' even while admitting that they may not have been composed by a single person.[19]

Over the past century a vast scholarship on the Qu Yuan authorship question has accumulated, and the origins of all these poems continue to be debated. One of the most productive lines of enquiry in the past several decades, however, has shifted the focus of attention from Qu Yuan himself to the better-understood compilation of the anthology in the Han. In China, Huang Linggeng has edited an exhaustive new redaction of the Wang Yi commentary itself, in which he identifies many inconsistencies and transcription errors. Meanwhile, several Western scholars have highlighted the creative embellishments on the Qu Yuan legend introduced successively by Han editors. A recent article by Monica Zipki, for instance, illustrates how the *Chuci zhangju* imposes a rigidly 'gendered hermeneutics' on the more fluid gender roles of Chu religion. Moreover, Du Heng has summed up much recent work in her study 'The Author's Two Bodies', which distinguishes between the individuals who produced the *Elegies* and the authorial figure of Qu Yuan as established in the Han.[20] Though many questions remain, there is increasing agreement that the Qu Yuan question needs to be understood from a broader perspective within the evolving cultures of Chu and Han.[21] In this

[19] My approach to the anthology is inspired by that of Okamura and his close attention to formulaic language and composite structure throughout the poems. But recognizing the complexities of the text does not actually lead us to identify any alternative authors or compilers beyond the traditional account, so it remains convenient to describe the poems as 'Quvian' in spite of the manifold uncertainties that remain.

[20] It is telling that both of these useful articles use the original name of the anthology in their titles (rather than referring to Qu Yuan directly). See Zipki, 'Wanton Goddesses to Unspoken Worthies: Gendered Hermeneutics in the *Chuci zhangju*'; Du, 'The Author's Two Bodies: The Death of Qu Yuan and the Birth of the *Chuci zhangju* 楚辭章句'.

[21] Consider how the Chinese and Japanese authors in a recent edited volume (Ōno Keisuke, ed., *Soji to Sō bunka no sōgōteki kenkyū*) tend to agree on this point.

light, rather than wrestling further with the Qu Yuan question itself, we may be able to understand the anthology better by proceeding to discuss the later pieces in the anthology instead.

Song Yu and the Han Poets in the Elegies

After Qu Yuan, the key author of the *Elegies* is Song Yu, never as highly regarded but nearly as influential for the literary tradition. Song Yu is mentioned in a short epilogue to Qu Yuan's biography as one of his epigones in the state of Chu before its conquest by Qin, but otherwise there is no information about his life except a few clues in later poems where he figures as a speaking character. Thus we have far less reliable information about his life than about Qu Ping. Even his name can be interpreted as a fiction. Song is the name of an ancient state centred in the region of modern Henan province, and descended from the Shang dynasty. Yu means 'jade' and as such is frequently used to represent virtue and excellence. So the name 'Song Yu' can be interpreted as signifying 'the excellent man from Song', and represents a kind of alternative tradition of poetry within Chu culture.

Song Yu's literary achievement, though not quite on a par with Qu Yuan's, is impressive overall and would certainly rank him as one of China's great, foundational poets, were it not that his biography is such a lacuna. In the *Elegies*, two great works, the 'Nine Phases' and 'Summons to the Soul', are attributed to him. Though sharing some features with the 'Li sao', the 'Nine Phases' is quite different in mood. It opens with a remarkable set piece on the sadness inspired by autumnal transformations that has been endlessly imitated and studied throughout the tradition. The 'Summons to the Soul' is also an extraordinary piece. Presented as a dialogue between a shaman and the Lord of Heaven, the main text is the ritual invocation to a lost soul. This is the earliest record of a ritual that persists today in China and Taiwan. It is full of vivid descriptions and powerful imagery, and, like 'Nine Phases', was enormously influential on the literary tradition afterwards. Apart from these two pieces, though, Song Yu is also identified as the author of a large number of *fu* poems on political and also erotic themes.[22]

---

[22] See the concise biography with extensive bibliography in Knechtges and Chang, *Ancient and Early Medieval Chinese Literature*, 1007–22.

Both of the poems attributed to Song Yu in the *Elegies*, though extremely different in content, prosody, and diction, share one key feature: rather than being composed in a mode of criticism or protest, they are for the most part eulogistic, being dedicated at least in part to praise of the sovereign. Moreover, they are explicitly located in a court context. The importance of these two works can also be seen in the influence on the later tradition. The 'Nine Phases' opens with a powerful description of the sadness that accompanies the onset of autumn, which would be cited and reused in countless poems. The 'Summons to the Soul' contains influential descriptions of a lavish banquet and musical celebration, but its concluding lyric lamenting the 'pity of spring' was particularly inspirational for later poets.[23]

In other words, though Qu Yuan and the 'Li sao' garner more praise and admiration, it may actually be Song Yu's works that were more influential on later poetry. The eulogistic dimension distinguishes Song Yu's compositions dramatically from the 'Li sao' or most of the poems attributed to Qu Yuan. But they were recognized as such by later readers, and 'Song Yu' was used as a critical term to distinguish elements of the *Elegies* beyond the writings of Qu Yuan himself, and indeed Song Yu was widely admired and cited by medieval poets.

Song Yu serves as a bridge to the Han authors included in the anthology, with whom he shares more in common than with Qu Yuan: Jia Yi (200–168 BCE), Dongfang Shuo (*fl.* 140–130 BCE), Zhuang Ji (2nd c. BCE), Wang Bao (*c*.84–*c*.53 BCE), Liu Xiang (79–8 BCE), and Wang Yi. A couple of these attributions are contested but all the later pieces seem to have been composed by Han courtiers. Like Song Yu's pieces, these are poets writing for an audience of the emperor and contemporaries, and lack the fierce independence of Qu Yuan at his best. On the other hand, they illuminate in various ways the struggle of Han scholars to refine literary expression as a way of representing their own new situation.[24]

One of the most appealing of these is the 'Summons to the Recluse', attributed only to the 'Lesser Mountain of Huainan', which seems to be either a pseudonym or a bibliographical classification designating a composition from that court. It is a brief piece written at court to

---

[23] See my study 'The Pity of Spring'.

[24] There are relatively few studies of the later pieces in the anthology. For one exceptional recent article that examines some of them in depth, see Bender, 'Figure and Flight in the *Songs of Chu (Chuci)*'.

summon back a fellow courtier who has departed the court to live in isolation in the mountains. Thus it self-consciously adopts the method of the 'Summons to the Soul' to a purely secular context. But the unnamed poet triumphs in this unlikely mode, vividly depicting the strangeness and terror of the natural world. The poem encapsulates in brief the way that Han poets transferred the inspiration of Chu poetry to their own situation.

Wang Bao was one of the leading *fu* poets of the Former Han. Few of his compositions have survived apart from a poem on the pan-pipes. His 'Nine Longings', though loosely inspired by the works of Qu Yuan, are profoundly different in style and form. They employ a metre closer to the *Book of Songs*, and are dense and compact compositions that portray individual angst and aspirations through cryptic imagery drawn primarily from canonical texts. Moreover, although Wang Bao employs some of the same motifs of shamanic flights through the heavens, in these poems 'Heaven' may be merely a metaphor for the imperial court itself.

Jia Yi, Dongfang Shuo, and Zhuang Ji are all writing within the tradition established by Qu Yuan, but with a new emphasis on depicting the injustice of their own period. Collectively they express the frustration of ambitious writers upset that the Han emperors have failed to recognize their own talent. Jia Yi's own biography parallels Qu Yuan's, in that he was known as a youthful prodigy who offended his colleagues and so was removed from court, so he had a strong personal basis for his poem on this theme. Zhuang Ji also writes in 'Lamenting Time's Fate' of the unfairness of being born under the Han, and lacking the opportunities for success of ministers under the Zhou. Dongfang Shuo was known for his humorous pieces and his 'Seven Remonstrances' are noteworthy for some of the very rare flickers of humour in the anthology.

Liu Xiang's 'Nine Threnodies', by contrast, constitute one of the most ambitious works in the anthology. Elaborating on Qu Yuan's models, particularly the 'Li sao' and 'Nine Avowals', in a highly self-conscious and allusive manner, Liu incorporates a number of different topics beyond the plight of the neglected courtier. He is one of the few Han poets (apart perhaps from the author of 'Far Roaming') to write dramatically about the theme of Daoist transcendence, and also draws exuberantly on historical allusion to suggest the parallels between Han rulers and the various kings and emperors of the Zhou. Liu seems to write with more self-confidence than many of his contemporaries, perhaps because he belonged himself to the imperial family and was therefore less subservient to the current regime.

The very last composition in the anthology is the 'Nine Yearnings' of Wang Yi. Wang Yi was the compiler of the anthology and of its commentary, so in many ways he is the lens by which we view all of these texts, relying whether explicitly or not upon his interpretations of the earlier poems. More than any other compositions in the anthology, they seem to represent a conscious attempt at pastiche of a Quvian voice by a poet far removed from Qu Yuan's original circumstances. We can appreciate the 'Nine Yearnings', not so much as an original poetic composition in the sense we might take for granted, but rather in a postmodern vein as compositions playing with the themes of the earlier *Elegies*; as in the second poem of the series, with its long catalogue of animals from the natural world, concluding unexpectedly with a variety of insects pestering the protagonist as they crawl and flitter around him.

Song Yu and the Han poets, then, represent some of the perennial themes of imperial Chinese culture: the scholar staking out an identity in relation to the all-powerful state when possible, while relying for personal satisfaction on the consolations of nature and the liberating potential of Daoism, all the while commenting self-consciously on their plight in a poetic language shaped by classical erudition.

Literary Characteristics of the Elegies

Though they are full of vivid depictions of their social, cultural, and material milieu, the *Elegies* have continued to be read because of their rich verbal expression. Though the English translation represents these aspects only in part, an overview of its literary characteristics is essential to an understanding of the anthology.

RHETORIC

Perhaps the most distinctive characteristic of the *Elegies* is the set of metaphorical substitutions or what one may loosely call 'allegory' (*bixing*), a whole system of imagery drawn from the natural world and other sources, used to represent the poet's inner

feelings and thoughts by symbolic means.[25] For instance, one of
the most striking features of the *Elegies* is the constant reference
to herbs and flowers, some important examples of which are iden-
tified at the glossary at the end of this volume. Qu Yuan frequently
uses the names of fragrant herbs such as 'angelica' or 'sweet clo-
ver' to represent his own inner virtue, inherited directly via the
royal lineage of Chu. But this is only one of a wide variety of
poetic substitutions used throughout the *Elegies*, including the use
of shamanic flight and other religious iconography with political
implications.

A complementary feature of the poems is the recurrence of cer-
tain themes throughout, what one may call the 'topoi' or set topics
of the anthology. In some cases these are the result of deliberate and
conscious imitation, but in others poets may jointly be drawing on
a body of shared poetic material. For convenience, it is easy to take
the 'Li sao', say, as the model for the autobiographical narrative of
the estranged courtier. But the same topos opens the 'Summons to
the Soul', where we encounter yet another rendition of Quvian self-
presentation. It is very likely that all these poems were part of
a larger universe of poetry in a similar style, much of which has
been lost.[26] When we discover similar passages in several of the
Elegies, they may not reflect direct borrowing but rather the use of
a shared heritage.

Aside from the fundamental Quvian topos of the 'estranged cour-
tier', one elaboration of the same theme is the 'topos of the world
upside-down'.[27] This topos becomes particularly prominent in the
Elegies composed under the Han, where it is used to convey the
bureaucratic officials' sense that the state of contemporary politics is
inverted from the idealized, Confucian state they envision. A corres-
ponding theme is that of the 'discovery of hidden talent'. One of the
most prominent themes in the entire anthology is the poet's desire for

[25] Pauline Yu has pointed out important differences from allegory in Western litera-
ture (*The Reading of Imagery in the Chinese Poetic Tradition*), but the term is indispensable
in dealing with the *Elegies* because of the etymological sense of 'saying something other
[than what you mean]'.

[26] So far, few of these have overlapped directly with the *Elegies* in style or content, but
the recently discovered collection of bamboo strips held by Anhui University is said to
contain new materials that may enlighten us further.

[27] The phrase was borrowed from Trask's translation of Curtius by Knechtges in *The
Han Rhapsody*.

a sovereign to employ him, and this is frequently expressed by a litany of historical examples, such as Lü Wang mentioned above, or Ning Qi, elevated to a ministerial position by Duke Huan of Qi when he was feeding his ox.

A related rhetorical device shared by most of the *Elegies* is the use of historical allusion and citation. Beginning with the 'Li sao' itself, nearly all the poems refer back to sage-emperors of the past like Yao and Shun, said to have governed the realm with ideal justice. The Han poems, in particular, refer increasingly often to the *Book of Songs*, using it as an additional source of authority.[28] Another related device is the quotation of popular proverbs, which occurs most obviously in some of the oldest pieces in the anthology, the 'Li sao' and parts of the 'Nine Avowals'.[29]

The Han poems in the anthology best demonstrate the integration of *Elegies* with the older *Book of Songs* tradition. Allusions and quotations from the *Book of Songs* steadily increase in frequency as one progresses through the anthology. This is in large part the result of the canonization of the *Book of Songs* as a standard text of the Confucian rule in the Han. It is also a vivid indication of how Chinese poetry would continue to develop as a synthesis of these two separate fountainheads, the *Songs* and *Elegies*.

STYLE

The *Elegies* are rich in figures of speech and other literary artifice, much of it unprecedented in the *Songs*.[30] One of the most fundamental is the use of parallel couplets like this one from 'Crossing the River Jiang' in the 'Nine Avowals':

> The broadsword I carry gleams and glitters,
> my cap pierces the clouds, ascending aloft.

Or this one from 'Fisherman':

> All the world is soiled, I alone am pure;
> all the people are drunk, I alone am sober.

---

[28] 'Nine Phases', line 153, already does so explicitly. Though its dating is unclear, this passage in particular could easily date to the Han.

[29] For instance, 'Rueful Remonstrance', line 67, quotes the proverb 'the man whose arm is broken nine times makes a doctor', also known from the *Zuo zhuan*.

[30] See the valuable study by Tang Bingzheng, 'Qu fu xiuci juyu'.

Classical Chinese poetry typically employs this kind of parallelism and eschews enjambment, the continuation of a single sentence beyond a single line.[31]

The *Elegies* are written entirely in verse, but in a number of different forms, almost all of which use a rhythmic particle such as *xi*. This seems to reflect their origins in actual musical performance and is one of the features that distinguish the Chu style from other Chinese poetry. There is no way of representing this accurately in translation, but I normally indicate the appearance of a particle like this with the en-dash: '–'. It can be understood as a pause or caesura that contributes to the broader rhythm. It is particularly obvious in the metre of the 'Nine Songs', where it appears in every line. In keeping with their origins, perhaps in actual religious ritual, these poems have the most obvious musical form of rhyme and repetition. Other poems employ more complex metrical forms, such as 'Sublimating Sorrow' and 'Heavenly Questions', consisting of rhyming quatrains. Some of the 'Nine Avowals', and most of the Han poems in the anthology, contain long passages of dozens of lines all following the same rhyme. On the other hand, 'Divination' and 'Fisherman' are written in an irregular verse form that is similar to that of the *fu* genre popular in the Han (see below).[32]

Another distinctive feature of the *Elegies* is the frequent use of 'descriptive compounds' (in Chinese, *lianmian ci*). These are disyllabic words composed of two Chinese characters, whose meaning normally is not an extension of the meanings of the individual words, and which is descriptive of a state of affairs, such as 'loftily looming' or 'precipitously spiralling' or 'diversely disposed'. Following the method established by earlier translators of Chinese poetry, I normally attempt to translate these into alliterative or assonant phrases in English, to preserve some of the rhetorical effect of the original poetry.[33] Occasionally this may have odd aural effects in English, but

[31] A valuable consideration of this feature and its broader significance is the essay by Andrew Plaks, 'Where the Lines Meet'.

[32] My analysis of the rhyme schemes is reflected in line breaks within poems, which normally reflect changes in rhyme as well. To identify these I have generally followed Wang Li, *Chuci yundu*, and Luo and Zhou, *Han Wei Jin nanbeichao yunbu yanbian yanjiu*. I have occasionally ignored the rhyme and divided stanzas according to content, however, as this is not a linguistic study.

[33] For a detailed discussion of this method, see Knechtges, 'Problems of Translating Descriptive Binomes in the *Fu*'.

it is nonetheless preferable to the simplification of a single adjective like 'high' or 'beautiful'.

The use of these rhyming or alliterative compounds can be seen as a special case of the repetition of related or synonymous words throughout the anthology, a feature which has been discussed extensively by modern scholar Tang Bingzheng (1910–98). Tang notes that in extreme cases this extends to the repetition of three synonymous terms in a row. A remarkable example may be found in lines 135–6 of the 'Li sao':

> Caltrops, carpetgrass, and cocklebur now fill your chamber –
> unlike, alone, and apart, you refuse to be demeaned.

The three wicked weeds represent the unscrupulous flatterers who have monopolized the king's attention. They contrast dramatically with the three adjectives describing the hero's, Qu Yuan's, uniqueness and separateness. This kind of verbal repetition is a fundamental component of the poetic language of the *Elegies*, as the poets use it to build an elaborate mood over the course of many lines and stanzas, much as an oil painter might apply many successive layers of paint in subtly varying hues.

GENRE

The *Elegies* are highly varied in form and content, but retrospectively have been understood as constituting a distinctive genre in Chinese literature, the early form of the *fu* or 'rhapsody', dominant in the Han dynasty and a major vehicle of expression long thereafter. *Fu* poems frequently include multiple, fictional speakers in dialogue with one another; elaborate descriptions of material objects and sensuous pleasures; a lengthy scale comprising hundreds or even thousands of lines; and the setting of autobiographical material within descriptive and narrative frames. The 'Li sao' itself became the model for the rhapsody of the long, individual journey.[34] The fictional dialogues of 'Fisherman' and 'Divination' would become a standard framing device for the *fu*. Finally, the extravagant description of hunting, feasting, and music in 'Summons to the Soul' and 'Greater Summons' would be elaborated upon in countless court poems on related topics.

---

[34] Hawkes's classic article 'The Quest for the Goddess' discusses the journey theme as a religious one that is gradually secularized. As discussed here, though, I find these distinctions arbitrary, with religious elements persisting much later in poetry, and secular politics intruding much earlier.

Some of the greatest and most influential poems of the *fu* tradition
date to the Han dynasty, contemporary with the composition of many
of the Elegies. These include a number of poems dealing with Qu
Yuan himself. Jia Yi wrote a *fu* lamenting Qu Yuan when he himself
was dismissed by Emperor Wen (see the introduction to 'Rueful
Oath' below, attributed to Jia Yi as well). Yang Xiong (53 BCE–18 CE)
was a prolific and influential writer, who early in his career composed
a 'Contra-Sao' criticizing Qu Yuan for committing suicide rather
than continuing to struggle in politics.

Why, then, were none of these poems included in the *Elegies*? The
modern scholar Li Zhi has decisively resolved this question, with his
compelling argument that the unifying principle of compilation is
that all the poems in the *Elegies* are written in the voice of Qu Yuan.[35]
In other words, what unifies the poems it that they are all 'Quvian' in
style and voice. Thus the heroic, quasi-divinized figure of Qu Yuan
overshadows the entire anthology from beginning to end.

---

[35] See his book *Chuci yu zhonggu wenxian kaoshuo*.

NOTE ON THE TEXT

THE standard edition of the *Elegies* is the *Chuci buzhu* (Elegies of Chu with supplementary commentary) compiled by Hong Xingzu (1090–1155). This edition is based on Wang Yi's original edition, the *Chuci zhangju* (Elegies of Chu with chapter-and-verse commentary), but has additional commentary supplemented by Hong himself. Hong's commentary is sometimes useful, especially in its citation of other early texts, but its greater importance lies in its preservation of the *Chuci zhangju*. Though various Ming-dynasty (1368–1644) printings of the *Chuci zhangju* also survive, none is demonstrably earlier than the *Chuci buzhu*.

Han historian Sima Qian, as mentioned above, quotes in his biography of Qu Yuan the entire text of 'Embracing the Sand', but not even a single line of 'Li sao'. Considering how generous he is in his quotations of other literary works like the much longer poems of Sima Xiangru, this suggests that he may not have had a legible text of the entire poem. Half a century later, Liu Xiang, the great scholar and imperial archivist of the late Former Han, seems to have organized the 'Li sao' and other works attributed to Qu Yuan, since there is an entry for twenty-five poems by Qu Yuan in the catalogue of the imperial library completed by him and his son Liu Xin. Liu Xiang is also said to have compiled a set of poems by Qu Yuan in sixteen fascicles (*juan*), but again it is unclear exactly how these were constituted.[1]

It is clear that we do not have the *Elegies* in its original form. One important hint can be found in the table of contents of the *Chuci buzhu*, which also preserves an alternative ordering belonging to a lost version of the anthology, *Chuci shiwen* (Elegies of Chu with interpretative commentary), which was probably compiled in the Tang by an unknown editor. Regarding the original compilation of the anthology, Tang Bingzheng has presented the most systematic and compelling

---

[1] Huang Linggeng has also made the intriguing proposal that this sentence actually refers to a recompilation of the 'Li sao' text itself. While his thesis remains unproven, the evidence he provides demonstrates conclusively to me that none of our editions of the *Elegies* preserves anything close to the original form. See Huang, *Chuci yu jianbo wenxian*, 48–9.

theory. Tang employs the contents of the *Chuci shiwen* to recon-
struct how the *Chuci zhangju* anthology was compiled as the result of
an accretive process during the Han dynasty.[2] He then goes on to
suggest a convincing division into five stages, originating with Qu
Yuan and Song, progressing gradually through the court of Huainan,
to Liu Xiang, through the hands of other Han scholars culminating
with Wang Yi, and still continuing after his time.

Tang Bingzheng's proposal more or less represents the consensus
of the best modern scholarship, seeing the *Elegies* as the product of an
accretive process. One notable insight in Tang's discussion is that in
some respects, it is actually the later works in the anthology that present
the most difficulty for us—his fourth and fifth groups. For instance,
the 'Greater Summons' was already a puzzle to Han readers, and
similarly the attribution of the 'Rueful Oath' to Jia Yi is uncertain.
Even if future scholarship makes a different determination about the
origins of these poems, then, this structure helps to confirm their
more marginal status during the Han. By contrast we see that there
was actually some consensus about the status of most works attrib-
uted to Qu Yuan by the Former Han.

Another striking feature of the *Shiwen* order is that it raises the
'Nine Phases' to a position of high status, placing it second in the
anthology as a whole. This long, repetitive, unwieldy, often frustrat-
ing poem has not been accorded much respect in modern scholar-
ship. Many modern editions actually omit it entirely, including only
works attributed to Qu Yuan himself. But as we have seen above,
'Nine Phases' has been enormously influential in the Chinese liter-
ary tradition, as have the works attributed to its putative author,
Song Yu.

Huang Linggeng, one of the greatest contemporary scholars of the
Elegies, follows the *Shiwen* order in his magnum opus, the five-volume
Chuci zhangju shuzheng. This translation is based primarily on Huang
Linggeng's text and commentary, though I have not always accepted
his emendations. This ordering of the poems, though not necessarily
the original one, provides a suggestive framework for viewing the
poems as medieval Chinese readers did.

---

[2] Tang Bingzheng, '*Chuci* chengshu zhi tansuo'.

Conventions of This Translation

There are a number of existing translations of the *Elegies*. The most important, and the only complete translation into English of the whole anthology, is that of David Hawkes. Hawkes's translation was begun when he was a student in Beijing in the 1940s, first published in 1959, and then republished as a Penguin paperback in 1985. The original translation is a splendid work in the tradition of English sinology, written in smooth and polished English verse. Hawkes's 1985 edition takes account of new discoveries and has much expanded notes and introductions which are full of important insights into the texts and their historical background. He refrained, however, from making substantive revisions to the translation itself.

Aside from Hawkes's sole complete translation into English of the entire *Chuci zhangju* text, there is also an excellent version in French by Rémi Mathieu. Following the model of both these scholars, this volume translates the entire anthology, since it is only by reading the poems in the context of the whole anthology that we can understand their historical development. There are other translations of the 'Li sao' and other prominent pieces in the anthology. Gopal Sukhu has recently published a complete translation of the Zhu Xi text of the anthology, and there are numerous translations of the 'Nine Songs', in particular. The examples of two translators have been particularly inspiring for me: Arthur Waley's versions of the 'Nine Songs' and 'Greater Summons', and Paul W. Kroll's rendering of 'Far Roaming'.

The *Elegies* present many challenges that will never obtain final resolution, beginning with the word *ci* in the title of the anthology. This pivotal term hints at the significance of the anthology in Chinese cultural history, as a repository of a singular poetic genre. While the term *ci* can mean simply 'words' or 'statements', in practice it frequently referred in ancient China to statements charged with prayerful or critical import, such as prayers offered up to ancestors, legal accusations, or remonstrances against a ruler. Balancing these opposing considerations, I follow several previous scholars in rendering the *ci* as 'elegy', originally a metrical form of Greek and Roman poetry, but in English more commonly the name of a long and mournful poem like Thomas Gray's 'Elegy in a Country Churchyard'. The *Chuci*, likewise, has its own distinctive metre, and many of its contents also have a funereal dimension (especially the 'Summons to the

Soul', but also many of the poems reflecting on Qu Yuan's drowning).[3] Thus *Elegies of Chu* as an English title pays respect both to the anthology's geographical origins and to its place within the literary culture of imperial China.[4]

I have also translated many proper names rather than merely romanizing them. For interested readers the Glossary-Index provides the original Chinese terms. Many of these names of deities and places seem to have been chosen in part because of their literal meanings. For instance, the obscure term 'Qianying' in the 'Far Roaming' is identified in the Han commentary as a 'water deity'. Since there is no corroborating evidence for this proposition, and Wang Yi does not seem to have known much about the actual origins of the 'Far Roaming', it is possible that this is a textual phantom, and no deity was ever worshipped by this name in ancient China. So I translate 'Qianying' as 'Dark Frailty', interpreting the term tentatively as a personification of the Daoist principle that fragility triumphs over rigidity.

One area where precision is of special importance in translating the *Elegies* is with respect to the flora and fauna of the anthology. Qu Yuan in the 'Li sao' itself laments of his contemporaries that they are 'Not even capable of distinguishing among the grasses and trees' (line 273). At the same time, the plethora of obscure terms, in particular the names of aromatic herbs, can be daunting to reader or translator, and these are identified in the glossary at the end of this volume. One of the central challenges for the translator is the key symbolic term *lan*, which in modern Chinese means 'orchid', and which has sometimes been rendered that way in previous translations of the *Elegies*. While the orchid is also a symbol of beauty and nobility, though, it is fundamentally different from the plant to which *lan* actually refers, the *Eupatorium chinense*, in that the *Eupatorium* is a genus of visually quite unprepossessing, low-lying shrubs with small clusters of white or purple flowers. The reason Qu Yuan refers to the *lan* and a few

---

[3] What makes the parallel between the *sao* (the poetic genre of the *Elegies* and later imitations) and 'elegy' particularly productive is the fact that both are genres defined by a combination of a distinctive metre and also melancholy subject matter. See, for instance, the essay by Gregory Nagy, 'Ancient Greek Elegy'.

[4] The Hungarian scholar Ferenc Tökei may have been the first to apply the term 'elegy' in his study of the *fu* genre, *Naissance de l'élégie chinoise*. More recently Waters applied the term to the 'Nine Songs' specifically (*Three Elegies of Ch'u*), and Mathieu's exquisite French translation of the entire anthology is entitled *Élégies de Chu*.

other key plants so often is not because of the visual splendour—which they in fact lack—but because of their fragrance, used throughout the *Elegies* as one of the primary symbols of inner beauty, moral virtue. I translate here instead with the less common Anglicization of the genus name, 'eupatory', literally meaning 'of good paternal lineage'.

Finally, the use of brackets in sinological translations is almost always misleading; the implication is that the part outside of the brackets is a straightforward or literal translation, but this is in fact never the case. Thus I eschew the use of brackets throughout.

Notes to the poems (both textual and explicatory) are placed at the end of the volume and are indicated by the presence of the line number. Since the line number is indicated at every tenth line, if one of these lines also has a note, the line number is italicized in the main text. Line breaks between stanzas normally follow the rhyme changes in the original poems. Citations to major sources in the footnotes are given to English translations, when available and pertinent. Following standard sinological practice, citations of Chinese texts normally give both chapter or fascicle number and page number, separated by a full stop. Translations from Chinese texts in the footnotes are my own unless otherwise noted; Wade-Giles or other romanizations in the translated sources have been tacitly converted to Pinyin.

SELECT BIBLIOGRAPHY

This bibliography provides key sources in English for further study of the anthology and related topics.

Selected English Translations of the Elegies

Hawkes, David, trans. *Ch'u Tz'u: The Songs of the South*. London: Oxford University Press, 1959. Paperback edition: Boston: Beacon Press, 1962. Revised edition: *The Songs of the South. An Anthology of Ancient Chinese Poems by Qu Yuan and Other Poets*. Harmondsworth: Penguin Books, 1985.

Kroll, Paul W. 'On "Far Roaming".' *Journal of the American Oriental Society* 116.4 (1996), 653–69.

Lim Boon Keng. *The Li Sao: An Elegy on Encountering Sorrows by Ch'ü Yüan*. Shanghai: Commercial Press, 1935.

Mair, Victor. 'Heavenly Questions.' In idem, ed., *The Columbia Anthology of Traditional Chinese Literature*, 371–86. New York: Columbia University Press, 1994.

Sukhu, Gopal. *The Songs of Chu: An Anthology of Ancient Chinese Poetry by Qu Yuan and Others*. New York: Columbia University Press, 2017.

Waley, Arthur. 'Hymn to the Fallen' and 'The Greater Summons'. *Chinese Poems: Selected from 170 Chinese Poems, More Translations from the Chinese, The Temple, and The Book of Songs*, 35–42. London: George Allen and Unwin, 1946.

Waley, Arthur. *The Nine Songs: Study of Shamanism in Ancient China*. London: Allen & Unwin, 1955. Rpt. San Francisco: City Light Books, 1973.

Waters, Geoffrey R. *Three Elegies of Ch'u: An Introduction to the Traditional Interpretation of the Chu tz'u*. Madison: University of Wisconsin Press, 1985.

Yang Hsien-yi and Gladys Yang, trans. *Li sao and Other Poems*. Peking: Foreign Languages Press, 1952.

Translations of Relevant Sources from Early China

Abbreviations Used in Notes:

Analects. See under Legge, James.
Book of Changes. See under Wilhelm, Richard.
Book of Documents. See under Legge, James.
Book of Songs. See under Waley, Arthur.
Classic of Mountains and Seas. See under Birrell, Anne.

Birrell, Anne. *Classic of Mountains and Seas.* London: Penguin, 1999.

Campany, Robert Ford. *To Live as Long as Heaven and Earth: A Study and Translation of Ge Hong's Traditions of Divine Transcendents.* Berkeley: University of California Press, 2002.

Crump, J. I., Jr. *Chan-Kuo Ts'e.* Oxford: Clarendon Press, 1970.

Durrant, Stephen, Wai-yee Li, and David Schaberg. *Zuo Tradition. Zuo zhuan* 左傳. *Commentary on the 'Spring and Autumn Annals'.* Seattle: University of Washington Press, 2016.

Graham, A. C. *The Book of Lieh-tzŭ: A Classic of the Tao.* New York: Columbia University Press, 1960, 1990.

Knechtges, David R. *Wen xuan or Selections of Refined Literature,* Vol. 1: *Rhapsodies on Metropolises and Capitals.* Princeton: Princeton University Press, 1982.

Knechtges, David R. *Wen Xuan or Selections of Refined Literature,* Vol. 2: *Rhapsodies on Sacrifices, Hunting, Travel, Sightseeing, Palaces and Halls, Rivers and Seas.* Princeton: Princeton University Press, 1987.

Knechtges, David R. *Wen Xuan or Selections of Refined Literature,* Vol. 3: *Rhapsodies on Natural Phenomena, Birds and Animals, Aspirations and Feelings, Sorrowful Laments, Literature, Music, and Passions.* Princeton: Princeton University Press, 1996.

Lau, D. C. *Mencius: Revised Edition.* New York: Penguin, 2003.

Legge, James. *The Lî Kî.* Two volumes. Oxford: Clarendon Press, 1885.

Legge, James. *The Chinese Classics, with a Translation, Critical and Exegetical Notes, Prolegomena, and Copious Indexes.* Five volumes. Oxford: Clarendon Press, 1893-5.

Legge, James. *Confucian Analects.* In *The Chinese Classics,* Vol. 2.

Legge, James. *The Shoo King or the Book of Historical Documents.* In *The Chinese Classics,* Vol. 3.

Legge, James. *The She King or the Book of Poetry.* In *The Chinese Classics,* Vol. 4.

Liao, W. K. *The Complete Works of Han Fei tzŭ: A Classic of Chinese Legalism.* Two volumes. London: Arthur Prosthain, 1939.

Mair, Victor H. *Wandering on the Way: Early Taoist Tales and Parables of Chuang Tzu.* Honolulu: University of Hawai'i Press, 1998.

Major, John, et al., trans. *The Huainanzi: A Guide to the Theory and Practice of Government in Early Han China.* New York: Columbia University Press, 2010.

Nienhauser, William H., Jr, ed. *The Grand Scribe's Records,* Vol. 1: *The Basic Annals of Pre-Han China.* Bloomington: Indiana University Press, 1994.

Rickett, W. Allyn. *Guanzi: Political, Economic, and Philosophical Essays from Early China.* Two volumes. Princeton: Princeton University Press, 1985-98.

Waley, Arthur. *The Book of Songs: The Ancient Chinese Classic of Poetry*. Edited with additional translations by Joseph R. Allen. New York: Grove Press, 1996.

Watson, Burton. *Records of the Grand Historian: Han Dynasty*. Revised edition. Two volumes. Hong Kong and New York: *Renditions* and Columbia University Press, 1993.

Wilhelm, Richard. *The I Ching, or Book of Changes*. Rendered into English by Cary F. Baynes. Third edition. Princeton: Princeton University Press, 1967.

Other Useful Sources on the Elegies *and Early China*

Allan, Sarah. *The Heir and the Sage: Dynastic Legend in Early China*. San Francisco: Chinese Materials Center, 1981. Revised and expanded second edition: Albany: State University of New York Press, 2016.

Allan, Sarah. *The Shape of the Turtle: Myth, Art, and Cosmos in Early China*. New York: State University of Albany Press, 1991.

Bender, Lucas Rambo. 'Figure and Flight in the *Songs of Chu (Chuci)*.' *Asia Major* 32 (2019), 1–31.

Birrell, Anne. *Chinese Mythology: An Introduction*. Baltimore: Johns Hopkins University Press, 1993.

Chan, Timothy W. K. 'The *Jing/zhuan* Structure of the *Chuci* Anthology: A New Approach to the Authorship of Some of the Poems.' *T'oung Pao* 84 (1998), 293–327.

Chan, Timothy W. K. 'Wang Yi on Integrity and Loyalty.' In *Considering the End: Mortality in Early Medieval Chinese Poetic Representation*, 7–40. Brill: Leiden, 2012.

Cook, Constance A., and John S. Major. *Defining Chu: Image and Reality in Ancient China*. Honolulu: University of Hawai'i Press, 1999.

Du Heng. 'The Author's Two Bodies: The Death of Qu Yuan and the Birth of the *Chuci zhangju* 楚辭章句.' *T'oung Pao* 105 (2019), 259–314.

Hawkes, David. 'The Quest of the Goddess.' *Asia Major*, n.s. 13.1–2 (1967), 71–94; rpt. in Hawkes, *Classical, Modern and Humane*, ed. John Minford and Siu-kit Wong, 115–41. Hong Kong: Chinese University Press, 1989.

Knechtges, David R., and Taiping Chang, eds. *Ancient and Early Medieval Chinese Literature: A Reference Guide*. Four volumes. Leiden: Brill, 2010–14.

Lawton, Thomas. *New Perspectives on Chu Culture during the Eastern Zhou Period*. Washington, DC: Arthur M. Sackler Gallery, Smithsonian Institution, 1991.

Lewis, Mark Edward. *The Flood Myths of Early China*. Albany: State University of New York Press, 2006.

Loewe, Michael, and Edward L. Shaughnessy, eds. *The Cambridge History of Ancient China: From the Origins of Civilization to 221 B.C.* Cambridge: Cambridge University Press, 1999.

Schimmelpfennig, Michael. 'The Quest for a Classic: Wang Yi and the Exegetical Prehistory of his Commentary to the Lisao.' *Early China* 29 (2004), 109–60.

Schneider, Laurence. *A Madman of Ch'u. The Chinese Myth of Loyalty and Dissent*. Berkeley: University of California Press, 1980.

So, Jenny F. 'Chu Art: Link between the Old and New.' In Cook and Major, eds, *Defining Chu: Image and Reality in Ancient China*, 33–47.

Sukhu, Gopal. *The Shaman and the Heresiarch: A New Interpretation of the Li sao*. Albany: State University of New York Press, 2012.

von Falkenhausen, Lothar. 'Chu Ritual Music.' In Lawton, *New Perspectives on Chu Culture during the Eastern Zhou Period*, 47–106.

Williams, Nicholas Morrow. 'The Pity of Spring: A Southern Topos Reimagined by Wang Bo and Li Bai.' In *Southern Identity and Southern Estrangement in Medieval Chinese Poetry*, ed. Wang and Williams, 137–63. Hong Kong: Hong Kong University Press, 2015.

Williams, Nicholas Morrow. 'Tropes of Entanglement and Strange Loops in the "Nine Avowals" of the *Chuci*.' *Bulletin of the School of Oriental and African Studies* 81 (2018), 277–300.

Williams, Nicholas Morrow. '"Roaming the Infinite": Liu Xiang as *Chuci* Reader and Would-be Transcendent.' *Tsing Hua Journal of Chinese Literature* 20 (2018), 49–112.

Williams, Nicholas Morrow. 'Sublimating Sorrow: How to Embrace Contradiction in Translating the "Li sao".' In Maghiel van Crevel and Lucas Klein, eds, *Chinese Poetry and Translation: Rights and Wrongs*, 181–99. Amsterdam: Amsterdam University Press, 2019.

Williams, Nicholas Morrow. 'Shamans, Souls, and Soma: Comparative Religion and Early China.' *Journal of Chinese Religions*. 48.2 (2020): 148–73.

Yü Ying-shih. '"Oh Soul, Come Back!" A Study of the Changing Conceptions of the Soul and Afterlife in Pre-Buddhist China.' *Harvard Journal of Asiatic Studies* 47 (1987), 363–95.

Zipki, Monica. 'Wanton Goddesses to Unspoken Worthies: Gendered Hermeneutics in the *Chuci zhangju*.' *Early China* 41 (2018), 333–74.

Scholarly References

The guide below is not intended to be comprehensive but merely to identify the principal texts and scholarly sources employed in this translation.

The anthology was transmitted to us via the *Chuci zhangju* compiled by Wang Yi, whose myriad failings and inconsistencies have been alluded to above. Even the *Chuci zhangju* itself does not survive independently in an early edition, only in Ming reprints of Song woodblock editions.[1] The standard text for most purposes is the *Chuci buzhu* text compiled in the Song, which cites a large number of variants for both the text itself and the Han commentary of the *Chuci zhangju*. However, the supplementary commentary by Hong Xingzu is uneven in quality. In late imperial China the most influential version of the *Chuci* was Zhu Xi's *Chuci jizhu*. Ming and Qing editions followed Zhu Xi's selection, omitting most of the Han poems.

Some of the poems (the 'Li sao', six of the 'Nine Songs', 'Nine Avowals: Crossing the River', 'Divination', 'Fisherman', 'Nine Phases', 'Summons to the Soul', 'Summons to the Recluse') were also included in the sixth-century anthology *Wen xuan*, so important variants are preserved in the numerous extant versions of that anthology, notably the *Wen xuan jizhu* manuscripts.

The best edition of the entire anthology today is the *Chuci zhangju shuzheng* by Huang Linggeng, which attempts to restore the original configuration of the *Chuci zhangju* as best as possible. Aside from collating the various versions of the commentary, Huang frequently adds his own judgements regarding the interpretation of the main text as well, comparing a vast range of other commentaries and early sources, including recently excavated manuscripts.

Apart from this text, other commentaries are cited in the notes only when I have followed their emendations or interpretations rather than the most obvious reading of the received text or the straightforward explanation of the Han commentary. Some of the most useful of these have been the *Tianwen zuanyi* of You Guoen; the revised edition of Jiang Liangfu's *Qu Yuan fu jiaozhu*; and the commentary to all the poems by Tang Bingzheng et al. Premodern commentaries between the Song and Qing often recycle and repeat much important information—as one would expect, since they were mainly intended to facilitate access to the main poems of the anthology, not to provide critical analysis contrasting with previous scholarship. This situation changes, however, in the Qing dynasty, when a number of *kaozheng* scholars provide helpful emendations, two of the most original and insightful being Xu Wenjing and Yu Yue. For a comprehensive survey of Chinese scholarship on the *Elegies*, see Yi Zhonglian, *Zhongguo Chuci xue shi*, though reception history is itself a thriving field and more up-to-date studies of particular scholars are also appearing frequently.

---

[1] Notably the 1518 edition of Huang Shengceng, the 1571 edition of the Furongguan, and the 1586 edition of Feng Shaozu. See also Hawkes, 'Ch'u-tz'u'; Knechtges and Chang, eds, *Ancient and Early Medieval Chinese Literature: A Reference Guide*, 1:128–39.

Japanese scholarship on the *Elegies* is often very helpful as well, because of the way that Japanese scholars skilfully balance fidelity to the textual tradition with new critical insights. The work of Okamura Shigeru and Kominami Ichirō, in particular, has been helpful in shaping my overall approach. For a survey of Japanese scholarship on the *Elegies*, see Xu Zhixiao, *Riben Chuci yanjiu*.

PRIMARY TEXTS

Chuci buzhu 楚辭補注. Compiled by Wang Yi 王逸 (*fl.* 114–20). Edited by Hong Xingzu 洪興祖 (1090–1155). Based on the Jiguge 汲古閣 edition, collated with *Sibu congkan* edition and *Wen xuan*. Punctuated by Bai Huawen 白化文 et al. Beijing: Zhonghua shuju, 1983.

Chuci zhangju shuzheng 楚辭章句疏證. Compiled by Wang Yi 王逸 (*fl.* 114–20). Edited by Huang Linggeng 黃靈庚. Ordering based on the anonymous *Chuci shiwen* 楚辭釋文. Five volumes. Beijing: Zhonghua shuju, 2007.

COMPILATIONS

Chuci huibian 楚辭彙編. Edited by Du Songbo 杜松柏. Compilation in ten volumes. Taipei: Xin wenfeng, 1986.

Chuci wenxian congkan 楚辭文獻叢刊. Edited by Huang Linggeng 黃靈庚 et al. Compilation in 100 volumes. Beijing: Guojia tushuguan chubanshe, 2014.

COMMENTARIES AND TEXTUAL STUDIES

Dai Zhen 戴震 (1724–77). *Qu Yuan fu Dai shi zhu* 屈原賦戴氏注. *Xuxiu siku quanshu*.

Ding Yan 丁晏 (1794–1875). *Chuci Tianwen jian* 楚辭天問箋. Taipei: Guangwen shuju, 1975.

He Jianxun 何劍熏. *Chuci xingu* 楚辭新詁. Chengdu: Ba Shu shushe, 1994.

Huang Linggeng 黃靈庚. *Chuci yiwen bianzheng* 楚辭異文辨證. Zhengzhou: Zhongzhou guji, 2000.

Huang Linggeng 黃靈庚. *Chuci jijiao* 楚辭集校. Three volumes. Shanghai: Shanghai guji chubanshe, 2009.

Huang Linggeng 黃靈庚. *Chuci yu jianbo wenxian* 楚辭與簡帛文獻. Beijing: Renmin wenxue, 2011.

Huang Linggeng 黃靈庚. *Chuci wenxian congkao* 楚辭文獻叢考. Three volumes. Beijing: Guojia tushuguan chubanshe, 2017.

Jiang Liangfu 姜亮夫. *Chuci shumu wuzhong* 楚辭書目五種. Beijing: Zhonghua shuju, 1961. Rpt. *Jiang Liangfu quanji* 姜亮夫全集, Vol. 5. Kunming: Yunnan renmin chubanshe, 2002.

Jiang Liangfu 姜亮夫. *Chuci tong gu* 楚辭通故. Four volumes. Ji'nan: Qi Lu shushe, 1985.

Jiang Liangfu 姜亮夫. *Chongding Qu Yuan fu jiaozhu* 重訂屈原賦校注. In *Jiang Liangfu quanji*, Vol. 6.

Jiang Liangfu 姜亮夫. *Er Zhao jiaozhu* 二招校注. In *Jiang Liangfu quanji*, Vol. 6.

Jin Kaicheng 金開誠, Dong Hongli 董紅利, and Gao Luming 高路明, eds and comm. *Qu Yuan ji jiaozhu* 屈原集校注. Two volumes. Beijing: Zhonghua shuju, 1996.

Lin Geng 林庚. 'Tian wen lunjian' 天問論箋. In *Lin Geng Chuci yanjiu liangzhong* 林庚楚辭研究兩種, 169–294. Beijing: Qinghua daxue chubanshe, 2006.

Liu Yongji 劉永濟 (1887–1966). *Qu Fu tongjian* 屈賦通箋. Edited by Liu Yongji 劉永濟. Beijing: Zhonghua shuju, 2010.

Ma Maoyuan 馬茂元 et al. *Chuci zhushi* 楚辭注釋. Wuhan: Hubei renmin chubanshe, 1985.

Ma Qichang 馬其昶 (1855–1930). *Qu fu wei* 屈賦微. *Xuxiu siku quanshu*, Vol. 1302.

Mao Qiling 毛奇齡 (1623–1716). *Tianwen buzhu* 天問補注. *Xuxiu siku quanshu*, Vol. 1302.

Nie Shiqiao 聶石樵. *Chuci xin zhu* 楚辭新注. Shanghai: Shanghai guji, 1980.

Qian Chengzhi 錢澄之 (1612–93). *Zhuang Qu hegu* 莊屈合詁. Hefei: Huangshan shushe, 1998.

Shen Zumian 沈祖緜 (1878–1969). *Qu Yuan fu zhengbian* 屈原賦證辨. In *Chuci huibian*, Vol. 1.

Tang Bingzheng 湯炳正 et al., eds. *Chuci jinzhu* 楚辭今注. Second edition. Shanghai: Shanghai guji chubanshe, 2012.

Wang, Chia-hsin 王家歆. *Chuci jiuzhang jishi* 楚辭九章集釋. Taipei: Shangwu yinshuguan, 1980.

Wang, Chia-hsin 王家歆. *Jiubian yanjiu* 九辯研究. Taipei: Taiwan shangwu yinshuguan, 1986.

Wang Fuzhi 王夫之 (1619–92). *Chuci tongshi* 楚辭通釋. In *Chuanshan quanshu* 船山全書, Vol. 14. Changsha: Yuelu shushe, 2011.

Wang Li 王力 (1900–86). *Chuci yundu* 楚辭韻讀. Shanghai: Shanghai guji, 1980.

Wang Yuan 汪瑗 (d. c.1566). *Chuci ji jie* 楚辭集解. Kyōto daigaku Kanseki senpon sōsho 京都大學漢籍善本叢書, 5–6. Kyoto: Dōhōsha, 1984.

Wen Yiduo 聞一多 (1899–1946). *Chuci jiaobu* 楚辭校補. Taipei: Huazheng shuju, 1977.

Wen Yiduo Chuci yanjiu lunzhu shizhong 聞一多楚辭研究論著十種. Hong Kong: Weiya shuwu, 1973.

Xu Huanlong 徐煥龍 (d. 1653). *Qu ci xisui* 屈辭洗髓. In *Chuci wenxian congkan*, Vol. 48.

You Guoen 游國恩 (1899–1978). *Lisao zuanyi* 離騷纂義. Beijing: Zhonghua shuju, 1982.

You Guoen. *Tianwen zuanyi* 天問纂義. Beijing: Zhonghua shuju, 1982.

Yu Xingwu 于省吾 (1896–1984). *Zeluoju Chuci xinzheng* 澤螺居楚辭新證. Beijing: Zhonghua shuju, 2009.

Yu Yue 俞樾 (1821–1907). 'Du Chuci' 讀楚辭. *Chuci wenxian congkan*, Vol. 68.

Yu Yue 俞樾. 'Chuci renming kao' 楚辭人名考. *Chuci wenxian congkan*, Vol. 68.

Zhou Gongchen 周拱辰 (17th c.). *Lisao caomu shi* 離騷草木史. *Xuxiu siku quanshu*.

Zhu Ji 朱冀 (Qing dynasty). *Lisao bian* 離騷辯. *Chuci huibian*, Vol. 9.

Zhu Jihai 朱季海 (1916–2011). *Chuci jiegu* 楚辭解故. Beijing: Zhonghua shuju, 1963.

Zhu Junsheng 朱駿聲 (1788–1858). *Lisao fu buzhu* 離騷賦補注. 1882; reprinted in *Chuci wenxian congkan*, Vol. 65.

Zhu Xi 朱熹 (1130–1200). *Chuci jizhu* 楚辭集注. Shanghai: Shanghai guji chubanshe, 2001.

OTHER WORKS CITED

Allan, Sarah. *Buried Ideas: Legends of Abdication and Ideal Government in Early Chinese Bamboo-Slip Manuscripts.* Albany: State University of New York Press, 2015.

Allan, Sarah. '"When Red Pigeons Gathered on Tang's House": A Warring States Period Tale of Shamanic Possession and Building Construction Set at the Turn of the Xia and Shang Dynasties.' *Journal of the Royal Asiatic Society* 25 (2015), 419–38.

Bielenstein, Hans. *The Bureaucracy of Han Times.* Cambridge: Cambridge University Press, 1980.

Chen Hung-to 陳鴻圖. 'Lun *Chuci zhangju* yunwen zhu de xingzhi yu shidai' 論《楚辭章句》韻文注的性質與時代. *Tamkang Journal of Chinese Literature* 39 (2018), 1–31.

Chen Zhi. 'A Study of the Bird Cult of the Shang People.' *Monumenta Serica* 47 (1999), 127–47.

Cheng Sudong 程蘇東. 'Liudong de wenben: Liu Xiang "Hongfan wuxing zhuanlun" yiwen kaobian' 流動的文本：劉向〈洪範五行傳論〉佚文考辨. *Zhonghua wenshi luncong* (2017.1), 261–314.

Chūbachi Masakazu 中鉢雅量. *Chūgoku no saishi to bungaku* 中国の祭祀と文学. Tokyo: Sōbunsha, 1989.

Curtius, Ernst Robert. *European Literature and the Latin Middle Ages.* Translated by Willard R. Trask. Princeton: Princeton University Press, 1973.

Cutter, Robert Joe. 'Saying Goodbye: The Transformation of the Dirge in Early Medieval China.' *Early Medieval China* 10–11 (2004), 67–129.

Diaoyu ji 琱玉集. *Xuxiu siku quanshu* 續修四庫全書.

Diwang shiji 帝王世紀. Edited by Lu Ji 陸吉. In *Ershiwu bieshi* 二十五別史. Ji'nan: Qi Lu shushe, 2000.

Erkes, Eduard. 'Ho-shang-kung's Commentary on Lao-tse.' *Artibus Asiae* 8 (1945), 119, 121–96; 9 (1946), 197–220; 12 (1941), 221–51.

Fangyan jiaojian 方言校箋. Edited by Zhou Zumo 周祖謨. Beijing: Zhonghua shuju, 1993.

Goldin, Paul. 'On the Meaning of the Name Xi wangmu, Spirit-Mother of the West.' *Journal of the American Oriental Society* 122 (2002), 83–5.

Guben Zhushu jinian jizheng 古本竹書紀年輯證. Edited by Fang Shiming 方詩銘 and Wang Xiuling 王修齡. Revised edition. Shanghai: Shanghai guji chubanshe, 2005.

Guoyu jijie 國語集解. Original commentary by Wei Zhao 韋昭 (204–73). Compiled by Xu Yuangao 徐元誥 (1876–1955). Beijing: Zhonghua shuju, 2002.

Han shu 漢書. Beijing: Zhonghua shuju, 1962.

Han Wei Liuchao biji xiaoshuo daguan 漢魏六朝筆記小說大觀. Shanghai: Shanghai guji chubanshe, 1999.

Hawkes, David. 'Ch'u-tz'u 楚辭.' In Michael Loewe, ed., *Early Chinese Texts: A Bibliographical Guide*, 48–55.

Hightower, James Robert. 'Ch'ü Yüan Studies.' In *Silver Jubilee Volume of the Zinbun Kagaku Kenkyûsho*, 192–223. Kyoto, 1954.

Hoshikawa Kiyotaka 星川孝清. *Soji no kenkyū* 楚辭の研究. Kyoto: Yodokusha, 1961.

Hu Shih 胡適. 'Du Chuci' 讀楚辭. *Dushu zazhi* 1 (1922), 2–3. Rpt. in *Hu Shi wenji* 胡適文集, 3:73–8. Beijing: Beijing daxue chubanshe, 1998.

Huang Hsing-tsung. *Science and Civilisation in China*, Vol. 6: *Biology and Biological Technology*, Part V: *Fermentations and Food Science*. Cambridge: Cambridge University Press, 2000.

Huang, Kuan-yun. 'Poetry, "The Metal-Bound Coffer", and the Duke of Zhou.' *Early China* 41 (2018), 87–148.

Jao Tsung-i 饒宗頤. *Chuci dili kao* 楚辭地理考. Shanghai: Shangwu yinshuguan, 1946; rpt. in *Rao Zongyi ershi shiji xueshu wenji* 饒宗頤二十世紀學術文集, 11:73–210. Taipei: Xin wenfeng, 2003.

Jao Tsung-i 饒宗頤. *Chuci yu ciqu yinyue* 楚辭與詞曲音樂. Rpt. in *Rao Zongyi ershi shiji xueshu wenji*, 16:367–444.

Jiang Liangfu 姜亮夫. '*Shi ji* Qu Yuan liezhuan shuzheng' 史記屈原列傳疏證. In *Jiang Liangfu quanji* 姜亮夫全集, 8:1–28. Kunming: Yunnan renmin chubanshe, 2002.

Jiang Liangfu 姜亮夫. 'Chu Ying du kao' 楚郢都考. In *Jiang Liangfu quanji*, 8:226–34.

Kinney, Anne Behnke. *Exemplary Women of Early China: The Lienü zhuan of Liu Xiang*. New York: Columbia University Press, 2014.

Knechtges, David R. *The Han shu Biography of Yang Xiong (53 B.C.– A.D. 18)*. Tempe, Ariz.: Occasional Paper No. 14. Center for Asian Studies, Arizona State University, 1982.

Knechtges, David R. 'Problems of Translating Descriptive Binomes in the *Fu*.' *Tamkang Review* (Autumn 1984–Summer 1985), 329–47.

Kominami Ichirō 小南一郎. *Soji to sono chūshakushatachi* 楚辞とその注釈者達. Kyoto: Hōyū shoten, 2003.

Kroll, Paul W. *A Student's Dictionary of Classical and Medieval Chinese*. Leiden: Brill, 2017.

Laufer, Berthold. *Sino-Iranica: Chinese Contributions to the History of Civilization in Ancient Iran: With Special Reference to the History of Cultivated Plants and Products*. Chicago: Field Museum of Natural History, 1919.

Li Hui-lin. *Nan-fang ts'ao-mu chuang: A Fourth Century Flora of Southeast Asia*. Hong Kong: Chinese University Press, 1979.

Li Zhi 力之 (Liu Hanzhong 劉漢忠). *Chuci yu zhonggu wenxian kaoshuo* 《楚辭》與中古文獻考說. Chengdu: Ba Shu shushe, 2005.

Lin Geng 林庚. '"Li sao" zhong cuanru de wenzi' 離騷中竄入的文字. In *Lin Geng Chuci yanjiu liangzhong* 林庚楚辭研究兩種, 102–6. Beijing: Qinghua daxue chubanshe, 2006.

Luo Changpei 羅常培 and Zhou Zumo 周祖謨. *Han Wei Jin Nanbeichao yunbu yanbian yanjiu* 漢魏晉南北朝韻部演變研究, Vol. 1. Beijing: Kexue chubanshe, 1958.

Maenchen-Helfen, Otto. 'Are Chinese *hsi-p'i* and *kuo-lo* IE Loan Words?' *Language* 21.4 (1945), 256–60.

Maspero, Henri. Review of Conrady and Erkes, *Das älteste Dokument zur chinesischen Kunstgeschichte, T'ien-wen…die 'Himmelsfragen' des K'üh Yüan*. *Journal Asiatique* 222 (1933), 59–74.

Maspero, Henri. 'Le Ming-t'ang et la crise religieuse chinoise avant les Han.' *Mélanges chinois et bouddhiques* 9 (1948–51), 1–70.

Mayor, Adrienne. *The Poison King: The Life and Legend of Mithridates, Rome's Deadliest Enemy*. Princeton: Princeton University Press, 2010.

Milburn, Olivia. *Cherishing Antiquity: The Cultural Construction of an Ancient Chinese Kingdom*. Cambridge, Mass.: Harvard University Asia Center, 2013.

Mori Yasutarō 森安太郎. *Kōtei densetsu: Kodai Chūgoku shinwa no kenkyū* 古代中国神話の研究. Kyoto: Kyōto joshi daigaku jinbungakukai kan, 1970.

Nagy, Gregory. 'Ancient Greek Elegy.' In *The Oxford Handbook of the Elegy*, ed. Karen Weisman, 13–45. Oxford: Oxford University Press, 2010.

Okamura Shigeru 岡村繁. 'Soji to Kutsu Gen—hīrō to sakusha to no bunri ni tsuite' 楚辭と屈原—ヒーローと作者との分離について. *Nihon Chūgoku gakkai hō* 18 (1966), 86–101.

Okamura Shigeru 岡村繁. 'Soji bungaku ni okeru "Shūshi" no ichi' 楚辭文学における「抽思」の位置. *Tōyōgaku* 16 (1966), 9–18.

Ōno Keisuke 大野圭介, ed. *Soji to So bunka no sōgōteki kenkyū* 『楚辞』と楚文化の総合的研究. Tokyo: Kyūko sho'in, 2014.

Pan Fuh-Jiunn 潘富俊. *Chuci zhiwu tu jian* 楚辭植物圖鑑. Second edition Taipei: Maotouying, 2014.

Plaks, Andrew H. 'Where the Lines Meet: Parallelism in Chinese and Western Literatures.' *Chinese Literature: Essays, Articles, Reviews (CLEAR)* 10.1/2 (1988), 43–60.

Riegel, Jeffrey K. 'Kou-mang and Ju-shou.' *Cahiers d'Extrême-Asie Année* 5 (1989), 55–83.

Schimmelpfennig, Michael. 'Qu Yuans Weg vom wahren Menschen zum wirklichen Dichter: Der Han-zeitliche Kommentar von Wang Yi zum *Li sao* und den *Liedern von Chu*.' Ph.D. diss., Heidelberg, 1999.

Schlegel, Gustave. *Uranographie chinoise*. Two volumes. Leiden: Brill, 1875.

Schuessler, Axel. *ABC Etymological Dictionary of Old Chinese*. Honolulu: University of Hawai'i Press, 2007.

Shi ji 史記. Beijing: Zhonghua shuju, 1959.

Shirakawa Shizuka 白川静. *Kodai no bungaku* 古代の文学. In *Shiraka Shizuka chosaku shō* 白川静著作集, Vol. 8. Tokyo: Heibonsha, 2000.

Shisanjing zhushu 十三經注疏. Originally published in 1815. Rpt. Taipei: Yiwen yinshuguan, 1980.

Taiping yulan 太平御覽. Beijing: Zhonghua shuju, 1960.

Tang Bingzheng 湯炳正. 'Qu fu xiuci juyu' 屈賦修辭舉隅. In *Qu fu xintan* 屈賦新探, 292–369. Ji'nan: Qi Lu shushe, 1984.

Tang Bingzheng 湯炳正. 'Chuci chengshu zhi tansuo' 《楚辭》成書之探索. In *Qu fu xintan*, 85–109.

Tang Bingzheng 湯炳正. *Chuci leigao* 楚辭類稿. Chengdu: Ba Shu shushe, 1988.

Tökei, Ferenc. *Naissance de l'élégie chinoise: K'iu Yuan et son époque*. Preface by Paul Demiéville. Paris: Gallimard, 1967.

von Falkenhausen, Lothar. 'Chu Ritual Music.' in Lawton, *New Perspectives on Chu Culture during the Eastern Zhou Period*, 47–106.

Wang Guanguo 王觀國 (*jinshi* 1119). *Xuelin* 學林. Beijing: Zhonghua shuju, 1988.

Wang Guowei 王國維. 'Yin buci zhong suo jian xiangong xianwang kao' 殷卜辭中所見先公先王考. *Guantang jilin* 觀堂集林, 9.409–37. Beijing: Zhonghua shuju, 1973.

Wang Ping. 'Sound of the Maple on the Yangzi River: A Topos of Melancholia in Early to Medieval Chinese Poetic Writing.' *Tang Studies* 26 (2008), 13–38.

Wang Zhongjiang. *Order in Early Chinese Excavated Texts: Natural, Supernatural, and Legal Approaches*. Houndsmill, Basingstoke: Palgrave Macmillan, 2016.

Wen xuan 文選. Six volumes. Shanghai: Shanghai guji chubanshe, 1986.

Wilhelm, Hellmut. 'The Scholar's Frustration: Notes on a Type of "Fu".' In John K. Fairbank, ed., *Chinese Thought and Institutions*, 310–19, 398–403. Chicago: University of Chicago Press, 1957.

Wilhelm, Richard. *The I Ching, or Book of Changes*. Rendered into English by Cary F. Baynes. Third edition. Princeton: Princeton University Press, 1967.

Wilkinson, Endymion. *Chinese History: A New Manual*. Fifth edition. Cambridge, Mass.: Harvard University Asia Center, 2018.

Williams, Nicholas Morrow, ed. *The Fu Genre of Imperial China: Studies in the Rhapsodic Imagination*. York, UK: Arc Humanities Press, 2019.

Xin xu jiaoshi 新序校釋. Compiled by Liu Xiang 劉向. Beijing: Zhonghua shuju, 2001.

Xu Wenjing 徐文靖 (1667–1756?). *Guancheng shuoji* 管城碩記. Beijing: Zhonghua shuju, 1998.

Xu Zhixiao 徐治嘯. *Riben Chuci yanjiu lungang* 日本楚辭研究論綱. Beijing: Xueyuan chubanshe, 2004.

Yan Changgui 晏昌貴. *Wugui yu yinsi: Chu jian suo jian fangshu zongjiao kao* 巫鬼與淫祀——楚簡所見方術宗教考. Wuhan: Wuhan daxue chubanshe, 2010.

Yang Lien-sheng. 'A Note on the So-Called TLV Mirrors and the Game Liu-po.' *Harvard Journal of Asiatic Studies* 9.3/4 (1947), 202–6.

Yang Lien-sheng. 'An Additional Note on the Ancient Game Liu-po.' *Harvard Journal of Asiatic Studies* 15.1/2 (1952), 124–39.

Ye Shuxian 葉舒憲, Xiao Bing 蕭兵, and Chŏng Chae-sŏ 鄭在書. *Shanhai jing de wenhua xunzong: 'Xiangxiang dilixue' yu dong xi wenhua pengchu* 山海經的文化尋踪：「想像地理學」與東西文化碰. Two volumes. Wuhan: Hubei renmin chubanshe, 2004.

Yi Zhonglian 易重廉. *Zhongguo Chuci xue shi* 中國楚辭學史. Changsha: Hunan chubanshe, 1991.

Yi Zhou shu huijiao jizhu 逸周書彙校集注. Shanghai: Shanghai guji chubanshe, 2007.

Yishi 繹史. Compiled by Ma Su 馬驌 (1621–73). Four volumes. Ji'nan: Qi Lu shushe, 2002.

You Guoen 游國恩. *Chuci lunwen ji* 楚辭論文集. 1955; rpt. Shanghai: Gudian wenxue chubanshe, 1957.

Yu, Pauline. *The Reading of Imagery in the Chinese Poetic Tradition.* Princeton: Princeton University Press, 1987.

Zhang Shuguo 張樹國. 'Han chu libian Chuci yu *Shi ji: Qu Yuan Jia sheng lie zhuan* de cailiao laiyuan' 漢初隸變楚辭與《楚辭‧屈原賈生列傳》的材料來源. *Zhonghua wenshi luncong* 28.1 (129), 61–99.

TIMELINE

Shang dynasty founded	*c.*1570 BCE
Zhou conquest of Shang	*c.*1045
Fall of Western Zhou, Spring and Autumn era begins	770
Wu Zixu commits suicide	484
Confucius dies	479
Warring States era begins	*c.*476
Death of Fuchai, final king of Wu	473
Reign of King Huai of Chu begins	328
King Huai held captive by Qin	299
Reign of King Qingxiang of Chu begins	298
King Huai dies in captivity	296
Chu capital Ying annexed by Qin	279
Reign of King Qingxiang of Chu ends	263
Chu destroyed by Qin	223
Qin unification and founding of new empire	221
Han dynasty founded by Liu Bang	202
Jia Yi dies	168
Emperor Wu reign begins	141
Liu An commits suicide	129
Sima Xiangru dies	117
Emperor Wu dies	87
Historian Sima Qian dies	86
Liu Xiang born	79
Liu Xiang charged with cataloguing imperial library	26
Liu Xiang dies	8
Wang Mang interregnum begins	9 CE
Han restored as Later Han	25
Wang Yi compiles the *Elegies* with commentary	*c.*120
Fall of Later Han	220

ELEGIES OF CHU

1. SUBLIMATING SORROW (LI SAO)
QU YUAN

I. Self-Introduction

Heir and scion of the High Lord Gaoyang, –
2   my resplendent begetter was called Boyong.
When Jupiter was ascendant in the first lunary cycle –
4   on the twenty-seventh day I descended from Heaven.

That splendid one observed and determined my initial bearing –
    and first bestowed on me an exquisite name.
He named me Righteous Principle –
8   with the cognomen of Spirit Harmony.

In splendid profusion do I possess inner beauty –
10   further complemented by consummate manner.
Adorned with river lovage and reticent angelica –
    I entwine autumn eupatory for my pendants.

In time's ceaseless torrent I cannot keep the pace –
    I fear the years and decades will not suffice me.
At dawn I gather magnolia from the hillsides –
16   at dusk I cull the dormant slough grass.

Day and night flit by me without pause –
    springs and autumns pass on in progression.
Just as the plants and trees must wither and fall –
20   so I fear that anyone admirable must grow old at twilight.

If not by relying on health and discarding the dross –
    how else to alter this condition of ours?
Charging forth unfettered upon a sterling steed,
    come, I'll lead the way on the journey ahead.

II. Spirit Paragon

25 The Three Sovereigns of old were pure and refined –
    for in them did all the fragrances abide.
So I mingle lush fagara and dainty osmanthus –
    not weaving together only sweet clover and angelica.

The ancients Yao and Shun were unwavering and resolute –
30   because they followed the Way they could pursue their path;
But Jie and Zhow behaved with reckless abandon –
         for they had taken a misway, and had their footsteps forestopped.

I think of those sycophants who indulge in passing pleasures –
         on a path that is dark and dismal, danger-filled and declivitous.
I do not fear that my own person suffer privation and peril –
36   only that the illustrious carriage should meet with disaster!

Restless I scurry and scamper, both ahead and behind –
38   to keep in step with the traces of the former Kings.
39 Lord Calamus does not perceive my inwardmost feelings –
40   but instead believes the slander, and flares up with fury.

Though I know that loyal counsel can bring calamity –
42   yet I must endure what comes and not desist.
I refer to the Ninefold Heavens as my witness –
44   all this is the fault of Spirit Paragon!

At the beginning he had made a pledge to me –
         but later he broke faith, altered course, chose another.
The separation itself is not what I suffer most –
         I only grieve for Spirit Paragon's many changes.

III. *Flowers of Virtue and Weeds of Slander*

I would irrigate nine patches of pure eupatory –
50   then plant one hundred acres of sweet clover.
Marking plots for the peony and gooseneck –
         combining there asarum and fragrant angelica.

Hoping that the branches and leaves will grow superior and lush, –
         I await the proper moment for them to be culled.
Though they wither and fade what woe is that to me? –
56   I grieve only for all those blossoms choked by weeds.

Though all the others vie for advance, grasping and greedy –
         never will I be sated with striving and seeking.
Other men, I know, judge each other so as to justify themselves –
60   in their hearts each aroused by avarice and envy;

Swiftly they gallop and race, scamper and chase –
    but that is not what my heart hastens for.
Old age inexorably encroaches upon me –
    and I fear my own fair name will not endure.

At dawn I drink the dew descending from the magnolia tree –
    at dusk sup from the bursting blooms of the autumn
        chrysanthemum.
Since my inner self is truly fair and refined in essence –
    though my skin sallow from starvation I will not grieve.

Plucking the roots of trees to weave with angelica –
70   threading the creeping fig with fallen pistils,
I raise up osmanthus braided with sweet clover –
    splicing garlic and snowparsley to dangle in garlands.

Resolutely I follow the figure of the upright men –
    not such models as vulgar people of this age conform to.
75 Should I not find accord with the men of this age –
    I would follow the model bequeathed by Peng and Xian.

Grieving that human life is constant toil –
    I heave a long sigh and check my tears;
Though I pursued refinement and grace, I am reined and curbed –
80   my honest admonitions at dawn already slandered by dusk.

81 How they slander me for my sweet clover pendants –
    and even more so for my culling of angelica.
But this is what in my heart I know to be right –
    though I face nine deaths yet will I never repent!

I resent Spirit Paragon for his immense indifference –
    his obliviousness to people's inner minds.
All the ladies envy my eyebrows exquisite as moth wings –
    and so defame me with propensity to vice.

The vulgar people of this age excel in cunning –
90   they violate the rule of compass and square, and alter the order;
91 They reject the plumb-line to pursue instead the deviant –
    vying in conformity and collusion as their only measure.

Dispirited, downcast, dejected, foiled and forestalled –
    alone I endure the desperate troubles of these times.

I would rather die at once or perish in exile –
   but I cannot bear to continue in this state.

For 'the bird of prey does not join the flock' –
   since antiquity it has ever been thus.
How can circle and square make mutual accord? –
100   how can men travel by different ways towards harmony?

Bending my heart and suppressing my will –
   I bear with this blame that I may at last be rid of shame.
On behalf of the pure and untainted, I would die for the straight path –
104   that was ever praised by the ancient sages.

I regret that in perusing the way I was not acute –
   having stood long in place, now I will go back,
Turning the carriage onto the opposite road –
108   so long as I have not already travelled too far astray.

Pacing my steed past the riverbanks of eupatory –
110   racing past fagara hillsides, where can I pause to rest?
Advancing, I do not succeed but only suffer blame –
112   retreating, I will return to perfect my original apparel:

Trimming water-chestnut and lotus to fashion my robe –
   gathering rosemallow blossoms to fashion my skirts;
115   Enough now of those who do not understand me! –
   so long as my own passions are sure and sweet.

High stands my crown, soaring up precipitously –
   broad sweep my pendants, intricately arrayed;
My fragrance and my lustre contaminated and impure –
120   yet my luminous substance has still not waned!

Now all at once I turn around and let roam my gaze –
   I will travel to observe all within the Four Margins;
My pendants are diversely disposed and intricately ornate –
   the fragrance wafts sweetly, growing ever more apparent.

In human life each takes his own pleasure –
   I alone admire self-perfection and make it my measure;
Even though I am vivisected I will not waver –
   for I know in my heart I deserve no demerit.

IV. Lady Xu

129 Lady Xu the Shamaness clings closely to me –
130   scolding me repeatedly and saying:
    'Gun lost his life for his honesty and frankness –
132   ultimately he perished in the wilds of Mount Plume.

    'Why are you immoderately righteous, so avid of perfection –
        so grandiose and solitary in your proud demeanour?
    Caltrops, carpetgrass, and cocklebur fill the royal chamber –
        unlike, alone, and apart, you refuse to conform.

    'You cannot convince all the people one household at a time –
        for who can rightly discern our inner convictions?
    The worldly collude and aid only their cronies –
140   so why must you remain alone? Why not heed my words?'

V. Lord Shun

141 Instead I take the ancient sages as my intermediaries –
    alas, that by following my heart I have come to this!
    Crossing the Yuan and Xiang to journey southward –
        I approach Shun of Many-Faceted Majesty and set forth my
            plaint:

145 'When Qi obtained the Nine Phases and Nine Songs –
        the Xia were devoted to debauchery and self-indulgent;
    They did not look out for trouble or plan for the future –
148   so his five sons were ruined in family strife.

    'Archer Yih was a dissolute man who overindulged in hunting –
150   but succeeded in shooting the great boar.
    Thus the consequences of rebellion rarely end peaceably –
152   for Han Zhuo in turn envied his master's home.

153 'Ao possessed in his person massive strength –
    but he unleashed his desires without any restraint.
    Each day further devoted to debauchery, he forgot himself –
    and so it was that his head was toppled.

    'Jie of the Xia dynasty often violated order –
    and so ultimately he too met with calamity.

And Hou Xin had men pickled and ground into paste –
160   so the sovereignty of Yin did not last long.

'Tang and Yu were upright, both reverent and pious –
162   and the Zhou cared for the Way and did not deviate.
They promoted the worthies and employed the talented –
        they adhered to the plumb-line-straight rule without partiality.

'Glorious Heaven, never partial or fawning –
        observing a person's virtue, will employ and further him.
Thus men of sagely virtue and upstanding conduct –
168   will be accorded employment in the sublunary realm.

'Peering backwards so as to perceive what lies ahead –
170   considering and noting the limits of man's schemes:
What man deserves to be employed if he be not dutiful? –
        and who deserves to be obeyed if he be not good?

'Even though I imperil myself and risk my own demise –
        I still perceive my beginnings and so regret nothing.
It was because the mortise was not to scale, the tenon not set straight –
176   that the most upright men of old were ground into paste!'

Redoubling sighs and suspirations, I am shrouded in sorrow –
        I grieve that I have not met with the right moment.
Culling the soft leaves of sweet clover I wipe the tears –
180   that soak my collar billow upon billow.

On my knees with hem outstretched, I set forth my plaint,
182   assured of my own mastery of the righteous path:
I yoke jade dragons and I ride upon a phoenix –
        now the tempest rises and I will soar aloft!

VI. *Quest for a Consort in Heaven*

At dawn I release the brake at Silver Pillar –
186   at dusk I arrive at the Hanging Garden.
I'd like to tarry a while by the divine threshold –
        but the day all of a sudden is come to dusk.

I command Xihe, sun's charioteer, to tighten the reins –
190   embarking for Mount Tarryhere but not yet near.

Though the road is long and seems to have no end —
    I will seek throughout the world above and below.

I let my steed drink at the Pool of Affinity —
194   I gather up the reins at Sunrise Mulberry.
195 I pluck a branch of Dimming Wood to block the sun —
    I wander where I please and roam at leisure.

Before me I have Prospect Shu as advance scout —
198   behind me Flying Lian brings up the rear.
Towering simurghs watch as my vanguard —
200   the Master of Thunder warns of the unknown.

I command the Phoenix to fly out ahead —
    and follow behind it day and night.
The whirlwind gathers itself up and then disperses —
204   leading clouds and coronas comes to welcome me.

In tempest and tumult they split and fuse again —
    in iridescent splendour they plummet and then rise.
I command the High Lord's watchman to release the latch —
    but he just leans on Heaven's portal staring back at me.

As the season dims to dusk I prepare to depart —
210   knotting up recondite eupatory I linger a while.
The worldly are confounded and corrupt, discerning nothing —
    in their jealousy and rancour they miss all that is beautiful.

213 At dawn I cross over the Whitewater —
    climb up Skywind and tether my horse there.
Suddenly I look back and my tears flow down —
216   I lament that there is no lady on the Mound of Gao!

I rush back now to visit the Palace of the Spring —
    Snap off a jade branch to add to my ornaments.
So long as a flourishing bloom has not yet perished —
220   I'll look for a lady below worthy of bestowing it.

I command Fenglong to ride upon the clouds —
222   in quest of the goddess Fu Fei.
I undo my accoutrements and prepare to make my vow —
224   I send out Plainspoken Paragon to be my agent.

Frequent and fraught are our partings and unions –
   now this wrangling rift makes it hard to move her.
At dusk she returns to sojourn at Desperation Rock –
228   at dawn she rinses her hair at Wei Basin.

Preserving her beauty with all overweening pride –
230   she finds delight ever in profligate pleasure;
Though she is truly fair, yet she lacks propriety –
   so I must depart, reject her, and shift my suit.

I spy, seek, and find amid all the Four Extremities –
   roaming the Heavens till I finally descend.
I gaze towards Chalcedony Terrace, sublimely soaring –
236   and see there the peerless daughter of the Yousong clan.

I send the serpent eagle as my matchmaker –
   but he cautions me of ill to come.
The turtledove calls out to me as I depart –
240   but I loathe its insinuations and intrigues.

In my heart I still hesitate, dither, and delay –
   I would like to advance myself but cannot.
The phoenix has already received my token –
244   but I fear the Highlord Gaoxin has preceded me.

I'd like to find a perch afar but have no place to rest –
   instead I must meander and drift along, roaming detached;
So long as Shaokang has not yet married –
248   the two Princesses of the Youyu clan are still available.

My intermediary is weak and my matchmaker clumsy –
250   I fear their pleaful speeches may seem specious.
The worldly are confounded and befouled, envying the talented –
   wilfully they eschew all that is beautiful and call it ugly.

The inner sanctum remains secret and secluded –
   nor has the sagely king yet been enlightened.
Harbouring these passions that cannot be expressed –
256   how could I endure with these through all eternity?

VII. The First Divination

I gathered jade-like rushes along with bamboo strips and tablets –
258   commanded Spirit Aura to divine for me.
He spake: 'Two forms of beauty will certainly become allied –
260   can someone truly sublime remain unyearned for?

'Considering the vastness of the Nine Continents –
    can this be the only place there is a Lady to court?'
He spake again: 'Strive to go far off and have no doubt –
264   what seeker of beauty would discard one like you?

'What manner of place has no fragrant plants at all? –
    Why do you continue to pine for your home of old?
The world is blind and benighted, dazzled by brilliance –
268   who is there who can perceive the good or ill in us?

'People's likes and dislikes are not entirely the same –
270   but this cabal of mediocrities is by far the worst.
At every house they put on mugwort to fill their sashes –
    and decry the recondite eupatory as unfit for adornment.

'Not even capable of distinguishing among the grasses and trees –
    they can scarcely discern the proper balance of jade emblems;
They would fill their incense pouch with lumps of ordure –
    yet still profess the lithesome fagara is not sweet!'

VIII. The Second Divination

I'd like to follow the auspicious augury of Spirit Aura –
    but still hesitate in my heart, dithering and delaying;
Since Shaman Xian will descend at dusk –
280   I hold up the sacrificial rice and fagara as I await him.

The hundred gods fill the air as they prepare to descend –
    teeming from the Nine Semblances they welcome me.
Majestic in fiery splendour he displays his numinousness –
    and reports to me of the auspicious case:

Saying, 'Strive to ascend and descend, travelling above and below –
    seeking to accord with the square and compass!
Tang and Yu were earnest and sought agreement –
288   with ministers like Yi Zhi and Gaoyao they could achieve harmony.'

If in their inner feelings they were fond of perfection –
290   then what need to employ a go-between?
Yue was pounding earthen walls in the crags of Fu –
292   when Wu Ding employed him without a qualm.

While Lü Wang was brandishing a butcher's knife –
     he found his true métier by meeting King Wen of Zhou;
Again while Ning Qi was idly singing a ditty by the carriage –
     Duke Huan of Qi overheard and appointed him as aide.

I'll use the years I have before it is too late –
     so long as I know my moment has not yet passed:
I only fear the shrike will cry out first –
300   and cause the hundred grasses to lose their fragrance.

IX. *Reconsidering the Journey*

My garnet medallions dangling I soar sublime –
     while the masses of men are muddled and oblivious.
How untrustworthy are the members of that clique! –
     I fear that out of jealousy they will wreak destruction.

The times are chaotic and confused, mutating and devolving –
     how is there any way to make them stay?
Eupatory and angelica are changed and lose their fragrance –
     calamus and sweet clover become mere cogongrass.

Why is it that the aromatic herbs of olden times –
310   are now become nothing but wormwood and mugwort?
Can there be any other cause for this calamity –
     than the harm done by neglecting virtue's practice?

I thought that eupatory blossoms were something dependable –
314   in fact they had a fine appearance but no substance.
They disdained their own beauty to conform to the vulgar –
     that they might be ranked high among all the other blossoms.

Fagara specialized in sycophancy and self-conceit –
318   and prickly-ash sought to enter the sachet of adornments.
When they vie for advancement and sweat for success –
320   how can such fragrances be respected?

Conforming and submitting to the trends of the time –
    who can endure without devolving into error?
Observing how even fagara and eupatory have come to this –
    what more need be said of mere gooseneck or river lovage?

Only these pendants of mine still deserve to be prized –
    but trusting in their beauty is what brought me to this.
Scents wafting sweetly will scarcely wither –
    that fragrance till now has not yet been obscured.

Modulating, moderating the tone to suit my own pleasure –
330   I'll roam a while further in search of a lady.
So long as my appearance is properly embellished –
    I'll reel, and roam, and rove both below and above.

According to Spirit Aura's fine augury for me –
    on that fortunate day I prepare to depart.
I snap off a carnelian branch to serve as my oblation –
336   distil the splintered carnelian to serve as my victuals.

Driving winged dragons on before me –
    join chalcedony and ivory to make my chariot.
If hearts divided can never be united –
340   I'll travel far off so as to make myself remote.

Swerving on my path towards Kunlun –
    the road extends far off and circles all around.
Lifting up clouds and nimbuses that block out the sun –
    my jade chimes resound with sonorous ring.

At dawn I loose the brake at Heaven's Ford –
    at dusk I arrive at the western pole.
Phoenixes winging alongside hold up dragon pennants –
    aloft they soar and skim on pennons outstretched.

Now I scurry across the land of Sinking Sands –
350   till by the River Scarlet I halt in hesitation.
I beckon the Flood Dragon to ford me past the ocean,
352   summon the Sovereign of the West to ferry me thither.

The road toward the far horizon is full of hardship –
    I command countless chariots to attend me on the flank.

I pass Broken Mountain and turn towards the left –
356   still aiming at the ocean in the West for my rendezvous.

I join my carriage with one thousand chariots –
    jade axles parallel we charge on together.
I yoke eight dragons before me, sinuously circling –
360   hold up cloud pennants that twirl and whirl around me.

Though I check my own ambitions and rein in my steed –
    my spirit races aloft towards indiscernible infinity.
363 I perform the Nine Songs and I dance the sacred Shao –
    I spend the day idling in leisure and delight.

Rising into the heavens in a blaze of radiance –
    for an instant I peer back down towards my homeland.
The driver is wistful and my steeds look woeful –
    idly gyring to and fro, I gaze back and advance no farther.

Envoi

369 All is done, alas, all done!
370 There is no one in the realm who knows me –
    why should I still pine for my old home?
372 Since there is none here with whom to rule in harmony –
    I shall follow Peng and Xian to the place where they abide.

2. NINE PHASES
ATTRIBUTED TO SONG YU

I. *Autumn Meditation*

Alas! How sorrowful is the breath of autumn:
  how desolate its sigh! – which makes grasses and trees shed their
    leaves and die.
We are disconsolate and doleful – as if travelling afar,
  as gazing on rivers from high mountaintops – or saying a farewell.

In the measureless vastness – of heaven above, the air is pristine.
Silent and unperturbed – the floods recede and the waters clear.

What pain and pangs redouble our sighs –
  as the chill air assaults us.
What trauma and trouble, how raw the regret –
10   departing the old to face the new.
A penniless gentleman I – rough and ragged,
  no profession and ambitions unsettled.
Immeasurably far – will be this friendless journey;
  swathed in sorrow – and only myself for solace.

Swallows flit and flutter as they set off for home –
  cicadas stay still and silent without a chirp.
17 The wild geese trumpet a tune as they journey south –
  the demoiselle crane whistles its mournful cry.
Alone and alert till dawn without sleeping –
20   I grieve while the crickets keep busy all night.
Time passes inexorably past the mean –
  yet I linger here still with nothing accomplished.

II. *Longing for the Sovereign*

Mournful, afflicted, fearful, distraught – I abide alone in the world;
  yet there is a beauty – from whom my longings are inseparable.
Departing my land and leaving my domain – a traveller venturing afar,
  even further I roam and wander – no destination now.

For my liege only am I longing – but I cannot change him,
　　in his uncomprehending state – what is to be done?
Brooding in resentment – ever more pensive,
30　　my heart anxious and unquiet – I forget even to eat.
I wish only to see him once – to tell of my intent;
　　but the heart of my liege – is not in accord with mine.
My carriage now readied – I set off back homewards;
　　because I cannot meet him – my heart is wracked by worry.

Leaning upon the carriage-rail – I heave a deep sigh;
　　my tears pour down in torrents – drenching the crossbar.
Utterly depressed and dejected – I find no success,
　　my mind clouded in chaos – lost in confusion.
Lamenting my own plight – without limit,
40　　though my thoughts are in turmoil – yet I am true and
　　　　incorrupt.

III. Grieving for the Seasons

The four seasons were set apart by mighty Heaven –
　　but I grieve especially in the chill of Autumn.
Bright dew has fallen on the hundred grasses –
　　while the mallotus and parasol trees wither.
Departing the refulgent splendour of the bright sun –
　　I enter the endless dark of the long night.
Relinquishing the fragrant foliage at its bloom –
　　wasted and wan, I pine and fret.

Autumn's premonition in the bright dew –
50　　winter deepened with the deadly frost,
Subduing the wanton wildness of high summer –
　　all foiled, forestalled, receding, retreating.
The leaves wither away and have no hue at all –
　　the bare boughs form a lattice interlocking.
Their colours grow bold and brilliant before they fade –
　　bare trunks begin to show as the leaves brown and fall.
How pitiable these the bare branches starkly protruding –
　　their living forms desiccated and degenerating.
Pondering that chaotic confounding of forms about to fall –

60   how I regret missing the moment to find my place!
       Seizing the tracer-horses' bridle I press upon the reins –
           I'll roam easy and free, dither and dally here.
       How swiftly the years have passed, now nearing expiry –
           I only fear I will not be able to fulfil my life's span.
       And mourn that my birth was not timely –
           for I fell into this world of disorder and disarray.
       I linger in tranquillity, standing solitary –
           while crickets chirp in the western palace;
       Uneasy and anxious, tremulous and troubled –
70   how can there be so many facets to one grief?
       Gazing up at the full moon I heave a sigh –
           till dawn stroll on beneath the serried stars.

IV. Finding the Way

       How I suffer as the blossoms of sweet clover once piled high –
           now are scattered and strewn in the courtly chamber.
       Why do those many-petalled blooms bear no fruit –
           but scatter along with the wind and rain?
       I had thought my liege alone was adorned in sweet clover –
           in fact he could not tell it from another fragrance.
       Ruing that these strange ponderings of mine cannot be told –
80   instead I will depart my lord and take flight heavenward.
       Mourning and tormented, my heart sore and sorrowful –
           I only wish to see him once more and make myself manifest.
83   I will have no more resentment at this parting-in-life –
           though inner feelings are knotted up, grief ever sharper.

       Why should I not be downcast as I long for my lord? –
           the gates surrounding my lord are ninefold.
       Fierce hounds yelp and yowl at me, and snarl when
           I approach –
           the barriers and bridges are blocked and impassable.

       High Heaven overflows with autumn downpours –
90   when will Sovereign Earth be dry again?
       I alone keep solitary vigil bereft of vivifying moisture –
           gazing at the clouds that drift past I sigh without cease.

V. Upsetting the Order

Why do the vulgar of this age craft their deceptions –
94   rejecting the plumb-line rule and altering the order?
They decline the sterling steeds and do not ride them –
     while whipping on jade and nag to take to the road.
Could it be that our age lacks a single outstanding steed? –
     No, it is only that there is no true master of riding.
I know well this rein-master is not the right man –
100   for the steeds leap and bolt till they have vanished.
Mallard and goose peck at the millet and waterweeds –
     while only the phoenix soars ever closer to the heavens.

When tenon is rounded and mortise square –
     they surely mismatch and cannot be joined.
All the species of birds have a place to climb and perch –
     the phoenix alone searches vagabond, without place to pause.
I would gag myself and have no more words to speak –
     though I once received the generous favour of my lord.
Lord Tai was ninety before attaining eminence and glory –
110   truly he had not ever met his match before then.

Say, oh thoroughbred racer – when will you return?
     Say, oh propitious phoenix – where can you perch?
Altering tradition, changing the old ways – the world declines;
     the experts of today – elevate even the flabbiest of
        steeds!

While thoroughbreds go into hiding and are not seen –
     the royal phoenix flies far up high and finds no perch.
Even bird and beast know to cherish mutual obligation –
118   why should noble men abide with their due merit unknown?

A thoroughbred does not plead for the harness to satisfy
     ambition –
120   nor does a phoenix consume carelessly to sate its gluttony.
When the sovereign exiles you and does not recognize you –
     though you long to be loyal how can it be achieved?

Though I aim only for serenity, eschewing all acclaim –
     yet I dare not forget the favour that I knew once.

Melancholy and grief have caused these wounds –
    have shrouded me in interminable gloom.

VI. *Abiding in Poverty*

Frost and dew descend on me, mingling with misery –
    I waver and quaver but cannot find success.
Hail and snow plummet pell-mell upon me –
130   I know that I must soon meet my fate.
I wish I could by compromise obtain fair treatment –
    but remaining in this waste land I'll die among the weeds.

Though I'd like to forge a path of my own –
    the roads are barricaded and impassable.
I hope to follow the way and race on at steady pace,
    yet I cannot tell whither it leads.
When along the road I find myself deluded and astray –
138   I strive to calm myself a while in study and in song.
Because of my simple nature I am irritable and impatient –
140   I can never attain calm and composure.

141 How I admire the supremely spirited Shen Baoxu –
    I only fear that in this age people are not so resolute.
Why do the mass of men craft such contrivances –
    destroying rules and measures, altering the order?
I alone am loyal and upright, and not easily swayed –
    for I revere that teaching bequeathed by past sages.
To abide in a defiled age by earning eminence and honours –
    is no object for my heart to delight in!
As for lacking devotion while possessing fame –
150   I'd rather abide in poverty yet preserve my ideals.

Though I sup on insipid fare I'll still eat my fill –
    though I don awkward garb still keep myself warm.
How I aspire to the manner bequeathed by that poet in the *Songs* –
154   I vow like him to shun the 'bread of idleness'.
155 By honesty satisfied and sated, no other means at hand –
    I will remain in this boundless, barren land.
But with no robe or fur to ward off the winter –
    I fear death could come before I see the springtime sun again.

VII. Days Depart

In the stillness of the long night at autumn's end –
160   my heart enwrapped and enwreathed in sorrow,
the springs and autumns pass into the distance, the sun high overhead –
       I condole myself for this disquiet and distress.
The four seasons pass in succession and the year comes to an end –
       Yin and Yang cannot be shared simultaneously.
The sun has dimmed to dusk and soon will set –
       the moonlight wanes steadily until it ceases.
The year now passes precipitously on towards its end –
       old age encroaches steadily, decay extends its sway.
My heart was stirred to delight enjoying ever-greater favour –
170   but now I am steeped in melancholy and despair.
My inner self wrung and wrenched with gloom and woe –
       I weep for my state and heave another sigh.

The years accumulate past numbering as the days depart –
       while old age looms vast upon me I cannot rest.
As all things shift ineluctably, I long to advance,
       but instead must linger and languish here, halting in hesitation.

VIII. Hoping for an Audience

How they surge and swell, the clouds above! –
       rushing forward to block and obscure the bright moon;
By right of my loyalty's pure radiance, I deserve an audience –
180   but through this murk and miasma I have no way to pass.

I wish that the sun could shine forth in glory –
       but the clouds, dimming and darkening, obscure it.
Truly I cannot dally here but long to be loyal to my lord –
       yet other men with pollution and corruption besmirch him.

The upright deeds of sages Yao and Shun –
       illuminate the void and vastness all the way to Heaven.
How severe and steep must have been men's jealousy –
       to slander even sages with lacking parental virtue.

Sun and moon once shone brilliantly –
190   but with dimming of day jade's flaws become apparent.

How much worse for the affairs of a single state –
    now sundered into many by rift and rupture.

193 Those men wear lotus jackets which are richly resplendent –
    but billowing out broadly, cannot be belted back.
He prides himself in glorious mien and also martial courage –
    but frustrates his advisors who were noble and upright.
He detests, resents, condemns the virtuous and fine –
    and prefers servants of passionate intensity.
The many trudging drudge-like are promoted further –
200   while worthy men are far removed and face demise.
The peasants cease their ploughing and dally in pleasure –
    but I fear that the farm crops will wither and rot.
As controversies grow numberless and selfishness is rife –
    I must grieve for the perils and the ruin to come.
Though all in the world are indistinguishable in their boasting –
    they are blind to the difference between fame and ignominy.

Now I refine my dress and peer into the mirror –
    for the future how could I seclude and conceal myself?
I'd like to send a message with a shooting star –
210   but all passes in a moment's flash and I lose the pace.
Finally blocked and barred by the drifting clouds –
    all below is a murky maelstrom without light

IX. *Reflecting on Antiquity*

Yao and Shun could elevate the talented in every case –
    reclining upon a pillow they succeeded by spontaneity.
Truly they were not resented by anyone under Heaven –
    at heart they had no need to cavil or take caution.
Just so on a thoroughbred racer prancing and pacing –
    the driver need not ever apply a heavy whip.
Truly walls and ramparts cannot be relied on –
220   even weighty armour bears little benefit.
Though I bend in deference and duty, I have no destination –
    but wallow in misery, wretched and woeful.
A man lives between heaven and earth like a wayfarer –
    if his task is not accomplished then all is for naught.

I'd rather sink into isolation with no audience at court –
　　but at least spread my name through the realm.
In all this tumult and transformation I cannot find a patron –
　　but flounder foolishly and further trouble myself.

In this vast universe that extends to the infinite –
230　　swiftly I soar upwards but towards what end?
In this kingdom there are fine steeds but no one expert at riding –
　　so why fret and frown about searching once again?

Ning Qi sang a ditty beneath the king's carriage –
234　　Duke Huan of Qi heard and recognized him.
Without a master like Bole to recognize talent –
　　who today could employ or praise men of their ilk?
Distraught, my tears stream down in worry and woe –
　　I can only fix my resolve to find success:
Abundant in earnest sincerity I aim to be loyal –
240　　but jealousy runs rampant and prevents me.

Envoi

I would fain give my unworthy body up and depart –
　　letting my thoughts float free amid the clouds:
Riding on the spiralling swirlings of the vital pneuma –
　　I will chase the close configurations of the sky spirits;
Will drive the rippling revolutions of the silvery coronas –
　　pass over the sundry spirits mustering en masse.
To the left the Vermilion Bird wafts winging by –
248　　to right the Azure Dragon creeps uncoiling past.
I dispatch the booming bolts of the Master of the Thunder –
250　　guide forward the whirring whirlwinds of Flying Lian.
Ahead of me the coaches and carriages jingle-jangle –
　　behind the luggage train trundling slowly along,
Bearing cloud pennants that curve and coil –
　　with cavalry guard fanning out far behind.

My design is of true devotion and will not alter –
　　merely to advance and achieve some merit.
Relying on awesome Heaven's kind blessings –
　　may his majesty be preserved ever unharmed.

3. NINE SONGS
ATTRIBUTED TO QU YUAN

I. Supreme Unity, Sovereign of the East

On this auspicious day – of stars propitiously arrayed,
Reverently shall we entertain – His supreme Majesty.
Wielding the broadswords – with hilt of jade,
  clinging and clanging resound – his nephrite gems.
On agate-studded seat – weighted with jade,
  we gather, prepare, raise – the ruby-like blossoms.
Presenting melilotus-scented chops – on bed of eupatory,
  we offer osmanthus-scented wine – and fagara liqueurs.

Raise the mallet – and beat the drums,
10 slow the rhythm a bit – and sing on gently.

Set out the mouth-organs and zithers – and sing out loud!
Divinities swing and swivel – in bewitching robes,
  a fragrance sweet and sultry – fills the court.
The five tones sound in profusion – and rich harmony,
  our lord is delighted – what joy and contentment for all!

II. Lord Amid the Clouds

Bathing in eupatory waters – hair sprinkled in sweet scents,
2   Gorgeously arrayed in many colours – like iridescent jade.
3 The god sways and spins – and then stops,
    his brilliance gleaming and glistening – without end.
5 He advances steady and tranquil – to the Palace of Long Life;
    his glory is equal to – that of sun and moon.
Carriage drawn by dragons – in the regalia of the High Lord,
    now he soars overhead – and circles all around.

Divinity in its brilliant splendour – now descends,
10   and rush far off and up – into the clouds.
Gazing down upon Jizhou – and far beyond,
    crossing the Four Oceans – towards what destination?
How I long for my lord – and heave a great sigh.
    I am sore at heart – suspiring in sorrows.

III. Lady of the Xiang River

You do not advance – but dither and delay,
For whom do you stay fixed – upon that isle?
Your beauty is wondrous to behold – so fittingly adorned.
Swiftly I ride – on my osmanthus-scented vessel.
You calm the Yuan and Xiang – they have not a ripple;
  you cause the waters of the Jiang – to flow along serenely.

How I wait in hope for her – but she does not come.
As I blow the panpipes – who is longing for me?

I drive a winged dragon – proceeding northward,
10 Then turn my route – to Dongting Lake.
With creeping fig for canopy – enfolded in sweet clover,
  calamus for my flagpoles – and eupatory banners.
I gaze towards the farthest shore – of Cenyang,
  cross the great River – and send forth my spirit.

Though I send forth my spirit – it does not arrive,
Ladies bid and beckon – and heave sighs on my behalf.
My tears pour down in torrents – flux and flow.
  This hidden longing for my lord – turns me inside out.

With oars of osmanthus – planks scented of eupatory,
20 I slice through ice floes – and banks of snow.
Just like plucking the creeping fig – from out of the water,
22 or picking lotus blossoms – from the treetops:
When hearts are not aligned – the matchmaker works in vain;
  when love is not sufficient – a lover is discarded lightly.

25 The shallow rapids speed – across the stones,
While the winged dragon – skits rapidly along.
You were not faithful to our troth – I will ever be bitter;
  you did not keep the rendezvous – told me you were not free.

At dawn you rush along – past riverbend,
30 at dusk you slow the pace – at northern islet.
Birds perch – upon the roof;
  water circles – below the palace.
33 I have tossed my halfmoon of jade – away in the River;

I have left my pendants – on the shores of the Li.
I gather blossoms of ginger-lily – from the fragrant isles,
    to bestow upon – her handmaidens.
The moment cannot be – recaptured,
    so let us roam and ramble – and dally in delight.

IV. Mistress of the Xiang

The High Lord's child descends – to the northern islet,
2   Her gaze glinting in the distance – fills me with sorrow.
I hear the gentle rustling – of the autumn wind,
    Dongting's waters ripple – as the tree leaves fall.

5 Climbing through the white bulrushes – I gaze far off,
    Meeting at the propitious hour – when the evening is outstretched,
Why would birds flock – together in the waterclover,
    or nets be placed – up in the trees?

There is angelica in the Yuan – eupatory in the Li,
10   I long for the young lord – but dare not speak.
Gazing as far as – to the hazy horizon,
    I watch the flux – of the streaming current.

Why do elaphure nibble – in the courtyard?
14   What are the krakens doing – at water's edge?
At dawn I race my steed – from River's bend,
    at dusk I cross – to the western shore.
I heard the Fair One – summon me,
    and I will speed my car – to depart by her side.
I built a chamber – here in the waters,
20   I thatched for it – a ceiling of lotus.

With walls of calamus – yard of purple stoneseed,
    planting fragrant fagara – I construct my palace:
with osmanthus purlins – and eupatory eaves,
    magnolia lintels – and angelica chambers.
I weave the creeping fig – to form a canopy,
    split sweet clover for eaves – till all is prepared.
With white jade – to serve as clamps,
    we set in place oreorchis – to make it fragrant.
Thatching with angelica – a roof of lotus,
30   interwoven with – sweet asarum.

Gathering the hundred plants – to fill the yard,
    building out of far-spreading fragrance – my house and gate.
The Nine Semblances all together – come to welcome her,
34   the gods arrive all at once – like so many clouds.

I toss my sleeves off – into the River,
   bequeath my singlet – to the shores of the Li.
I gather ginger-lily from – the sandbars and reefs,
   that I may bestow it – on the one so far away.
The moment cannot be – captured of a sudden,
40   so let us roam and ramble – and dally in delight.

V. *Greater Controller of Destinies*

Open it wide – the gate of Heaven!
Splendidly I ride forth – upon the dark clouds.
Commanding the whirlwind – to be my vanguard,
  ordering the tempest – to sweep the dust away.

Lord, gyrating in flight – you descend;
Passing beyond Sky Mulberry – I will follow you.
The vast profusion and plenty – of all the Nine Provinces,
  how could long life or early death – be decided by me?

Flying high above – and soaring serenely,
10 I ride the untainted air – I drive the Yin and the Yang.
You and I – speed along at the same pace,
  leading you, Lord on High – to the Nine Chasms.

My deified robes – trailing tenuous behind,
My jade pendants – splendorously sparkle.
With one Yin – and then one Yang,
  none of the people knows – what is done by me.

Plucking the soma – and blossoms of jade,
I will bequeath them – to the one from whom I am divided.
Old age imperceptibly encroaching – has already arrived,
20 if we cannot approach – then we must be estranged.

Riding the dragon – with its thunderous roar,
Bearing up high – charging into Heaven;
I weave together the osmanthus branches – and stand still,
  but only long yet more keenly – ensorrowing myself.

Ensorrowing myself – but what to do?
If only we could go on as now – without fading.
But after all human life – has its necessities:
  who can effect – these partings and these unions?

VI. Lesser Controller of Destinies

Autumn eupatory – and selinea,
Arrayed throughout – the courtyard.
Verdant leaves – and unadorned branches,
   their overflowing fragrance – surrounds me.
For men of course will have – their own sweethearts,
   Lord Calamus, why ever – must you suffer from worry?

Autumn eupatory – blooms abundant
With verdant leaves – and purple stalks.
Though they fill the courtyard – beautiful ladies,
10   suddenly your eyes lock – with mine.

Arriving without words – departing without speech,
You ride the whirlwind – borne on cloud pennants.

No grief is more grievous than – a parting in life;
No joy more joyous than – new acquaintance.

With robes of lotus – and sash of sweet clover,
Suddenly you come – swiftly you depart;
Resting in the evening – in the precincts of the Divine,
   whom else to meet – at the margin of cloud?

With you I will roam – on the Nine Rivers,
20 Through the blast of wind – raising waves upon the stream.
21 With you I bathe – at the Pool of Affinity,
You dry your hair – on a sunlit knoll.
I long for my Beauty – who does not come,
   facing the winds in my frustration – I sing out boldly.

With your peacock-plumed canopy – and halcyon flags,
26 You ascend the Ninefold Heavens – seizing the comets there.
Holding upright your long sword – you aid the young and fair:
   you, Lord Calamus, alone are worthy – to bring justice to all.

VII. *Lord of the East*

Luminously it appears – there in the East,
Shining upon my balustrade – at Sunrise Mulberry.
I urge my steed forward – drive steadily on,
    as a gleam appears – abruptly in the night.

Dragons lead my chariot-shafts – as I ride upon the lightning,
With cloud-pennants – swaying sinuously behind.
I heave a long sigh – and prepare to ascend;
    my heart lingers in longing – I gaze back on my love.
Ah! How the sound and beauty – please us,
10   till the audience in its ecstasy – forgets to go home.

The zither strings are taut – we strike the drums in unison,
12 Sound the bells – on their chalcedony frame.
Play the bamboo flutes – blow the mouth-organ,
    longing for that surrogate of spirit – so worthy and fair.
Flitting up into the air – with featherlike facility,
16   they declaim poems – and dance in unison.

They follow the pitches – accord with the rhythm,
Till the coming of the deity – occludes the sun.

Robes like clouds in the blue – jackets like white haloes,
20 Raising the long quiver – I shoot down the Wolf of Heaven.
Wielding my bow – I fall back and dive below,
    grabbing the Northern Dipper – to pour an osmanthus libation.
Seizing the reins – I soar again on lifted wing,
Journeying off – east into boundless heaven.

VIII. Sire of the Yellow River

1　Together with you I'll roam – the Nine Rivers,
　　While the gale wind raises – torrential waves.
　　Let us ride a water carriage – with lotus canopy,
　　　　driving twin dragons – and triple wyverns.

　　Ascending Mount Kunlun – and looking in all four directions,
　　My heart flew up – exhilarated and alive.

　　Now as day nears dusk – I'm reluctant to return,
　　Still feeling such longing – nostalgia for the farthest shore.

　　Your chambers are of fishscales – in dragon sanctums,
10　　towers of violet molluscs – in vermilion palaces:
　　What is that god about – here beneath the waves?

　　Riding a white sea tortoise – chasing the dappled fish,
　　Together with you I'll roam – on the reefs of the Yellow River;
　　Adrift in the currents – coming down together.
　　Clasping your hand – to depart for the East,
　　　　I'll send you off, my Beauty – to the southern shore.
　　The waves surge and swell – in welcome,
　　　　fish shoal upon shoal – escorting us home.

IX. *Spectre of the Mountains*

Somebody is faintly visible – up on the hillspur,
2 Dressed in creeping fig – adorned with lady-lichen;

Now she winks modestly – now a splendid smile:
'You adore me – for my goodness and delicate beauty'.

Riding a crimson leopard – she follows a striped raccoon-dog,
On magnolia cars – we weave osmanthus banners.
Adorned in oreorchis – bearing fine asarum,
    plucking a spray of flowing fragrance – to give to my beloved.
'I abide in a secluded bamboo grove – where I never see the sky.
10   The road is rough and hard – and I cannot come till later.'

Standing alone and unique – upon this hill,
    clouds glide past – far beneath her.
All is shrouded in obscurity – and darkness at noon.
    The East Wind blows – and sacred spirits rain down.
Oh, Spirit Paragon, stay! – dally here and forget to go home;
    the season is late – whose splendour will remain?

Gathering the tricolour bloom – here in the mountains,
Where boulders pile precipitously – and kudzu vines tangle and entwine,
'I resent that young lord – I am so wretched I forget to return.
20   you once cared for me – but now have no time for me.'

That goddess in the mountains – fragrant as ginger-lily,
Drinking streams from amid the stones – shaded in pine and cypress,
'You once cared for me – but then doubts arose.'

The thunder thrashes and clashes – down the rain rushes and gushes.
Gibbons howl and wail – and call out again in the night.

The wind soughs and sighs – keening, crying through the trees:
'For my love of that young lord – I have met only with sorrow.'

X. *Martyrs of the Realm*

Wielding glaives of Wu – clothed in rhinoceros armour,
Chariot wheels interlock – and close weapons cross.

The banners block out the sun – our opponents like clouds.
Our arrows cross and fall – soldiers vie to advance.

They broach the ranks – they invade our lines,
The steed to left is slaughtered – the righthand one cut down.

Both chariot-wheels buried – the four steeds are fettered.
Lift the jade baton – to strike the sounding drums.
Heaven in its time struck down – our proud spirits enraged,
10 Valiant men were slaughtered – bodies discarded on the open plain.

11 We departed but did not return – we travelled but did not arrive;
One moment of action on the plain – then a journey impossibly far.

Bearing our broadswords – and longbows of Qin under arm,
Heads cut away from our bodies – our hearts remain unchastened.
Truly you were brave – and also fought with prowess;
    to the end your resolve and fortitude – could not be overcome.
Though the bodies may die – your spirits are divine,
18   and your earthsouls and skysouls – will be heroes among the dead.

XI. *Rite for Souls*

Complete the ceremony – join in the sound of drums,
    pass the petals along – and dance in turn;
Comely maidens sing – and dally in delight:
    in spring the eupatory – in autumn the chrysanthemums;
Forever without dying ever – till the end of time.

4. HEAVENLY QUESTIONS
ATTRIBUTED TO QU YUAN

I. Formation of the Universe

It was said:

I

Regarding the beginnings of the primordial age,
    who recorded the events and told us of them?
Before all above and below had taken shape,
    what way was there to investigate it?

2

When light and dark were still indistinct,
    who could fully comprehend them?
In that chaotic congeries of semblances,
    how could anything be differentiated?

3

How were dawn's light and night's dark
    formed separately and created?
Of Yin, Yang, the Three Conjoined:
    which is original and which is altered?

4

The Heavenly Sphere divided ninefold,
    how can its circumference be measured?
What craft was responsible for it?
    Who could have created it in the beginning?

5

Where are the axle and mainstays attached?
    Where is the fulcrum of Heaven placed?
How do the Eight Pillars support the Earth?
    Why is the Southeast truncated?

6

Regarding the margins of the Nine Heavens:
    where are they placed and where do they connect?

Though corners and interstices are many,
who can know their number in full?

7

Into what sections is Heaven partitioned?
   How are the Twelve Stations divided?
To what entity are subjoined the sun and moon?
   How are the serried stars disposed?

8

Rising out of Sunny Vale
   to lodge at Murky Strand,
From dawning all the way to dusk,
   how many miles does the sun travel?

9

What power possesses nocturnal radiance
   that it may die and then grow back again?
What advantage does it constitute
   that a rabbit is perceived within its belly?

10

Lady Tangent never mated,
   so how could she obtain Nine Sons?
Where does the Sire of Might reside?
   Where do the gentle airs abide?

11

What is it that closes when darkness descends?
   What is it whose opening brings light?
When the Horn Portal has not yet risen,
   where does the radiant spirit hide?

II. Heroes from the Age of Floods

12

Were Gun not appointed to control the floods,
   why would the masses have elevated him?
The officials said: 'Why be anxious?
   'Why not test him with the challenge?'

13

As for the giant tortoises drawing and leading,
  how did Gun follow their example?
When he had achieved the desired task,
  why did the Lord still punish him?

14

When imprisoned at Plume Mountain till his death,
  why was the corpse not displayed for three years?
When Prince Yu was born from Gun's belly,
  how were these metamorphoses contrived?

15

Continuing the legacy of his predecessors,
  Yu ultimately accomplished the task of his father.
Why, to further the effort and advance the work,
  did he use such different stratagems?

16

The abyss of the floodwaters most deep,
  how could he block the flow?
When he divided the earth into nine levels,
  how could he further build it into embankments?

17

How did the Responding Dragon measure them?
  How were rivers and oceans traversed?

****
****

18

What did Gun himself construct?
  What did Yu himself achieve?
In the crack and the clash, the fray and fury,
  why did the earth buckle down to the southeast?

III. On the Geography of the World

19

How are the Nine Continents arranged?
  How were the rivers and valleys carved out?

Though waters run east they do not overflow:
    who knows the reason behind this?

20

East and west, south and north:
    which direction extends the farthest?
If south and north form an ellipse,
    how much further do they protrude?

21

The Hanging Garden of Kunlun's Peaks:
    in what locale may they be found?
The nine walls of the Tiered Palisade:
    how many miles high do they stand?

22

Who is it who passes through
    the Gates of the Four Directions?
When the Northwest opens up wide,
    what kind of air blows through it?

23

Why does the sun not reach its mark
    till Xihe lifts the reins of the sun carriage?
What does the Torch Dragon illumine?
    What flickers on the blossoms of the Dimming Wood?

24

What place is warm in the wintertime?
    What place freezes in summer?
Where is there a forest of stone?
    What beast is capable of speech?

25

Where is the coiled dragon
    diving with a terrapin on its back?

****
****

26

The fierce hamadryad of nine heads,
    where does it go so swiftly and suddenly?

What place is there without death?
   Where do the giants abide?

27

Waterlily blossoms branching ninefold
   and soma flowers: where are they to be found?
When a snake swallowed an elephant,
   how gigantic must it have been?

28

Blackwater and Mystic Base and
   Mount Triperil: where can they be found?
Though years till death may be prolonged,
   when must longevity come to an end?

IV. Heroes of the Xia Dynasty

29

Where is the home of the mermen?
   Where do the griffins abide?
How did Archer Yih shoot down the suns?
   How were the suncrows deplumed?

30

Yu exerted himself to complete the task,
   he descended to watch over all four parts of the earth.
How did he find that lady of Mount Soil,
   and mate with her at the Platform of Mulberries?

31

Caring for that maiden, he made a match
   in order to perpetuate himself;
Why did he who relished such unlike flavours
   so hasten for dawn's consummation?

32

When Qi was replaced by minister Yi as heir,
   that one too in the end met his doom.
Why was it that Qi was so beset by anxiety,
   and yet succeeded in evading captivity?

33

Since all obeyed and bowed unto him,
    and none did harm to that man's body,
Why did Qi overthrow the Lord Yi,
    though his sire Yu had rendered blessings to all?

34

Qi had sped to make audience with the High Lord,
    chanting the 'Nine Phases' and the 'Nine Songs';
Why did that diligent son rupture his mother,
    and, dying, make new division in the earth?

35

The High Lord sent down Archer Yih for the Yee tribes,
    and he purged the evil from the people of Xia.
But why did he shoot at the Sire of the Yellow River,
    and take the nymph of the Luo River as his wife?

36

With mighty bow of nacre and keen gauntlet
    the giant boar he shot dead;
Why did his sovereign Lord not approve
    of that generous offering?

37

When Han Zhuo seduced Pure Fox,
    that beguiling consort conspiring with him,
Why was it the hide-piercing Archer Yih
    suffered that they plot to devour him?

38

When blocked at Desperation Rock while travelling westward,
    how was it that he managed to cross those cliffs?
When Gun was transformed into a yellow terrapin,
    how did the shaman bring him back to life?

39

Though all were sowing black millet and sticky millet,
    there they planted only reeds and cresses;
Why is that after they had fled and taken refuge,
    when Gun was ill only his consort Xiu Ji nursed him?

40

Necklace and tiara glittering in a white nimbus,
    why did Chang'e display such magnificence?
How did she discover the precious elixir
    that could not be kept secret?

41

Heaven is configured horizontal and vertical:
    when Yang energy disperses then you die;
Why did the mighty bird cry out,
    and how was it deprived of mortal frame?

42

When Pingyi summons the rain into being;
    how does he cause it to be created?
As for that body possessing two torsos,
    how was a deer implanted on it?

43

When the mountain-bearing turtles start to dance,
    how do they hold them in place?
When ships are crossing over land,
    how are they kept moving through space?

44

When Ao arrived at the doorstep,
    what was he seeking from his brother's wife?
Why did Shaokang on the chase with hounds
    end up decapitating only one of these?

45

When Lady Tangent was sewing an undershirt,
    why did she share lodgings with Ao?
Why did Shaokang behead the wrong one,
    so that the lady met with harm instead?

46

When Shaokang prepared the army for ambush,
    how did he strengthen it sufficiently?
When Ao capsized the vessels of Zhenxun,
    by what route did he defeat them?

47

When Jie assaulted Mount Meng,
  whom did he obtain there?
Why was Lady Moxi abandoned by him,
  and why did Tang destroy Jie for it?

48

While Shun dealt with discontent within the household,
  why did his father keep him a bachelor?
Why did sagely Yao not inform the groom's own clan Yaw
  when marrying off to Shun his two daughters?

49

When the sprouting of events is at its start,
  how can one begin to sense its scale?
The agate-studded tower had ten storeys;
  who was it who completed it?

50

When she ascended to the throne as Lord,
  by what means was she elevated, Nü Wa?
As for the body she possessed,
  who crafted and constructed it?

51

Shun was subservient to his younger brother,
  but ultimately met with harm;
In spite of Xiang's cur-like, reckless person,
  why was he not endangered or ruined?

52

Shun of Yu had obtained, from ancient times,
  territory ending at the Southern Marchmount;
Who would have predicted that at this place
  he would encounter the two young noblemen?

V. The Shang and Its Ancestors

53

When with swan-shaped tripods and ornamented jade
  Yi Zhi made offering to his Sovereign Lord,

Heavenly Questions

Why was he tasked with the plot against Jie of Xia,
    which only resulted in his death and destruction?

54

After the supreme lord Tang descended to observe,
    and on earth had rendezvous with Yi Zhi;
Why, when Jie was punished by exile to Tiao,
    did the people rejoice greatly?

55

While his concubine Jian Di was at the altar,
    why did Highlord Ku find it fitting?
For the gift proffered by the dark bird
    why was she so gratified?

56

When Wang Hai upheld the virtue of Ming,
    he showed the same excellence as his father;
Why was he then murdered by the Youyi Clan
    while tending the cattle and sheep?

57

How by timely showing of the shield dance
    did he draw his rivals into friendship?
With plump torso and delicate complexion
    how did they then fatten him up so?

58

The lowly oxherds among the Youyi Clan,
    how did he come upon them?
When they ambushed him upon the couch,
    how was it that his life was spared?

59

Wang Heng too upheld the virtue of his father Ming,
    but where did he obtain the tame oxen?
After going to bestow ranks and rewards,
    why did he return from them in vain?

60

As Twilight Wei followed the old paths,
    so that the Youdi were not content,

Why, as with the 'owls roosting in the brambles',
   did he betray his son with untrammelled passions?

61

The muddled younger brother, joining in adultery,
   endangered and damaged his elder.
Though he changed his shape to dissimulate and deceive,
   why did his progeny still enjoy rapid increase?

62

When Cheng Tang journeyed east
   until he arrived at the Youshen Clan,
Why did he make a request of that lesser official
   and so obtain a propitious consort?

63

It was from a tree at water's margin
   that they had obtained that little child;
Why did they then, detesting him,
   cause him to depart escorting a Youshen bride?

64

When Tang emerged from the double springs,
   of what crime had he been found guilty?
When he could not muster courage to assault the Sovereign,
   who was it that spurred him on?

VI. Founding of the Zhou Dynasty

65

When they met at dawn to make the war compact,
   who was it that accomplished their common oath?
When the birds grey and black cluster in flight
   what is it that causes them to join together?

66

When the army assaulted Zhow's very body,
   Lord Dan did not approve of the act.
Why did he personally survey the setting forth,
   while all sighed in admiration at Zhou's mandate?

67

When all under Heaven had been allotted to the Yin,
　　by what authority did they rule?
When in turn success was followed by destruction,
　　by what crime was their fall incurred?

68

Contending to dispatch the weapons of war,
　　how did King Wu accomplish it?
Advancing in stride, striking on both flanks,
　　how did he take command of all?

69

When Lord Zhao completed his excursion
　　reaching as far as the southern lands,
What good to him was it in the end
　　that he met there the white pheasant?

70

Why did King Mu, so clever and covetous,
　　choose to pursue his world-spanning journey?
When he had mastered all under Heaven,
　　what was it that he went searching for?

71

When the uncanny couple were selling their goods,
　　what did they call out in the marketplace?
Who was it that King You of the Zhou executed
　　so as to obtain his concubine Bao Si?

72

As the Mandate of Heaven revolves and reverses:
　　wherefore chastening, wherefore succour?
Duke Huan of Qi convened the lords nine times,
　　but he too was murdered in the end.

73

That figure of Zhow, the sovereign king:
　　why was he so disturbed and so confounded?
Why did he resent his own aides and helpers,
　　and surrender to slanderous gossip?

74

Why did his advisor Bi Gan revolt,
  only to be crushed and ruined?
Lei Kai was obsequious and obedient,
  and yet received enfeoffment.

75

Why does the constant virtue of the sages
  yet conclude in such contrary ways?
Sire Mei was ground into meat paste,
  Master Ji made a charade of madness.

VII. Manifestations of Virtue through the Ages

76

Hou Ji was the primary son,
  so why did the High Lord revile him?
When he was discarded on the ice,
  why did the birds keep him warm?

77

Why was he, with mighty bow and arrows,
  able beyond all others to lead the people?
Since he once startled his lord, grievously and piercingly,
  how after all did he arrive at enduring success?

78

When Prince Chang exclaimed upon the decline,
  wielding the whip and showing mastery,
Why did he command that the Qi altars be re-established,
  while capturing the mandate of Yin's realm?

79

When he transported his prized possessions towards Mount Qi,
  why did people follow along with him?
As for the bewitching lady of Yin-Shang:
  why was she so reviled by them?

80

When Zhow presented him the bloody paste,
  the Prince of the West protested up to Heaven;

Was it because he personally addressed the Lord on High,
    that the mandate of Yin was rebuked and never restored?

81

When Master Wang was in the market,
    how did Chang recognize him there?
Wielding a sword and raising up a cry –
    why did the sovereign rejoice therein?

82

When King Wu set forth to assault Yin,
    what was it that had infuriated him?
When he bore his spirit tablet to join in battle,
    what was it that spurred him on?

83

For what reason could it have been that
    his brother was hanged in the Northern Forest?
What was it that stirred the Heavens and shook the Earth,
    and who was still in awe and fear?

84

When awesome Heaven has located its Mandate,
    on what grounds may we suggest reproach?
When Zhow already offered the rites to all under heaven,
    why did this result in his own overthrow?

85

At first the minister of Tang was Zhi,
    but later this one took on the responsibility of counsellor.
Why did he ultimately serve as officer for Tang,
    to honour the offerings of the ancestral succession?

86

The meritorious scion Helu was born of Meng,
    but was cast away in his youth.
Why was he so mighty and practised in arms,
    that he could spread his reputation far and wide?

87

When Peng Keng brewed the pheasant soup,
    why did the Lord consume it?

Achieving extraordinary longevity,
   why was he still so long distressed?

88

When the central states were governed by Earl Gong,
   why was the sovereign angered?
How could the paltry lives of bees and ants
   possess such might as to endure?

89

When they startled a woman while gathering vetch,
   why did a deer protect them?
North as far as the winding currents,
   meeting there why did they nonetheless rejoice?

90

When the elder brother met with a rabid dog,
   what was it the younger one was seeking?
Though bartering for a hundred chariots,
   why was he left ultimately without estate?

Epilogue

91

A bolt of lightning in the twilight sky:
   what worry rankled the returning?
If their lord's authority they did not respect,
   why did they make further demands of him?

92

When men hide and skulk in caverns,
   what more is there to say?
When a king has seen his fault and changed his ways,
   what else can be advised?

93

The army of Jing achieved a meritorious deed,
   but how was it to endure?—
As Guang of Wu contested the realm,
   though they were long victorious over us.

94

Why did they encircle the shrines and trample the altars,
    even offending the very tomb mounds?—
It was that wantonness, that wildness,
    which led to the appearance of Sir Wen.

95

I would like to warn the master Du Ao
    that he will not long survive;
Yet after the throne has been usurped
    how can loyalty's lustre shine on?

5. NINE AVOWALS
ATTRIBUTED TO QU YUAN

I. Rueful Remonstrance

With rueful remonstrance I communicate my misery –
    relieving my indignation by relating my convictions;
Were this portrayed as merely a pretence of loyalty –
    I would point to azure Heaven as my witness.

I decree the Five Elemental Deities judge the proper balance –
6   direct the Six Ancestral Powers to respond and obey.
I cause the mountains and the rivers to guard and attend me –
    mandate that Lord Gaoyao assess my uprightness.

Expending all my loyalty and integrity to serve my lord –
10   I end up estranged from the crowd, treated like a blister or boil.
Neglecting to fawn or flatter, I have turned my back to the masses –
    I only await a perspicacious lord to understand this.

Both words and deeds may be put into practice,
    but my convictions and countenance I will not alter.
Examining the vassals, none is superior to his liege –
    and the proof of all this is indeed not far from us.

My duty is first to my lord and then to myself –
    but alas! by the others I was resented.
I think solely of my liege and not of any other –
20   yet still by the base multitudes I find myself reviled.

To keep a mind in focus without a quaver –
    indeed is not something that can be guaranteed.
I am fiercely devoted to my liege and not to any other –
    but that is the path that leads towards my ruin.

In longing for the sovereign none matches my loyalty –
    for I am indifferent even to poverty or disrepute.
Serving my sovereign I would have no other –
    but I have gone astray and cannot find the gate to favour.

What crime is devotion that it should suffer such punishment? –
30   nor was this what I aimed for in my heart.
I acted apart from the crowd and so was overturned and undone –
    subjected to mockery by the many.

Meeting with such blame and suffering slander –
    though I make my case I cannot dispel all that.
My dejection and despair I find no way to communicate –
    I am so beset by obstacles I cannot make this plain.

My heart is steeped in sadness, discontented and dismayed –
    there is none to perceive the good or ill inside me.
My intricate orations I cannot finish, cannot transmit –
40   I wish I could relate my will but cannot find the route.

I retreat in quiet reticence no one can penetrate –
    advance in clamorous call that no one hears.
I tell of the dejection and dismay that have made me distraught –
    in my heart remain loyal through this fruitless toil.

Once long ago I dreamt that I was ascending to Heaven –
    but my soul midway had no means to ford across.
47 So I caused the Honing God to divine it for me –
    he spake: 'Some ambitions come to their limit and have no support;

'If you are isolated ever, staying separate and unlike' –
50   he spake again: 'even your lord you long for, you cannot rely on.
Just as "the mouths of the multitude can melt metal" –
    from the beginning it has ever been thus, so now you face peril.

53 ' "Once scalded by the soup, you blow to cool even pickled meat" –
    so why not alter your ambition accordingly now?
You want to climb to Heaven while discarding the ladder –
    that way the order of things will remain as it ever was.

'All are hurried and harried, divided of mind –
    why then should they be your companions?
They strive for the same end but by different routes –
60   why should they be considered your allies?

'The filial son Shensheng of Jin –
    his father believed in slander and deprecated him.

Practising stubborn loyalty without wavering –
64   Gun's merit and industry were without success.'

I had heard how an act of loyalty can engender spite –
      but carelessly used to call that exaggeration;
67 How 'the man whose arm is broken nine times makes a doctor' –
      But only now do I appreciate how true that is.

For the tethered arrow and mechanical traps are set above –
70   and webs of gauze and mesh unfurled here below;
They place the nets and snares with my lord in their sights –
      I'd like to be beside him but no place stands ready.

I'd like to delay further, to dally and implore him –
      but I fear to repeat my fault and meet catastrophe.
I'd like to soar up high and to perch far off –
      as my lord will not ask where I am going.

I'd like to race across but have lost the path –
      firm in my ambition though I cannot bear it.
My back and breast are divided but share in the agony –
80   my heart is care-coiled and entangled in sorrow.

Pestling magnolia petals and culling the sweet clover –
82   I powder the lush fagara for my ration.
I seed the river lovage and plant chrysanthemums –
      if only the spring sun could preserve their dry fragrance!

I fear the object of my devotion still is not faithful –
      thus I make a solemn declaration of my inner self.
I hoard these charms that I may endure alone –
      I'd like to multiply my musings and make myself remote.

II. Crossing the River

In my youth already I was fond of rare attire –
    now I am old in years but not enfeebled;
The broadsword I carry gleams and glitters –
    my cap pierces the clouds, ascending aloft.

Myself bedecked in moon-bright pearls – adorned with precious jade;
    the worldly are befuddled and corrupted, and none can know me –
So I race high above without looking back;
    I drive a cerulean spirax – with white wyverns for trace-horses.

Along with Him of Many-faceted Majesty I visit – the Pleasance of
    Jasper.
10   we climb up Mount Kunlun – and sup on blossoms of jade.
I equal Heaven and Earth – in longevity,
12   and match the Sun and Moon – in radiance.
Only I lament that the southern folk do not appreciate me –
14   as at dawn I cross over the River and the Xiang.

I climb up the Islet of E and then turn to look behind –
    endure the gale that has lasted – from autumn and winter.
I canter my horse past – hills and riverbends,
18   park my carriage – at the square grove.

Riding my fenestrated barge upstream the Yuan –
20   Wu paddles in unison beat upon the waves.
My craft lingers long and advances no further –
    slowed by the winding currents it pauses in place.

In the morning I set off from Crooked Bank –
24   in the evening I rest at Stellar Yang.
So long as my own heart is proper and undeviating –
    however isolated and remote I find myself I will not suffer.

Passing Xu Cove I pause, perplexed –
    I am lost and know not whither I am wending.
Deep in the woods, far off and lost in obscurity –
30   where gibbons black and white abide.

The mountains rise vertiginously and block out the sun –
    but underneath all is murky and rainswept.

Hail and snow fall in unceasing frenzy –
    an enveloping veil of clouds clings to the eaves.

Encompassed by grief, my life lacks any joy –
    enduring the darkness, abiding in the mountains.
I cannot change my mind and join with the vulgar –
    so I know this bitter grief will trouble me to the end.
A carriage-hailing madman once had his head shaved –
40   while Mulberry Door sauntered along naked.

Loyal men are not always recruited –
    the worthy not always employed.
Sir Wu met with catastrophe –
44   Bi Gan was ground into paste.

Just as in previous ages it was thus for every man–
    why should I so resent the men of today?
I will keep to the proper road and will not waver –
    though enduring till death this darkness recurring.

ENVOI

Simurgh and phoenix, birds of fine augury,
    perch ever further away –
50 While swallow and sparrow, crow and magpie,
    nest within the palace and upon the altar –

The magnolia withers outdoors
    and dies in the woods and thickets –
While rank and reeking occupy all positions,
    and the sweet-smelling have no chance to approach –

Yin and Yang have changed their places,
    and the time is not right –
Though keeping faith I have fretted and faltered,
    but now at last I hasten onward –

III. Lamenting Ying

Heaven, though magnificent, is not constant in its mandate –
    what disorder and disasters now befall the hundred clans!
I myself was forced into flight and self-concealment –
    right in mid-spring I journeyed to the East.

Leaving my old home and travelling far away –
    following the Jiang and Xia rivers into oblivion.
Departing the gates of the kingdom with piercing anguish –
    it was the morning of the first day that I set out.

Leaving my capital of Ying, departing from my home –
10   dazed and dumbfounded by measureless melancholy,
Oars paddling in parallel, yet dithering and delaying –
    I mourn that I will never again meet with my lord.

I gaze at the tall catalpa trees and heave a deep sigh –
    my tears stream in torrents, they fall like hail;
Passing the mouth of the Xia and drifting westward –
16   I look back towards Dragongate but cannot see it.

My heart languishes in longing, grieving and anguished –
18   half-blinded I cannot tell where I have trod.
Following the winds and waves, flowing with the current –
20   now adrift and astray, I live on as an exile.

21 Riding the swelling, surging waves of Lord Yang –
    swept away all at once, where will I moor next?
My feelings are knotted up, clotted and indissoluble –
    thoughts tightly wound, closely bound, undisentangleable.

I will direct my craft downcurrent –
    over Lake Dongting and down the Jiang.
27 Departing this place of our abode since antiquity –
    now I'll roam awhile and then come east.

Ah! How my numinous soul longs to return –
30   why would I forget to go back in just one instant?
31 I turn my back to Xia Cove and direct yearning westward –
    lamenting that my former capital is ever farther removed.

Ascending the high embankment to gaze into the distance –
    for a while I relax my sorrowful heart.
Sorrowful in spite of the prosperity and plenty of my province –
36   I grieve for the customs inherited on the banks of the Jiang.

As I coast on these waves of Yang spirit, whither am I wandering?
    Through the torrents crossing southward, where am I wending?
I had not thought those great palaces would become grave mounds –
40   nor those two east-facing gates be overgrown with weeds.

My heart has been miserable longer than I can tell –
    anxiety and grief passing one after another.
How far off goes this road from Ying –
    The Jiang and the Xia can hardly be crossed.

45 It seems as though I've not been away more than overnight –
    though by now nine years have passed while I cannot return.
My misery shrouds and clouds me and cannot be pierced –
    I am chagrined and shaken, disheartened and downcast.

The delicate and dainty seem to enjoy their delights –
50   but in truth are weak and frail, and will not endure.
My fidelity deep and lasting, I long to proceed –
52   but envious men run rampant and block my way.

How noble were the deeds of Yao and Shun –
    their brilliance shines unceasing straight to Heaven.
But the masses of slanderers envy and resent me –
56   and taint me falsely with ungenerousness.

My lord detests, resents, condemns the virtuous and fine –
    and prefers servants of passionate intensity.
The many trudging drudge-like are promoted ever further –
60   the worthy men are far removed and near demise.

ENVOI

Letting my sight go far off, and my gaze roam free –
    I only hope I may return some day.
Birds flock back to their old home –
64   'When the fox dies it always faces its old burrow.'
It was not by my own fault that I have been exiled –
66   and never in all the days and nights will I forget!

IV. Unravelled Yearnings

My heart is shrouded in anxious yearning –
  long sighs of loneliness that heighten the hurt.
Yearnings knotted and clotted up, undisentangleable –
  I endure a night that is without end.

5 I grieve at the autumn wind that alters the appearances –
  how the Pole is askew, and wanders off course.
Ever I think of Lord Calamus, so easily angered –
  haggard at heart, I moan in melancholy.

I would like to rise up at once and dart across –
10   to observe the faults of others while settling myself.
I gather my inner feelings to set forth in words –
  and lift them up to present to the Beautiful one:

Long ago my lord spoke to me words of sincerity –
  saying our rendezvous would be at twilight.
But in the middle of the passage he broke faith –
  and reversing course set another resolve.

He flaunted before me his beauty and goodness –
  and made a show of his exquisite loveliness,
But his words to me were not true –
20   for he sought only to provoke me.

I would take the moment to examine myself –
  but my heart trembles with sorrow and I dare not.
I lag on in grief and hope to advance –
  my heart care-killed, woeful, wounded.

The sorrows I met with, I would now set forth in words –
  but Lord Calamus feigns deafness and will not hear.
Discerning men are never flatterers –
  which is why the many see in me their own ruin.

What I had related from the first was clear and right –
30   so why has it all now been forgotten?
Why do I alone delight in honest speeches –
  desiring the beauty of Lord Calamus should be illuminated?

I look towards the Three and the Five as my models –
34   I aim at Peng and Xian as my companions.

What ambition then can I not achieve –
    though my repute travels far I cannot easily be hurt.

Goodness does not come to us from outside –
    and fame cannot be fabricated.
What can be gained without a venture?
40   How before the blooming does one reap a harvest?

THE LESSER SONG

Though I unravel my yearnings to my Beauty –
    day and night I have no way to prove it.
43 He flaunted before me his beauty and goodness –
    he spurned my words of counsel and would not hear.

THE AIR

There is a bird that comes from the South –
    to perch north of the Han.
Noble and lovely, splendid in its beauty –
    it abides apart and alone in a foreign land.
Ever alone and without a flock –
50   not even a wise messenger by its side.
The way is far and ever more unknowable –
    I would like to put myself forth but cannot.
Gazing at the northern hills, I stream forth tears –
    and over the flowing waters, heave a deep sigh.

Nights ever shorter near the first month of summer –
    and yet each day's dawning seems to last a year!
I think of the path towards faraway Ying –
    my soul flies back there nine times in a night.

I did not know if the road would be crooked or straight –
60   southward I recognized the moon and serried stars.
I would follow the path away but cannot find it –
    only my soul recognizes the road and hurries forth.

How faithful and true is my numinous soul! –
    but the hearts of other men are not like mine.
My go-between is weak and the messenger cannot pass –
66   they do not even recognize my appearance.

ENVOI

Through great rapids and jetting currents
    I ride back up the river and bays –
Gazing back desperately I journey south,
70   thinking to ease my heart –
But boulders square as chariots towering
    thwart my desire –
Strayed and diverted from the rule I strive for,
    prevented from further advance –

I dither and dally, loiter and tarry,
    sojourn in North Lodge –
Wounded by worries, visage distraught,
    truly must I hasten hence –
Melancholy sighs torment my spirit,
80   my dream-soul yearning for what is far away –
The road is far and this place is dark,
    I have no messenger to send for me –

Out of my yearnings midway have I made this orison,
    so as to rescue myself –
My anxious heart will not be contented,
    for to whom may I tell these words of mine? –

V. Embracing the Sand

In the full fire of early summer –
    when grasses and trees grow ripe,
Mourning my aspirations, with grief unending –
    swiftly I travelled towards the southern lands.

I was dazed – by that remote and lonely scene,
    the profound calm and the utter stillness.
Knotted in woe, entangled in grief –
    I was constantly confounded by new misery.

Mastering emotion I achieve my ambition –
10   though deeply wronged I will restrain myself.
Those men may whittle the square to make it round –
    but the enduring measure cannot so be replaced.

To alter the initial and original pathway –
    would be that which is most scorned by the noble man!
Once clarified and delineated, once inscribed in ink –
    the model determined should not be changed.

To be sincere in character and proper in substance –
    is that which is most celebrated by the great man;
If artful Chui had not hewn wood with such artistry –
20   who could know he had attained the proper way?

Just as when deep patterns are set in darkness –
    but blind men say they are not even visible;
Or when Li Lou sees into every subtlety –
24   even where the sightless saw no light at all.

Men alter white and make it black –
    invert what is above and place it below.
Phoenix and simurgh are held in bamboo cages –
    chicken and duck dance together in the air.

Blending indiscriminately jade and pebbles –
30   the mediocre measure all by their own rule.
Oh, this clique of men is petty and unyielding –
    how can they fail to see what is splendid in me?

My duty is grave and my burden is great –
    but I am trapped in place and cannot proceed.

Though I clasp nephrite, clutch priceless jade –
    I have no one to show them in my plight.

The hounds of the hamlets yelp in their packs –
    they yelp at what they cannot comprehend.
So with these men who are neither elite nor elect –
40   for they are common in manner indeed.

In both cultivation and character they are weak within –
42   that herd of men do not recognize my singular quality.
Though this fresh timber is stored and hoarded–
    none of them recognizes all that I possess.

45 Treasuring humaneness and pursuing duty –
    in care and candour I am well supplied;
But if I cannot meet a Shun-like sage –
    who will appreciate my motives and my manner?

Since ancient times some men have not conformed –
50   who can say what was the reason?
Men like Tang and Yu lived long ago and far away –
    too remote even to gaze after in admiration.

Correcting regret and reforming discontent –
    I restrain my feelings and rein myself in.
Though I meet with misfortune I will not change my course –
    I only hope my striving has a worthy model.

Proceeding on my path I make a stop in the North –
    the sun is already dimming as dusk approaches.
Though I would ease my angst and assuage this grief –
60   I am confounded instead by the calamity of fate.

ENVOI

Onward rush the Yuan and the Xiang,
    gushing along in separate streams –
The long path is occluded in darkness,
    the road disappears in the distance –

Possessing fine character, embracing deep passions,
    I lack only witness to my ability –
For Bole the connoisseur has perished,
68   and fine steeds can no more be discerned –

In the lives of the myriad people,
70   each has his own disposition –
With mind fixed and ambitions broadened,
    what is there that I should fear for? –

Grief deepening, I mourn,
    with long sighs and sobs –
Men are confounded and corrupted, and know me not,
76   nor can any tell what lies in the heart of another –

For I know that death cannot be evaded,
    so I will not seek to cherish life –
But show clearly to all men of nobility:
80   that I will make of myself a model –

VI. *Yearning for a Beauty*

Yearning for a Beauty –
    I can only stand in a daze, wiping my tears.
The matchmaker is thwarted and my path blocked –
    I cannot weave my words together to win her.

All my honest counsel incurs only trouble and abuse –
    tripped up, trapped in, I cannot communicate it;
Awake until the dawn, I would release my inner feelings –
    but my aspirations are buried, bound, unsayable.

I'd like to send a message by the drifting clouds –
10   I meet with Thunder Spirit Fenglong but he refuses.
So I employ a homing bird to make my speech –
    how swiftly it ascends and yet how hard to reach her!

Of old Lord Gaoxin was a venerable spirit indeed –
14   I'd meet the dark bird and send him a message through it.
I ought to shed integrity and join the vulgar –
    but am ashamed to change my conviction or bend my will.

Alone I face the years and suffer this misery –
    for relying on the heart there is no way to change her.
I'd rather live out my doleful, woeful days –
20   for what prospect is there of any alteration?

Though I know this carriage-route will not achieve my end –
    I still cannot change my guiding rule;
Though my carriage be overturned and the steeds toppled –
    myself hobbled, forlorn, and heartsick on this other path;
I rein in my rapid courser and change my ride –
26   my handler Zaofu drives them for me.
I pass on, proceeding in promenade but never rushing –
    enjoying the sunlight while I await the proper time.
I point to Mount Bozhong at the western rim –
30   and accept the tawny hue of twilight as my rendezvous.

At the start of spring in the new year –
    the bright sun comes steadily into view.
I will sweep away ambition and indulge in delight –
    all along the Jiang and Xia rivers, charm away my cares.

Culling sweet angelica from the spreading foliage –
    plucking dormant slough grass from the oblong isles:
I lament that I cannot convey this to the ancients –
    with whom can I share delight in these fragrant blooms?

I separate the swaths of knotweed and the uncouth herbs –
40   prepare the flowers to weave as my sash adornments,
My adornments resplendently replete, twisting and twirling –
    now are changed and disarranged, withering and wilting.
But I dither and dally here to charm away my cares –
    observing the unnatural ways of the southern folk.

With secret exultation deep within my heart –
    I'll not wait long to manifest my discontent.
My fragrance and my lustre have been mingled and intermixed –
    Ah! But there is a sweet flower that blooms from within:

A dense, rich perfume that is inherited from afar –
50   and permeates all and manifests far beyond.
Ardour and honour are truly hard to preserve –
    though I stay in hiding my reputation will be known.

I send out Creeping Fig to serve as a matchmaker –
    but she dares not lift her heel to climb up the tree.
Then I rely on Lotus Bloom to serve as a go-between –
56   but she dares not draw up her skirts or drench her feet.

Though I climb up high I still cannot find satisfaction –
    though I dive underwater I achieve nothing.
After all I will not submit my own person –
60   but linger here long, dithering in delay.

The designs of previous sages were broadly beneficent –
    I would not choose to change their guiding rule.
My mandate now to reside in obscurity, I will depart –
    I only hope it is before the sun has set.
Forlorn and friendless, alone in my southern journey –
66   I ponder still the example of Peng and Xian long ago.

VII. *Regretting Past Days*

Regretting past days when I enjoyed His confidence –
    and received the royal mandate to use poems to enlighten;
How I upheld the deeds of our predecessors to instruct those to come –
    and expunged each doubtful crux from the laws of state:
The kingdom was wealthy and strong, laws firmly established –
    affairs delegated to loyal ministers, prosperity gaining;
Then essential matters were thrust into my confidence –
    and even though I erred and failed, I was not punished.
My heart was simple and sincere, and did not slip –
10   but then I met with slanderers who envied my success.
My sovereign checked his anger and merely detained me first –
    not yet sure whether he would grant favour or not.
But they bewildered and beguiled his wise mind –
    by falsehood, fraud, cheating, and chicanery.
He did not confirm or consider things, nor investigate the truth –
    but expelled me far away without another thought;
He trusted flatterers and sycophants, the confounded and confused –
    while castigating those great in spirit and boldness.
Why is it that a loyal minister untainted by vice –
20   should suffer exile and accusation, and endure such wrong?
How I regret his confidence in me, our intimacy like light and shadow –
    now that I am cast into obscurity and oblivion.

Facing the fathomless deeps of the Yuan and Xiang –
    I must bear with things and sink into the current.
Ultimately I must let my body perish and my name be erased –
    only regretting that my lost liege could not be enlightened.
My liege, who followed no fixed rule and failed to examine facts –
    he rendered the burgeoning blossoms of his court a desolate
        waste.
How can I express my feelings and convey my loyal sentiments? –
30   Tranquil in mind, I accept death rather than live by compromise.
Only since he was misled and muddled, deceived and deluded –
    has he left his loyal minister without any means to act.

Among the ministers of the past, Baili Xi was once a prisoner –
    and Yi Yin cooked in the royal kitchen.
Lü Wang had been merely the butcher at Dawnsong –

36   and Ning Qi sang as he fed the oxen.
      Had they not met Lord Tang and King Wu, Dukes Huan and Mu –
        who in the world would even have known of them?

      The King of Wu trusted in slanderous words and did not
        discriminate –
40   after he let Zixu die the King too met with disaster.
      Sir Jie stood faithfully by the barren trees as they burned –
        But Duke Wen realized his error and went in search of him.
      He sealed up the mountain and forbade entrance –
        commemorating the genial grace of Jie's surpassing virtue.

      He thought of how that longtime friend had stayed by him –
        and wept for him in the white silk of mourning.
      Some men are faithful and sincere, and die for their integrity –
        others spew out deception and lies, but are never doubted.
      He did not examine or reflect, nor ascertain the facts –
50   but listened to the hollow words of the slanderers.
      Fragrance and lustre are jumbled and confused –
        who else will work day and night to distinguish them?

      How swiftly do the fragrant herbs perish –
        for the mildest frost they must be well prepared.
      Truly that man is not percipient, but bewildered and benighted –
        allowing the toadies and sycophants to profit ever more.
      From ancient times excellence has been envied –
        even sweet clover and ginger-lily libelled as indecorous;
      Envying sweet fragrance and ravishing beauty –
60   and enchanted by Homely Crone, imagining themselves fair;
      Though Xi Shi's fair complexion stands before them –
        slander and jealousy rush in to take her place.
      I strove to relate my ardour and make plain my deeds –
        never expecting to meet instead with blame and chastisement.
      My ardour and my grievance are displayed as bright as the sun –
        articulated and arrayed in heaven like the stars.
      Riding a sterling steed I gallop gladly on –
        or setting aside reins or bridle let the current carry me.
      Aboard a raft I'll drift downstream –
70   without boat or oars I must fend for myself.
71 As to betraying the laws and norms to govern at will –

there would be no difference from this present regime.
I'd rather die at once and fall into oblivion –
    for I so fear that doom and disaster will recur.
Before concluding this plaint I'll enter the abyss –
    regretting only my benighted lord will never know!

VIII. Ode to the Tangerine

Tree prized by lord and sovereign,
2   the tangerine, their willing subject –
Granted its destiny it is immoveable,
4   growing only in the Southern realm –

Deeply rooted and hard to transplant,
    because it concentrates its will –
Green leaves and flowering white
    magnificent and delightful –

Overlapping branches pointed and pricked,
10   and spherical fruits hanging full –
Verdant yellow hues intermingled
    in glistening array –

Its colours brilliant, interior pristine,
    of a type conforming to the Way –
With flourishing fragrance, a paragon of propriety,
    splendid with no hint of ugliness –

Ah! Truly your youthful ambition
    has something excellent in it –
Standing alone and immoveable,
20   how can one not rejoice in this? –

Deeply rooted and hard to transplant,
    containing more than is required –
Standing alone in opposition to the world,
    obdurate and unyielding –

Sealing its mind and staying cautious,
    it never fails or errs –
Possessing virtue without partiality,
    peer of Heaven and of Earth –

I hope to share the lifespan
30   of this abiding friend –
Its splendid isolation incorruptible,
    rigidly and rightly patterned –

Though in years still young,
    it can serve as teacher to its elders –
35 For deeds comparable to Bo Yi,
    extol it as our paragon! –

IX. *Grieved by the Whirlwind*

Grieved by the whirlwind that strips bare sweet clover –
    my heart is tangled up in wrong and wounded within.
Some beings, delicate, are deprived of their nature –
    other voices, though seeming subtle, are first to sing out.
5 Why do I reminisce about the case of Peng and Xian –
    hoping that such mighty ambitions will not be forgotten?
In spite of ten thousand blows their ardour cannot be contained –
    for how long can what is false and forged remain?
Bird and beast cry out and summon their kin –
10 grasses green and withered, ranked together, have no scent.
Fish may interlace their scales to signal their distinction –
12 but mighty krakens conceal their gorgeous patterning.
13 For sowthistle and shepherd's purse do not share a field –
    eupatory and angelica are hidden and fragrant alone.
For a comely person can remain ever finely cultivated –
16 and over the successive ages sustain himself.
How far away and beyond can my ambition reach –
    compatient with the clouds that drift hither and thither.
My far-reaching aims have stirred a certain feeling –
20 I composed this lyric in order to clarify all this.

Truly a comely person must endure solitary yearnings –
    plucking the ginger-lily and fagara to adorn himself.
Heaving repeated sighs, alas, alas –
    obscure and alone, full of yearning and worry,
Streams of tears sweep down in numbing sorrow –
    in my grieving state I do not slumber until dawn.
Through the trackless vastness of the long night –
    I try to hide but cannot rid myself of woe.

Awakening, leisurely and languorously I circle round –
30 roam a while free and easy, and guard myself.
Grieving with a great sigh of my deep melancholy –
    my spirits are sulky and sullen but I cannot rest.

I'll intertwine my thoughts and feelings into pendants –
    weave my sorrows and suffering to make a vest.
I'll take a spray of Dimming Wood to block the light –
    follow along the drifting breezes wherever they go.

Though I conceive a faint sense of him I cannot see him –
    my heart churns and surges as if boiling over.
Gripping onto my pendants and collar, I surrender ambition –
40   dejected, doubting, dismayed, I set out on my journey.

The season rushes rapidly towards ruin –
    time passing steadily towards its destination.
Bulrushes and asarum wither and split in pieces –
    the fragrances vanished, sundered from one another.

I lament that this melancholy mind cannot be made right –
    proving that these words can no longer be relied upon.
I would rather die at once and enter oblivion –
    I cannot bear to endure with this unending sorrow.

A solitary man may sing and wipe away tears –
50   an exile once departed will not return.
Who, indeed, can ponder it and not feel grief –
52   reflecting on the story of Peng and Xian.

Climbing up the stony ridge to gaze afar –
    the road fades off in the distance, still and desolate.
Entering, no answer or shadow or even an echo –
    yet I listen, observe, and imagine all in vain.

Steeping and stewing in melancholy without release –
    abiding in bitter pain that I cannot dispel.
My heart is bridled and reined in and cannot stay whole –
60   my spirit revolves and reels, ever more entangled.
My vision is merged obscurely with the ineffable horizon –
    across a vastness blurred and boundless beyond all form.
Even a voice that is faint will likely find its response –
    but though a person is pure he still may not succeed.

So far away, so imperceptibly infinite, that it cannot be
    measured –
    so faint, so ethereal and impalpable, that it cannot be
    ensnared:
Sorrow, wounding and wasting, has filled me with lasting gloom –
    though I soar the vast empyrean I find no delight.
I cross the great waves and drift with the zephyrs –
70   thinking to lodge in the place where Peng and Xian abide.

Climbing up the lofty crags and the plunging banks –
72   I pause at the very peak of a womanly fogbow;
Nearing the blue heavens I unspool a rainbow –
    then for an instant brush against the sky.
I sip the heavy dew that drifts from the source –
    taste from the frost's shimmering sheen;
I lodge in the Cave of Winds to rest myself –
    but suddenly am stirred by an aching regret.
Standing on Mount Kunlun I peer into the mist –
80   hide myself on Mount Min by the pristine Jiang.
I fear the gushing rapids that crash and clash upon the rocks,
    as I hear the sound of its waves plashing and splashing.

In wild tumult and commotion without any guide –
    a nebulous haze of chaos without any plan;
Through a vast and vertiginous space, with no path to follow –
    racing along hither and thither where can I stop?
Floating on and drifting along, now skyward now to earth –
    winging into the distance, now left and now right.
While floods spurt past me ahead and behind –
90   I trust the right time will come along with the ebb and flow.

Watching the flaming airs that scorch past –
    I gaze upon the mists and rains that lift about me;
Ruing the frost and snow falling around me –
94   I listen to the tides that strike upon the shore.
I'll borrow from the time that's left to travel on –
    laying on my crooked crop of withered brambles;
I'll seek out the place where loyal Sir Jie survives –
    see the banished traces of princely Bo Yi.
My heart's measure modulated, I will not depart –
100   but inscribe my intent though it go unfulfilled.

It is said:
How I resent what has come of my hopes in days of yore –
    and mourn the hardships others will face hereafter.
Drifting on the Jiang and Huai till I enter the sea –
    I'll join Wu Zixu and satisfy my own inclinations;
Gazing towards the cays and islets of the Yellow River,
106   I grieve for the resolute traces of Shen Tudi.

Many times I remonstrated with my lord but he did not hear –
108   though I take on a stone again what will it profit me?
My feelings are knotted up, clotted and indissoluble –
110   thoughts tightly bound, closely wound, undisentangleable.

I. Self-Introduction

How straitened and simple are the customs of this age –
    if only I might rise up weightless and roam afar!
My body insubstantial and frail, I have no means at hand –
    how can I find a vessel to drift heavenward?

Facing the defilement of disorder, virtue blemished and besmirched –
    pent up in solitary sadness, whom can I tell?
Disturbed, unnerved, all night unable to sleep –
    my lone soul distressed and bereft until the dawn.

Pondering the infinite space between Heaven and Earth –
10   I grieve for the unending hardship of human life;
Those who have gone before I cannot equal –
    of those yet to come I can learn nothing.

Pacing hither and thither with thoughts of the remote –
    dejected, defeated, depleted, passions gone astray:
My thoughts vague and unsettled, slipping away untethered –
    my heart is pained by melancholy and my griefs multiplied.

II. On the Immortals

My spirit departs in a start and does not return –
    my body may wither and wilt but I'll persist still.
Inward I ponder and reflect on propriety and virtue –
20   seeking the very sources of the proper pneuma.

In the vast, vacant, silences I enjoy tranquillity's delight –
    in serene non-action I find myself fulfilled.
23 I have heard report of the immaculate traces left by Red Pine –
    if only I could carry on in the manner of his legacy!

I cherish the supreme powers of the Perfected Ones –
    admiring those who rose to transcendence in past ages.

They were transformed and departed, never to be seen again –
    yet their fame and name remain, growing ever more prominent.

I marvel at Fu Yue, whose spirit lodged in the Nascence Stars –
30   I envy Han Zhong who attained Unity.
My body is serene, pristine, advancing into the far spaces –
    departing from the mass of men to disappear in seclusion.

Pursuing the mutations of the pneuma, I rise up further –
    precipitously my spirit soars along in its uncanny guises;
Occasionally a shadowy semblance appears from afar –
    my essence passes to and fro with incandescent gleam.

Absconding from grimy vapours and from all blessing or blame –
    never will I return to the old capital.
Freed of the myriad ills and no longer anxious –
40   no one in the world knows where this journey ends!

III. *Preparing for the Journey*

I am disquieted that the seasons of Heaven rotate in succession –
42   that the radiance of spirit refulgent advances ever westward.
A slight frost descends and sinks downward –
    I mourn the fragrant plants so soon to wither.
I'll idle here a while and wander on at will –
    though enduring the long years with nothing attained.
Who will enjoy with me the blossoms that remain? –
    at dawn I face into the wind and put forth my feelings.
Our ancestor Gaoyang is somewhere beyond my ken –
50   how can I make of him the model for my journey hence?

IV. *The Refrain*

Springs and autumns pass abruptly on without stopping –
    how can I linger long in this old abode of mine?
Xuanyuan cannot be reached or relied upon –
    so I consort instead with Prince Qiao for my enjoyment.
55 Consuming the Six Energies and drinking midnight mists –
    gargling pure Yang energy and swallowing dawn roseclouds;
Preserving the pristine purity imparted by divine illumination –
    letting essential energies enter and filthy impurities depart.

Coasting on the balmy breezes to roam where they lead me –
60   I reach Southern Nest in just a single breath.
There I see the Prince and sojourn with him –
62   inquiring how to unify vitality and to modulate potency:

He says:
      'The Way can be received –
        but cannot be transmitted.
65   So minute it has no interior –
        so vast it has no bounds.
      Don't let your soul be agitated –
        but rather act spontaneously.
      Unify your vitality, concentrate spirit –
70   maintaining them through the nighttime.
      "Respond to things only by vacancy" –
72   do not move in advance of them.
      Let each kind achieve fullness –
        this only is the gate of Potentiality.'

V. Self-Cultivation

I heard this most precious message and then departed –
    making haste to continue in my journey.
Joining the feathered men on Cinnabar Hill –
    I paused in the homeland of the immortals.
At dawn I rinsed my hair in Sunny Vale –
80   at dusk I washed my body in ninefold Yang.
81 I swallowed the subtle liquor of Flying Font –
    I consumed the sweetest blossoms of sacred jade.
My complexion lustrous, my countenance glossy –
    my essence pure, exquisite and newly vigorous,
My substance refined and dissolved till it becomes ethereally fine –
    my spirit drifting through infinite space bursts into omnipresence.

VI. The Flight to Heaven

The southern lands possess the splendid virtue of fire –
    beautified by the cinnamon tree that blooms in winter.
Those mountains are desolate and drear, without a living beast –
90   the plains are silent and solitary, without a single man.

91 Sustained by skysoul and earthsoul I ascend the auroras –
       concealed in drifting cloud I complete my climb.

     I order the watchman of Heaven to open the gate for me –
       he pulls open the tiered portal and welcomes me in.
     I summon Fenglong to serve as my vanguard –
96   and ask where Grand Tenuity abides.
     Concentrating manifold Yang powers I enter the palace of the High
          Lord –
98   reach the Calends Star and from it observe the ethereal city.
     At dawn I loose my carriage-brake at the court of Grand Decorum –
100   only at dusk do I approach Mount Yuweilü.

     I set my own car alongside a myriad chariots –
       multitudes roaming at random, racing side-to-side.
     I drive eight dragons before me, sinuously snaking –
       upholding cloud pennants that coil and unfold.
     I stand erect the many-coloured banners of the vivid rainbow –
       the five colours mingle and shine splendiferously.

     My shaft-horses sinuously swerve, plunging and soaring –
       my trace-horses tauten and slacken, haughtily charging.
     The steeds gallop to and fro in pandemonium –
110   spread out in riotous array and then advance en bloc.
     I seize the reins and hold the whip erect –
112   for now I go on to visit Curling Frond.
113 Passing by Supreme Illumination I veer to the right –
       Flying Lian rides ahead to guide my way.
     Tendrils of sun appear on the horizon not yet bright –
116   I transverse the Pool of Heaven along the equator.

                    VII. The Gods of the Sky

     As the Lord of Winds serves as my vanguard –
       the grimy vapours dissolve into freshness and purity.
     Phoenixes winging alongside hold up dragon pennants –
120   I meet Reaper of Rushes along with the Sovereign of the West.

     Seizing onto comets to drape as my feathered banners –
       I grab the handle of the Dipper to brandish as my flagpole.

Distinguishing this motley melange, ascending and descending –
    I navigate through jetting fog and billowing waves.

At this moment, dusky and dim, the shade pervading –
126   I summon the Mystic Warrior to charge before me.
127 Behind him Civil Flourishing is dispatched to lead my attendants –
    he appoints the lower gods who race along, wheelhubs clattering.

The road extends without end to the remotest places –
130   gradually I slow the pace and advance even higher.
To the left the Master of Rains I dispatch to serve alongside –
    on the right the Lord of Thunder I make my bulwark.

I would pass beyond the world and lose my will to return –
    let my thoughts be free to meander, roaming at will:
Delighting in my own interiority, finding beauty in myself –
    enjoying temporary pleasure and content on my own.

VIII. *Southern Idyll*

Crossing azure cloudspace in my realmless roaming –
    suddenly I peer back down towards my lifelong home.
My driver is seared by longing, I grieve too in my heart –
140   the carriage horses on both sides look back and cease to go.

Thinking of a lifetime's friends, images come to mind –
    I heave a deep sigh and wipe my tears.
I would drift away, roaming upon a whim, and rise into the remote –
    for now I'll contain my ambitions and repress myself.

Aiming towards the Spirit of Fire I race directly –
146   for I am heading towards the Southern Semblances.
Perusing the measureless vastness beyond all bound –
    on the churning, surging currents I let myself flow.

Zhurong cautions me to turn around my carriage-bar –
150   so I rush to summon the simurgh and welcome Lady Fu.
Performing 'Pool of Affinity' and presenting 'Cloud Carried' –
152   the two goddesses attend the song of the Nine Shao.

I cause the Spirit of the Xiang River to play the zithern –
154   command the Ocean Eminence to dance alongside Pingyi.

The mystic wyvern, wyrm, and kraken rise together –
156   their bodies snaking sinuously, curving and coiling.

Feminine fogbows, delicate and lovely, curve yet further –
        simurghs flutter and glide, soaring upwards in flight.
The melange of marvellous melodies never ceases or slows –
160   while I set forth on my wanderings without a worry.

IX. *Transcendence*

Releasing and then rejoining the tallies to race ahead –
162   passing beyond the furthest margin where the Frigid Gate stands:
Overtaking the rushing winds to reach the pure springs –
164   I join Zhuanxu among the many-tiered glaciers.

165   Passing by Wondrous Abyss by a deviant byway –
        riding over the cosmic nodes I gaze back down;
167   I summon Dark Frailty and meet with him –
        he goes before me and straightens out the path.

Passing hither and thither amid the Four Margins –
170   circumnavigating the Six Penumbras;
Rising up to the final fissures –
172   descending I observe the Mighty Chasm.

To depths precipitously plummeting beyond any Earth –
        soaring to prodigious heights beyond all Heaven;
I gaze at shimmering swiftness seeing nothing –
        listen to the thunderous roar but hear nothing;
I pass beyond non-action to the ultimate clarity –
178   *joining the primal origin as my neighbour.*

7. DIVINATION
ATTRIBUTED TO QU YUAN

When Qu Yuan was first exiled,
For three years he was not seen again.
Though plying all his knowledge and striving with utmost loyalty,
Still he was obstructed and thwarted by calumny.
Troubled at heart and confused by worry,
He did not know whom to follow next.

So he went to see the Great Diviner Zheng, saying:

'There is something I am unsure of:
I would like to have it settled by you, master.'

10 The diviner then prepared the bamboo strips and brushed the
       tortoise shell,
Saying: 'How would you like to be instructed?'

Qu Yuan replied:
'Should I be simple and sincere, honest and forthright,
       unaffected but still dutiful?
Or hurry along hither and thither,
       and so on without end?
Should I hoe and harrow the grasses and rushes,
       labouring away at the plough?
Or should I roam alongside the Great Man
20   to establish my reputation?
Should I speak of justice without compunction,
       though it endanger my own life?
Or should I share in the vulgarity of the rich and mighty,
       just to eke out a living of my own?
Should I rise up to the heights transcendent,
       to preserve and perfect myself;
Flatter and fawn, curry and cajole,
       with insincere smiles and glib giggling,
          to do favours for ladies?
30 Should I be righteous, upright, proper, and true,
       preserving my purity;

Or adapt as unctuously and slip as smoothly
    as lard or leather
        encircling a pillar?

Should I rise up regally like a thousand-league stallion,
    or flap and flutter like a duck in a pond,
        rising and falling with waves,
            just to save my own skin?

Should I race in harness with thoroughbred,
40   or follow the tracks of an old nag?
Should I pair wings with the golden crane,
    or compete for grub with chicken and mallard?
Which way will be auspicious and which malign?
    Which one to choose and which to reject?

This world is turbid and troubled, and cannot be made pure:
    a cicada's wings are deemed heavy,
        a thousand tons merely a trifle;
48 the Golden Bell is shattered and discarded,
        while terracotta trumpets blare out like thunder.
50 The slanderers rise to celebrity;
        but worthy men remain unknown.
Alas, alas, that all are silent –
    no one knows of my fidelity and rectitude.'

The Diviner then let go of the stalks and declined politely, saying:

'Sometimes a foot is still too short;
    sometimes an inch a bit too long.
All matters have regions of inadequacy,
    and wisdom has its zones of ignorance.
There are places that divination cannot touch,
60   where spirits are not permitted to pass.
Use your mind and heart to accomplish your intention:
    neither by tortoise shells nor yarrow stalks can you know your fate.'

8. FISHERMAN
ATTRIBUTED TO QU YUAN

When Qu Yuan was first exiled, he wandered by the rivers and pools, chanting as he walked past marsh and riverbank, his countenance wasted by melancholy, while his frame and demeanour were withered and rotten. The Fisherman saw him and asked: 'Are you not the Master of Three Clans? How is it that you have come to this?' Qu Yuan replied:

> 'All the world is soiled, I alone am pure;
> All the people are drunk, I alone am sober.

That is why I was exiled.' The fisherman then said:

> 'The Sage does not become mired in objects,
>   but is capable of shifting along with the world.
> If everyone in the world is muddy,
>   why not stir up the muck
>   and raise your own waves?
> If all the people are soused,
>   why not dine on their dregs
>   and swallow their lees?
> What are these profound longings and lofty aspirations for,
>   but to get yourself exiled?'

Qu Yuan said: 'I have heard that:

> One who has just bathed must flick his cap;
> One who has just rinsed must brush off his clothes.
> How could I let an immaculate body such as mine
>   suffer the contaminations of objects?
> I would rather enter the current of the Xiang,
>   and be buried in the belly of the river fish;
> How can I let something pristinely white
>   suffer the besmirching and besoiling of the vulgar?'

The fisherman smirked and laughed. He slapped the side of the boat with the oar and departed, singing:

30 'When the waters of the Canglang run clear,
    then I can wash my hatstrings in them;
When the waters of the Canglang run muddy,
    then I can wash my feet in them.'

And he was gone without another word.

9. SUMMONS TO THE RECLUSE
ATTRIBUTED TO THE COURT OF LIU AN

Concealed deep in the mountains – the osmanthus trees
twine and twist, curling and coiling – branches interlacing.

The mountain haze looms aloft – beyond boulders jaggedly jutting;
in gorges and valleys, plunging precipitously – rapids swell.

Troops of gibbons black and white howl – tigers and leopards roar.
Seizing onto a sprig of osmanthus – you linger a while.

The prince who has gone wandering – will not return,
while grasses of spring flourish – dense and verdant;

At the sunset of the year – there is nothing to detain you,
10   And the tree cicadas clitter sadly – *tsyew, tsyew, tsyew.*

So vast – and vertiginous
   the mountains steeply scarped;
Your heart lingers there – pained and perplexed,
Wondering – in bewilderment
   disturbed – and distressed,
      in the caves of the tigers and leopards:
so deep in the forest underbrush –
   that the man who enters must tremble with fear:

Amid those perilous escarpments, precarious cliffs –
20   jagged boulders jutting sharp and sheer,
Where elliptical boughs weave together –
   in woods gnarled and knotted with age.

Green coco-grass complements the trees –
   bulrushes swish and sway.
The white deer and the roebucks –
   stand and leap and stand again,

Raising antlers high – jutting and jagged,
   shivering and quivering – in the blistering chill.
All the macaques – and bears black and brown,
30   must suffer – from longing for their own kind.

Seizing onto a sprig of osmanthus – you linger a while.
   tiger and leopard spar – bears growl black and brown.
Fowl and beast are startled – and stray from their kin.
Ah, Prince! – you must return;
In these mountains – you may no longer tarry.

10. SUMMONS TO THE SOUL
ATTRIBUTED TO SONG YU

Prologue on Earth

In my youth I was pure, honest and virtuous –
   and the body befitting its duty will never be bedimmed.
Though directed by this supreme virtue –
   I was compelled by the vulgar to join the rank and polluted.
My supreme lord had no way to perceive my supreme virtue –
   so I must ever meet with disaster, enduring sorrow and grief.

Prologue in Heaven

The High God told Shaman Yang:
'There is a person down below,
   whom I would like to aid.
10 His skysoul and earthsoul are divided and scattered.
You must make a divination of yarrow stalks on his behalf.'

Shaman Yang replied:
   'As dream-diviner,
      the command of your supreme Lordship is hard to fulfil,
         but if the divination must be done on his behalf,
I only fear that if he perishes first
   there will be nothing left to be done.'

The Summons

18 And then Shaman Yang sent down the summons:

Oh soul – return, return!
20 You have departed from your lasting frame,
   what will you do in the four quarters? –
Make residence in the abode of delights,
   and depart from all those pernicious things –
Oh soul – return, return!
For in the East you cannot lodge –

There giants a thousand fathoms tall
    are searching out your soul –
There ten suns rise in succession,
29   melting metal and dissolving stone –
30 The people there are long accustomed to that heat,
    but your soul gone thence will deliquesce –
Oh, return, return!
    For there you cannot lodge –

Soul! – Return, return,
You must not stay in the South –
36 Men with tattooed brows and blackened teeth
Take human flesh for their sacrifices,
    grind up bones into paste –
Moccasins and pit vipers proliferate and fester,
40   and giant foxes sprint thousands of leagues –

41 The fierce hamadryad of nine heads –
    passes here and there, swift and sudden,
Swallowing men to satisfy its heart –
    Return, return! –
You must not tarry there any longer –

Oh, soul! – return, return!
For the Western lands are full of harm.
48   there the Sinking Sands flow for one thousand leagues –
You will be swirled into the pit of thunder,
50   that grinds, disintegrates, and cannot be stopped –

Even if by good fortune you escape,
    beyond it is a boundless expanse –
Where the scarlet ants grow big as elephants,
54   and the black bees giant as gourds –

55 There the five staple crops do not grow,
    you will scavenge only brambles and oatgrass –
The earth there scorches you,
    when you seek out water there is none to be found –

Wending and winding without fixed abode,
60   vast and wide without any limit –
Return, oh, return!

I fear you only bring yourself harm –
Oh soul, return, return!
For in the North you cannot stay –
There sheets of ice soar sheer above,
    snow flurries over thousands of leagues –
Oh, return, return!
For there you cannot abide long –

Oh soul, return, return!
70 You should not ascend into Heaven –
Tigers and panthers guard the nine gates,
    they gnaw to death ordinary men –
There a giant with nine heads
74   lifts up nine thousand trees –
The wild dogs and wolves eye you hungrily,
    passing to and fro in ravenous packs –
They dangle you in the air for their delight,
    then fling you into a deep pit –
They dispatch your life to the High Lord,
80   and only then do you get your rest –
Return, return!
    If you travel there I fear you will perish.

Oh, soul! Return, return!
You must not descend to the City of Darkness –
The Earthking guards nine gates,
    and his horns are keenly cusped –
With his mighty shoulders and bloody thumbs,
    sprinting and springing, he catches his prey –

Tigerheaded monsters with three eyes,
90   bodies shaped like mighty bulls –
For all these human flesh is a delicacy.
Return, return!
I fear you are only bringing yourself harm –

Soul—return, return!
Come within these lofty gates –
The expert sorcerer is summoning you,
    leading with backward-facing steps –
The bamboo baskets from Qin with threads from Qi,

99   silken webs of Zheng as well –
100 The paraphernalia of summons are all ready now,
    he calls out loud and wails your name! –
Oh soul, return, return!
Come back to your old home –
Though all four quarters of Heaven and Earth
    are rife with scoundrels and slayers of men –
Here in resemblance to life is prepared your chamber,
    soundless, still, and serene –
With lofty palaces and spacious chambers,
    banister upon banister, bower upon bower –
110 Tiered terraces, embedded baldachins
    so tall they overlook the mountains –
Lattice windows lapped in vermilion
    are carved in square patterns –
For the winter cosy niches to stay in,
    in summer chambers to keep chill –
Streams and channels flood forth and swirl back,
    the flowing waters gurgle and gush.
118 Sunlit breezes brush the sweet clover flowers,
    and sway the thickets of eupatory –
120 Passing through the palace into the sanctum,
    vermilion canopies and bamboo mats –

122 Stone-burnished chambers trimmed with kingfisher plumes,
    carnelian hooks dangling –
124 Gem-laden quilts of kingfisher and phalarope feathers,
    each shimmering with equal radiance –
Reed-mats and tabby silks cover the walls,
    and canopies of gauze hang outstretched –
128 Tassels red and motley, damask and tsatlee,
    interwoven with precious jades and demi-discs –

130 Within these rooms are to be seen
    countless things exquisite and strange –
Eupatory-scented tallow lights the candles,
    gorgeous faces are ready too –
Double rows of eight musicians attend your rest,
    and are replaced each evening in turn –

From all the Nine Fiefdoms come demure ladies
    many, teeming, en masse –
Their elaborate hairpieces all of different design,
    they truly fill up the palace –

140 Their faces and figures are wonderfully arrayed,
    serving a time they are soon replaced –
Behind their soft faces they are steadfast of heart,
143   and speak honestly their own minds.
Their winsome features and superb figures
    fill up the cavernous bedchamber –
Their moth-like brows a lustrous vision,
    a glance from them makes sparks fly –

Exquisite faces, lustrous skin,
    with a peek, a glance, a gaze –
150 In detached villas and high hunting tents,
    they attend the lord at leisure –

152 Halcyon canopies, phalarope-plumed curtains
    decorate the lofty palaces –
Crimson walls and cinnabar floors,
    with purlins of dark jade –

Looking overhead you observe the chiselled beams,
    painted with dragons and snakes –
Sitting in the palace and leaning on the balustrade,
    you peer down at winding pools –

160 There the lotus have just started to bloom,
    intermingled with water chestnut –
Purple-stemmed water mallow
    adorns and embroiders the waves –
Wearing dress with patterns rare as leopard-skin,
    attendants wait on the riverbanks –
Canopied, windowed carriages have arrived,
    footsoldiers and cavalry stand in formation –

Eupatory planted by the doors,
    gem-like wood forms the hedges.
170 Oh, soul! Return, return,
    what do you so far off hence? –

The whole clan has assembled,
    and the delicacies are of many kinds –
174 Rice, broomcorn millet, early-ripening wheat,
    mixed with yellow foxtail millet –
Seriously bitter, salty, sour,
177   spicy, or sweet flavoured –
The tendons of a fattened ox,
    well-done and fragrant –
180 Mixing sour and bitter flavours
    presented in a stew from Wu –
Boiled tortoise and roasted veal,
    savouring of sugarcane juice –
Pickled swan and stewed duck,
    with fried goose and oriole –
Open-air chicken and tortoise soup,
    piquant but not pungent;
And twisted crullers and honeycakes,
    as well as sugar puffs –
190 Opalescent potions with spoonfuls of honey
    filling up winged goblets –
Pressing out the dregs for the chilled libations,
    fresh and cool as they are poured –
The ornate winecups are all set out
    for the gem-glistening liqueurs –
Return, return! To your old palace,
    where you are honoured not endangered.

Before the choice cuts and meats are finished,
    musician girls line up before you –
200 Setting up the chimes, striking the drums,
    they perform new songs –
'Crossing the River' and 'Plucking Water Chestnuts',
203   and sing out 'Sunlit Knoll' –
Once the beauties turn tipsy,
    their faces blush crimson –
Peering at them frolicking in the light,
    your gaze ripples off of them –
Clothed in damasks and donning taffeta,
    alluring and yet not strange –

210 Their long hair in glossy fringes
    trails down in seductive disarray –

In two lines of eight they stand parallel,
    ready for the dances of Zheng –
Delicately and gingerly they exchange bamboo poles,
    strike the table and depart –
With mouth organ and zither in wild harmony,
    they strike the resounding drum –
The palace shakes with astonishment
    as they start the 'Frenzied Chu' –
220 With Wu songs and Cai ditties,
221   they sound the Great Pitch of the inverse scale –

Gentlemen and ladies seated amongst one another,
    they are confused and cannot be distinguished –
Undoing and setting down their ribbons and tassels,
    the different ranks are muddled all together.
All the seductive entertainers of Zheng and Wei
    come forward to perform en masse –
And at the finale of the 'Frenzied Chu',
    stand alone in the front –

230 With bamboo tallies and ivory draughtsmen,
    you prepare for Six Sticks –
232 Divided into teams, they advance in parallel,
    pressing the opponent fiercely –
Having made an owl and won a draw,
    you call out the 'five white' –
Advancing and repelling, retreating or approaching,
    you use up all the daylight –
Striking the bell and rocking the frame,
    they play the catalpa zither –

240 Delighting in wine without pause,
    debauched day and night –
With eupatory-scented tallow lighting the torches,
    incised oil-lamps laid in order –

Inditing in verse their utmost yearnings,
    pristine as scent of eupatory –

Men have their own higher aspirations,
    their hearts conjoined in recitations –
Pouring out the drink they achieve the utmost joy,
    and delight alike the ancestors and departed.
250 Oh soul! return, return,
    come back to your old home –

Envoi

As spring brings in the new year –
253   in haste I ride off southward.
Carpetgrass and waterclover have matching leaves –
    and angelica blooms.
The route crosses the Lu River –
257   deep shrubbery on the left.
Charging past ponds and pools –
    we gaze far over the plain.
260 The dark stallions race in quartets –
    together making one thousand steeds.
Beacon fires spread upwards –
    dark figures rise.
Marching through, running then halting –
    driving ahead at a gallop.
I stop the chargers and line them up –
    turning the chariots back to the right.
Entering the marsh alongside the king –
    we contend for first and last.
270 My lord and king shoots first –
    and kills the black rhinoceros.
272 As fiery radiance replaces the night –
    Time cannot be stayed.
Plashy eupatory covers the path –
    till this road disappears.
Limpid flow the waters of the Jiang –
277   with maple trees above.
My vision penetrates one thousand leagues –
    the pity of spring in my heart.
280 Oh Soul – return, return, return,
    and grieve for the Southland.

11. NINE LONGINGS
BY WANG BAO

I. Righting the Occasion

1 I did not meet – the Polestar's course,
    so I am abased – thwarted and disheartened.
  How deeply I grieve – miserable and melancholy,
    though I would reach the highest rank – I lack the means.
  Riding sun and moon – I will rise up on high,
6   though my heart stray back – to Hao and to Feng.
7 Perusing all through – the nine corners of the realm,
    I slow so as to sojourn – in the Eupatory Palace:

  By angelica threshold – and herb-scented chambers,
10   I go forth wafting – the fair fragrances.
  Amid osmanthus towers – and sweet clover halls,
    belvederes and avenues – crisscrossing around us,
  Collecting and guarding – jewels and gold,
    the palaces are filled – with the finest of jade.
  Osmanthus rivers – gurgle and gush,
    raising up currents – immense and unending.
  Aged tortoises – dance with joy,
    venerable cranes – soar up circling.
  But leaning on the balustrade – I gaze afar,
20   thinking of my sovereign – I do not forget.
  Drowning in despair – I cannot express,
    this regret festers – ever in my heart.

II. Opening a Route

Will Heaven's gate – or Earth's vestibule
    ever allow entry to – the worthy man?
In chaos and confusion – no orthodoxy remaining,
    how to distinguish – those who harbour virtue?
5 Weary even in daylight – I grieve only for this:
    with whom can I – converse in confidence?
Grieving phoenixes – have departed far off,
    while tame quail – abide in this vicinity.
The paddlefish and whale – are concealed in the dark,
10   but minnows en masse – cavort by the riverbanks.

Riding on the spirax – I ascend the sunlit pneumas,
12   on a chariot of ivory – I rise upwards.
At dawn I set out from – the Pamir Mountains,
14   at evening I arrive – at the unflickering gleam.
In the north I sip from – Flying Font,
    southward I cull the – mystic mushrooms.
Roaming through each of – the serried constellations,
    circumnavigating the Polestar – I idle a while.
With crimson colours – and robes of ochre,
20   halcyon hues and opaline silks – for my tunics,
Loosing my pendants – rich and resplendent,
    I hold erect my broadsword – forged by Gan Jiang.
While shimmering snakes – follow behind,
    and chasm-spanners – pace alongside:
Inspecting as I pass – the Hanging Garden,
26   I approach and examine – Chalcedony Gleam.
There I open up the chest – to inquire of the divining slips:
    but the reading implies – that I am destined to misery.

29 Braiding together sweet clover – making permanent farewell,
    I prepare to depart – from the one for whom I yearn.
With the floating clouds – I'll roam and range,
    guiding me on a path – destination unknown.

Gazing at the horizon – enshrouded in cloud,
34   I listen as thunder – thrashes and clashes.
A secret sorrow – stirs within me,
    frustrated, forsaken – I rue my state.

III. Excellence Endangered

The forest cannot contain – the chirping cicada,
　　nor can I linger any more – upon this isle.
Instead I'll indulge in the moonlight – to ready my carriage,
　　cull jade blossoms – and otherwise perfect myself.
Twining the flowing angelica – in twisting trails,
　　I will depart from these folk – and roam afar.
Traversing Mount Tai – and the watchtowers of Wei,
8　　I will pass the Nine Crooks – of Ox and Oxherd.
I'll idle a while enjoying the sun – dallying and dithering,
10　　while a gleaming lingers – to roam all around.
I gaze up towards Supreme Unity – and heave a sigh,
　　relax the reins – and allow myself a rest.
Bathing in the bright sun's – resplendent rays,
　　travelling further and further – through the vastness of space.
Gazing back up the arrayed comets – blink past in a blur,
　　I regard the dark clouds – drifting along in sequence.
17 As the Mighty Treasure revolves – with thunderous roar,
　　the pheasants all crow out – in response.
Through boundless space – I pursue my ambition,
20　　only anxious that my heart – is mired in melancholy.
I pace my steed – to the flying pylons of Heaven,
　　and observe whether – there are peers to join me there.
But finding no one – worthy as a single filament,
　　I yearn alone – downcast and despairing.

IV. Enlightening the World

The world is corrupt – its people ignorant and blind:
    so I disobey my Sovereign – to regain the genuine.
Riding upon a dragon – sublimely soaring,
    I spiral skyward – to reach the world above.
Donning gorgeous robes – of tangerine-hued hems,
    I wear flowered jackets – wafting sweet aromas.

Climbing up the ram's horns – of the swirling vortex,
8   I drift upon the Milky Way – for my own delight.
Settling my inner spirit – to be calm and collected,
10   I enjoy communing – with gods and men.
Shooting stars plummet down – like rain,
    advancing to gaze and observe – climbing hillocks and hummocks;
I gaze upon my old country – which looks clouded and dimmed,
    how could I be willing – long there to abide?
My resolve and longings are defeated – my heart woefully faltering,
    I shorten the reins – and halt in hesitation.
I have heard the subtle songs – of the White Maiden,
18   I listen to the royal consort – blow the reed-organ.
My soul is wrung by woe – and moved to sorrow,
20   my innards tied in knots – coiled and contorted.

Seizing these pendants – diversely displayed,
    I heave a sigh from above – and condole with myself.
I send off Zhurong – to be my forerunner,
24   and order Refulgent Clarity – to open the gate ahead.

Driving six krakens before me – I climb upward,
    straightening my steed – I enter into the void.
Passing through the Nine Provinces – in search of a match,
    who is there with whom – I can spend my remaining life?
All at once I look behind me – to the West Pleasance,
30   observe hills square as carriages – towering overhead.
Pouring down tears profusely – in cascades coursing,
    how I grieve for my sovereign – for spirits betrayed!

V. Honouring Virtue

In the last month of spring – in the warmth of the sun,
    every grass springs up – in flourishing rows.
I grieve that – the eupatory full-grown
    now lies strewn – all across the ground.
The river lovage too – is discarded and lost,
    the magnolia – crushed and buried.
Reflecting back upon – all that is past and gone,
    how many men have – met with disaster:
Wu Zixu's corpse – floated in the Jiang,
10   and Master Qu – drowned in the Xiang.
In time's cycle I – ponder this ever more,
    my inner heart still – suffering from regrets.

Gazing over the Huai River – surging and churning,
    rushing over the banks – and then departing;
Roaming my wooden raft – down along the stream,
    surging eastward – clashing and plashing.
The krakens and dragons – lead me along,
    the dappled fish – climb up the rapids.
I pluck out the rushes – to lay out as my seat,
20   I select the lotus blossoms – to make my canopy.
The billows leap up – around my pennants,
    and I interweave with them – the wild grasses.
My cloud banners – rush ahead like lightning,
    now hurrying, scurrying – now dithering, dallying:

The Sire of the Yellow River – opens the gates,
    and welcomes me – to delights and joys.
Looking back and longing – for the old capital,
    I endure this frustration – hardship and heartache.
I lament that this life – is like floating duckweed:
30   drifting in the current – rootless to the end.

VI. Guarding Merit

The autumn wind blows – *siew, siew,*
    stirring up fragrance – and swaying the twigs,
Through the faint frost – I peer into the distance,
    sick unto death – I hear the cicadas call.
The dark bird – has already departed,
6   soaring in flight – up to the spirit mound.
I gaze at the gullies – clouded and dim,
    where bears black and brown – growl and snarl.
Yao of Tang, Shun of Yu – no longer survive,
10   what cause have I – to tarry here for long!

Overlooking the abyss – vast beyond all bound,
    I look back at the forest's – impenetrable haze.
Straightening out my – mantle and robes,
    I'll ride the dawn cloudwisps – soaring southward.
I mount the clouds – whirling and wheeling,
    steadily and ceaselessly – find myself strengthened.

I decide to rest – upon the eupatory banks,
    but my aim is frustrated – I pine and ponder.
My copious capacities – blackened and besmirched,
20   I long for my sovereign – so I cannot rest.
My body already lost – yet my will survives,
    lacerated with regret – wounded by woe.

VII. Longing for Loyalty

1 Ascending to divinity in nine stages – I let my spirit roam,
    where modest ladies sing – of the dawn's faint appearance;
3 I lament that the mound of power – is encumbered by vines,
    which criss-cross in varied forms – of rampant overgrowth.
    The faithful branches grow stunted – and wither away,
    while crooked carriages ascend – the clouds of fortune.
    My will is shaken – and quavers in awe,
    my heart broken and battered – I lament my fate.

    Riding upon a black wyvern – I journey northward,
10 turning my route – towards the Pamir Mountains.
11 Joining together the Five Planets – to lift up my banner,
    raising vapours and pneumas – as my pennants.
    Crossing over the vast silence – sprinting and dashing,
    I look upon the central states – shrouded in darkness.
    The Mystic Warrior strides – past water's source,
16 to rendezvous with me – amid southern lushness.

17 Climbing up Floriate Canopy – upon the surging Yang force,
    I'll roam and ramble a while – dispersing illumination.
    Gripping the Treasury and Tower – I sip sweet liquors,
20 And rely on the Great Gourd – to restore my provisions.
    When I am done with recuperation– I depart for the remote,
    releasing the jade brake – and journeying westward.
    Truly the custom of this age – is to revile the just,
    so I could scarcely tarry – in this place.
25 Waking I rend my breast – with an endless yearning;
    my heart is occluded by angst – I am wounded within.

VIII. Cultivating Delight

Considering the benighted, blighted – values of this world,
    I am dejected and distraught – with nowhere to take refuge.
I grieve that the customs of the age – are topsy-turvy,
    so I will unfurl my wings – and soar aloft:
Driving eight dragons – sinuously snaking,
    I hoist rainbow pennants – swaying and swirling.
Surveying the central realm – vast and wide,
    steadily, serenely winging my way – I mount upwards.
Coursing down Weakwater – that glimmers faintly,
10   turning to dally on – the sandbars and the islets.
I curb my carriage – to seek an understanding friend,
    in quest for a wise ruler – I enquire for a teacher too.
No way is so to be prized – as submitting to genuineness;
    my own arts are envied – for how they bring delight.

Thus I have departed – to cavort in the southern lands,
    following a dark path – to the Nine Semblances.
I traverse fire and flames – for a thousand leagues,
    pass the Many-Crowned Mountain – that spires high above.
I ford the rivers and seas – instantaneous as a cicada moulting,
20   cross over the northern bridge – to make my long farewell.
Obscured by floating clouds – day turns to dusk,
    and dust flies up – in whirling, whorling haze.
Reposing in Yangcheng's – spacious mansions,
    my appearance is aged – but within I am not fatigued.
My thoughts bright as the dawn – I suddenly awaken:
    to examine myself – here where I am:
I think of the past success – of Yao and Shun
    fortunate to obtain the counsel – of Gaoyao.
I grieve that the Nine Provinces – lack a sovereign;
30   bowing over the crossbar with a sigh – I composed this poem.

IX. Uprooting and Insight

Sorrow, alas! I sigh and suffer –
    still refining and repolishing my feelings:
I would bloom up as the coltsfoot –
    after leaves and branches have withered.
Nowadays clay tiles and gravel are presented as prizes –
6   Sui's pearls and He's jade discarded.
Leaden knives are honed for the court –
    while Supreme Buttress is dulled and abandoned.
The noble stallion droops both ears –
10   faltering, halting midway up the hill.
A lame donkey is yoked to the carriage –
    and malingerers grow ever more numerous.
The refined and pure must abide in darkness –
    those most revered are ground down like sand.

The phoenixes no longer soar in the sky –
    but quail and turnix ascend to the heights.
Riding on rainbows, driving coronas before me –
    I'm borne forth by clouds' transformations.
Blazing firebirds prepare the way –
20   followed behind by green serpents.
Marching and galloping through the osmanthus woods –
22   charging and surmounting the 'bend in the hillside';
The hillocks and hummocks dance and leap –
    the gullies and valleys sing sorrowful songs.
With divine compositions and mystic poems –
    the music is performed in mutual harmony.
I delight in this for myself –
    and who could further add to it?
Regarding all around me the manners of this age –
30   I realize the net of order has rotted away.
Rolling up my adornments I prepare to depart –
    my tears streaming forth in floods.

Envoi

The resplendent gate opens – the earth below is illuminated.
Rotting tree stumps are cleared away – so eupatory and angelica appear.
35 The Four Toadies were expulsed – only then could Yu be lord.
Sagely Shun governed – further clarifying the traces of Yao.
Whosoever could match them – only such a ruler would I serve.

12. SEVEN REMONSTRANCES
BY DONGFANG SHUO

I. On First Being Exiled

Qu Ping was born within this kingdom –
    but matured in the wilderness.
His speech was plain and uncouth –
    and he had no powerful supporters.
Shallow in knowledge, straitened in capacity –
6   wisdom and experience both scant;
He repeatedly counselled schemes to bring advantage –
    only to be resented by the other courtiers.
Because the King did not perceive his own future benefit –
10   Ping at last was cast into the wilderness;
And thinking back and reflecting on his errors –
    saw nothing he would have done otherwise.

The vulgar crowds joined in cliques –
    his Highness was inundated in error;
Artful slanderers stepped to the forefront –
    while worthy men were silenced and removed.
The sages Yao and Shun have already perished –
    who now could be deemed loyal and upright?

High mountains soar and spire above –
20   the rivers flow on rushing and gushing,
The day of my death is soon approaching –
    when I am ensnared alongside elaphure and deer.

Alone now – overburdened,
    lodging on the open road,
All the world is alike –
    so who is there to tell of my plight?

Rebuking and repulsing the mighty condor –
    men fraternize instead with hooters and howlets.
Slashing apart tangerine and pomelo –
30   they plant instead orchards of hairy peach.

But one slender bamboo, delicate and supple –
    lodges itself amid the rivers and pools:
Above its burgeoning foliage keeps off the dew –
    below its refreshing cool draws in the breeze.
Truly indeed he is not suited to the times –
    for he shares with bamboo and cypress a mind apart.

Those who have gone we cannot hope to equal –
38   and those to come we cannot prepare for.
39   'Azure Heaven lofty and limitless' –
40   you have no aid nor succour for me.
How I regret that my liege is unaware –
    let me die first and so be done with this!

II. Drowning in the River

Pondering the successes and failures of the past –
    I note the wrong incurred by cliquish calumnies:
Yao and Shun, the sagely, were generous and good –
    so later ages praised them and did not forget.
While Duke Huan of Qi erred in arrogating authority –
    Guan Zhong's loyalty still burnished his fame.
Duke Xian of Jin was beguiled by the concubine from Li –
    The filial Shensheng still met catastrophe.
King Yan of Xu enacted policies of compassion and propriety –
10   but Duke Wen of Jing saw his chance and so Xu fell.
The tyrannical Zhow finally lost his throne –
    for the Zhou overcame him with the aid of Lü Wang:
They revived the mores of antiquity to distribute merit –
    enfeoffing the martyred Bi Gan in his funerary mound.
The sagely and meritorious admired and attached themselves –
    as the days proceeded they gradually formed a compact,
Comprehending the laws and decrees and enacting principles –
18   as eupatory and angelica, though reticent, still exude their
        fragrance.
I suffer because the others all envy me –
20   So Master Ji was percipient and feigned madness.
I do not look back towards the earth and lust for fame there –
    rather my heart is distraught and depressed, and I grieve within.
Binding together sweet clover and angelica to make my adornments –
24   but when I visit the salted-fish seller they lose all fragrance.
Righteous vassals keep proper deportment and action –
    but nonetheless meet with slander and are cast away.
The customs of the age move on, steadily devolving –
    so Bo Yi starved at Mount Shouyang;
Even the noblest and finest are not accommodated –
30   yet when enough time had passed Shu Qi's fame grew.
The drifting clouds spread farther, the darkness encompassing us –
    causing even sun and moon to lose their brightness.
Loyal ministers are steadfast and willing to counsel the sovereign –
    but slanderers and sycophants cause ruin by his side.
The autumn grasses are flourishing and soon to bear fruit –
    but then a faint frost descends and the night falls.

The winds of autumn are harsh and destroy life –
    the hundred grasses sprout but not for long.
The many share in jealousy for worthy men –
40   the lone sage stands apart and is easily ruined.
He harbours plans and stratagems but never finds employment –
    abiding in the crags and caves guards himself in secret.
Success and merit are crushed and do not last –
44   so Wu Zixu died and was not buried.
Our age adapts to customs and so continues to devolve –
    swaying in the wind, the people march in lockstep.
Loyalty and honesty retreat, suffering disdain and defeat –
    hypocrisy advances and finds a fitting place.
Though I repent for my past errors it is already too late –
50   mere loyalty does not suffice to earn success.
Now our guiding models have long been abandoned –
    all strive for personal gain only and reject the public good.
Yet I will never waver but will die for my liege –
    only regretting I cannot live out my proper span.
55 I will drift downstream upon my rafted boats –
    hoping that my sovereign might at last awake from ignorance.
I grieve that faithful words grate on his ears –
58   regret that Master Shen sank himself into the River.
I hoped to put to use what I had learned before –
60   but met instead with a sovereign who was not perceptive.
If he does not become aware then it is hard to guide him –
    for he cannot tell the horizontal from the vertical.
He listens to the wicked ministers' flimsy stories –
    and so will prevent this kingdom from enduring long.
He abolishes the rules and ignores the laws –
    deviating from the perpendicular of the plumb-line.

After this worry and despair I have come to my senses –
    suddenly as fire overtaking autumn fleabane.
The project of the state, once lost, will not be saved –
70   no need to speak of my own calamity and suffering.
They provoke division and dissent, the cliques of conspirators –
    what hope is there for a gentleman who proceeds alone?
Every day I am contaminated further till I do not know myself –
    even that minuscule as autumn down changes its countenance.

When many trivialities accumulate, the chariot-axle snaps –
    so slanders against Qu Yuan were sundry and his burden great.
He faced the drifting currents of the Xiang and Yuan –
78   but feared to follow the waves all the way to the east.
Embracing stones and pebbles he drowned himself –
80   he could not bear to see his sovereign deceived and beguiled.

III. Indignant at the World

The world is mired in confusion and cannot be ordered –
  the vulgar are hoisted high and appointed hodge-podge.
Men pure as gleaming dewdrops are slaughtered and destroyed –
  while those corrupted to the core flourish daily.
Though hooters and howlets flock together –
  contemplative cranes fold in their wings and retreat.
Fleabane and wormwood come right in and straddle between bed
    and cover,
  while pony aster runs wild and spreads further each day.
They casually discard medicinal angelica and sweet asarum –
10 what kind of a world is it that appreciates no fragrance?
11 For the way of the Zhou was level and open –
  but now is weedy and rank, steep and treacherous.
Our ancestor Gaoyang is cast in the dirt without a cause –
  Yao and Shun defiled and distorted, slandered and reviled.
Who is it who will affirm the truth of these matters? –
16 even the Eight Masters perhaps could not do so.

Mighty Heaven will preserve its majesty –
  and Sovereign Earth will endure for ages.
I will clothe myself in the pure and white, and roam freely –
20 assuming a hue utterly unlike those polluted blossoms.

Xi Shi is lithe and lovely but cannot find an audience –
22 Homely Crone stumbles and shambles but stays in attendance.
Osmanthus borers can find no secure place to abide –
  knotweed mites do not recognize the sweetness of the mallow.
Abiding in this foul world of corruption and confusion –
  how now may I achieve my own ambition?
My thoughts have their own burden, that of departing far away –
  which is not such as the mass of men could comprehend.
Fine stallions hoof and haw, overturning the carriage –
30 only by Sun Yang's approbation will their talent be applied.
Lü Wang was wretched and helpless, without even a livelihood –
  till he met King Wen and could realize his ambition.
Ning Qi was feeding oxen and seeking ditties of Shang –
  Duke Huan heard him singing and did not neglect him.
Meeting with maidens tending mulberries on the road –

36 Confucius found himself advised by them as he passed by.
    I alone am betrayed and assailed and waylaid –
        my heart haggard and harried, my thoughts in turmoil.
    Pondering Bi Gan and his unqualified loyalty –
40   I grieve too for Wu Zixu's vigilant devotion.

    I mourn for Master He, another hero of Chu –
        his priceless jade was mistaken for mere stone.
    He met with Kings Li and Wu who were not percipient –
44   and for this sole failing had both legs severed.
    Petty men now occupy the seats of power –
        regarding the loyal and righteous as if they were inferior.
    They have transformed the order and the laws of the former sages –
        they delight in conspiratorial whispers and rash decisions.
    Making intimates of toadies and sycophants, estranging the wise and
        worthy –
50   they would describe Nymph Lü as ugly and vile.

    Delighting in the fond and familiar, he disparages the distant –
        scarcely able to distinguish black from white.
    Since I have not been able to deploy my heart and sentiments –
        I have no place to take refuge, between here and the horizon.

    I focus my own spirit in order to enlighten myself –
        but still am blocked out, boxed in by night's encroachment.
    Of my years I have already passed the greater half –
        but still I am hindered and hampered, delayed, abeyed.
    I would soar high aloft and find a far-off perch –
60   but I fear I'll be enmeshed and perish in defeat.
    Alone, wronged, wrecked, I have no means to continue –
        I grieve for my vital spirit and precarious survival.
    Majestic Heaven is not simple in the destinies it allots us –
        and so nothing in my life has been dependable.
    I would like to sink myself into the currents of the Jiang –
66   to slip between the torrents and depart far away.
    I'd rather join the mud and mire beneath the rivers and seas –
        than to look for long on this lutulent world.

IV. Resentful Thoughts

Worthy gentlemen are ruined and must reside in reclusion –
    while the honest, correct, and dutiful remain unwelcome.
Wu Zixu offered his counsel and so lost his life –
    Bi Gan was loyal so his heart was eviscerated.
Jiezi Tui carved himself open to feed his lord –
    so virtue is further forgotten, and resentment deepens.
Actions plain and honest are labelled black as night –
    thorns and brambles spring up to fill a forest.

The river lovage is discarded in desolate alleys –
10   ignoble pigweed pervades the East Wing of the Palace.
Worthy men are deprecated and disregarded –
    slanderers and toadies advance and join in cliques.
Hooters and howlets advance in tandem and squawk as one –
    but the phoenix soars far higher than all of them.
I would like to depart for once and journey off –
    but the path is impassable and I find no escape.

V. Mourning My Plight

My abiding melancholy and misery I can tell no one –
    burning, yearning, in worry and woe.
Inwardly I reflect on myself but am not ashamed –
    for my proper stance is firm and does not falter.
In reclusion for three years, I still could not decide –
6   but the season rushes rapidly towards ruin.
I grieve my lifetime was inadequate to achieve my aim –
    still hoping for just one audience before I depart.
I mourn that human affairs are full of misfortune –
10   subject to Heaven's mandate, destined by the Pool of Affinity.

I have suffered affliction and can find no ease –
    as if my heart must face suffocating heat.
Ice and burning coals do not remain together –
    so too my life will not last much longer.
Grieving alone, risking death, lacking pleasures –
    yet I must cherish these years before they expire.
I mourn that I cannot return to my old abode –
    resent that I must depart from my own home.
Birds and beasts are startled and leave their flocks –
20   then fly aloft and loose a sorrowful cry.
21 The fox turns toward its old burrow when it dies –
    what man does not return to his authentic passions?

The men of former days now are distanced and swiftly
       forgotten –
    while new ones are drawn close and ever more familiar.
No one can act properly under the shroud of darkness –
    nor will men serve others without requital.

It pains me that the masses of men are so conformist –
    myself I'll ride the whirlwind and roam afar.
29 Crossing over Mount Heng it seems deserted –
30   I'll while away the time to forget my worries.

I mourn those empty words that had no substance –
32   am pained that 'many mouths can melt metal'.
Passing my old home I take one look behind –
    weeping, sighing, suspiring, tears drench my sleeve.

I press white jade to form my countenance –
    clutch precious jadestones to construct my heart.
Vile airs rush in and I am stirred within –
    but I show forth my jade-like countenance that radiates beyond.

How the clouds in the blue surge and swell –
40   a film of frost falls with a drenching chill.
A gentle breeze drifts along, hither and thither –
    then a harsh gale blows by blaring and bawling.

I have heard the southern lands are fortunate and long to go there –
    upon reaching Mount Guiji I rest a while.
45 I visit Han Zhong and spend the night with him –
    enquiring where the way to Heaven may be found.

I borrow the drifting clouds to send me along –
    and hold up coronas as my pennants.
I drive green dragons and race ahead –
50   aligned in awesome array, through boundless void.

Thrown into the vast abyss where can I go –
    crossing the trackless wilderness without direction?
It pains me that the many are so untrustworthy –
    I'd rather depart the crowds and rise aloft.

Climbing up the mountain ridges I'll gaze far off –
    admiring the osmanthus that blooms in winter.
Perceiving the fires of Heaven that burn resplendent –
    I listen for the sounds of the waves in the great gullies.
59 Guided by the Eight Mainstays I make my own way –
60   swallowing midnight mists to prolong my life.

Abiding in discontent and frequently yearning –
    I consume the mellow fruits of the flowering trees.
I drink the morning dew of osmanthus and ginger-lily –
    hew the cinnamon wood to make my chamber.

Assembling tangerine and pomelo to build my abode –
    I arrange the magnolia together with fagara and privet.
The demoiselle crane trumpets alone in the night –
    mourning the sincere devotion of this solitary survivor.

VI. Lamenting My Fate

I lament my destiny did not suit this moment –
 I grieve for the many troubles of the kingdom of Chu.
In me I harbour passions that are pure and stainless –
 but I met with an anarchic age and suffered slanders.

I detest how, although the upright and good behave correctly –
 yet the world is confused and corrupted, and knows them not.
Why must sovereign and vassal lose one another? –
 riding up the Yuan and Xiang rivers till they diverge.

I have tested the waters of the Miluo and the Xiang –
10 I know time's passage is fast and irrevocable.
I grieve that separation and dispersal together form disaster –
 so I have shifted my body and estranged myself.

13 Residing deep within the gates of a wondrous lodge –
 tunnelling through the boulders I hide myself in the grottoes.
Joining the krakens to form my companions –
 alongside divine dragons I find a place of rest and calm.

How precipitously spire upwards the mountain peaks –
 my numinous soul follows along, winding and wheeling;
I swallow the pure waters and submerge myself in the depths –
20 the sun moves ever more remote and is only faintly visible.

I lament that my body's frame is now divided and isolated –
 my spirit bereaved and baffled has no place to abide.
23 For Fagara and Eupatory are not willing to change course –
 my soul has gone astray and cannot find the route.

I had wanted to establish rules such that no thing goes awry –
 but even in destruction and death I will find contentment.
I grieve that the Kingdom of Chu is fallen into ruin –
 lament that Spirit Paragon has been rigid in error.

For the customs of our time are beguiled and misguided –
30 even I am confused and confounded, and have lost the route.
31 Pondering those who governed wisely their domains –
 far away I cross the Jiang and depart to remote lands.

33 Thinking of 'Lady Xu the Shamaness clinging closely' –
 my tears stream down in torrents of my pent-up sadness.

I have decided to die rather than live on –
    for though I search again how can I find my goal?

I frolic in the pure waters of these torrential streams –
    gaze up at the precipitous spirals of the high mountains.
I rue the crimson slopes of the Mound of Gao –
40   though I lose my life I will never return.

VII. *Unwise Counsel*

1   I resent Spirit Paragon for his immense indifference –
    how inconstant he is in upholding his own integrity.
    I mourn that Mount Tai has become no more than a mound –
    how even the rivers and streams now run dry!

    I would take this chance to exert my own will freely –
    but I fear violating the sacred and encroaching on taboo.
    Ultimately I master my passions and choose isolation and aloneness –
    but I am miserable and melancholy, and mourn my own state.
    Now jade and pebble must share a single casket –
10 fish eyes be stitched together with pearls and gems.
    The broken nag and swiftest steed can no longer be distinguished –
    the worn-out ox pulls ahead, with chargers as his trace-horses.
    As the years roll on relentlessly I make myself ever more remote –
    as my lifespan passes on without cease I grow ever more frail.

    My heart is downcast and dejected by trouble and wrong –
    I long to soar above but lack the hope of success.
    For the custom of this age is to practise only artifice –
    ruining the square and compass by change and misuse.

    Men reject the finest thoroughbred to ride upon –
20 while driving instead worn-out nags upon the road.
    There will always be more than one thoroughbred in this world –
    but there is only a single Wang Liang to judge.
    Seeing that the rein-master now is not the right one –
    a spirited colt must depart to a far land.

    If we try to right the tenon without measuring the chisel –
    I fear the compass and square will never conform.
    I would rise up aloft and not speak more of this world –
    though I fear my deportment and deeds have lacked propriety.

    The bowstring once released will not go taut again–
30 who can tell where the arrow has hit?
    Without facing peril that the kingdom will be overthrown –
    who can tell if men are worthy enough to face death?

    The vulgar may promote mere flatterers and praise the profligate –
    while the practice of virtue is flaunted but not achieved.

The worthy and good are overlooked and have no allies –
    friends and clans are formed and cliques esteemed.

Heterodox sayings are flaunted and deviousness is rife –
    the proper way is viewed askew, not chosen as the norm.
Righteous gentlemen go into hiding and seclude themselves in
      secrecy –
40   while the flatterers and connivers ascend to the Hall of Light.

41 Men reject what Peng and Xian had found their pleasure and delight –
    they destroy the plumb-line and ink of the Artful Chui.
Jade-glinting bamboo is jumbled together with stalks of hemp –
    the crossbow fires bolts of fleabane to strike at hide targets.
They drive lame donkeys without even a whip –
    how can they ever reach the end of their route?
Attempting to angle with a straight needle –
    what fish will they ever catch that way?

Bo Ya snapped his very zither strings –
50   for he had no Zhong Ziqi to listen to him play.
Master He bore forth his uncarved jade and so wept blood –
    for he had found no artisan to chisel it for him.
Like tunes may form a harmony between themselves –
    like kinds conform to one another.
The flying birds cry out for their own flock –
    the deer cries searching for his friend.

So strike a Gong note and a Gong one echoes –
58   play a Jue note and a Jue stirs.
The tiger howls and the winds rise from the valley –
60   the dragon rises and auspicious clouds appear.

Thus the square and the round have different shapes –
    their forms cannot be interlocked together.
Master Lie concealed himself and abided in desperate straits –
    because there was no place in the world worthy of refuge.
The myriad birds all have their lines and formations –
    alone the phoenix flutters on without a place to perch.
Enduring a foul world where I cannot fulfil my aim –
    I would lodge myself in crags and caves and so find refuge.
I'd like to close my mouth and never speak –
70   for I once received rich favour from my sovereign.

I alone am preciously poised but in my heart harbour poison –
    mired in melancholy, having no way to turn.

Thinking back on these three years and their hoarded yearnings –
    I'd like to have one audience and to present my words.
But I cannot reach my sovereign to show off my orations –
    who in all the world could enlighten him?

My body endures agony and daily grows more distraught –
    my feelings downcast and dejected cannot be restored.
Among the masses there is none with whom to discuss the Way –
80   I grieve that my inner spirit can never be made known to all.

Envoi

1 'Simurgh and phoenix, birds of fine augury, perch ever further away' –
       while here we rear only goose and mallard.
   The chickens and ducks fill the courtyard and the altar –
4   toads and frogs play in Floriate Pond.
   The Litheloined steed has galloped off and disappeared –
6   I am left to race upon a humpbacked camel.
   The leaden dagger is wielded at court –
       Supreme Buttress cast off into the outer reaches.
   They weed out the mystic mushrooms –
10   and cultivate instead rows of tawdry taro.
   Tangerine and pomelo withered and decayed –
       bitter plums meanwhile dangle lusciously.

   Clay bowls and jugs ascend to the Hall of Light –
14   the Tripods of Zhou were lost in the deep abyss.
   Since ancient times the world has ever been thus –
       why resent especially the faults of our contemporaries?

13. NINE THRENODIES

I. Facing Anarchy

1   That scion and progeny of his majesty Boyong –
     namely, the august and incorruptible Qu Yuan,
  Spoke thus: My originating sire was Lord Gaoyang –
     my lineage linked with Chu's King Huai;

  I, Yuan, by birth bestowed the charge of fealty and duty –
6   with boundless bounty also inherited virtuous name:
  A name and sobriquet commensurate with Heaven and Earth –
8   their resplendent sheen on par with the serried stars.

9   I imbibed the finest essences and expelled the turbid airs –
10   athwart the wicked world I sought no concessions.
  With integrity in act and speech I would not grovel –
     so I was cast out and much slander endured.

  His majesty believed fictions and banished truth –
     refused to reason with me but yielded to passion.
  Viscerally indignant and outraged, I checked my anger –
     my will warped and wavering, as I am demoted leftward:

  Mind muddled and befuddled, he granted me nothing –
     his person harried and hampered, he approached me not.
  Departing from Spirit Paragon, ambitions consigned to failure –
20   I sing by the shores of pools and on the riverbanks.

  Though fagara and osmanthus are toppled in their rows –
     because I am firm in faith I will regain integrity.
  Slanderous men are legion, swarming into prominence –
     why not at least release my inner feelings?

  We first made our compact in the temple court,
     but that trust he did betray mid-course.
  Clutching eupatory and sweet clover, asarum and angelica –
     I roam in the meadows and scatter them there.

29 My voice keens with sorrow as I long for the Mound of Gao –
30   my heart rent and rueful as I yearn for my former land.
I would find an occasion to deploy myself –
    but the paths are deluged and diluvial, the true way submerged.

My countenance is stained with darkness, wounded, wasted –
    my spirit fractured, battered, and decrepit with age.
My sleeves flit and flutter in the rush of the breeze –
    robes drenched and doused in the all-covering dew.

I proceed along the rapid streams of the Jiang and Xiang –
    descending along with the converging torrents;
Then dally for a while on a mountain knoll –
40   where the passing stormwinds surge and sputter.

I race my carriage past the wondrous rocks –
42   I canter my steed by Lake Dongting.
At the hour of dawn I set out from Silver Pillar –
44   at dusk pitch camp at Stonewall.

With lotus canopy and water-chestnut car –
    my pylons made of periwinkle shells, my court of jade.
My pendants woven of creeping fig, mats studded with lapis lazuli –
48   my robes covered in fishscales, my sleeves luminously haloed.

I climb Mount Dragonmeet and fall back to earth –
50   I depart the former Capital deliberately.
Thinking of the old ways back at Southern Ying –
52   I feel my viscera transported back nine times each night.

The rolling waves surge up billowing and breaking,
    my body turning and churning in flow back to the east.
My heart suffers the pangs of a ceaseless longing –
    my thoughts are occluded with the setting of the sun.

The white dew falls rife in senseless profusion –
    the autumn winds shriek with tempestuous wail.
My body will drift forever and not return –
60   my soul, departed into the distance, grieving ever.

THRENODY

Just like the rapids of the stream,
    when they crash upon the rocks –

The waves meet rolling and roiling,
   and surge up in baleful bursts –

Swiftly rising, shaking and quaking,
   rolling currents pouring downwards,
     striking the cragged stones –
Coursing criss-cross, plashing and splashing,
   interweaving revolutions interlacing,
70   impeding all approach –

Facing anarchy, confronting disaster:
   for my honest counsel I suffered blame –
But I leave behind my writings, I raise these insignia,
   bequeathed to those who come hereafter –

II. Departing This World

Spirit Huai, the numinous, does not know me –
    Spirit Huai does not hear of me;
I turn to face Spirit Huai's august ancestors –
    complain of Spirit Huai to the spirits and ghosts;

But Spirit Huai will make no pact with me –
    hearing only the fawning phrases of others.
My own phrases match in excellence Heaven and Earth –
8   and attract to me the spirits of the four seasons.

Addressing sun and moon, I make them shine yet more brilliantly –
10   seize upon Twinkling Indicator as pledge and witness;
Music-master Kuang standing by to aid my righteous statement –
    I command the wise Gaoyao to listen alongside.

By the tortoise-shell cracks my name reads Righteous Principle –
14   according to the hexagrams I style myself Spirit Harmony.
From youth already I had a magnificent integrity –
    as I matured my virtue only grew firmer and purer.

I do not obey the fashion of a wayward course –
    but rectify my own intent, trusting in my will.
I do not warp the guy-line to pursue the crooked –
20   but subject my feelings to the demands of proper action.

I correct my actions till they are righteous as jade –
    I retrace the tracks laid down by the august carriage.
The masses make fawning faces and obscure the light –
    the august carriage is upturned and concealed in dark.

The carriage midway must turn volte-face –
    the steeds of the charabanc are startled and run wild.
The wielders of the reins can no longer control them –
    they must turn the yoke and press at the shafts.

Breaking from their bit and bridle to charge ahead –
30   only at evening do they cease flight and dare to pause.
31 Broad and long is the path, but no one is following it –
    no one drives past within a thousand leagues.

Since I was defeated, ruined, and forced to sink away –
   I cannot find any way to ascend back into the world.
Yet no matter how base or wretched I may be myself –
   I only lament that the august carriage cannot be righted;

Departing the gates of the kingdom with righteous aims –
   I long that he once be enlightened and grant me a return.
What I lament is only my driver's hardships and regrets –
40   repeatedly meeting peril and suffering disaster.
In these nine years I have not been able to go back –
42   I long to roam beneath the waves along with Peng and Xian.
I lament that Music-master Yan wafted by the islets –
   following in the endless current of the Miluo River.

I keep to the river's course, with its weaving and winding –
   I strike upon a rocky corrugation and traverse sideways.
The waves plish and plash, and stir up a whirlpool –
   I must course the long rapids with their lutulent flow.

49 Crossing a turbid tributary and descending below –
50   I long to go back upstream and to return.
Vessels braving the darkness race in tandem –
   but I dally and dither, and daily drift further away.

Oaring my boat down and voyaging across –
   fording the currents of the Xiang and ending up South.
I stand on the margin of the Jiang and sing out long –
   my melancholy keen and my suspirations many.
My feelings bewildered and befuddled, I know not how to return –
   but my spirit roams free and charges high.
My heart anxious and agitated, nostalgic and yearning –
60   my soul gazes yearningly back, but I depart alone.

THRENODY

I long for my old country,
   my heart pining in separation –
In the half-light of dusk,
   secluded in sorrow –

65 Departing from Ying and roaming eastward,
   who is still worthy to admire? –

Slanderous men forming cliques and parties,
   such was the disaster that befell us –

In the rushing, rolling river waters
70   there lies my heart's desire –
Gazing backwards on the road to Ying,
   where I know I will never return –

III. Resentful Thoughts

Enduring worry and distress, shadowing and enshrouding me –
    my resolve is blocked and barred, but not abandoned.
My body is exhausted and enfeebled, and I long for the daylight –
    but the sun darkens to dusk and I remain in mourning.

Pitiful as the orphan abandoned in the empty hall –
6   miserable like the wronged chick in the withered poplar:
A lone hen cries from the high ramparts –
8   the calling pigeon nests in mulberry and elm;

A dark gibbon that is lost deep in the wood –
10   I alone am cast out and exiled far away;
11 A traveller worn out on the road that leads to Zhou –
    his wife at home longs after him in her frustration.

I have exerted fealty and loyalty without straying –
14   my plain feelings pristine as a roll of silk;
I have shone radiant as the sun and moon –
16   the patterns of my person resplendent as jade.
My grief at being buried and displaced, I cannot reveal it –
    the thoughts I feel, sunk and oppressed, I cannot expose.
My fragrance wafts afar, and yet at last will perish –
20   as my fame, dispersed and dissolved, cannot be displayed.

I turn my back to the jade portal and I charge onward –
22   Alas, I suffer blame and incur disgrace.
Like Guan Longpang who was decapitated –
24   or Prince Bi Gan ground up into paste;

I think of the altars of hearth and land facing peril now –
    but they have made me their enemy and I am hated.
I yearn for this country of mine that faces destruction –
    but myself suffering blame will complete the disaster.

As when the black blowfly falsifies true substance –
30   or Lady Li of the Jin misused a passion;
I fear that ascending the steps I will meet with peril –
    so I retreat into hiding in a remote courtyard.

With the yelping and whelping of the petty officials –
    this court is grown over with weeds and cannot be governed.

35 By violating propriety and provoking with remonstrance –
    I only end up suffering blame and sustaining suspicion.

    Culling the selinea with osmanthus and ginger-lily –
38   watering liquorice root via a stagnant ditch;
They submerge the fragrant angelica in a putrid well –
40   discard rhinoceros horn in bamboo baskets.

They seize a Tangxi sword to slice at tumbleweed –
42   and wield keen Gan Jiang to chop their meat.
Culling the water weeds in the hide of leopard –
44   they shatter the jade of Master He with a wooden pestle.

In this age chaos and confusion have not yet been cleared up –
    the world is beset by disorder not yet to be understood.
I'd like to dally here and await a better time –
    but I fear the season has already come too late.

Considering these men who relinquish integrity to go with the flow –
50   my heart is agitated, anxious, and unsteady.
I'd rather cruise along the River Yuan, wafting at whim –
    sweeping and swerving from the Jiang to the Xiang.

THRENODY

53 Carriage rumbling up the hills,
    thoughts pained –
The traveller hastens anxiously along,
    with no place to abide –

Criss-crossing the bare plains,
    searching out the borderless void –
Riding a stallion, galloping a racehorse,
60   to relieve my sorrows –

Bringing my old bones back home,
    even if I have no one to talk to –
I extend my plaint and depart far off,
64   to waft away on the Xiang –

IV. Faraway Departure

1 My resolve is bitterly concealed, knotted in frustration –
     grieving my lone grief, entangled by this wrong.
    My innards are rent in chaos and confusion –
4   I weep on endlessly as a millstone revolving.

    Sighing and suspiring in my passion, I long ever back –
     while trusting in the supreme majesty to prove me right.
    Joining the Five Marchmounts and the Eight Spirits –
8   I address the Nine Qi and the Six Ancestral Powers.

    I point to the serried constellations and make plain my hurt –
10   I complain to the Five Elemental Deities and state my plaint.
    The Northern Dipper is my intermediary –
12   Supreme Unity listens on my behalf.

    Thus I speak:
    I will follow the proper path of Yin and Yang –
14   drive on the level, steady route of Sovereign Earth.
    Adorned by the sinuous spirals of the Azure Dragon –
     I wear the coruscating curves of the vaulting rainbow.

    Grasping onto the resplendent gleam of the comets –
18   I hold as well the Vermilion Bird and the Simurgh.
19 I roam in the refreshing briskness of Pristine Spirit,
20   I don cloud robes that stream aloft behind me.

    I lean on jade blossoms and vermilion pennants –
     dangling the translucent pearl of the full moon.
    I lift coronal banners hovering and covering me –
     plant my ceremonial flag of yellow and carmine.

    My person is utterly pure and bears no flaw –
26   for I inherited supreme propriety from my resplendent begetter.
    Still regretting all the discord that has gone before –
     I cross the Miluo River and pass downstream.

    I ride the mighty waves and traverse southward –
30   following the smooth currents of the Jiang and Xiang.
31 I reach the foaming whitecaps of Lord Yang –
     descend the rocky rapids and land upon an islet.

A ridge looms high above and blocks my sight –
   clouds hang murky and obscure what lies before.
The mountains stand taller than can be compassed –
   their vertiginous vastness oppresses me.

The snow falls heavily and covers the trees –
   clouds gather close and surge below.
Between the hills the narrow defiles are sombre and steep –
40   the boulders sharply protruding block out the sun.

I grieve for my old homeplace and feel indignant –
   having departed my own land so long ago.
My back to Dragongate I ride the Yellow River –
44   atop the great mound, I gaze back towards the mouth of the Xia.

Crossing in my boat, fording the Xiang –
   my ears ringing and tingling, I felt anxiety grip me.
The waves are thundering as they circle round –
   crashing and splashing, breaking higher and higher.

This road proceeds so far it can have no end –
50   a circuit so vast in extent it can hardly be identified.
I take the sun and moon to point out the Polestar –
   for a brief moment of respite I feel my longings eased.
The water's currents reach far into the sightless deep –
   so remote I cannot make out their east or their west.
I follow the wind and wave down to north and down to south –
   the murky twilight fog looming drearily everywhere.

The sun descends into the remote darkness of the west –
   the road is long and far, and I by miseries beset.
I would pour the sweet ale to ease my apprehension –
60   yet I cannot disentangle these *sao*-like sorrows.

THRENODY

61 As the gale gusts and puffs,
       dust scatters and spreads –
   Plants and trees shed their leaves
       in the wasting season –

   Being overthrown, meeting disaster,
       no hope of succour –

Long I chant and sigh,
 my tears unceasing –

I set forth my suffering and recite a poem,
70 hoping to preserve myself –
Plunging down in the current,
 each day swept further away –

V. Cherishing Heroes

When I peruse the 'Li sao' of Master Qu –
    my heart breaks with sadness, a long-borne anguish.
I cry out piercingly in the vast silence –
4   look back on my carriage driver also sick at heart.

To purge flattery and slander and regulate wickedness –
    excising the stain and besmirchment of the vulgar;
To cleanse the muck and mess of rebellion and strife –
8   eliminating the taint and pollution of the uncivilized.

I harbour a pure fragrance and possess sweet clover –
10   I adorn myself with the scent of river lovage,
Seize the lush fagara and the ginger-lily –
12   crown myself with floating clouds lifting high above.
I climb the high ridge and gaze in the four directions –
    peruse the garden of angelica in its pristine order.
I visit the eupatory banks and sweet clover grove –
    agape at jade and stone towering overhead.

I lift up splendid blossoms with their resplendent gleam –
    densely the fragrance drifts along, their beauty immaculate.
19 I weave together osmanthus bark, so soft and tender –
20   I lace together calamus, sweet clover, and magnolia.
The fragrance sweet as this cannot find employment –
    discarded in a forest grove it is stifled and dies.

I following Prince Qiao in his aerial course –
    as Shen Tudi descends into the watery abyss;
25 Like the immaculate beauty of recluses You and Yi –
    or Jiezi Tui who retired to the mountains:

Shensheng met with doom in the state of Jin –
    Master He offered jade to Jing but ended by weeping blood.
Zixu had his own eyes plucked out to watch Wu's fall –
30   for his honesty, Prince Bi Gan was savagely maimed.

I would like to humble myself and to prostrate my body –
    but my heart is wounded and I cannot find my place.
Square and round diverge and cannot be aligned –
    compass and plumb-line have separate forms befitting use.

I wish to while away the time until the proper moment –
    but the day already fades away and is soon to set.
As time moves steadily on, the sun advances –
    as the years vanish away yet the sun passes on.

In vain I compromised to mingle with the vulgar –
40   but the inner sanctum was still kept barred to me.
I await a seasonable breeze, a brisker form of inspiration –
    to pass beyond this fog as dense as a cloud of dust.

Though I offered virtues pure as the turtledove –
    they were besmirched by slander, ruinously rife.
Silently I follow the breeze and concede cravenly –
    still I hesitate to advance myself.

As my heart is keenly pained, knotted in grief –
    fraught with feelings, agonized and afflicted.
I pluck the creeping fig on the hillsides –
50   gather safflower blossoms from the islet in the river.

51 I gaze towards the Mound of Gao and heave a sigh of grief –
    sobbing over and over out of clinging nostalgia.
53 No man laden with sorrows can serve as ridgepole of the state –
    the sun fades into the void, sinking to oblivion.

THRENODY

The Jiang and Xiang flow along lusciously,
    currents streaming ceaselessly on –
Tossing, tumbling, buffeting billows,
    churning, trembling, whirling –

My fearful heart revolves without rest,
60   an anguish suffuses, infuses me –
The wrong consuming me cannot be expressed,
    forever I'll endure this indignation –

Meeting that moment I faced disaster,
    but what else could I have done? –
65 My suffering heart distressed and desolate,
    the tears pour down in torrents –

VI. Melancholy and Suffering

How I grieve at heart, distressed and desolate –
2   lamenting that my country has suffered calamity.
Since nine years ago I departed I have not returned –
    but bereft, distressed, alone I travel on southward.

Yearning for the enduring customs and proper teachings –
    my heart is torn by doubt but cannot accept these today.
I traverse the wild grasslands and cry out in the wind –
    stepping leisurely and calm to an alcove in the hills.

I roam the mountains and the plains, the riverbanks and the marshes –
10   secluding myself in desolation to find solitude and quiet.
I lean upon the boulders there and shed my tears –
    wasted and withered by anxiety and lacking any joys.

Climbing a precipitous peak I gaze far off –
    and peer out as far as to Southern Ying.
The mountains stretch far off beyond even the horizon –
    my journey extends on and on without any ending time.

17 Listening to the dark crane that calls at dawn –
    high up in the sharp crags of the hilltop,
Alone my indignation builds along with both sorrow and delight –
20   I roam upon the river's islets and sing steadily.

21 Three Birds fly up from the Southland –
    observing their resolve I long to go north as well.
I would like to send a message with those Three Birds –
    but they depart in such flurried haste I cannot.

I would shift my resolve and alter my integrity –
    but my heart is troubled and constricted, and I cannot leave.
Outwardly I dilly-dally in my roaming and my visits –
    inwardly I am wrought with worry and holding in grief.

I'd like to idle for a moment in temporary oblivion –
30   but my heart grows ineluctably more vexed and conflicted.
31 I'd like to borrow a reed-organ to relieve my worry –
    my thoughts are knotted up and hard to loosen.

I chant the 'Li sao' to send forth my thoughts –
    which were not yet completed in the 'Nine Avowals'.

Ever sighing in sorrow, feeling my frustration –
    my tears gather side by side in equal streams.

I grieve that bright pearls have been tossed in the mud –
    while fish eyes—mistaken for gems—are keenly treasured;
Classing nags and mules alongside sterling stallions –
40   confusing the diverse and various for the base and bestial.

41 Creeping kudzu entangles the osmanthus tree –
    hoot owls gather upon the magnolia branches;
Dwarves and dolts converse within the palace temple –
    while the paragons of men are banished to the hillsides.

Detested now is the panpipe Shao that was bequeathed from lord Shun –
46   most popular is the discarded mode of the Frenzied Chu.
Those men would sink the tripods of Zhou in the Jiang and the Huai –
48   and boil terracotta kettles in the inner sanctum.

Men long in their hearts to maintain tradition –
50   but it cannot be preserved forever.
Turning back onto that southern road –
    I continue my journey even in dark of night.

How I yearn to be on that road to Ying –
    and gaze back in rueful fondness;
My tears fall in streams that course together—
56   my sobs descend flood after flood.

THRENODY

From high on the mountain I gaze in hope,
    but I am miserable at heart –
Verdant grasses lush around me,
60   yet my tears fall like a cascade –

I linger in yearning and look northward,
    and weep without cease –
My keenness thwarted and my might overthrown,
64   I am stranded in the turbulent flow –

Considering my state, oppressed and bereft,
    who is there for my soul to seek? –
The carriage driver is enervated and enfeebled,
68   as if drifting in the current –

VII. Lamenting My Destiny

Long ago my Resplendent Begetter had an admirable resolve –
2   he enjoyed raising talent and illuminating worth.
His inner feelings were refined, and pure, and immaculate –
    and his demeanour superb, and true, and without blemish.

He exiled flatterers and servile slanderers –
    dismissed the gossipmongers and the toadying lackeys;
Cultivated the loyal and just, the upright and sincere –
    summoned the honourable and good, the perspicacious and wise.

His heart's capacious kindness could not be measured –
10   his passions were as placid as a tranquil pool.
The wayward and wicked were expelled and not admitted –
    while the honest and willing were kept safe and not banished.
He chased the lowly stratum to the rear of the court –
14   and welcomed Fu Fei at the Yi and Luo rivers.
He abscised the slanderous knaves from the inner palace –
16   culled the ilk of Lü and Guan from out in the underbrush.

In the forest groves there were no resentful men –
    on the banks of the rivers there were no recluses.
19 The descendants of the three villains were banished and exiled –
20   Yi Yin, Gaoyao, and their like filled the imperial lodge.

But now surface is transformed into reverse –
    undergarments worn inside out as robes of state:
Now Wan of Song is the intimate ranked between the pillars of the
    great hall –
24   the Dukes of Zhou and Shao banished as far as the remote
    barbarians.

He reverses the speedy stallions and redirects their course –
    while charging forth on steeds of donkey and mule.
The lady of Cai is dismissed and cast from behind the curtain –
28   a savage woman welcomed to court in satin and brocade.

Righteous Qing Ji is imprisoned in an underground cell –
30   craven Chen Buzhan sent to the front lines of battle;
31 Our lord smashes the Sounding Bell of Bo Ya –
    takes up the common cither and plays its strands instead.

33 He guards jadelike pebbles in a golden casket –
  but discards crimson jadestones in the very courtyard.
Han Xin is left defending in an infantryman's breastplate and
      helmet –
  while the cadets are made generals and sent to storm cities.

Angelica and river lovage are discarded on the islets –
  gourd-carved ladles rot in bamboo baskets.
39 The unicorn is fugitive in the ninefold marsh –
40 a sloth of bears cavorts in the imperial park.

He plucks blossoming boughs and amethyst flowers –
42 plants thorny limebush, nettles, and brushwood in their
      place;
He uproots the calamus, sweet clover, and the blackberry lily –
  but cultivates pigweed, hyssop, and ginger.
I regret how different this era is from that one –
  men's thinking past and present is not alike.
Some sink in the current and never reach their goal –
  others righteously impassioned never make their virtue known.

I lament that I was born at this inopportune moment –
50 only to suffer slander and submit to blame.
Though I am forthright and honest in presenting my resolve –
  my lord misprizes, wrongs, and finally discards me.

Truly I prize the rich scent of flowering blossoms –
  but now these are regarded as putrid;
Though I treasure fagara for its fair fragrance –
  now it must endure disorder and suffer revilement.

THRENODY

Now that his superb majesty has perished,
  gone and never to return –
In the hills it is dark and perilous,
60 the road back to Ying is far indeed –

Slanderers are vitriolic in accusation,
  but to whom may I offer a plaint? –
This traveller will never arrive at his destination,
64 and who is there to tell? –

Chanting in the journey, multiplying sighs,
  calling out alas, alas —
Embracing my grief, enduring this woe,
  how hapless and hindered am I —

VIII. *Yearning for Antiquity*

Dark and gloomy are the deep woods –
    and the trees murkily massed.
The mountains stand serrated with perilous peaks –
    the hills rise up far off and block the sun.

The grief in my heart is wounding and wrenching –
    I peer into the distance and let my tears fall.
The winds sough *sao*-like and shake the boughs –
    the clouds drift past in spiralling riffs.

Grieving, my life has no more pleasure to it –
10   melancholy, worries overwhelm me here in the hills.
At dawn I dally and dither on the long slope –
    at evening I wander at will and sleep alone.

My tresses are unkempt and tangled in knots –
    my body exhausted by baleful disease;
My soul is anxiously strained and travels southward –
    my sobs drench my collar and soak my sleeves.

My heart is tugged by longing of which I cannot tell –
    voice choked up and I cannot speak.
Departing the ancient towers of the Ying capital –
20   I navigate the Xiang and Yuan rivers to my remote banishment.

I ponder my country's affliction and peril –
    how men worship the spirits and gods out of proper order:
I mourn that my ancestral lineage will be severed –
    confused and conflicted at heart I grieve for my own state.

For now I'll roam over the mountains and valleys –
    rambling and ranging around the banks of the Jiang.
I look over the deep pools and whistle a while –
    dillying and dallying here I'll observe all the world.

The subtle words of the 'Li sao' my stimulus –
30   I hope that Spirit Paragon will once become aware;
Returning my carriage back to Southern Ying –
    I'll redirect my carriage-gauge to its original state.

The road is long and far, and hard to travel on –
    it grieves my heart so I cannot bear it.

He has rejected the canons and disciplines of the Three and Five –
36   destroyed the exemplary record of the 'Great Plan'.

Casting off the compass and square, rejecting the measure –
        he mistakes the balanced judgement and acts at will.
Those who wield the rope and ink are discarded –
40   while the stooping and servile win favour and attend at his side.

The sweet pear withers amid the flourishing grasses –
        pigweed and brambles are planted in the central square.
Xi Shi is rebuked in the northern court –
        while hideous hags attend the pillars of state.

Wu Huo is made an intimate and drives alongside –
46   the Duke of Yan demoted to work as stable hand.
Kuai Kui ascends to the Pure Chamber –
48   Gaoyao is abandoned out in the wilderness.

Now I have seen all this and must forever sigh in grief –
50   I would like to ascend the terrace but I deliberate in doubt.
Sailing down the Whitewater I will soar up high again –
        then I linger in leisure there, and make my long farewell.

THRENODY

Long I linger on the slate hill,
        by the pond's deep waters –
Taking my ease on an islet of the Han,
        letting my tears fall in torrents –

Now Zhong Ziqi and Bo Ya are dead,
        who can form the proper sounds? –
If not by fleeing moonward like the Gossamer Maid,
60   how else to relieve this grief? –

Sorrow redoubled, I sigh and sob,
        my heart divided, disintegrating –
Looking back towards the Mound of Gao,
        my tears course down in cascades –

IX. Far Roaming

I grieve for my nature, that cannot be altered –
  though rebuked and punished, I will not be moved.
My garb gleams resplendent, utterly unlike the vulgar –
  my aspect has a lofty dignity and a glory superb.

Just like Prince Qiao ascending the clouds –
  borne along on crimson ethers, piercing the high empyrean,
I'd like to partake in the longevity of Heaven and Earth –
  to compare in splendour with the Sun and Moon.

I ascend Mount Kunlun and face towards the North –
10   all the divinities of the realm come to visit there.
Selecting spirits and gods from the Ultimate Yin –
  I ascend the portal of Heaven by the mystic watchtowers.

I turn around my carriage and veer towards the West –
  raising my rainbow banners at the jade gates.
Driving six dragons over Mount Triperil –
16   I summon the Four Spirits from the Nine Shores.

I harness my chariot on the western hills –
  crossing the precipitous gorge journey south.
19 Pointing straightway to the Boundless Capital –
20   I pass Zhurong at the vermilion sea of the South.

Skewing the Jade Balance in the scorching flames, –
22   bypassing the two lodges of Affinity Pool and Sunny Vale.
Passing through the formless melange and reaching furthest East –
24   I tie my Six Dragons at Sunrise Mulberry.

I gaze all around upon the Four Seas –
  descending and then rising, preparing to ascend the heights.
I call the Nine Spirits to circumnavigate the Pole –
  raise rainbow pennants to summon and direct them.

Driving simurgh and phoenix to roam in the skies –
30   I follow mystic cranes and blazing firebird.
Peacocks glide past sending me off –
  I summon the swans to gather at Chalcedony Gleam.

Arrayed are the palace of the gods and its hunting park –
  ascending to Hanging Garden I am dazzled with wonder.

Tying on branches of jasper and various adornments –
    I stand upon the evening star and follow the Sun.

Braving the startling thunder to drive with the violent lightning –
    I join the hundred spectres by the Northern Dipper.
Whipping on the Lord of Winds as my vanguard –
40   I capture the mystic spirit in the Fathomless Abyss.

Tracing back the high breeze, circling around –
    I observe the outer current in the North.
Setting forth my invocation to Zhuanxu –
44   I consult Wondrous Abyss at Sky Mulberry.

45 Turning back my carriage, I depart for Eminent Hill –
    making my declaration to his lordship Shun at Silver Pillar.
47 Crossing in my willow boat to Mount Guiji –
    I meet Shen Xu at the Five Lakes.

Seeing the customs current at Southern Ying –
50   my own body perishes in Yuan and Xiang.
Gazing back dimly at my old country –
    its age of confusion and corruption has not yet ended.

I harbour the fragrant odours of eupatory and angelica –
    but men are envious of their flourishing and cull them.
The king unfurls a crimson canopy that rustles and swishes –
    but the breeze brushes faintly by, covering him.

The sun is shining clear as it departs to the West –
    I look back towards its sparkling rays.
I will pass the days in leisure, for a brief moment –
60   why grieve *sao*-like and make myself antique?

THRENODY

Just like the flood dragon
    floating upon the clouds –
Roaming rampant over vast voids,
    through the fog of boundlessness –
Torrents tumbling, chaotically careening,
    through thunder booming and lightning flashing,
        swiftly I rise above! –

Ascending the void, crossing the darkness,
    scattering pollution, sailing in purity,

70 I enter the palace of the Gods –
   shaking my wings, brandishing my feathers,
   I race with the winds and sprint with the rains,
73   roaming the Infinite!

14. LAMENTING TIME'S FATE
BY ZHUANG JI

1 I lament time's fate, that I could not share that of the ancients –
    oh, why in this life have I not met with the right moment!
    Those who have gone before I cannot draw upon to guide me –
4   and no way to make a rendezvous with those who are to come;
    My ambitions wrongfully frustrated cannot be realized –
    so I project my inner passions by composing a verse.
    The nighttime burns so bright I cannot sleep –
    I have come this far ever harbouring a hidden grief.
    My heart is shrouded and smothered so as I cannot tell –
10   what other man is there with whom to share wise counsel?
    In defeat, dejection, and doubt I meander and languish –
    but old age encroaches inexorably upon me.

    Enduring here in melancholy, secluded and sequestered –
    my ambitions are buried, blocked, and doomed to failure.
    The road is beset and barricaded, and there is no way to pass –
    the streams of the Jiang are broad and there is no bridge.
    I would like to reach the Hanging Gardens of Mount Kunlun –
18   and cull the jade blossoms of Mount Concentration.
    I seize the elongated branches of the jasper trees –
20   I gaze towards Pawlonia Sheet beyond Skywind.
    Weakwater's rapids race on and form an obstacle –
    the way is blocked halfway and I cannot pass further.
    Against that force I cannot surmount the waves to make a crossing –
    nor have I wings that I might soar aloft.
    Thus I must suffer in silence and I cannot reach my aim –
    but only dither and delay, hesitating and hovering here.
    Disappointed, devastated, dejected, consumed ever with yearning –
    my heart is entangled in woe and wounds that only increase.
    Delaying and deferring here I'll pause a while –
30   though I'm out of provisions and ever more famished.
    In this remote region I clutch to one fond image in solitude –
    yearning ever more for my old home.
    In this remote, vast silence I have no friend –
    no one to share with me what fragrance remains.

Day's brightness turns to dusk and sunset nears –
    I grieve that my lifespan will not last long.
My carriage is hobbled and my steed is weary –
    puttering in the same ruts I cannot move ahead.
If I can no longer be welcomed in this foul world –
40   who knows if it is better to advance or to abscond?
My crown towers aloft and pierces the very clouds –
42   my sword is beauteously begemmed and freely brandished.
My robes are spaciously outspread and loftily aligned –
    my left sleeve catches on far Sunrise Mulberry;
My right lappet brushes against Broken Mountain –
    the six corners of the universe do not suffice for my roamings.
47 Above I share mortise and tenon to work alongside Fu Xi –
    below I match compass and square with Shun and Yao.
I would honour integrity and make majesty my model –
50   but my ambitions are still base compared to Yu and Tang.
Though I know only defeat I will not alter my deportment –
    nor let the wicked and warped deform what is right.
Those in the world act in unison and favour only allies –
    measuring alike a single peck and a whole bushel.
Other men, aligned in conformity, stand shoulder to shoulder –
    but the worthiest distance themselves and go into hiding.

For the phoenix they have prepared a quail-size cage –
    though he folds in his wings still he cannot be contained.
His Divine Majesty is not enlightened –
60   how can I tell of my plaint and exert myself in loyalty?
The vulgar are envious and defame the worthies –
    is there anyone to appreciate my deeds and devices?
I would express my aims and unravel my wronged feelings –
    but how am I to know what is fair and what is foul?
Jade sceptre and disc are mistaken for clay cauldron and pot –
66   homely Long Lian and chaste Meng Ju share a palace chamber.
All the world takes this for the custom of ancients –
    thus I must endure sorrow and pain, and ever be frustrated.
In dark isolation I turn and cannot sleep –
70   nothing but trouble and despair fills my breast.
My soul races carefree through the imperceptible distance –
    while my heart is sadness-swept by this great wrong.

My will is frustrated and foiled, and I cannot find ease –
   the road is dark and tenebrous, and most impassable.
From utter solitude I guard my own obscure nook –
   regret-wracked and sighing in despair.

My sadness through the long nights trails on unending –
   my spirit boils up in billows of indignation.
Though I possess a spangled sabre, I cannot wield it –
80   though having compass and square I cannot employ them.

I gallop my lightning charger through the central court –
   yet how can I follow to the end that distant road?
If you cage long-tailed gibbons within a narrow pen –
   what right have you to doubt their agile swiftness?

As if you were driving lame tortoises to climb up a mountain –
   I knew all along you would not rise to success.
87 Casting off Guan Zhong or Yan Ying to employ slaves instead –
   can this be called a policy of moderation and balance?

Adamantine bamboo is tossed together with stalks of hemp –
90   the crossbow fires arrows of fleabane to strike at leather.
Bearing up and shouldering this burden in a space barely a yard –
   I cannot even stretch out my waist.
93 All around I am harried and intimidated by crossbows and nets –
   above tugged and torn by hunters' lashed arrows;
My shoulders are pinched together and cannot bear it –
   stifled and suffocated I can barely breathe.

Wu Guang cast himself into the fathomless abyss –
   but suffered no blemish nor besmirching from the world.
Who, though a peerless paragon, could long endure this?
100   I'd rather retire myself and endure in poverty.
I'll dig out pillars in a hillside to make my chamber –
102   make my garments of the riverbed beneath it.
I'm drenched in the fog and dew that drizzle down at dawn –
104   an enveloping veil of clouds looming under the eaves.
Irises and rainbows multiply in the dawn cloudwisps –
   at night the rain floods down in torrents.
In the bleak and vacuous void I cannot return –
   sorrowfully I gaze afar over the endless plain.

While I plunge the bait down into the mountain brook –
110   I long to meet with the transcendents high above:

With Red Pine I'll become friends –
    joining Prince Qiao as my companion.
113 I enlist a langur monkey as my vanguard –
    with white tigers attending before and behind.
The clouds and mist drift along into the dark –
    I ride a white deer and dally in delight.

My pilgrim, ill-come soul in its lonely sojourn –
    hurries on its journey never to return.
Abiding in the ethereal heights and journeying ever farther –
120   still I waver in my resolve, am wounded by remorse.

Simurgh and phoenix soar past clouds in the azure sky –
    so high even lashed dart or arrow cannot touch them.
The flood dragon conceals itself in the whirling vortex –
    its body unsnared by net or trebuchet.
They know not to risk death by swallowing the bait –
    better to plunge beneath the pristine waves.
I'd rather hide in seclusion and keep disaster far away –
    for then what hurt or outrage could be done to me?
Wu Zixu died and so established his integrity –
130   Qu Yuan plunged into the Miluo River.
Though his body was dissolved he was not altered –
    for loyalty and fealty cannot be changed.
Though my heart is troubled and tumultuous, yet my character
        remains upright –
    treading on plumb-line and ink I will not go to excess.
Measuring by the balance-beam I will not be partial –
    in evaluating the trivial or weighty I will not err.

Rinsing off the blemishes and besmirchments, wildness and wantonness –
    ridding myself of taints and constraints, I return to the true.
My physical frame is spotless and my substance pure –
140   inside I am radiantly immaculate, and modest, and incorrupt.
Now I am sated and content even without employment –
    for I shall go into hiding apart, and make myself remote.
I'll bury my traces and conceal my tracks –
    in detached, lone solitude with scarcely a sound.

Though lithe and refined, yet suffering trouble and venom –
    thus I will show my indignation and express my woe.
The times are tenebrous and murky, and the end is night –
    I suspire in grief and lacking even my good name.
Bo Yi starved to death at Mount Shouyang –
150   in the end he died in reclusion and never thrived.
Had Lord Tai not met King Wen's favour –
    then never in life would he have flourished.
Harbouring amethyst and ivory, with pendants of carnelian –
    I would like to present this fine array but none will admire them.
Life between Heaven and Earth is like a moment passing –
    all at once, sundered and undone, and never made complete.
A foul vapour assaults me in my body and my limbs –
    illness, angst, and heartache arise in me all together.
I only wish I could see once more the bright sunlight of springtime –
160   but I fear I may not live to complete a full span of years.

15. RUEFUL OATH
ATTRIBUTED TO JIA YI

How I grieve for old age that makes me daily more decrepit –
    the years recede so swiftly and do not return.
I climb into the azure heavens and rise above –
    pass over the myriad mountains and reach beyond.

Viewing the crooks and curves of the rivers and waterways –
    crossing the deluge of the Four Seas,
I seize onto the Northern Pole and take a rest there –
8   sipping on the midnight mists to sate my thirst.
The Vermilion Bird aloft I made my vanguard –
10   driving on behalf of Supreme Unity the ivory car.

The Azure Dragon twists and twines as my left tracehorse –
12   White Tiger charges ahead as my right sideracer.

Vaunting Sun and Moon as my own canopy –
    carrying jade maidens in the rear carriage;
I gallop and I soar through the trackless voids –
    I rest and recline on the crags of Mount Kunlun.

Enjoyment at its very apex I am not yet satisfied –
    I'd like to frolic and cavort along with illustrious spirits.
I'll cross over the Cinnabar River and ride along –
20   revering the customs bequeathed from the mighty Xia.

21 In an instant the golden crane rises up –
    I recognize each nook and crook of mountain and river.

Rising up once more –
    I perceive the roundness of Heaven and the squareness of
      Earth.
Overlooking the myriad inhabitants of the central states –
    I surrender myself to the idle currents of the whirlwind.
27 Then at last I arrive in the land of Shaoyuan –
    Red Pine and Prince Qiao are there beside me.
Those two fine sirs strum the zithern and tune it to perfection –
30   I especially praise them for their pure tone of Shang.

Now in perfect tranquillity and finding my own joy –
    I drink in the myriad vapours and soar up once again.
Thinking of how I'd live long and as a transcendent evermore –
    far better to return straightway – to my quondam abode.
The golden crane awaits the moment to find a perch –
    tiny wrens flock together to harry it.
Divine dragon abandons the water and abides upon land –
    where he is cut to size by the very ants.
But if golden crane and divine dragon should be so –
40   how much worse for the worthy men that meet a disordered age!

As life wanes steadily I grow daily more frail –
    and keep shifting hither and thither without rest.
The vulgar men wallow in the current without cease –
    the many assemble in error and skew what was straight.

Some gather clandestinely and advance without scruple –
    others reside in obscurity and bury themselves in the depths.
They labour to judge capacity but without any acuity –
    like choosing a balance as a tool to plane wood.

Some shift their stance by hasty compromise –
50   others speak out directly, honest and unswerving.
I grieve that sincerity and truth are not even recognized –
    as if floss-grass were intertwined with silk to make a rope.
Thus the vulgar men are benighted and blinded –
    dazzled by the difference of white and black, fair or foul.
Neglecting tortoiseshell and jade in the hills and pools –
    instead they join in cherishing the tawdriest of pebbles.
Sire Mei offered his sincere counsel, so his body was minced into paste –
58   Lai Ge satisfied every demand and so was employed by the state.
How I lament that men of goodness exert all their integrity –
60   but in return endure abuse by the petty men.

Bi Gan presented the wisdom of his loyalty and so had his heart cut out –
    Master Ji let his locks flow free and feigned madness.
The rivers reverse their course and the springs run dry –
    trees are divided from their roots and grow no taller.
It is not that I value my person or fear disaster –
    I only grieve that losing my life would achieve nothing.

It is done, alas!

68 Have you not seen:
The phoenix and the simurgh soaring high above –

70 perch only in the land of a great and virtuous ruler.
Tracing the four Poles and circling all around –
they descend only once they have perceived real virtue.

As for the divine powers of those sages –
distanced from the dirty world, they guarded their own being.
If you put reins upon the unicorn and tame him –

76 then how is he any different from any goat or hound?

16. GREATER SUMMONS
ATTRIBUTED TO JING CUO

Green springtime fades,
    the bright sun shines down –
Spring vapours burst forth revived,
    the myriad creatures are startled –
A shade assails them, passing everywhere:
    do not flee there, soul! –
Oh earthsoul and skysoul, return,
    go not far and yonder –

Come back, oh soul!
10 Go neither east nor west,
    neither south nor north!
For in the East is the great Ocean,
    where whelming waters flow and flux –
Wyvern and dragon share the currents,
    curling down and careening up –
The fog and rain pour down profusely,
    glistening and gleaming white –

Do not go east, oh soul!
For Sunny Vale is forlorn –
20   Do not go south, oh soul!
For in the south are thousand-league flames,
    and poisonous vipers outstretched –
The hills and ridges are treacherous and harsh,
    with tigers and leopards creeping –
25 Striped-fish, sea bleak, newt-foxes,
    king cobras all menacing –
Do not go south, oh soul!
    sand-spitters will ravage your body –

Do not go west, oh soul!
30 In the west the level sands
    stretch on boundless and bare –
Beasts with boarlike head and glaring eyes,
    their manes in wild disarray –

Bear long claws and sawlike teeth,
    and snigger hysterically –
Do not go west, oh soul!
    for it is full of menaces to life –

Do not go north, oh soul!
For in the north are the cold mountains,
40   the scarlet flash of the Torch Dragon –
The waters of Dai cannot be forded,
    plunge unfathomably far –
The sky is of brightness incandescent,
    but the chill freezes a man solid –
Do not venture there, oh soul!
    All the way to the Northern Pole –

Return, earthsoul and skysoul,
    to ease and to tranquillity –
Indulge yourself in Jing and Chu,
50   with calm and with contentment –
Satisfying your whims and exhausting desires,
    let your heart and mind find ease –
For your whole life enjoy longlasting bliss,
    with the span of your years prolonged –
Come back, oh soul!
    For this bliss is beyond all words –

The five grains are completed by a sixth,
58   laying out the water-bamboo –
The meats in the tripods, well-cooked, fill your sight,
60   seasonings balanced and fragrant –
Adding grey crane, pigeon, and swan,
    flavoured with stew of wild dog –
Come back, oh soul!
    Indulge in all these tastes –

Fresh tortoise and sweet chicken,
66   blended with Chu yogurt –
Minced suckling pig, gall-bitter dog meat,
    thin-sliced ginger –
Wu pickles of artemisia and wormwood,
70   not oversteeped, nor too weak –

Oh soul! return, return,
    and indulge in all that you like –

Grey crane sauté, boiled goose,
    roasted quail, all laid out together –
Fried carp, braised oriole,
    all presented, selected, and offered you –
Oh soul! return, return,
    allurements are all prepared for you–

Four-time-fermented liqueurs well-aged,
80   not harsh to the throat –
Clear and fragrant libations
    are a delight to the palate –
A sweet ale from Wu of white malt
84   alongside a pure Chu wine –
Oh soul! return, return,
    be not anxious, be not afraid –

Dai, Qin, Zheng, and Wei:
    let the singing reed-organs play out –
Fu Xi's 'Propitious Phases' with
90   the 'Shang Harmonies' from Chu –
91 Singing along with 'Sunlit Knoll',
    the bamboo flutes of Zhao piping –
Oh soul! return, return,
94   to relish the Sky Mulberry zither –

Two lines of eight join in the dance,
    accompanying lyrics and rhapsodies –
Striking the bells and modulating the chimes,
    the entertainers play the envoi –
99 The four superior modes all vying for mood
100   exhaust the variations of melody –
Oh soul! return, return,
    audience and singers are all prepared –

With vermilion lips and radiantly white teeth,
    they are lovely and alluring –
Alike in virtue, fond of modesty,
    both expert and elegant –

Plump flesh on ethereal limbs,
  joined harmoniously in diversions –
Oh soul! return, return,
110 take ease and comfort here –

Lovely eyes well-formed for smiling,
  mothlike eyebrows outstretched –
Countenance comely and proper,
  childlike with blushing cheeks –
Oh soul! return, return:
  be quieted and eased –

All gorgeous, tall, generous of manner,
  exquisite and alluring –
With rich-layered cheeks and close-hung ears,
120 the curve of their brows perfectly circular –
Overflowing hearts and poised deportment,
  their sweet charms unfurl –
Minute waists and elongated necks
124 arch like belt hooks –
Oh, soul! return, return,
126 let your yearning and resentments go –

Placid within, yet keen of mind,
  and so in their movements too –
Powder-white and kohl-black
130 enhancing scented sheen –
Long sleeves brushing faces,
  they compel their guests to stay –
Oh, soul! return, return,
134 and delight in this night –

With azurite hue, level eyebrows,
  lovely eyes in lovely face –
Their dimpled cheeks and peerless teeth
  readily smiling and ridibund –
Their flesh is full, frames weightless,
140 with delicate and dainty limbs –
Oh soul! return, return,
  and indulge in every comfort –

In magnificent mansions, spacious and grand,
    splendid with cinnabar-tinted palaces –
There are private halls in the southern chambers,
    and towers rising over the courtyard –
147 There are winding rooms and porticos for strolling,
    suited to domestic animals too –
Whether racing carriages or roaming on foot,
150   there is a pleasance for hunting in spring –
Jade-studded wheelhubs and gilded crossbeams,
    resplendent with floral patterning –
And angelica and eupatory and cinnamon
    luxuriantly shading the paths –
Oh soul! return, return,
    to indulge every wish and whim –

There peacocks fill the gardens,
    tame phoenixes and simurghs –
Demoiselle crane and swan-goose flock at dawn,
160   joining adjutant stork and oriole –
Great swans flutter by in succession,
    halcyon kingfishers queuing by –
Oh soul! return, return,
    where phoenixes fly overhead –

165 Your lustrous sheen and tranquil face,
    flush with ruddy health –
You will preserve your body
    and prolong your life –
Your extended clan filling the court,
170   rich in honours and titles –
Oh soul! return, return,
    your whole household is ready –

Roads criss-crossing over a hundred leagues,
    men come to serve numerous as clouds –
175 Doughty lords of the Three Jade Discs,
    governing with godlike judgement –
Attending in earnest all the casualties and infirm,
    ensuring orphans and widows are comforted –
Oh soul! return, return,
180   to put in order the first and the last –

On a thousand footpaths through field and town,
    the people multiply and prosper –
183 Harmonious rule embraces each class of people,
    so virtue and beneficence are made evident –
First there is authority and later resplendent patterning,
    all is decent, and splendid, and bright –
Oh soul! return, return,
    that rewards and punishments may all be just –

Your name and influence, like the sun,
190 illuminate all within the four seas –
Your virtuous repute is coeval with Heaven,
    the ten thousand peoples are all in proper order –
North as far as the Darkslope,
    south as far as Jiaozhi –
West to mountains rugged as goat's entrails,
    east extending up to the sea –
Oh, soul! return, return,
    that you may elevate worthy gentlemen –

Proclaiming edicts, advancing exemplary conduct,
200 prohibiting cruelty and brutality –
Promoting the talented to the apex of authority,
    abrogating chastisements and inquisitions –
The upright and superior stand in high office,
    as if impelled by Lord Yu of old –
The best and finest of men hold the reins of power,
    and their beneficence flows down to all –
Oh, soul! return, return,
    act for country and state –

How majestic and mighty, splendid and superb,
210 Heaven's virtue illustrious –
211 The Three Excellencies solemn and steadfast
212 ascend and descend within the court –
All the enfeoffed lords arrive,
214 the nine dignitaries stand at attention –
The archery targets are all set forth,
216 the bulky quintains are prepared –

Taking up their bows with arrows underarm,
   they bid farewell and depart, deferential —
Oh, soul! return, return,
220   exalt the Three Kings above all —

17. NINE YEARNINGS
BY WANG YI

I. Suffering Blame

Sadness – and sorrow!
Misery – and woe!
Heaven bore me – in this moment of darkness;
    I suffered slander and smears – and met with unjust blame;
My heart is worried and worn – while my mind can find no rest.
    Preparing the carriage and horses – I set out on an idle drive.

Circling through all Eight Extremities – traversing all Nine Provinces,
    I seek out Lord Xuanyuan – search for him of Many-Faceted
        Majesty.
Distanced from the passing world – removed beyond vision's limits,
10   I seize onto my pendants and jetstones – hesitate upon the road.

I admire how Gaoyao – established the canons and counsels;
Deem exquisite how the Lord of Winds – received the auspicious
    charts.

13 How I lament that in my own life – I have met with the Six Evils.
    discarding my own jade-like substance – in a muddy ditch,
Hurrying along, wandering bewildered – I race through forest and
    swamp.
    treading anxious and uneasy – I proceed past hillock and ridge.
My carriage thills shattered – my horses are gouty and lame.
    Flustered and fazed I stand – tears streaming down in torrents.

Yearning for a King Ding or a Wen – sagely, perspicacious, and wise;
20   I grieve that Kings Ping and Fuchai – were deluded, mistaken,
        and ignorant.
When Lü and Fu were appointed to office – Shang and Zhou thrived;
22   but when Ji and Pi usurped control – Ying and Wu proved hollow.
Looking upwards I heave a long sigh – and my breath is choked and
    broken;
    misery leads me to the point of fainting – when I start to breathe
    again.

Tiger and rhinoceros war – there in the courtyard;
    wild dogs and wolves battle – right alongside me.

Cloud and fog commingle – the sun is obscured in darkness;
    the whirlwind rises – scattering dust and dirt.
Running along hurry-scurry – now to east, now to west:
30   I would like to hide away – but where should I proceed?
I long for the sanctum of the divine – secluded, manifold, and deep.
    I'd like to use all my integrity – but in this impasse find no means
      to do so.
I gaze towards my old home – but the route is crooked and curving;
    unsettled by melancholy thoughts – I aim to persevere.
35 My soul bereft, anxious, oppressed – I still cannot sleep,
    my gaze fixed and unwavering – remaining wakeful till the dawn.

II. Indignant at the Sovereign

The chief minister – is haughty and aloof,
    while his assembled officers – flatter and fawn.
Oh, alas! – in all this trouble and turmoil,
    master and servant – together meet the deluge.

The pulse plants and the grapevines – flourish and spread,
    while aromatic angelica – is thwarted and barren.
Vermilion and violet – are confused and commingled,
    till no longer can anyone – distinguish between them.

Taking refuge here – in the crags and caves,
10   I long constantly – for remote tranquillity.
I sigh for all my cares – for him who is blinded and baffled,
    though I exert my will – I attain no prominence.

He has discarded – the Jade Dipper,
14   rejected and lost all sight of – its handle and pivot.
My heart – is inflamed and infuriated,
    it is only because of this – that I am anxious.
17 Ahead of him he detests – Qiu and Xun,
18   behind him looks down on – Peng and Wu.
I should imitate these – two sets of tracks,
20   but I know not where – to lodge myself.

Singing and chanting – out in the wild,
22   above I perceive – the jade-cog and pearl-star.
The brilliant fire star – tilts to the west,
24   while the braces and buttresses – slump lower.
The thunderbolts crash – with a clang and a clap,
    hail and sleet – fall flurry after flurry.
The bolts of lightning – flicker and flash,
    chill winds blow – with sorrow and desolation.
The birds and beasts – are startled into flight,
30   and follow one another – to burrow and perch.
Mandarin ducks – chirp to one another,
    foxes skulk – in troops together.
I grieve that I – am separate and sole,
    abiding alone – without a companion.
The mole-cricket – chirps in the east,
    the leafhoppers – shrill in the west.

The centipede crawls – along my hems,
   hawk-moth caterpillars reach my chest.
Insect and slinker – assault me on both sides;
40   how miserable and wretched – is my state!
Standing still – doubtful and dismayed,
   my heart is knotted and tangled – ravaged and ruined.

III. Detesting the Age

Roaming hither and thither – by the islets of the Han,
    searching for the River God's – numinous daughters;
I sigh that in this kingdom – there is no good man,
    the matchmakers are doltish – quarrelsome and querulous.
Thrushes line up – twittering toadyingly,
6   the warbling of magpies – deafens me.
Possessing luminous gem – and precious jades,
    I wish to flaunt them – but there is no buyer.
Thus I set forth – advancing northward,
10   summon my friends – as travelling companions.
11 The sun is hidden by haze – and sheds no light;
    silent, tenebrous, and dim – no thing to be seen.

So I will race off – and charge up high,
    for I seek to consult – the luminous Fu Xi.
Round the islets of the Yellow River – drifting to and fro,
    my course has altered – for the time is out of joint.
Crossing over the glaucous ocean – to journey eastward,
    I bathe and purify myself – in the Pool of Heaven.
19 I enquire of his Supreme Illumination – the essentials of the Way.
20   He says: 'Nothing more precious – than humaneness and
      dutifulness'.
My thoughts now pleased and joyful – I journey back,
22   and meet King Wen of Zhou – at Bin and at Qi.
Grasping jade blossoms – I make my oath,
    and as the sun is soon to set – my heart aches with grief.
For Heaven-appointed blessings – will not come again,
    yet to contravene my duty – would betray myself.
Traversing the Long mountain range, crossing the deserts,
28   I pass Cinnamon Car – and the Heli River.
Reaching Mount Kun – I rein in my stallion,
30   roaming free and easy there – I dither and dally.
Gargling liquors of jade – I quench my thirst,
    munching on mystic mushrooms – I ease my hunger.
Residing in that boundless space – companions are scarce,
    displaced, discomfited, distraught – I seem to lose myself.
I gaze towards the Jiang and the Han – in their tremendous tumult,
    but my heart is wrenched and wrought – and wounded with longing.

Now with dawn's – faint gleam approaching,
    all is covered in dust – that has not been wiped clean.
Consumed by worry, I have no time – to sleep or to eat,
40   and can only repeat my groans – rumbling like thunder.

IV. Condoling with the Sovereign

I lament that this age is – one of mass mediocrity,
    and serpentine words of slander – hum and hiss about me.
The multitudes cease not – to fawn and flatter,
    compromise and inconstancy – their only rule.
The greedy and corrupt – form together in cliques,
    while the honest and fair – are alone and apart.
Swans hide there – amidst the thorns and nettles,
    while pelicans take their perches – atop the canopy of state.
Sweet cicely – grows green and glaucous,
10   but liquorice root – withers and decays.
Regarding all this – fabrication and confusion,
    I feel my mind – distanced and removed:
Ambling, rambling – amid the shrubbery and gardens,
    tracing back those – field and foot paths,
Rivers and valleys – plunge fathomless down,
    hills and ridges – are rugged and rocky.
The forests – tower far over me,
    the groves – mass darkly about me.
Frost and snow – lie in thick layers,
20   the ice has hardened – in one gapless web.
East and west – south and north,
22   I have no place – to return for refuge.
Taking shelter in the shade – of withered trees,
    I creep amongst – the rocky caves.
25 I circle aimlessly – crippled and confined by the cold,
    I abide alone – and my ambitions cannot be fulfilled,
        as my years wane – my fate is harried and haltered.

Hurried and hastened, chased and chastened – I suffer ever from shame.
    bearing worry, oppressed by age – my melancholy never turns to joy;
30 My beard and hair grown wild with worry – my temples tinged with white.
    I long for the divine favour – to bathe at once in that moisture,
I clutch to blossoms of eupatory – I grasp at jasper-like ginger-lily.
    await Heaven's dawning – while still in hesitation and doubt,
As the clouds lurk murkily above – and the lightning flits and flashes;
    the lonely hen is startled – and chirps *gow-gow*.
My thoughts dark and depressed – my liver as if sliced and scraped,
    infuriated, embittered, dispirited – whom to tell of my complaint?

V. Encountering Disaster

I grieve for Master Qu, who met with disaster,
    and plunged his jade-like body – into the waters of the Xiang and Mi.
Why was the state of Chu – so hard to reform?
    even up till now – it has not yet been transformed.
5 No man there has the will – to match the 'lamb's fur' model;
    rather they vie in flattery and fawning – slander and dissension.
They point to righteousness and dutifulness – as if they were
      crooked,
    they malign jade discs – as if they were mere pebbles.
Owls and hawks consort – in the ornate rooftops,
10   the golden pheasant perches – amid thickets of brushwood.
Rising up, straining, speeding – I charge on ahead,
    braving the slander and curses – of the petty men.
Borne up by the clouds in the blue – I ascend above,
    till I reach that place where – resplendent brightness abides.

Treading the avenues of Heaven – and charging far,
    I step amid the Nine Yang – and play and frolic there.
Crossing over the Milky Way – I journey on south,
18   watering my horse – at Riverdrum.
Clouds and coronas plentiful – hide and hinder me,
20   Triaster and Heart are reversed – sending me topsy-turvy.
Coming upon a shooting star – I ask the way,
    and looking back it points me – to follow the left.
23 Crossing the Mullet's Mouth – and charging onward,
    my driver goes astray – and loses the track.
Then rashly careening – we arrive all askew,
    on a separate path – far from sun and moon.
My ambition blocked and frustrated – where can I proceed?
    I grieve the one I sought – could not be my companion.
Clambering up the staircase to Heaven – I peer below,
30   and see in Yan and Ying – my onetime abode.
My will is to roam free and easy – my desire to return,
    but the many are steeped in pollution – dark and dismal.
My thoughts are stifled and strangled – twisted and tangled,
    and my tears stream down in showers – and in torrents.

VI. Mourning Disorder

Alas for me – what grief, alas!
    confusion and chaos – perpetually perpetrated:
Floss-grass and silk – are on the same loom,
    cap and sandals – are tied by the same laces.
5 Hua Du and Song Wan – attend the banquets,
    the Dukes of Zhou and Shao – are made to trundle firewood.
The white dragon – becomes a shooting target,
8   the numinous tortoise – is taken prisoner.
Confucius – was trapped and thwarted,
10 Zou Yan – held captive in the shadows.
Oh, when I – do think of these things,
    I would flee and hide – to live in reclusion.

I'll climb up – the high mountains,
All the way to – the monkeys and gibbon;

Then go back down – into deep gullies,
Where nethermost – lurk vipers and snakes.

To the left I see – the shrikes screeching,
To the right notice – the owls hooting.
Fearful and faint – tired and out of breath,
20 leaping and jumping – swinging and swaggering.

Wandering and wending – over the central plain,
I look up to Heaven – and redouble my sighs.
The oat-grass and the wool-grass – grow lush and luxuriant,
24 rank rushes and reeds – proliferate.
The deer trip by – pittering and pattering,
    sand-badger and ferret-badger – squiggling and squirming.
Sparrow hawk and kite – skimming the skies,
    a bevy of quail – flutter and flurry by.
Alas that I – am isolated and alone,
30 and have no one – no peer or companion.
Though I would rather – loll and linger longer,
    the sun advances – towards the twilight.

The mystic crane – that soared aloft,
    has already departed – into lazulite gloom.

The orioles are – warbling and whistling,
    the mountain magpies – chirruping and chirping.
Swan and egret – raise their pinions,
    returning geese – begin to make their way.
My ambition I now – have suddenly recognized,
40   that I yearn still – for the sacred capital.
Donning my sandals – I prepare to set forth,
42   and stand awaiting – the great illumination!

VII. *Grieving for the Age*

In summer's celestial splendour – and divine radiance,
    creative energy is set free – bright and untainted.
The wind wafts past – warm and gentle,
    the hundred grasses burgeon – and blossom splendidly.
5 Blue rocket and sowthistle flourish – lust leaves lengthening,
6   but asarum and angelica wither – ignored and unknown.

Pitying those loyal and worthy men – who met with destruction,
    now I too face untimely death – to be crushed and pulverized.
These times are decadent and disturbed – all confused as watery gruel,
10   and I lament that in this age – there is none who knows me.
I consider however in antiquity – how heroic and noble men
    were dismissed and degraded – entrammelled and imprisoned too:
Guan Zhong was held by – fetters and manacles,
14   Baili Xi was sold as a slave – and then traded himself back again.
Meeting Duke Huan and Duke Mu – they were recognized and
        promoted,
    their talent and virtue thus – were allotted proper places.
As for me, I'll dally here – and console myself
    enjoying zither and brush – in idle entertainment.
Oppressed by the narrow confines – of these central states,
20   I'd rather travel off to join – the Nine Yee abroad.
Passing over the five ridges – precipitously perched,
    I'd look off to the floating crags – spiring and soaring.
Climbing cinnabar mountains – and fiery plains,
    I park my carriage – at Huangzhi.
Meeting Firelord Zhurong – I question and consult him,
26   and he praises me – for effecting non-action.
Then reversing course – I set off northward,
28   where I meet the Tortoise God – and share joyful feast.
I'd like to reside in tranquillity – and satisfy myself,
30   but my heart is broken with sorrow – and I cannot do it.
Setting aside my reins – I whip on my steeds,
    when all at once the whirlwind stirs – and the clouds drift by.
Boarding an airborne craft – I pass over the oceans,
    joining Anqi Sheng – at Mount Penglai.
Following the ladder to Heaven – I advance north,
36   ascending to Supreme Unity – by the Jade Stair.

I tell the White Maiden – to play the reed-organ,
38   while the Huntress harmonizes – with song and ditty.
Their voices high and keening – in ethereal accord,
40   with mellifluous melodies – and dexterous dances.
All rejoice and relish in – the utmost in pleasure,
    but I feel a longing that – makes me mourn alone.
Recalling Zhanghua Palace – I heave a deep sigh:
    my mind persists in pining – with regret that remains.

VIII. *Lamenting the Turning Year*

When autumn skies – are cool and fresh,
    the mystic airs – rise crisply above:
The North Wind – has a piercing chill,
    the grasses and trees – pale and wither.
The cicadas chirp – *joo, joo, joo*,
    and locusts prepare – for metamorphosis.
The year rushes hastily on – towards the nightfall,
    and time's passage – make me saddened, distraught.
I grieve that the vulgar – are confused and corrupted,
10   blinkered and blind – wanting in worth.
They treat as treasures – mere grains of sand,
    they discard even – night-shining pearls.
Fagara and nephrite – are blackened and besmirched,
    instead with cocklebur – they fill their chambers.
Straightening my robe – and loosening my belt,
16   I wield my splendid sword – the Inksun.
Climbing up into my chariot – I command my driver,
    to race off far as – the Four Margins.
19 As I enter the courtyard – I spy scorpions approaching,
20   and departing through the gate – I strike at a wasp.
In the alleyways there are – spider-centipedes,
    out in the villages there are – praying mantises.
Looking upon all these – ravenous beasts
    in my heart I feel – a piercing pain.

Here I think upon – Wu Zixu,
    there I admire that hero – Bi Gan.
Throwing away the sword – I doff my cap,
    contorted like a dragon – worming and writhing.
I conceal myself in secret – amid the hills and lakes,
30   creeping and crawling – in the dense underbrush.
Peering out among – the ravines and the streams,
    I see the flowing streams – spurt and spume.
Sea turtle and alligator – gambol and frolic,
    the mud-eel and sheatfish – teem and thrive.
The crowds proceed – above and below,
    aligned in rows – arrayed en masse.

I regret for myself – that I have no peers,
    but abide solitary – bereft and distressed.
The winter nights – are unending,
40   the falling snow – occludes the view.
But a magic gleam – sparkles and shimmers,
    will o' the wisps – flicker and flash.
My own high virtue – now thwarted and defeated,
    I regret the loss – of my own life's freedom.
Ensnared by sorrow – dark and despondent,
    what place is there – to express my feelings?

IX. *Furthering My Intent*

Ascending jade peaks – I roam free and easy,
    surveying the elevated hills – that spire aloft.
Osmanthus trees are arrayed – spreading out profusely,
    expelling purple blossoms – over branches unfolding.
Where in truth the giant roc – ought to abide,
    now are gathered instead – the petty wrens.
Magpies are startled – into chirping and chittering,
    I gaze back into the distance – in bitter anguish.

The sun and moon above – are occluded in dark,
10   the heavens hidden or reversed – ill auras pervading.
Alas, my sovereign – is not percipient,
    how can I display my integrity – and exert my loyalty?
Unfurling my wingfeathers – I surpass the vulgar,
    and roam in delirious detachment – cultivating my spirit.
I ride a sextet of flood dragons – snaking and slithering,
    coursing and climbing – up into the clouds.
Seizing upon a comet – as my pennant,
    grasping a whip of lightning – to drive ahead;
As morning dawns – over Yan and Ying,
20   at mealtime I reach – the circuitous springs.
Rounding the crooked nooks – and stopping in the North,
    I pause my chariot – at the southern border.
23 Visiting the Gods of Bright and Dark – I present offerings,
    revering the loyal and steadfast – I too grow more determined.
Passing by the Nine Palaces – I stop to observe each of them,
    admiring their hidden treasures – so precious and rare.
I encounter Fu Yue – riding upon a dragon,
    and arrange a betrothal – with the Weaving Girl.
29 Wielding the Fork-net of Heaven – to vanquish evil,
30   I draw the bow of Heaven – to shoot down vice.
Following the Perfected Ones – I soar off free,
    consuming Primal Essences – to survive forever.
Gazing off towards Grand Tenuity – awesome and mighty,
34   I glance at the Three Platforms' – sumptuous splendour.
They assist in governance – and moral edification,
    establish heroic deeds – and bequeath a legacy:

The sun flashes past – to descend in the west,
    but the way is infinitely far – the difficulty lamentable;
My ambitions remain stored up – and unachieved,
40   in disappointment and despair – I grieve at my plight.

Envoi

The court of Heaven is bright – clouds and coronas concealed,
2 The Three Luminosities shine – mirrored in myriad locales.
I rebuke the salamanders – and promote tortoise and dragon,
4 Lash away the plotting toadies – and assist the Trigger and Transverse.
Allying with Hou Ji and with Xie – I restore the achievements of Yao,
And lament only that there is no hero – yet to be my peer.

BIOGRAPHIES

The following sketches are arranged in order of importance from the point of view of the anthology itself. Thus I have placed Wang Yi third on account of his pivotal role as compiler and commentator, even though he is less highly regarded as author or historical personage than several others listed after him. Both the details of the biographies and the question of these figures' relationships to the anthology are complex ones that continue to spur critical controversy; for an overview of those controversies see the Introduction.

Qu Yuan (*fl. c.*300 BCE). Nobleman of the ancient state of Chu (centred in modern Hunan and Hubei provinces), Qu Yuan was a gifted orator who served at the courts of King Huai and Qingxiang, just as Chu was collapsing in the face of concerted assaults by the state of Qin. He drowned himself in the Miluo in protest at the king's misguided rule and trust in flattering toadies at court. Over one third of the works in the *Elegies* are attributed to Qu Yuan, but there are doubts and complications regarding these attributions. Regardless of the historical details, though, he remains the central figure in the anthology, since so many of the poems are dedicated to eulogizing him: the great martyr, poet, and overall culture-hero of early China.

Song Yu (3rd c. BCE). Identified as the author of a large number of memorable poems, ranging from the 'Nine Phases' and 'Summons to the Soul' in this volume to the 'Rhapsody on the Gaotang Shrine' and 'Rhapsody on Master Dengtu the Lecher' in the *Wen xuan* anthology. He is said to have been a student of Qu Yuan's who continued his legacy at the Chu court. But the poetry of Song Yu essentially lacks the spirit of protest and indignation so celebrated in the work of Qu Yuan, substituting for it lavish descriptive power, appreciation for sensuous beauty, and originality of metaphor.

Jing Cuo. Said to be a contemporary of Song Yu but otherwise little is known of him. The 'Greater Summons' is attributed to him very tentatively.

Jia Yi (*c.*200–168 BCE). A talented scholar promoted at a young age by Emperor Wen, but later opposed by his older colleagues at court and demoted to the position of grand tutor for the King of Changsha, belonging to the ancient territory of Chu in modern Hunan. The experience may have given him a unique affinity with Qu Yuan, whom he mourned in his famous 'Rhapsody of Lament for Qu Yuan', one of the earliest extant works to eulogize Qu Yuan—and perhaps for that reason excluded from the *Elegies*, for which the voice of Qu Yuan is primary.

Liu An, Prince of Huainan (179–122 BCE). Grandson of the Han founder Liu Bang, Liu An was a major force in the culture of early China through his compilation of the *Huainanzi* and other works. He held court at Shouchun (in modern Huainan city, Anhui province), which had been the final capital of

Chu. The Huainan court admired the poetry of Chu and continued to produce new writings in the same vein, so it played a pivotal role in preserving Chu poetry and establishing its importance in the Han. Liu An is not actually named as an author of any of the poems, but is identified as the presiding authority for the composition of the 'Summons to a Recluse', and has frequently been named as a candidate for composition of other poems in the anthology as well.

Zhuang Ji (2nd c. BCE). Little is known of him except that he is mentioned in the first paragraph of Han poet Sima Xiangru's biography as his contemporary and identified as a native of the Wu region. He is mentioned together with the writers Zou Yang and Mei Sheng, as 'travelling persuaders' of the time. His work 'Lamenting Time's Fate' is typical of Han poetry with its focus on the frustration of the poet born in the wrong time, but it contains memorable turns of phrase that were much admired by later writers.

Wang Bao (*c*.84–*c*.53 BCE). The only one of the three great *fu* poets of the Former Han from the Shu region (modern Sichuan), along with Sima Xiangru and Yang Xiong, who is represented in the *Elegies*. He was highly celebrated and surely prolific, but his few extant works make it hard to appreciate him accurately. These include a eulogy (*song*) entitled 'The Sage Ruler Obtains Worthy Officials' and a 'Rhapsody on the Panpipes', as well as a 'Disquisition of the Four Sages Debating Virtue', all of which are preserved in the *Wen xuan*. He died of illness on a journey back to his native region to offer sacrifices there.

Liu Xiang (79–8 BCE). Great-great-grandson of Liu Bang's youngest brother, Liu Xiang led an active political life with vicissitudes that recall Qu Yuan's own frustrations; he was imprisoned and had a close ally forced to commit suicide for their criticisms of the rising power of the eunuchs. But his larger achievements are all tied to his assignment in the final decades of his life to organize and catalogue the imperial library. With this son, Liu Xin, he established major bibliographical divisions and authoritative texts that continue to shape our knowledge of early China. This work included editing of an early form of the *Elegies* themselves, and his deep erudition is visible in every verse of the suite 'Nine Threnodies' that was later included in the anthology itself.

Dongfang Shuo. A successful writer and prominent wit at the court of Han Emperor Wu (r. 140–87 BCE). Though he must have been prolific in oral composition, at least, few of his works survive beside the 'Seven Remonstrances' in this volume. The notable exception is 'Replying to a Guest's Objections', a dialogue justifying his own service at court. Though neither is as humorous as one expects from his reputation, both present alternative sides of the essential dialectic of Han literature: balancing the need for loyalty and submission to authority with that of self-expression and resistance when necessary.

Wang Yi (*c*.89–*c*.158 CE). Scholar of the Later Han, who probably compiled the *Chuci zhangju* (Elegies of Chu with chapter and verse commentary) under the auspices of Empress Dowager Deng (81–121). Though the only extant commentary to the entire anthology is attributed to him, its nature is hybrid and probably also contains commentaries by other scholars as well. In his own 'Nine Yearnings' we may observe his self-representation as a loyal servant of the state, expressed in original and occasionally bizarre imagery. His son Yanshou was a more talented poet who drowned crossing the Xiang River at the mere age of 20.

EXPLANATORY NOTES

LI SAO

The 'Li sao' is a poem about a courtier estranged from his sovereign, exiled from his country, and pondering his future course, but this most basic level of meaning is not expressed directly in such terms anywhere within the poem itself. The poem opens with its protagonist asserting his divine, aristocratic ancestry and his richly symbolic names Righteous Principle and Spirit Harmony. The series of substitutions and symbols that open the poem prepare us for the mythological and religious turn, beginning with the shamaness Lady Xu, then the sage-king Shun from remote antiquity; the shaman-hero Spirit Aura; and finally Shaman Xian, again a mythical shaman-hero. These four figures together represent the religious dimension to Chu culture, revering both the sages like Shun, prominent throughout early Chinese culture as a model ruler, but also various semi-divine figures known for their magical powers of divination. Indeed, Qu Yuan's interactions with the last two interlocutors, Spirit Aura and Shaman Xian, both consist of him asking for a divination.

The essential key to the hybrid, even self-contradictory nature of the poem may be its title, 'Li sao', which has divided commentators for two millennia (see my 'Sublimating Sorrow'). The poem uses symbolic substitutions to describe both the courtier's lament and a cosmic journey, both political and mythological contents, at the same time. Rather than choosing a single interpretation, in reading the 'Li sao', we ought to be open to all these possibilities, and also be attentive to the poet's artifice.

The 'Li sao' text consists of 92 rhyming quatrains followed by a brief 'Envoi'. There is a loose narrative arc to the poem, including Qu Yuan's self-introduction, journey to consult with various religious or mythical authorities, and despairing conclusion, but there are not explicit divisions between sections. Primarily for the convenience of the reader, I have divided the text into nine sections, following the main content of the poem. Though arbitrary, these divisions do reflect the consistent use of ninefold divisions throughout the anthology.

2: Gaoyang ('Lofty Sunshine'), also known as Zhuanxu, was an ancestral god of Chu, referred to both directly and obliquely throughout the *Elegies*. The Han commentary identifies Boyong ('Sire of Merit') as the name of Qu Yuan's father, otherwise unknown. Though modern scholars have proposed various other identifications of Boyong, such as the fire-god Zhurong, the term 'Resplendent Begetter' (*huangkao*) has been shown to refer usually to the father or grandfather. Liu Xiang also uses this term twice in his 'Nine Threnodies', below.

4: The difficult term *sheti* refers to the first of the twelve counter-orbital Jupiter years. See Wilkinson, *Chinese History: A New Manual*, 516. The date given (the *gengyin* day) is not the twenty-seventh day of the month, but of the sixty-day cycle in an unknown year, so there is no way to identify the specific date. The *yin* is the third of the earthly branches, and twenty-seven is three cubed, so the birthday presented here is intricately associated with the number three.

8: 'Spirit' here translates *ling*, which could also be rendered 'numinous', and in the language of the *Elegies* is used to refer to the shaman's person or activities. Why Qu Yuan assigns himself these names, which are not corroborated by any other sources, is a major problem in *Chuci* studies. Premodern scholars like Wang Fuzhi (1619–92) proposed that they are synonymous with Qu's names Ping and Yuan. More likely, the two are symbolic names for the protagonist of the poem, similar to Qu Yuan but not identical with him. 'Righteous Principle' represents Qu Yuan's moral/political ideals, and Lingjun, 'Spirit Harmony', his religious/cultural heritage.

10: The keyword *xiu*, here rendered 'consummate', refers to the perfection of inner virtue, outer appearance, and also behaviour and governance.

16: All these fragrant plants have their own distinctive virtues: magnolia impresses by its size, the slough grass by its longevity.

20: 'Anyone admirable' is an intentionally vague term that may not designate any particular individual. Here it may refer back to the speaker, who has just described his own 'inner excellence' (actually the same term *mei*, conventionally rendered 'beauty').

25: There are various identifications of the Three Sovereigns. According to Han commentary they are historic sages corresponding to each of the three great dynasties of antiquity: Yu of Xia, Tang of Shang, and King Wen of Zhou (*Chuci buzhu*, 1.7); according to Zhu Xi, Shaohao, Zhuanxu, Gao Xin (*Chuci jizhu*, 171); according to Wang Yuan and Dai Zhen, prior rulers of the Chu state (*Chuci jijie*, 1.9b–10a; *Qu Yuan fu Dai shi zhu*, 1.2b). Finally, Sukhu identifies them with the rulers identified recently from excavated manuscripts (*Shaman and the Heresiarch*, 95; Cook, 'Three High Gods of Chu'). But it is worth noting that none of these gods appears elsewhere in the *Elegies*.

The meaning of numerous traditional terms like this was either lost and rediscovered, or simply invented, during the Warring States era. Considering the anthology as a whole, Zhu Xi's hypothesis is most convincing, since it is these three ancient god-lords who are demonstrably important throughout the anthology.

36: The illustrious (i.e. royal) carriage is synecdoche for the project of state-building of Chu.

38: See line 13 above for the metaphor of keeping in step. The righteous path of former sages is often represented as a kind of 'footprint'—see e.g. *Songs* 245/1: 'Well she sacrificed and prayed | That she might no longer be childless. | She trod on the big toe of God's footprint, | Was accepted and got what she desired.' Trans. Waley, *Book of Songs*, 244.

39: 'Calamus', also known as 'myrtle root' or 'sweet flag', is a fragrant herb. It is mentioned by this name in the 'Li sao' and in 'Unravelled Yearnings', in both cases in this personified sense apparently also referring to the sovereign.

42: 'Loyal counsel' translates *jianjian* here. The word *jian* occurs often in the *Chuci* and its meaning is disputed. Here *jianjian* needs to be understood as a reduplicative compound whose precise connotations may vary according to context, but whose meaning we can grasp from its usage in the eponymous Book of Changes hexagram #39: 'The king's servants face obstruction and obstacles, but it is not their fault'. For the broader significance of this hexagram in the *Elegies*, see also Sukhu, *Shaman and the Heresiarch*, 131–7.

44: 'Spirit Paragon' is the term used to refer to the sovereign in this poem, hence implicitly King Huai of Chu (though equally applicable to other kings).

56: This passage has traditionally been understood as referring to the sovereign's efforts to cultivate talented advisors, but could also be interpreted as referring to the transience of all things, among other possibilities.

75: *Zhou* 'accord' means 'to encircle, surround', but more abstractly, to be in accord with. It is also the name of the dynasty that established the governing principles to which Qu Yuan still adheres, and serves as another key word within this text.

81: The repetition of 'slander' (*ti*) from the previous line is an effective use of 'anadiplosis' to create a sense of transition between stanzas.

91: The metaphor of the plumb-line for the proper order of government, important throughout the *Elegies*, can be found in the Bible as well. See Amos 7:8–9: 'Then the Lord said, "See, I am setting a plumb-line in the midst of my people Israel; I will never again pass them by." '

104: The Han commentary cites the example of King Wu of Zhou, who approved of Bi Gan's conduct (Bi Gan being the loyal critic of Zhow).

108: This quatrain plays with the contrast between different kinds of 'roads' or paths through life. Huang Linggeng argues that 'return' here means specifically to return to one's origin, namely to die, rather than to return to court (*Chuci zhangju shuzheng*, 1.222).

112: The connotations of *fu* 'apparel' are rich. Though later it can mean simply 'clothing', in early texts its significance ranges from submission and custom, to a person's outer appearance and bearing.

115: The exclamation here anticipates the envoi of 'Li sao', creating a miniature loop within its larger narrative.

120: 'Fragrance' and 'lustre' both represent personal character and virtue, though lustre emphasizes the inner quality, while fragrance emphasizes its external expression. Cf. 'Yearning for the Beautiful One', line 47. In Qu Yuan's rhetorical system 'mixing' necessarily has pejorative connotations. Thus the quatrain contrasts the hero's solitary virtue (crown tall above the others, pendants distinctively arranged) to the indifferentiable mass of his rivals.

129: The Han commentary claims that Nüxu is Qu Yuan's sister, but in fact this was just an honorific term for a female shaman in ancient Chu.

132: This sympathetic view of the mythological ruler Gun, who failed to control the great flood, is unusual in early sources. Qu Yuan is, fittingly, appreciative of the nobility of failure.

141: The thematic concern with matchmakers, intermediaries, and messengers here reflects the social role of the shaman, mediating between humans and deities.

145: The *Classic of Mountains and Seas* and *Guicang* (an early divination book) both describe how Qi obtained from Heaven the royal music of the Nine Phases, Nine Songs, and Nine Summons. See Birrell, *Classic of Mountains and Seas*, 16.177.

148: This line may be related to the 'Song of the Five Sons', the younger brothers of Taikang of the Xia, which is included in the pseudo-Old Text *Book of Documents* (Legge, *Shoo King*, 153–6).

152: There are a number of different legends surrounding Yih, some contradictory. Perhaps the earliest stratum simply has Yih killing a monster: 'Yih the Archer and Chisel Tooth [Zaochi] fought in the Wilderness of Longlivedbloom [Shouhua]. Yi shot him dead.' (See Birrell, *Classic of Mountains and Seas*, 6.110.) The monster should probably be identified with the giant boar mentioned in 'Heavenly Questions', #36.

Han Zhuo was the minister of Yih who went on to murder him and usurp the throne, as is already implied here. See also 'Heavenly Questions', #37. For a full account see *Zuo zhuan*, Xiang 4, trans. Durrant et al., *Zuo Tradition*, 917.

153: Ao was the son of Han Zhuo. He is said to have committed adultery with Lady Tangent. See previous note and 'Heavenly Questions', #44–5.

160: The final ruler of Shang, Zhow, was also called Hou Xin. He is said to have killed worthy ministers like Bi Gan and Mei Bo. Bi Gan, in particular, is said to have been ground up into meat paste. Zhow received his comeuppance when King Wu defeated him at Dawnsong and established the Zhou dynasty instead.

162: This couplet cites the founding sages of Xia and Shang, Yu and Tang respectively, as precedents for Zhou authority. Yu figures prominently in the 'Heavenly Questions' as well.

168: For the 'sublunary realm', literally 'lower world', see *Songs* 195/1: 'The angry terrors of Compassionate Heaven | Extend through this lower world; | [The king's] counsels and plans are crooked and bad;— | When will he stop [in his course]?' (trans. Legge, *She King*, 330).

176: Here ends Qu Yuan's long speech to Shun. After citing many examples of just and unjust rulers, he concludes that the minister has to be fitted properly to the ruler just as in carpentry the tenon needs to match the shape of the mortise (socket) in which it is inserted.

182: The 'righteous path' is literally 'the middle and right' (*zhongzheng*), as in *Book of Changes*, hexagram #30, 'Li': 'The yielding clings to the middle and to what is right, hence it has success' (from the 'Decision Statements' commentary, trans. Wilhelm-Baynes, 536).

186: In this section the protagonist makes a magical journey through the heavens, while simultaneously searching for a bride. The significance of the brides is unclear, but loosely speaking they seem to represent various potential alternatives from Chu mythology and history, either for Qu Yuan's own personal quest or for his ideal ruler of Chu.

Silver Pillar is a free translation of the place name Cangwu. Though the name of a mountain in modern Hunan, this was identified as the burial place of Shun. The Hanging Garden was located on Mount Kunlun in the west, so this couplet describes a world-spanning trajectory.

194: The Pool of Affinity is said to be the place where the sun bathes, and the Sunrise Mulberry (Fusang) the place where it rises, hence both places are located in the extreme east.

195: 'Dimming Wood' (the Ruo Tree) is described best in the *Huainanzi*, in a section describing the geography of the Kunlun mountains: 'The Ruo Tree is to the west of the Jian tree. On its branches are ten suns; its blossoms cast light upon the earth.' See Major et al., *Huainanzi*, 4.157.

198: Prospect Shu (Wangshu) is the charioteer of the Moon and Flying Lian (Feilian) the God of Winds.

204: The whirlwind may be a divine power as well, like the various celestial spirits above. It is the leitmotif of the poem 'Nine Avowals: Grieved by the Whirlwind', below.

213: The water of the Whitewater, flowing out of Mount Kunlun, is said to bestow immortality, according to a passage of the *Huainanzi* quoted by the Han commentary (no longer in the received text).

216: Though *gaoqiu* can just mean 'High Hill', Huang Linggeng argues that it is actually the 'Mound of Gao', the burial mound of Gaoyang, Chu ancestor (*Chuci zhangju shuzheng*, 1.376).

222: Fenglong is a celestial god of the clouds, and Fu Fei a goddess, perhaps the daughter of Fu Xi, and later identified with the goddess of the Luo River.

224: According to the Han commentary, Plainspoken Paragon (Jianxiu) was an advisor of Fu Xi, but the term may also be an alter ego of Lingxiu, Spirit Paragon. 'Plainspoken' (*jian*) is a keyword throughout the *Elegies* (the character can be written either with the foot radical or or the speech radical).

228: Wang Fuzhi explains Desperation Rock (Qiongshi) as a mountain in the far west, and the Wei River as flowing from Mount Tarryhere, so that both indicate a remote location in the west. See *Chuci tongshi*, 1.230.

236: The Yousong clan was the clan to which belonged the founding lineage of the Shang dynasty. See *Songs* 304/1: 'The clan of [You]song was favoured; | God appointed its child to bear Shang.' Trans. Waley, *Book of Songs*, 320.

240: The serpent eagle is so called because it was said to produce venom. Thus this stanza contrasts two sorts of intermediaries, one truth-telling but inauspicious, the other beguiling but unreliable. I take this turtle dove to be related to the turtle dove used in a critique of sexual licence in *Songs* 58/3: 'Before the mulberry-tree sheds its leaves, | How soft and glossy they are! | O dove, turtle-dove, | Do not eat the mulberries! | O ladies, ladies, | Do not take your pleasure with men.' Trans. Waley, *Book of Songs*, 50.

244: Gaoxin is the Highlord Ku, said to be the successor to Zhuanxu (see e.g. 'Bamboo Annals', in Legge, *Shoo King*, 111). Both he and Highlord Jun, with whom he has been identified in modern scholarship, are reported in early texts to have several goddesses as wives, and hence to have gone ahead of Qu Yuan in his quest for the goddess. See Allan, *Shape of the Turtle*, 33–4.

248: Here Qu Yuan alludes playfully to a historical episode of the Xia, reported in a speech attributed to Wu Zixu in the *Zuo zhuan*, Duke Ai, 1.2 (Durrant et al., *Zuo Tradition*, 1835), and asserts that if Shaokang has not yet married the two daughters of the Youyu clan after fleeing from his enemy, Ao, then they should still be available for Qu Yuan himself. The Youyu clan is said to be the descendants of Shun.

256: The word *zhonggu*, here rendered 'eternity', is a rich term that occurs three times in the *Elegies*. Literally it means something like 'ultimate obsolescence'.

258: The rushes (as with yarrow stalks), bamboo strips, and tablets, all belong to the paraphernalia of divination. Spirit Aura is probably the same as Wu Fen, legendary shaman mentioned as one of ten who inhabit a magical mountain in the *Shanhai jing* (Birrell, *Classic of Mountains and Seas*, 16.174).

264: Cf. *Songs* 113/1: 'At last we are going to leave you | And go to that happy land; | Happy land, happy land, | Where we shall have our place' (trans. Waley, *Book of Songs*, 88). The slight linguistic parallel is made more significant by the analogy in content, since both poems are recommending departure for a better political environment. The resemblance is pointed out by Zhu Junsheng (*Li sao fu buzhu*, 22b).

268: This line is parallel to the Shamaness's caution in line 138 above. In both cases the first-person pronoun has to be understood as plural. The Han commentary explains 'dazzled by brilliance' as meaning simply 'confused', a paraphrase repeated by later commentators and modern dictionaries, but the literal sense is preferable.

270: This couplet opens with 'good and ill' repeated (in slightly different wording) from the end of the previous quatrain, a good example of anadiplosis. Lin Geng proposed that lines 269–96 are an interpolation ('"Li sao" zhong cuanru de wenzi') because the content reflects the concerns of Han scholars.

280: The sacrificial rice here is also mentioned in the *Shanhai jing* as appropriate for offerings to the divinities it describes (as in Birrell, *Classic of Mountains and Seas*, 1.5).

288: There is no obvious way to tell where Shaman Xian's speech ends, and commentators have long disputed this point. The simplest solution is to end the speech as quickly as possible, after just these two lines. Noting that the divination may be ambiguous, I take it that Qu Yuan goes on to elaborate on its meaning in his own language of historical allusion.

Zhi is the personal name of Yi Yin, minister to sage-ruler Tang. Gaoyao was the legendary minister of ancient sage-king Shun said to have established legal norms.

292: Early Shang ruler Wu Ding encountered Yue at the Fu Crags (located in modern Pingyang, Shanxi), hence his name Fu Yue. Wu Ding immediately appointed Yue minister and charged with him numerous tasks, as recorded in a dialogue between the two in the *Documents*. See Legge, *Shoo King*, 251.

300: *Tijue* could be either the shrike or the cuckoo, but it is the former whose call is associated with the seventh month, near the onset of autumn, as in *Songs* 154/3: 'In the seventh month the shrike cries; | In the eighth month they twist thread, | The black thread and the yellow' (trans. Waley, *Book of Songs*, 120).

314: The references to 'eupatory' and other fragrant plants here and in the succeeding quatrain have been treated by the Han commentary and later commentators as referring to specific courtiers of Chu, but this view is not incontrovertible. Rather than playing this ancient game of historical whodunit, an alternative view might be to understand this passage as moving to a darker stage of Qu Yuan's personal journey, in which even his beloved 'eupatory' is unsatisfactory.

318: Fagara and prickly ash are ambivalent in Qu Yuan's lexicon. Both have a pungent flavour, and are more pushy, parvenu types than the herbs of aristocratic idleness that he favours.

336: This passage is a miniature encapsulation of the themes of the 'Nine Songs' and should be read in tandem with them.

350: 'Halt in hesitation' is an alliterative compound (**long-la*). Depending on context it can emphasize either hesitation or pleasure or both.

352: The Sovereign of the West is identified in the Han commentary as Shaohao Zhi, ancestor of the Shang people and associated with a divine bird or phoenix.

356: The three quatrains above all refer to mythical places in the West. These may be related to the cult of the Xiwangmu or 'Spirit-Mother of the West'. See Ye Shuxian et al., *Shanhai jing de wenhua xunzong*, 1253; Goldin, 'On the Meaning of the Name Xiwangmu, Spirit-mother of the West'.

363: The Nine Songs were the royal music of Xia, and the Nine Shao (perhaps equivalent with the Nine Summons, *jiu zhao*) were the royal dances of

Shun. At the same time they were the inspiration, and model, for some of the *Elegies*, as their titles make clear. The full relationship between ancient music and the *Elegies* cannot be ascertained in detail, for lack of evidence, but remains tantalizing.

369: This section is identified as the *luan*, a term that usually means 'chaos', but can also mean 'put in order'. Here it is apparently a musical term that indicates a conclusion to the piece that has gone before. The use of the *luan* in the *Elegies* is extremely significant, providing structural connections that are unusual in early Chinese poetry (for instance, the *luan* element is generally absent from the *Book of Songs*).

372: The key term *mei* is a challenge to translation as its principal sense of 'beautiful, admirable' applies awkwardly to 'government' in English. And yet it encompasses an aesthetic quality as well and so should not be rendered simply as 'virtuous' or 'just'. I compromise with 'harmony'.

NINE PHASES

The word *bian* in the Chinese title of this piece, 'Jiu bian', is ambiguous. It has a political meaning of 'argument, suasion', but is also closely related to its homonym meaning 'transformation'. Complicating matters further, the title of this piece is also known as an ancient musical air from the Xia dynasty. In light of all these multiple significations, I render it here as 'phase' in accordance with its simple sense of change, iteration, but also with connotations of gradual revelation. The iterations of the song are meant to bring to light a complex state of affairs, not least the internal psychological state of the poet himself. While the 'Li sao' is presented in the voice of man estranged from the centre and removed from court, the 'Nine Phases' ends with an assertion of admiration for the sovereign. The hero's suffering and complaints all build up to his desire to be restored to a position of intimacy at court. In this sense it marks the beginning of a 'eulogistic' tradition in Chinese poetry distinct from that of the 'Li sao'.

I divide the text into nine sections plus an envoi, following the divisions made by Liu Yongji. Though the parallel this creates with the 'Li sao', 'Nine Songs', and other *Elegies* is artificial, it helps to illuminate the structure of the poem.

17: The geese call out harmoniously in *Songs* 34/3: 'On one note the wild-geese cry, | A cloudless dawn begins to break. | A knight that brings home his bride | Must do so before the ice melts.' Trans. Waley, *Book of Songs*, 30.

83: For the contrast between a 'parting in life' and a 'parting by death' see also 'Nine Songs: Lesser Controller of Destinies', line 13.

90: This passage relies on the traditional analogy between the moisture of rain and dew from Heaven and favour from the Emperor.

94: Cf. 'Li sao', lines 89–92.

118: This couplet is making a coherent point in very compressed fashion. Even birds and beasts are well aware of the *de* (sometimes 'virtue', but here obligation due in response to merit or favour) owed to them. Why should a worthy vassal continue to reside at court if his merit is not recognized, due favour not given? But the sense is hard to express within the confines of the *sao* metre. See Wang Fuzhi's paraphrase for a heartfelt appreciation of this couplet (*Chuci tongshi*, 8.384).

120: This couplet is open to other interpretations, but I see it as praising the behaviour of these two noble animals, who do not modify their behaviour automatically in order to sate their bestial desires.

138: This difficult line should perhaps be understood in light of *Songs* 260/8, in which the author asserts: 'I, Yin Jifu, have made this song, | Solemn as the pure wind, | Though Zhongshan Fu is ever anxious, | May it ease his heart!' (my translation). The content is similar and that passage uses this same term *song* (also 'recitation', 'remonstrance', etc.) for (English) 'song'.

141: Shen Baoxu was the Chu nobleman who stayed to fight for Chu when Wu Zixu departed, and later successfully pleaded with Qin to lend Chu support. Song Yu here praises the less-famous Shen Baoxu but not Wu Zixu, in contrast to some of the *Elegies* below.

154: *Songs* 112/1 says that a noble man does not enjoy the 'bread of idleness', meaning that he does not consume the crops produced by workers without labouring himself: 'If you did not hunt, if you did not chase, | One would not see all those badgers hanging in your courtyard. | No, indeed, that lord | Does not feed on the bread of idleness.' Trans. Waley, *Book of Songs*, 87.

155: Hong Xingzu cites the *Book of Rites*: 'The scholar is not cast down, or cut from his root, by poverty and mean condition; he is not *satisfied or sated* by riches and noble condition' (modified from Legge, *Lî Kî*, 2:409).

193: Cf. Qu Yuan's lotus garb in 'Li sao', line 113.

200: These four lines also occur in 'Nine Avowals: Lamenting Ying', lines 57–60, but 'Nine Phases' is likely the source.

220: Armour is ineffectual because only a ruler who has the confidence of his advisors and the people will succeed, regardless of his military might.

234: Cf. 'Li sao', lines 295–6.

248: The Vermilion Bird is the symbolic deity of the south, and the Azure Dragon of the east. This passage represents the triumphant procession of the hero and his attendants, recapitulating the cosmic journey in the 'Li sao' in miniature, until at the end the hero turns back towards home, duty, and king.

NINE SONGS

The 'Nine Songs' are probably the works in the *Elegies* with the most obvious appeal to modern readers, yet for various reasons also the most puzzling works in the anthology. The first obstacle to reading the 'Nine Songs' is the fact that the series actually contains eleven songs with distinct titles. The simplest explanation, as proposed by Wen Yiduo and others, is that the first and last of the songs, which are notably shorter than any of the others, serve as prologue and epilogue, respectively, to the suite as a whole.

The key to understanding the poems is to recognize the role of shamanism in their structure. The shaman is an intermediary between the human and divine realms, who himself or herself impersonates a god in order to meet with other divinities. This is why the poems employ the alternation of speakers, both human and divine, and so it is foolhardy to identify the particular speaker of any given line with too much confidence. The overall effect of the poems ought to be to confuse our sense of mortal selfhood, to blur the line that normally separates humanity from the divine.

The Han commentary claims that Qu Yuan took local folk songs from the southern regions where he was exiled, and revised them to make these pieces. Though this is probably no more than speculation based on their contents, it seems to have a grain of truth: the songs would appear to derive in some way from songs used in religious ritual in Chu, but have been revised and recomposed by some poet into a coherent sequence

I. SUPREME UNITY, SOVEREIGN OF THE EAST

This poem is the ritual proemium, introducing the other songs devoted to particular deities. It alludes to key elements of Chu religion familiar not just throughout the 'Nine Songs' but also in the 'Li sao' and other *Elegies*: the use of various fragrant plants and precious gemstones as emblems of divinity, and the performance of music and dance to initiate contact with the spirits. In particular, in the twelfth line the poem uses the essential keyword *ling* 'divinity', referring both to the gods being worshipped and the shamans whose function is to lead them down to earth and assume their identities.

Though this poem is relatively straightforward in content, the title is a puzzle. Taiyi, the Supreme Unity, is identified as the supreme divinity and origin of the cosmos in the Warring States-era 'Supreme Unity Arises from Water' text excavated from Guodian, Hubei in 1993. But here it appears in a more philosophical context, and it is unclear when Taiyi actually became an object of worship and devotion. Recently excavated materials suggest that Taiyi may also have been worshipped as a divinity in Warring States Chu. There is no explicit reference that would inform us of the deity's proper identity in the text of the poem itself. 'Sovereign of the East' is also a surprising appellation. The 'Li sao' (line 352) already refers to a 'Sovereign of the West', identified in the Han commentary as the ancestral deity Shaohao, son of the Yellow Emperor. These terms are obscure, but may reflect relatively late (Warring States or Former Han) attempts at rationalization of pre-existing religious systems, correlating various deities with the four directions and other cosmological complexes.

II. LORD AMID THE CLOUDS

This deity is normally identified with the god of the clouds, Fenglong, who appears frequently in the *Elegies*, including the 'Li sao' (line 200), 'Nine Avowals: Yearning for the Beautiful One', and 'Far Roaming'. This god is also mentioned as 'Lord of the Clouds' in some recently excavated texts from the Chu region. Other scholars have attempted to understand this god's name as a geographical designation, Yunzhong, representing the Yunmeng marsh, a central geographical feature of ancient Chu, and one with some sacred and ritual significance, being used as the king's hunting park. In fact, these two views are not necessarily contradictory: the geographical term might be named after the god in the clouds, or vice versa. Clouds are themselves a zone of ambiguity and liminality, not unlike marshes; both are productive sites of fertilizing moisture as well, not unsuitable for romance. Thus the deity in question could govern both the nebulous sky and marshy earth, two parallel regions of shifting and ambivalent substance.

2: Cf. *Songs* 108/2: 'There came a gentleman | Lovely as the glint of jade'. Trans. Waley, *Book of Songs*, 85.

3: The Han commentary identifies this *ling* as the shaman, Wang Fuzhi and others as the god: but for a participant in the ceremony it could only be both.

5: The Han commentary identifies the word *jian*, translated here as 'advances steady', as an expressive particle or 'empty word'. In fact, though, it is a potent keyword in the *Elegies*; already the name of hexagram #39 in the *Changes*, where is signifies 'obstruction', but not solely in a pejorative sense: 'Water on the mountain: | The image of OBSTRUCTION. | Thus the superior man turns his attention to himself | And moulds his character' (trans. Wilhelm-Baynes, *I Ching*, 152). Thus as a verb *jian* means not 'to obstruct' but to move slowly but deliberately towards a goal, in face of obstructions.

III. LADY OF THE XIANG RIVER

This song and the next one both have to do with goddesses of the Xiang River, one of the landmarks of Chu geography. Though there are various theories about the deity or deities to whom these songs are dedicated, there is ample evidence for the worship of a pair of river goddesses in Chu. According to one popular myth, the ancient sage Yao had two daughters named Ehuang and Nüying, whom he betrothed to Shun, his successor. A close examination of the poem, though, reveals that the identity of the goddess is only of modest significance. The poem's emphasis is on the shaman, on the ritual encounter with the divine. No blessings are requested, nor prayers offered to the divinity. Instead the focus is on the liminal condition of the encounter. The poem begins and ends in a state of delay and uncertainty.

22: The poet employs two parallel metaphors for the difficulty of finding the loved one, the trope of 'adynata'.

25: Cf. hexagram #1 in the *Book of Changes*: 'Nine the fourth place means: | Wavering flight over the depths. | No blame' (trans. Wilhelm-Baynes, *I Ching*, 9).

33: There is a romantic pun here with the 'halfmoon disc' *que* representing its homonym 'incompleteness'. See Tang Bingzheng, 'Qu fu xiuci juyu', 339–41.

IV. MISTRESS OF THE XIANG

This poem seems to correspond to the previous one, being dedicated to the other of the two goddesses, and the two even conclude with the same lines. This poem addresses the goddess directly as 'daughter of the High Lord (*di*)', announcing from the beginning the arrival of the deity. Towards the end of this poem, however, many deities converge upon the site of the altar, and it seems the protagonist has approached closer to the divine. In this sense 'Mistress of the Xiang' is a sequel that fulfils promises kept in abeyance in 'Lady of the Xiang River'.

2: The goddess is identified as a daughter of *di*, the ancient term for the supreme divinity which was later borrowed for the appellation of the earthly sovereign as well. *Chouyu* may be a compound here: 'distressed and despairing'; but alternatively can be read as a causative verb 'fills me with sorrow'. I find it impossible to choose between these two appealing alternatives.

14: Again an example of the trope of 'adynata' as in 'Lady of the Xiang River', lines 21–2.

34: The 'gods' here are actually the *ling*, 'numinousness', which may refer to the shamans performing the role of gods.

V. GREATER CONTROLLER OF DESTINIES

Siming or the 'Controller of Destinies' is a god of longevity who is known well from early sources, including the bamboo strips excavated from Chu, though he was also worshipped in other areas throughout the country. But the 'Nine Songs' contain two distinct songs dedicated to two 'controllers of destinies' in 'Lesser' and 'Greater' variants. Though evidence of the popularity of Siming in general is abundant, the second of these figures, the 'Lesser Controller of Destinies', has not been identified elsewhere. In the context of a suite of religious songs, the two titles could equally well be interpreted as referring to 'Greater and Lesser [Songs] to the Controller of Destinies'. The extant songs are of equal length (though according to one theory, four lines of the 'Lesser' song have been interpolated from 'Sire of the Yellow River'), but the terms might refer to importance, or musical accompaniment, or simply sequential order.

VI. LESSER CONTROLLER OF DESTINIES

In spite of the modesty of its title, this song concisely interweaves romantic longing, spiritual flight, and monarchical ideology. Lines 13 and 14, contrasting the grief of parting and the joy of newfound love, are a highly influential couplet for the whole tradition of romantic poetry in China, yet these are somehow integrated into a seemingly incongruous hymn to a powerful deity.

10: Dai Zhen identifies all the images up to this point as *xing*, 'stimulus', as in the *Songs*, meaning that they are neither intended to be representational depictions of a particular scene, nor serving simply as political symbols. Instead they may be helping to establish a setting for the poem proper.

21: The Pool of Heaven appears also in 'Li sao', line 163.

26: Dai Zhen points out that the comets are evil omens and so the god is catching them to restore order. See *Qu Yuan fu Dai shi zhu*, 2.10b.

VII. LORD OF THE EAST

The 'Lord/Lady of the East' (Dongjun) at first might seem to refer to the sun god, but this hypothesis is cast into question by line 18 of this poem, in which the coming of the god blocks out the sun. Thus the god is more likely to be Xihe, who is closely related to the sun, either as the charioteer driving the sun on its journey or as the mother of the ten suns. It is thus possible that the divinity is feminine, in which case the title would better be rendered 'Lady of the East' to match the Lady of the Xiang River above. On the other hand, the speaker towards the end adopts the persona of the hunter roaming among the stars, which seems more likely to refer to a male divinity. The first half of the poem indeed seems to describe the sun's journey across the heavens from the perspective of its charioteer. The second part describes the ritual ceremony of worship devoted to the god. The final part of the poem, however, describes a different kind of celestial journey, more from the point of view of the shaman rising up above the human world than from that of the deity himself/herself.

20: The Wolf is a single red star southeast of the Well constellation. Schlegel finds its significance in that, according to Chinese hunting lore, the wolf's trail was particularly easy to mark out. Similarly, the Wolf rose early in the evening after the first month of summer, late April or May in the Western calendar (*Uranographie chinoise*, 430–2).

VIII. SIRE OF THE YELLOW RIVER

This figure appears in numerous historical and legendary sources, sometimes identified with the rain god Pingyi. There is evidence of human sacrifice being offered to him, including the offering of young unmarried women to be his brides. According to a legend referred to in 'Heavenly Questions', quatrain #35 (see below), he was shot at by the famous archer Yih. This story, though a piece of popular folklore probably attached to these figures *ex post facto*, still sheds much light on the lore of the ancient religious figure. The Sire of the Yellow River is a water god but also a figure of transformation, whose very nature is that of crossing over between the aquatic and terrestrial, the divine and the human, the human and the bestial.

IX. SPECTRE OF THE MOUNTAINS

The 'spectre' of this poem is literally a *gui*, a word typically used to refer to the returning spirits of the dead or ghosts. Here it seems more likely to be a minor divinity of the mountains. There have been numerous attempts to identify him or her more precisely, none of them authoritative. Another complexity of this poem is that it appears to present a kind of love triangle, with a goddess, 'young lord', and shaman-speaker. Since it is also the only one of the 'Nine Songs' to employ the term Lingxiu, 'Spirit Paragon', which we have seen in the 'Li sao', we may reasonably speculate that the song also involves the same kind of jealousy as in that poem, where an inferior competitor has replaced the hero in the affections of the love object/deity. Another noteworthy parallel appears in the final line of the poem with the compound *li you* 'meet with sorrow' which is very close to the title 'Li sao'. Thus, 'Spectre of the Mountains' should be seen as an important link between the 'Li sao' and the 'Nine Songs', relating romantic dialogue with the divine to political intrigue.

2: 'Lady lichen' trails down from tree trunks and branches in long clumps resembling human hair.

X. MARTYRS OF THE REALM

At first the topic of this poem seems to be quite unlike that of the other 'Nine Songs', but a closer examination shows that it is appropriate within the suite after all. In Warring States China, people worshipped various gods who protected against vengeance wreaked by the souls of people who had suffered violent deaths. The 'Nine Avowals: Rueful Remonstrance' also mentions one of these, the Honing God (*li shen*), a deity worshipped for protection against the ghosts of those who have died by violence. A similar god is also mentioned in bamboo strips from the Jiudian and Baoshan sites in Chu, where it is identified by the name Wuyi.

The greater contrast between this poem and the others in the 'Nine Songs' is in the realistic depiction here of the soldiers' final moments, a rare example of war poetry in early China.

11: Cf. line 11 in 'Lesser Controller of Destinies' above.

18: The *Elegies* employ both terms *hun* and *po* for the soul, but rarely use the two in conjunction as here, so it seems worth making the technical distinction that the first represents Yang energy, the second Yin energy. After death the former returns to heaven and the latter to earth, hence my free rendering as 'skysoul' and 'earthsoul'.

XI. RITE FOR SOULS

This piece seems to serve as a conclusion to the 'Nine Songs' as a whole. Unlike the other pieces, it is not dedicated to any particular deity. The title signifies that, like the previous song, 'Martyrs of the Realm', this one is also dedicated to the pacification of souls, but these are not necessarily the souls of the dead (see 'Summons of the Soul' below); rather it is a rite on behalf of all our souls, an offering to restore wholeness. These five lines thus fulfil the ritual expectations of the entire series.

HEAVENLY QUESTIONS

This poem may well be the earliest of any of the *Elegies*. Most strikingly, quatrains 56–61 refer to certain Shang ancestors whose names have been confirmed in modern studies of the oracle bone inscriptions, even though the Han commentary misinterprets them as referring to other figures. It is also worth remarking that the historical references in the poem seem to peter out around the 6th century BCE, suggesting that this poem may date even earlier than Qu Yuan himself.

Though the questions treat a disparate set of topics and the narrative thread sometimes seems to be lacking, all the disparate materials of the poem ultimately relate to a central question about the relationship between Heaven and Man. The poet repeatedly asks whether Heaven punishes the wicked and aids the virtuous, or not; and if not, is there some other logic or justification behind the course of events? Thus, while some scholars have suggested that the questions in the poem are merely rhetorical or originally accompanied by fixed answers, it seems more likely that they are open-ended. In this sense it is closest to the spirit of the Book of Job: 'What is the Almighty, that we should serve him? and what profit should we have, if we pray unto him?' There are also numerous parallels for this interrogative mode, particularly the cosmological speculations at the beginning of the poem, to be found in the Vedic and Zoroastrian hymns.

Partly because of its age, and also because of the enigmatic nature of the text itself, which consists entirely of cryptic questions, the poem is exceptionally difficult to read or translate. My translation has relied heavily on the rigorous commentaries of modern Chinese scholars, above all You Guoen, Jiang Liangfu, and Huang Linggeng. Because of the strict organization into independent quatrains, notes are provided by quatrain number rather than line number.

The initial *yue* 'it was said', which normally indicates reported speech, is a formal usage also found in the *Book of Documents* and other ancient texts, and one of the linguistic features indicating an early date of the poem.

#2: The second half of this quatrain is closely related to the third chapter of *Huainanzi*, describing the nature of the cosmos 'Before Heaven and Earth were formed'.

#3: According to an early source, Yin, Yang, and Heaven cannot produce life independently, but all three must work in conjunction. See *Guliang zhuan*, Duke Zhuang, year 3 (*Shisanjing zhushu* edition, 5.6b).

#5: The Eight Pillars are apparently those placed below the earth (not supporting heaven). The Southeast is said in the *Huainanzi* (1.58) to have been truncated by the mighty Gonggong, who warred with Qu Yuan's ancestor Zhuanxu. But see also quatrain 18 and note below.

#6: In ancient Chu cosmology, Heaven was said to be divided into nine horizontal layers stacked vertically upon one another.

#7: The Twelve Stations are the twelve regions of the sky through which the sun passes on its course—the elliptic—and which in turn correspond to the twelve months. The stars are arrayed into the twenty-eight mansions.

#9: The 'nocturnal radiance' of the moon was associated with the growth and decline of the human soul (in particular the *po*, the earthsoul). The 'rabbit perceived' *gutu* has been interpreted in various ways, and might instead refer to a toad in the moon, but the matter is not settled.

#10: Though Lady Tangent seems to be a celestial or astrological deity here, her name is shared with that of Ao's wife in quatrain 54 below and I translate them identically (it is not an unusual phenomenon for mythical figures to recur in different stories and historical periods). But the myth referenced here is uncertain. The Nine Sons were eventually identified with the Tail constellation, representing the tail of the Dark Dragon in the eastern quadrant of the sky (see *Shi ji*, 27.1298). So Lady Tangent seems to be another name for this same constellation of which the Nine Sons form a part.

There are various interpretations of 'Sire of Might' (Boqiang), but the Han commentary's explanation that he is a god for those who have died by violence, just like the recipient of 'Martyrs of the Realm' in the 'Nine Songs', is a plausible one. Corresponding to the Tail constellation of Lady Tangent, he represents the neighbouring Winnow constellation. Thus this quatrain opposes mythic representatives of feminine fertility and masculine violence.

#11: The Horn Portal is the answer to the question above—as the Gate of Heaven, its opening and closing correspond to the onset and departure of daylight. It is the first of seven constellations composing the Dark Dragon, the eastern quadrant of the sky. Maspero argues that this quatrain is not trivial but poses a subtle problem of astronomy (in his review of Conrady and Erkes, 64).

#12: Gun, father of the sage-king Yu, is a shadowy figure in early mythology, and although the *Elegies* affirm his importance, neither they nor other early sources provide enough information to resolve these questions today. According to the *Documents*, the officials who appointed him to stop the floods were the personified Four Marchmounts of the four cardinal directions.

#13: This episode is not mentioned in other early sources. Commentators hypothesize either that Gun was aided by these animals in the dyke's construction, or that the dyke was somehow modelled on these animals. A later source tells us that: 'Yu exhausted his strength in cutting dykes and ditches and in conducting the courses of rivers and levelling mounds. The yellow dragon dragged its tail in front of him, while the dark tortoise carried green mud on its back behind him' (see Birrell, *Chinese Mythology*, 242).

#14: Gun's death at Plume Mountain is mentioned in the 'Li sao' as well (line 131). The *locus classicus* is in *Zuo zhuan*: 'Long ago when Yao executed Gun at Plume Mountain, his spirit was transformed into a yellow terrapin, and plunged into the Plume Abyss' (Duke Zhao, 7.7; cf. different translation in Durrant et al., *Zuo Tradition*, 1423). The text originally refers to a 'yellow bear', but this is more likely the *nai*, a mythical sea tortoise that recurs in ancient myth, hereafter rendered as 'terrapin'. The divination manual

Guicang reports that even after three years Gun's body did not decay, and that when cut with a Wu sword, he transformed into a yellow dragon (quoted in Guo Pu's commentary to *Shanhai jing jiaozhu*, 18.396, n. 4). There were also other myths regarding the birth of Yu prevalent in early China: see Allan, *Buried Ideas*, 153–5.

#15: This quatrain follows directly from the previous one to introduce Gun's son Yu.

#16: Yu is described in various sources as playing a pivotal role in establishing the geography of China, not least the 'Tribute of Yu' in the *Book of Documents*.

#17: Yu is supposed to have had help from a dragon in measuring out the land and rivers. See *Classic of Mountains and Seas*: 'Responding Dragon lives at the South Pole. He killed the gods Jest Much and Boast Father. But then Responding Dragon could not go back up to the sky. That is why down on earth there are so many droughts. When there is a drought, people make an image of Responding Dragon, and then they receive a heavy rainfall' (Birrell, 14.162).

#18: This event is referred to already in quatrain 5 above. There is a myth that the earth collapsed because of the violent contest of Gonggong and Zhuanxu, but Lin Geng points out (193) that it does not appear in pre-Qin texts, only in *Huainanzi*, and suggests instead that this line is descriptive of lightning. 'Kang Hui' is identified in the Han commentary as an alternative name for Gonggong, but may actually be an alliterative compound (see Tang Bingzheng, *Chuci leigao*, 291).

In context, the whole quatrain may imply that it was Gun's fault the topography of the earth was transformed. Often the organization of the poem is questioned by scholars who even attempt to rearrange it. But here there is a subtle and very effective transition from the efforts of Gun and Yu to control the flood, to the geographical arrangement that resulted.

#19: I take these Nine Continents as continents of the world, not the immediate provinces of the central plain (as in the *Book of Documents*). The rivers do not overflow, apparently, because there is a bottomless abyss into which they keep pouring, as mentioned in *Liezi* (see Graham, *The Book of Lieh-tzŭ*, 5.97).

#20: The *Huainanzi* provides potential answers to these questions: 'The expanse within the four seas measures 28,000 *li* from east to west and 26,000 *li* from south to north' (see Major et al., *The Huainanzi*, 4.155). The same passage provides information relevant to the succeeding quatrains as well.

#21: The 'Tiered Palisade' and 'Hanging Gardens' are both mythical sites within the Kunlun Mountains at the centre of the world.

#22: The Gates of the Four Directions are described in *Huainanzi*, where the answer seems to be the wind from the Broken Mountain. As with the preceding quatrain, see Major et al., *Huainanzi*, 4.156.

#23: I have inverted the order of the second and third lines of this quatrain to create an ABAB rhyme in keeping with the remainder of the poem. The Torch Dragon is a deity providing constant illumination. For Xihe, charioteer of the sun, compare 'Nine Songs: Lord of the East'; for 'Dimming Wood', see also 'Li sao', line 195.

#24: The stone forest, as well as the nine-headed serpent in stanza 26, are alluded to in conjunction in Zuo Si's 'Wu Capital Rhapsody' (see *Wen xuan* 5.225; tr. Knechtges, 1:411–13). Zuo Si's use of the images suggests that they were pure fantasy to him: 'Though there be a stone forest rugged and steep, | Each warrior would willingly bare his arm and reduce it to rubble. | Though there be a great nine-headed serpent, | All would gladly lift their feet and stomp it to the ground.'

#25: For the 'terrapin', see quatrain 14 above. Though this question remains obscure, it seems to refer to an episode involving water deities, and may also relate to the story of Yu handling the flood (see quatrain 13 above).

#26: The monstrous *hui* is glossed as a kind of snake, so it seems appropriate to use the term 'hamadryad', a synonym for the king cobra. Cf. 'Summons to the Soul', line 41. Note that in early China the question 'what place is without death' is not a fanciful one, considering the fad for 'immortality-seeking'. See e.g. *Classic of Mountains and Seas*: 'The Neverdie folk are to its east. Its people are black and they live to a great age. They never die. One author says they are east of the borechest country' (Birrell, 6.110).

#27: For details on the legendary snake see again *Classic of Mountains and Seas*: 'The Big Snake eats elephants and after three years it disgorges their bones. Gentlemen take a dose of this snake so they will never have heart disease or illnesses of the belly' (Birrell, 10.136).

#28: Blackwater and Triperil are place names attested in the *Classic of Mountains and Seas*. They figure in the 'Tribute of Yu' chapter of the *Classic of Documents* as well, where the Blackwater is identified as the western boundary of the realm, and said to flow past Mount Triperil (see Legge, *Shoo King*, 123, 125). The Han commentary says that *xuanzhi* is another mountain whose name I have translated loosely as 'Mystic Base'.

#29: These mermen are identified in the *Classic of Mountains and Seas*: 'there the people have a human face, hands, and feet, but a fish's body' (trans. Birrell, 12.147). Another proposal is that the term refers to the fish-like pangolin. My 'griffins' are also described in the *Classic of Mountains and Seas*: 'There is a bird here which looks like a chicken but it has a white head and rat's feet with tiger claws. . . . It also eats humans' (trans. Birrell, 4.63). Yih shot down nine of the ten suns, and the corresponding nine suncrows all died. However, the story is only presented in fragmentary form in the earliest sources. See e.g. *Huainanzi*: 'Yao therefore commanded Yih [the Archer] to slaughter Chisel Tusk in the water meadows of Chouhua, to kill Nine Gullet on the banks of the Xiong River, to shoot down Typhoon in the wilds of Greenhill, upward to shoot the ten suns and downward to kill Chayu, to chop Long Snake in two at Dongting Lake, and to capture Mound Pig in Mulberry Forest. The multitudes of people all were happy and established Yao as Son of Heaven' (trans. Major et al., 8.276). This is a central origin story elaborated on in the mythology of the Shang (see Allan, *The Shape of the Turtle*, 36ff.). I write the name of the Archer as Yih rather than Yi to distinguish from the ruler Yi mentioned below.

#30: For the verb 'to descend', cf. 'Li sao', line 4; in the *Elegies*, gods and men both arrive upon the earth by descending from heaven. This episode is also described in more positive terms in the *Book of Documents* ('Yi and Ji' chapter), where Yu says, 'Do not be like the haughty Zhu of Dan, who found his pleasure only in indolence and dissipation, and pursued a proud oppression. . . . I took warning from his course. When I married in Tushan, I remained with my wife only the days *xin, ren, gui*, and *jia*. When my son Qi was wailing and weeping, I did not regard him, but kept planning with all my might my labour on the land' (see Legge, *Shoo King*, 84–5).

There are various identifications of Tushan, 'Mount Soil' and of the lady from this place. Rather than investigate its geographical location, I take it as a symbolic location, since *tu* can have a neutral sense of 'route' but more commonly means 'to corrupt, defile'. For a vivid example of the pejorative usage, see *Zhuangzi*, where Bo Yi and Shu Qi assert 'Rather than ally with the Zhou and thereby besmirch (*tu*) our persons, it would be better to shun them and thereby preserve the purity of our conduct' (Mair, *Wandering on the Way*, 28.296). To preserve something of the ambiguity I use the comparable 'soil'. Cf. 'Lady Tangent'.

Whereas with Mount Soil this sense is not necessarily obvious, the 'mulberry' in the following line is an unambiguous sex symbol, because mulberry groves were employed as the sites of romantic trysts in early China. See Jean-Pierre Diény, *Pastourelles et magnanarelles: essai sur un thème littéraire chinois*.

#31: According to *Lüshi chunqiu*, Yu left his bride to stop the flood only four days after consummating the marriage. This is recorded in a fragment not part of the received text (Knoblock and Riegel, *Annals of Lü Buwei*, 674).

#32: My interpretation here follows the detailed analysis of You Guoen (*Tianwen zuanyi*, 193–4). Qi was the product of Yu's aforementioned union. He is said to have murdered Yi, Yu's minister to whom Yu entrusted the succession, in order to take the throne. Though early sources do not present a detailed account, these events are mentioned in the *Bamboo Annals* and elsewhere (see *Guben Zhushu jinian jizheng*, 2). This is one of the archetypal conflicts between 'the heir and the sage' discussed by Sarah Allan in her seminal study by that name. The questions here must refer to a version of the story that has not been preserved in other texts, so both the text itself and all the commentarial interpretations seem garbled.

#33: This quatrain apparently builds on the topics introduced in the preceding one, asking about the motives for Qi's usurpation, in spite of the benevolence of both Yi and Yu.

#34: The violent birth of Qi is not well attested, but can be found in at least one early source: 'Yu married the lady of Mount Soil, and stopped the flood waters. He opened up mount Xuanyuan, and was transformed into a bear. When the lady of Mount Soil saw this, she regretted it and departed. When she reached the base of high Mount Song, she was transformed into a stone. Yu said, "Return my child." The stone cracked open on the north side and gave birth to Qi.' This is from a fragment of the Mohist text *Sui Chaozi*, quoted in *Yishi*, 12.142.

#35: Yih the Archer was the ruler of the Youqiong people, here referred to as the Yee (sometimes a generic term for foreign peoples in northeastern China). Archer Yih defeated the Xia people when they were ruled by the imprudent ruler Taikang, thus inspiring the composition of the 'Song of the Five Brothers' in the pseudo-Old Text *Book of Documents* (Legge, *Shoo King*, 153–6). There may also be some confusion of mythology here. The term 'Sire of the Yellow River' (Hebo) seems in the earliest sources to be the name of a tribe competing with the Shang people, though later a deity and consort of the goddess of the Luo River, Fu Fei.

#36: This quatrain continues to discuss Archer Yih.

#37: For Han Zhuo see also 'Li sao', line 15. Pure Fox seems to be the name of one of the wives of Archer Yih whom Han Zhuo took for himself after he had overthrown Archer Yih by wiles and deceit.

#38: The *Zuo zhuan* includes the relevant line 'Archer Yih moved from Chu to Qiongshi [Desperation Rock] and, with the support of the Xia people, took over Xia rule' (Xiang 4, trans. Durrant et al., *Zuo Tradition*, 917; noted by Xu Wenjing in *Guancheng shuoji*, 16.280). The episode of Gun's transformation is mentioned briefly in *Zuo zhuan*, Zhao 7 (trans. Durrant et al., *Zuo Tradition*, 1423).

#39: The first line describes land crops and the second water plants. Xu Wenjing provides a novel and clear interpretation of this quatrain: Gun could plant only by the side of the water after he had been removed to Plume Abyss. His wife was named Xiu Ji, and she helped him in his hardship. See *Guancheng shuoji*, 16.281.

#40: The goddess Chang'e was said to have stolen a magical elixir from Archer Yih, and fled with it to the moon where she still lives. For this stanza and the next one we may ignore the fanciful interpretation of the Han commentary regarding certain immortals. That the subject is instead Chang'e was proposed by Ding Yan (see *Chuci Tianwen jian*, 34a/b; also You Guoen, *Tianwen zuanyi*, 243).

#41: The Han commentary identifies this with a story about Prince Qiao, who after death was transformed into a great bird that cried out and then flew away. But it is better to take it at its surface meaning, following the excavated bamboo-slip text 'Fan wu liu xing' (All things change their forms), quoted in Huang Linggeng, *Chuji jijiao*, 4.579, which asks about the general reasons that living beings cry out and then perish in turn. See also

Sukhu, *Songs of Chu*, 62; for full English translation, see Wang Zhongjiang, *Order in Early Chinese Excavated Texts*, 169–72.

#42: Pingyi is the Rain God, and the Thunder God, Flying Lian, was described by Guo Pu as a 'dragon bird with bird body and deer head' (note to *Shi ji*, 117.3034). According to some sources this is simply a monster (see Knechtges, *Wen xuan*, 1:136, note to line 330 of the 'Western Capital Rhapsody'). There has clearly been conflation of different myths in these sources, and I take the point of this quatrain to be rather in a query about the mysteries underlying these traditions. The deer god with two bodies seems similar to the strange deities depicted in the Zidanku Chu silk manuscript.

#43: For the sea turtles who carry continents on their backs, see the *Liezi* (Graham, *Book of Lieh-tzǔ*, 97).

Yu Yue argues that the source of land-crossing ships is the Confucian *Analects*: 'Yi was skilful at archery, and Ao could move a boat along upon the land, but neither of them died a natural death. Yu and Ji personally wrought at the toils of husbandry, and they became possessors of the kingdom.' See 'Du Chuci', 8a; *Analects* 14/6 (Legge translation, *Chinese Classics*, Vol. 1, 273).

#44: Beginning with this quatrain, we enter a sequence of questions all about a related series of events. For the strong man Ao, son of Han Zhuo, see 'Li sao', line 153, above, and Glossary. This quatrain refers to the story of the strong man Ao committing adultery with Lady Tangent. Shaokang is said to have killed Ao while hunting.

#45: This Lady Tangent, Ao's sister-in-law, is said by most commentators to be different from the goddess mentioned in quatrain 10. The same phenomenon occurs frequently, though, in part because these stories may not have originally been fixed in particular historical periods, much of which seems to be an artefact of Han scholars' labours. The story referred to here seems to be that Shaokang first attacked Ao at night and accidentally killed Lady Tangent; only later did he succeed in killing Ao, as referred to in the previous quatrain.

#46: Zhenxun was a kingdom whose rulers were of the same clan as the Xia royal house. The Xia ruler Xiang took refuge there, so Ao attacked them and killed him (see *Zuo zhuan*, Lord Ai, Year 1; Durrant et al., *Zuo Tradition*, 1835). This is apparently a metaphor, like 'ship of state'.

#47: Tang Bingzheng points out that 'Mount Meng' here is probably the same as Mount Min (*Chuci leigao*, 298–300). According to the *Bamboo Annals*, 'Jie attacked Mount Min, and at Mount Min they offered him two women, named Wan and Yan' (*Guben Zhushu jinian jizheng*, 17). It is interesting also to note the thematic repetition of the 'two brides', as in the princesses of the Xiang River.

#48: Shun was born at Yaw and so obtained his clan name from the place. Both Shun's family plotting against him, and the propriety of not informing Shun's parents are discussed in *Mencius* (trans. D. C. Lau, 5A.100).

Mencius explains that this was the only way that Shun could have been married, and also explains Shun's attitude to his brother Xiang. In a more rudimentary way, this quatrain addresses the same complex moral dilemmas as the more extensive treatment in *Mencius*. However, Huang Linggeng also points out that there is little evidence for this story outside of *Mencius*, and it may not agree with the source of this question (*Chuci yu jianbo wenxian*, 255).

#49: The Han commentary explains this quatrain by reference to the story of how Jizi criticized the extravagant final king of Shang, Zhow, for using ivory chopsticks, saying that this was a slippery slope: 'If he makes ivory chopsticks, then this will inevitably lead to using goblets of jade; after making the goblets, then he will long for exotic beasts from far-off lands to ride. The ruin of the imperial carriage and palaces begins from this, and they cannot be revived' (see *Shi ji*, 38.1609). In the event Jizi's prophecy was right and Zhow would later build a ten-storey tower decorated with precious stones. Yet it is also possible to understand this as an abstract question about a general issue: how drastic transformations can occur through gradual accumulation over time rather than a unique event.

#50: The Han commentary identifies the subject of the first couplet as Fu Xi, but Zhou Gongchen points out that there are several quatrains, such as 52 below, where the main subject is only identified in the latter couplet, so the former could also be referring to Nü Wa (*Li sao caomu shi*, 3.39b). There are various accounts of Nü Wa's form but they frequently involve her being half-snake. The insertion of Nü Wa here seems like a digression, but the next quatrain does continue along the theme of the bestiality of human character and bodies. There is also an echo of quatrain 42 above.

#51: Shun's younger half-brother Xiang 'The Elephant' and their father Gusou 'The Blind Old Man' together attempted to murder Shun, as apparently referred to more obliquely in quatrain 48 above.

#52: This quatrain is asking about Shun and his two sons Yigou and Jili, according to Liu Mengpeng (see discussion in You Guoen, *Tianwen zuanyi*, 290–2). Huang Linggeng elaborates on this new interpretation (*Chuci zhangju shuzheng*, 4.1136–9), suggesting the two men are Shun's son Shangjun (also known as Shujun) and the highlord Dan Zhu, Yao's son who did not inherit the throne. The *Classic of Mountains and Seas* mentions separately that Shun was buried at Mount Cangwu along with Dan Zhu, and also with his son Shujun (Birrell, 10.135, 15.167 respectively).

Thus, a series of questions relating to Shun's ascendancy and rule conclude with this quatrain interrogating the limits of his rule and the succession.

#53: According to the Han commentary, the quatrain as a whole is about Tang's minister Yi Yin, counsellor to Tang and later Shang kings, who is not explicitly mentioned till the next quatrain, there under the name of Yi Zhi. Some commentators understand 'Hou Di' here as the Lord of Heaven rather than Tang, but since Di is mentioned again in the following quatrain, it is much more straightforward to understand it as Tang in both cases. Or more precisely, in fact, Di refers *both* to the Lord of Heaven and the Sovereign Emperor of all Under Heaven, the Son of Heaven, so this is a distinction without a difference.

#54: Tiao is short for Mingtiao, where Jie, wicked final king of Xia, was exiled by Tang, founder of the Shang. See *Shi ji*, 2.88; Nienhauser, *Grand Scribe's Records*, 1:38.

#55: Jian Di is said in the *Shi ji* to be the younger concubine of Highlord Ku, mythic Shang ruler. She swallowed the egg of the Dark Bird, and then gave birth to Xie, ancestor of the Shang people. See *Songs* 303: 'Heaven bade the dark bird | To come down and bear the Shang, | Who dwelt in the lands of Yin so wide. | Of old God bade the warlike Tang | To partition the frontier lands . . .' (trans. Waley, *Book of Songs*, 320); cf. Allan, *The Shape of the Turtle*, 38–41, and Chen Zhi, 'A Study of the Bird Cult of the Shang People'. Jian Di belonged to the Yousong Clan, as in 'Li sao', line 238.

#56: The Youyi Clan were an ancient people located in modern Hu county, Shaanxi. This story is also mentioned in the *Bamboo Annals*: 'Prince Hai of the Yin was a guest with the Yi clan when he committed adultery. Mianchen, the King of the Youyi clan, murdered him and let go his oxen. Thus the ruler of Yin, Jia Wei, borrowed an army from the Hebo to attack the Youyi Clan, destroyed them, and killed their ruler Mianchen' (quoted in the commentary to *Shanhai jing jiaozhu*, 14.351). It seems that the following series of quatrains up to 60 and possibly 61 all refer to this story, though they refer to a number of plot details that have not survived in other texts and remain somewhat mysterious.

#57: Some premodern scholars identified these lines as referring to Shun's pacification of the Miao Clan in the 'Da Yu mo' chapter of the *Book of Documents* (see Legge, *Shoo King*, 62), but this may be a forged *guwen* text. Traditional commentaries do not offer convincing explanations of these lines, which seem to refer to another, unknown story about Wang Hai.

#58: According to the *Bamboo Annals*, Wang Hai's son Shangjia Wei attacked the Youyi in revenge (see note to quatrain 56 above). I take it that this quatrain is referring loosely to these events, though the syntax is obscure.

#59: Heng was Wang Hai's younger brother. The story behind this quatrain is obscure and interpretations vary widely even today.

#60: The former couplet refers again to Wang Hai's son Shangjia Wei. Wang Guowei and others have identified Youdi with Youyi, since the *Bamboo Annals* records Shangjia Wei's defeat of the Youyi. Shangjia Wei is also praised in a recently excavated text, the *Bao xun*. See Allan, *Buried Ideas*, 285–8.

For the owls flocking in the shrubbery, see *Songs* 141/2: 'There are brambles by the cemetery gate; | With owls roosting upon them' (my translation). This is said to be an accusation by a lady against an unwanted suitor, pointing out that even if no one else is there to watch indecent behaviour, the owls will be witness to it.

#61: This quatrain is taken by some commentators as referring back to the story of Shun and Xiang. While this is possible, it would be a needless repetition. I take it as potentially referring both to Wang Hai's family *and* to Shun's. In other words, it links together these disparate threads by posing a general question about the apparently inevitable conflict between brothers.

#62: With this quatrain we turn from the remote ancestors of the Shang dynasty to its founder Tang. Note that the progression also follows the parallel that Tang, like Wang Hai, is encountering an alien clan. The ancient kingdom of the Youshen Clan was in the region of modern Kaifeng, Henan province, and this episode is described in the *Annals of Lü Buwei* (trans. Knoblock and Riegel, 307).

#63: This passage refers to the Moses-like origin story of Yi Yin, also recounted in the same passage of the *Annals of Lü Buwei* (see previous note). He was discovered by a girl of the Shen Clan harvesting silkworms from the mulberry tree inside a hollow tree. On the consort of Tang, see also Kinney, *Exemplary Women of Early China*, 6.

#64: According to the *Shi ji* (2.88), Tang was imprisoned at the Terrace of Xia by Jie. Whether 'double springs' is the same place is unclear. Presumably the answer to the latter question is Yi Yin, Tang's great counsellor. Mori Yasutarō suggested that Tang was originally a sun deity, and the complex myths surrounding him were later rationalized into straightforward political lineages (see *Kōtei densetsu*, 13–29).

#65: This quatrain seems to refer to King Wu's founding of the Zhou and conquest of Shang at the battle of Muye. It relates to the depiction of the same events in *Songs* 236/8, which concludes: 'The captain was Shang-fu [Taigong Wang]; | Like an eagle he uprose. | Ah, that King Wu | Swiftly fell upon Great Shang, | Who before daybreak begged for a truce' (Waley, *Book of Songs*, 230). You Guoen cites Liu Mengpeng's helpful explanation: one of the good omens for King Wu's conquest of Shang was a fire that fell from Heaven and transformed into a crow (or a hawk, in the New Text *Documents*: see *Shi ji*, 4.121n.).

#66: Lord Dan, literally 'Uncle Dan', was the younger brother of King Wu and is more commonly known as the Duke of Zhou. This quatrain may refer implicitly to the story that King Wu personally decapitated Zhow's body and hung the head up on a flagpole (recorded in *Yi Zhou shu huijiao jizhu*, 36.346).

#67: This quatrain may be the clearest statement of the theme of the poem. Heavenly favour is granted to some, whether deservedly or not; when it is revoked, inevitably, what is the cause?

#68: Regarding the difficult term *jiyi* 'striking on both flanks', Huang Linggeng demonstrates the frequency of this term in contemporary military discourse (see *Chuci yu jianbo wenxian*, 270).

#69: According to the *Bamboo Annals*, King Zhao in the nineteenth year of his reign set out on a journey southward, where he came upon a rhinoceros and startled the pheasants and hares (see Legge, 'Annals of the Bamboo Books', in *Shoo King*, 149). According to another early source, in Chu he drowned after the lacquer boat he had received from the local people dissolved in the river (see *Diwang shiji*, 5.44, as quoted in *Shi ji*, 4.134n.).

#70: King Mu of Zhou, historically the fifth king of Zhou, was famous for his journeys to distant lands, and even so far as to see the Spirit Mother of the West, which are recorded in the mythic narrative *Mu tianzi zhuan* (Biography of King Mu). For this quatrain cf. 'Li sao', line 192.

#71: King You ['benighted'] was the final ruler of the Western Zhou. His unrestrained passion for femme fatale Bao Si led to his downfall. She was the adopted daughter of a man sentenced to execution, who offered her up to the king in exchange for a pardon. On Bao Si, see Kinney, *Exemplary Women of Early China*, 138–9.

According to *Accounts of the States*, King You's fall was anticipated by a children's ditty popular under the previous reign: 'With mulberry bow and willow quiver, | That will surely mark the end of the Zhou state!' A married couple were seen selling precisely these items, and they were captured and dragged through the streets (see *Guoyu jijie*, 16.473).

#72: Duke Huan of Qi was famous for convening alliances with the other states (not necessarily nine times, but frequently). The biography of Guan Zhong in the *Shi ji* mentions that he had helped Duke Huan to 'convene the feudal lords nine times', a kind of formula also used to describe the achievements of other leaders during the Warring States era (*Shi ji*, 62.2131). Yet his virtuous efforts at leadership and diplomacy ended in failure; Duke Huan perished, along with his wise advisor, after four wicked retainers revolted.

#73: This quatrain refers to the episodes of Bi Gan and Sire Mei, Zhow's loyal counsellors whom he executed, and who are mentioned by name in the two succeeding quatrains 74 and 75, respectively.

#74: This quatrain presents us with two opposing models of behaviour: Bi Gan protested at Zhow's corruption and was executed in a particularly grisly fashion, while Lei Kai was one of the flattering ministers of Zhow.

#75: Sire Mei and Master Ji were two ministers of Zhow, both of whom protested at Zhow's wickedness. But Sire Mei did so directly, and was executed in this gruesome way, while Master Ji feigned madness and survived to serve the Zhou—an unforgettable lesson for Chinese intellectuals throughout history. This quatrain provides a devastating conclusion to the whole section on the founding of the Zhou dynasty.

#76: This quatrain refers to the story of the mythic ancestor Hou Li, 'Lord Millet', and seems to correspond to *Songs* 245, which describes his virgin birth: 'She who in the beginning gave birth to the people, | This was Jiang Yuan. | How did she give birth to the people? | Well she sacrificed and prayed | That she might no longer be childless. | She trod on the big toe of God's footprint, | Was accepted and got what she desired. | Then in reverence, then in awe, | She gave birth, she nurtured; | And this was

Hou Ji.' In the third stanza, though, it describes how he was abandoned: 'Indeed, they put it on the cold ice; | But the birds covered it with their wings. | The birds at last went away, | And Hou Ji began to wail' (Waley, *Book of Songs*, 244–5).

#77: The Han commentary explains this quatrain with respect to King Wu's conquest of Shang, but Yu Yue provides a better explanation, relating these lines to the birth of Hou Ji as described in *Songs* 245/2, which might literally be translated: 'When he [Hou Ji] thus made manifest his numinous power, | The God on High was not at ease'.

#78: This seems to refer to King Wen of Zhou and the conquest of Shang, since King Wen's personal name was Chang. Mount Qi [my 'Tangent' in the name of Lady Tangent above] was a sacred site in the founding myth of the Zhou, as the place where Gugong Danfu and Jiang Yuan come to settle in *Songs* 237.

#79: According to the Han commentary, the first couplet refers to the settling at Mount Qi, and the second to Zhow's concubine Da Ji, killed during the Zhou conquest.

#80: The Prince of the West is King Wen of Zhou. This story is reported only in the *Diwang shiji* (5.40): Zhow tricked King Wen into eating his own son, in order to show that no sage would commit such a cannibalistic act. King Wen then protested to God on high.

#81: This quatrain refers to the well-known origin story of Lü Wang, hired to serve as chief advisor to King Wen when he was working as a butcher. This episode, so inspiring throughout the centuries to unappreciated scholars with unsanitary jobs, is referred to also in 'Li sao', lines 293–4.

#82: This quite straightforward quatrain enquires about King Wu's motivation for going into battle against the Shang. Quatrain 80 above has just provided one indication of an answer. According to the *Shi ji*, King Wu brought the spirit tablet of his father along with him and proclaimed that he was fighting on behalf of his father. But according to *Huainanzi*, he brought the actual corpse of his father. The term *shi* is ambiguous here between the two possibilities.

#83: The quatrain is more than usually obscure. The premodern commentaries following Han commentary generally relate it to Prince Shensheng of Jin, but no name is mentioned in the text. I follow instead Xu Wenjing's interpretation (*Guancheng shuoji*, 16.291) relating these lines to the story of Guan Shuxian, King Wu's younger brother, which keeps us in the same approximate period as the preceding and following lines. Guan Shuxian rebelled against King Cheng and was defeated and slain by the Duke of Zhou.

#84: As in quatrain 80, Shou should be understood as the style name of Zhow.

#85: The minister of Tang was Yi Yin, personal name Zhi, who figured prominently in section V of the poem above. The quatrain seems to ask why he was elevated to such a prominent role.

#86: These lines refer to Shou Meng (?–561), grandfather of the famous King of Wu, Helu, originally Sir Guang. The succession was contested among Shou Meng's grandsons, and Helu ultimately won the throne by murdering his cousin in cold blood, using a dagger concealed inside a fish (see *Shi ji*, 31.1463). Being 'cast away' refers to the fact that Sir Guang was the son of Shou Meng's eldest son, and so felt himself to be the rightful heir to the throne, but instead the throne was occupied by his cousin, King Liao, who was the son of Shou Meng's third son.

#87: Peng Keng is Peng Zu. He may also be the same person as the Peng of Peng Xian in the 'Li sao'. He was said to have cooked pheasant soup for Yao, bringing him longevity. Peng Zu himself was said to have lived 767 years, his lifespan encompassing the Xia, Shang, and Zhou dynasties. He still felt regret, though, because he could not live even longer.

#88: According to the Han commentary, the bees and butterflies represent the neighbouring tribes of the Man and Yi joining together to drive out the wicked King Li of Zhou (r. ?–*c.*841 BCE). The Han commentary then adds the amusing story that 'central' stands for a place known for its many-headed vipers who contest the crops.

It seems to have been Ma Qichang (1855–1930) who resolved the crux by pointing out that *gong* is not an adverb 'together' but rather a proper name, Earl Gong, personal name He (*Qu fu wei*, A.37a). According to the *Bamboo Annals*, it was Earl Gong who governed in place of the incompetent King Li (see Legge, *Shoo King*, 154). The quatrain also poses questions of greater generality: why should the king be upset if the lesser lords choose to collaborate rather than to undermine one another? And if it comes to a contest, can the lesser states (paltry as bees or ants) survive even while joined together?

#89: The commentary by Li Shan to the medieval anthology *Wen xuan* quotes a source called the *Gu shi kao* to provide the legend of Bo Yi and Shu Qi, the mythic Shang loyalists who starved themselves on Mount Shouyang (located south of modern Yongji city, Shanxi) rather than submit to Zhou. According to the legend, they only starved after a woman came to them and told them even the vetch they were harvesting belonged to Zhou, and so they could no longer consume even that (*Wen xuan*, 54.2438n.). Another source mentions that Heaven first sent a white deer to nourish them when they had been starving for seven days (*Diaoyu ji*, 12.29). For both these points, see Wen Yiduo, *Chuci jiaobu*, 55–6.

The 'winding currents' may refer to the rough waters of the Yellow River. Mount Shouyang, where Bo Yi and Shu Qi took refuge, is located near the sharp eastward bend in the Yellow River later known as 'Yellow River's Crook' (see Mao Qiling, *Tianwen buzhu*, 18b).

It is worth noting the coincidence that 'gathering vetch' is also the title of *Songs* 167, a moving poem about soldiers separated from their families while on an expedition.

#90: The Han commentary offers an explanation of this quatrain based on a story about the Duke of Qin and his younger brother Qian. It has no other extant source, but corresponds in part to *Zuo zhuan*, Duke Zhao, 1.8a, which mentions that Qian fled to Jin with one thousand chariots: 'Qian of Qin had been a favourite son of Lord Huan [r. 604–577] and was like a second ruler under Lord Jing [r. 576–537]. Their mother said to Qian, "If you do not depart, I fear that you will be sent away" (Durrant et al., *Zuo Tradition*, 1319). In the fifth month, on the *guimao* day (25), when Qian went to Jin, his chariots numbered one thousand.'

None of this fully explains the rabid dog, but Huang Linggeng cites (*Chuci zhangju shuzheng*, 4.1247) a proverb quoted in *Zuo zhuan*, Duke Ai, 12.4a: 'When a tall tree dies, there is nothing it will not fall upon; when the best dog in the domain goes rabid, there is no one it will not bite' (Durrant et al., *Zuo Tradition*, 1909). The proverb applies to the case of Qian as well, since he is identified as a talented and popular young man, and for that very reason a threat to his older brother.

#91: There are various proposals identifying the subject matter here. The Han commentary and Jiang Liangfu both see this section as returning to contemporary circumstances, or at least recent Chu history (*Chuci buzhu*, 4.117; *Chongding Qu Yuan fu jiaozhu*, 3.318–19). The latter interpretation seems to comport well with the literary effect of the bolt of lightning, which has not been identified as a historical allusion. In other words, the quatrain shifts the focus of the poem from heroes of the more remote past, especially the founders of Zhou, and towards the confrontations of Chu political history.

The theme of soldiers on campaign, longing to return home, is a common one in the *Songs*, as in 162/1: 'My four steeds are weary | The high road is very far. | Indeed, I long to come home; | But the king's business never ends. | My heart is sick and sad.' Trans. Waley, *Book of Songs*, 134.

#92: This quatrain might be inspired by an episode in *Zhuangzi* about a prince who took refuge underground. After three successive kings of the southern state of Yue were killed by their own subjects, it is said that: 'Prince Sou fled to the Cinnabar Caves, leaving the state of Yue without a ruler. The people searched for Prince Sou but could not find him, till finally they tracked him to the Cinnabar Caves. Prince Sou was unwilling to come out, but they smoked him out with mugwort and made him ride in the royal chariot. As Prince Sou held on to the straps to mount the chariot, he looked up to heaven and cried out, "A ruler! Oh, to be a ruler! Couldn't I alone have been spared from this?"' See Mair, *Wandering on the Way*, 28.286.

#93: Guang is the personal name of Helu, famous king of Wu who won the throne by murdering his uncle King Liao, and later led the state to its destruction by rival Yue. Before that, however, Wu established supremacy over Chu, invading its capital Ying in 506 BCE.

#94: Dou Bobi, the son of Chu king Ruo Ao (r. 790–764), had an adulterous liaison with a lady of Yun, which produced the son Ziwen, who became Lingyin, chief minister of Chu, from 664 to 637. But: 'Lady Yun had him abandoned at Meng Marsh. A tigress suckled him. When the Master of

Yun went hunting, he saw this and returned in fear. His wife told him what had happened, and he thus had the child brought back' (*Zuozhuan*, Xuan 4; Durrant et al., *Zuo Tradition*, 613). Ziwen's full name is Dou Guyutu, said to mean 'suckled by a tigress' in Chu dialect. The whole story is related at this point in the *Zuo zhuan* to provide the context for a ruinous rebellion by Ziwen's nephew Dou Jiao.

The 'tomb mounds' may refer to Wu Zixu's desecration of the tomb of King Ping of Chu during Wu's conquest of Chu (per Xu Wenjing).

#95: Du Ao (a.k.a. Xiong Jian, r. 676–675), briefly the ruler of Chu, attempted to kill his younger brother Xiong Hun and thereby eliminate a threat to his power. His brother escaped and later returned to usurp the throne from Du Ao and reign as King Cheng (r. 674–626). According to the standard chronology, both Du Ao and his younger brother were only small children when these events occurred, so the intrigues were presumably carried out in their names by advisors and regents. Decades later King Cheng himself was forced to abdicate and commit suicide. The poet concludes by asking yet again how it is that justice and virtue can be built upon a foundation of violence and betrayal.

NINE AVOWALS

The title of this suite of nine poems, 'Jiu zhang', could be interpreted simply as 'Nine Pieces [of Poetry]', but that would be a misleadingly bland title for a set of works that share a determination to assert the moral claims of the speaker in the face of a world of corruption. I follow instead the Han gloss of *zhang* as 'to illuminate, declare, avow', understanding the poems generally as being auto-biographical poems of self-expression. This suite contains some of the pieces most verifiably associated with Qu Yuan himself in the entire anthology: 'Lamenting Ying' and 'Embracing the Sand'. Both pieces are mentioned in Sima Qian's biography of Qu Yuan, and the latter is quoted in entirety therein. Yet neither the suite as a whole nor the individual poems are mentioned by Sima Qian, and several seem to postdate Qu Yuan considerably.

The nine poems are also composed in a variety of metres and are diverse in subject matter, though most resemble the 'Li sao' in being first-person narratives in the voice of a frustrated or exiled courtier, so they have frequently been employed as source materials for reconstructing Qu Yuan's biography. As with the 'Li sao', though, this procedure is hazardously circular. What unites all the 'Nine Avowals' is their collective affirmation of pride in the identity of the Quvian courtier: not necessarily Qu Ping himself, but also including later poets who model themselves on the hero of the 'Li sao'.

I. RUEFUL REMONSTRANCE

The title of this piece refers to two of the key and opposing themes of the *Elegies*: the poet's regret and ruefulness, on one hand, and the reproach to the sovereign on the other. The poem is more closely related to 'Li sao' in its overall structure than any of the other 'Nine Avowals' because it centres on a divination.

The pivotal, central section of the poem consists of the speech of the god in reply to the protagonist's query. Even though the content of the speech is not too startling, it is of great importance to the poem's overall structure and effect, since it provides a counterpoint, a separate voice speaking in dialogue with Qu Yuan. The divination here is directed towards the Li shen (my 'Honing God'), probably a god who protects those who died by violence, and who is well represented in excavated texts from Warring States Chu.

2: 'Convictions' translates *qing*, which is not simply 'feelings' but has a broader scope than any parallel English term.

6: The Five Elemental Deities are those of the four directions plus the centre, also corresponding to the Five Phases: Fu Xi, Zhurong, Shaohao (Sovereign of the West), Zhuanxu, and the Yellow Emperor. There is considerable debate in the precise identification of the Six Ancestral Powers, but Huang Linggeng shows that these refer to the ranking of sacrifices at the ancestral temple, constituting a collective term for the rites observed at the ancestral temple in honour of cosmological and ancestral divinities (*Chuci zhangju shuzheng*, 5.1271).

47: For the *li shen* (my 'Honing God', alternatively 'Whetstone God' or just 'God of Violence'), see also 'Nine Songs: Martyrs of the Realm' above; and *Zuo zhuan*, Zhao 7 (Durrant et al., *Zuo Tradition*, 1427).

53: 'Once scalded by the soup, you blow to cool even pickled meat' is apparently the Chinese equivalent of 'once bitten twice shy'.

64: This criticism of Gun for failing in spite of his virtues is similar to that of Lady Xu the Shamaness in 'Li sao', line 131. Gun was said to have failed in the task of flood-quelling assigned to him by the High God and so was punished and died.

67: Proverbial, as in *Zuozhuan*, Ding 13 (Durrant et al., *Zuo Tradition*, 1813).

82: Cf. 'Li sao', line 27: 'So I mingle lush fagara and dainty osmanthus.'

II. CROSSING THE RIVER

At first glance this poem seems to follow Qu Yuan's own story closely, as it traces a journey southward, referring to sites like E along the Yangtse River, and then other places on the Yuan and Xiang rivers further south of Chu, probably corresponding to the 'Jiangnan' region.

However, it would be unwise to read the narrative too literally. After all, the opening section of the poem presents the protagonist as a semi-divine hero with totemic possessions, and lines 9–12 describe a journey across the universe and assert the speaker to be on par with sun and moon.

10: 'Many-Faceted Majesty' refers to the ancient sage-king Shun, as in 'Li sao'. The 'Pleasance of Jasper' is the magnificent hunting park belonging to Shun in the lands of the immortals. With Mount Kunlun, these names identify the location as somewhere celestial.

12: These lines, echoed also in 'Nine Songs: Lord Amid the Clouds', were taken as emblematic of the aspirations and achievement of the *Elegies*: they form part of Liu An's appraisal of Qu Yuan, are quoted in Sima Qian's biography, and then are re-quoted continuously after that. As such they may be said to constitute a 'topos of celestial brilliance' in the *Elegies*.

14: The opening of this poem up to this line presents a different persona than most of the 'Nine Avowals', not the rejected courtier but a shaman hero more similar to the protagonist of 'Li sao'.

18: The Han commentary identifies Square Grove as a place name, but not its actual location. Jao Tsung-i points out that it may be a general term for a large forest (*Chuci dili kao*, A.122–4).

24: Both Wangzhu 'Crooked Bank' and Chenyang 'Stellar Yang' are proper place names with symbolic implications, located much further south than the places mentioned above. In other words, Qu had travelled westward from Lake Dongting, past Wangzhu, and then upstream along the Yuan River all the way to Chenyang.

40: The 'carriage-hailing madman' (Jieyu) is the famous 'madman of Chu' from *Analects*: 'Jieyu, the Madman of Chu, went past Confucius, singing: "Phoenix, oh Phoenix! | How is your virtue degenerated! As to the past, reproof is useless; but the future may still be provided against. Give up your vain pursuit. Give up your vain pursuit. Peril awaits those who now engage in affairs of government." Confucius alighted and wished to converse with him, but Jieyu hastened away, so that he could not talk with him.' See *Analects* 18/5 (trans. Legge, *Confucian Analects*, 332–3, slightly modified).

   Mulberry Door (Sang Hu) was one of a trio of eccentrics mentioned in *Zhuangzi*. After he died, his friends sang around his body without giving him a proper ritual burial. See Mair, *Wandering on the Way*, 60.

44: Sir Wu (Wu Zixu) and Bi Gan both anticipate Qu Yuan as loyal and crafty ministers murdered by their own sovereigns.

III. LAMENTING YING

This poem again seems to represent the intersection of poetry and verifiable history. The title would identify the poem as one composed in response to Qu Ping's exile from the capital of Chu at Ying (modern Jiangling in Hubei province). But two insightful scholars have offered different views. Wang Fuzhi (1619–92) proposed that the poem had to do instead with the abandonment of the old Chu capital, the opening lines referring to the disaster that befell Chu in 298 BCE, when Qin captured fifteen of Chu's cities. In the 20th century, Shirakawa Shizuka suggested that the poem referred not to Qu Yuan specifically but collectively to the shamans of Chu, being exiled by a new regime, an intriguing speculation that does not seem to accord well with the paucity of shamanistic imagery in the remainder of the poem. Both Wang and Shirakawa's intriguing proposals reflect the difficulty of otherwise tying the poem's narrative directly to Qu Ping's life. In sum, though the poem may refer to the actual destruction of Ying, it can also be read as symbolic of other losses.

16: The mouth of the Xia was close to the Chu capital at Ying. Dragongate is said in the Han commentary to be the eastern gate of the capital Ying, but this is obviously just inferred from the context of the previous line. Another 'Dragongate', located on the western reaches of the Yellow River, appears in the *Documents* (Legge, *Shoo King*, 127).

21: Lord Yang was a water deity, and the expression 'waves of Lord Yang' was a fixed expression in early texts. Perhaps the clearest explanation (though not necessarily a reliable one) is that of Ying Shao (2nd c. CE): 'Lord Yang was one of the various lords of antiquity. Because he had been punished [by the sovereign], he threw himself into the Jiang. His spirit then created great waves' (see *Han shu*, 87A.3519).

31: Xia Cove is the place where the Jiang and Xia rivers meet, site of modern Wuhan city. Due east of the capital of Chu at Ying, the speaker here gazes back westward towards his starting point.

36: I take this couplet as an example of *huwen* (reciprocal modification): in both lines Qu Yuan is lamenting the prosperity and high morals that have been lost.

40: The east-facing gates were a place of special significance within the ancient Chinese city, as suggested by their prominent appearance at the opening of five of the love songs in the *Book of Songs* (poems 89, 93, 137, 139, 140). This couplet is ambiguous with respect to tense, so while it could refer to the actual destruction of Ying, it might also be reflecting on the mutability of things, as in the old trope of 'oceans transforming into mulberry forests'.

45: For the usage of 'overnight' (*buxin*) in this couplet see *Songs* 159/3: 'The wild-geese take wing; they make for the land. | The prince went off and does not come back. | He must be spending the night with you'. Trans. Waley, *Book of Songs*, 127. See also Tang, *Chuci leigao*, 327–9.

50: This couplet employs descriptive terms appropriate for beautiful palace ladies, but probably referring more to sycophantic courtiers. The best gloss on it is a passage from Yang Xiong's 'Refuting Sorrow' (Fan sao), which might have been composed in response to it: 'In the harem pretty ladies vie in grace and charm, | Trying to outdo one another in elegance and beauty. | Since he knew of these ladies' jealous spite, | Why did he have to display his moth-eyebrows?' (see Knechtges, *Han shu Biography of Yang Xiong*, 15).

52: An identical line occurs in 'Nine Phases', line 242 (and line 239 there is similar as well). The remaining lines of the poem proper are also repeated in 'Nine Phases'. Since the *Chuci zhangju* only presents commentary to the 'Nine Phases' text, it seems likely that it is the passage here that is an interpolation.

56: This quatrain is identical with 'Nine Phases', lines 187–90.

60: This quatrain is identical with 'Nine Phases', lines 199–202.

64: This saying is also quoted in the *Book of Rites* (see Legge, *Lî Kî*, 2A.131). Cf. the use of proverbs in 'Rueful Remonstrance' above.

66: The ending highlights the theme of false accusation, which will be even more prominent in some of the later *Elegies*, such as 'Nine Yearnings: Suffering Blame'.

IV. UNRAVELLED YEARNINGS

This poem has a distinctive title with the same structure as 'Li sao', a verb–object phrase with both elements conveying melancholy interiority. It also has a complex structure divided up into four separate sections, whose titles seem to have musical significance. For an analysis of the poem's structure, see also my article, 'Tropes of Entanglement and Strange Loops in the "Nine Avowals" of the *Chuci*'.

5: The sense of this obscure line seems to be similar to that of the famous opening of the 'Nine Phases'.

20: This difficult quatrain presents a dramatic contrast that illustrates the message more often stated explicitly throughout the *Elegies*. The king 'boasts' of his fine qualities and presents a fine face to the world, but this façade is false, or at least incomplete, since he also lies to our protagonist. The passage is somewhat convoluted because Qu Yuan is sufficiently loyal that he cannot believe the king is as bad as his rivals at court; yet he still wants to make his explicit objection.

34: This couplet combines enigmatic references to the 'Three and the Five' and also to 'Peng and Xian'. Though the Han commentary confidently identifies the former as the 'Three Kings and Five Hegemons' (founding rulers of the Xia, Shang, and Zhou, and hegemons of Qi, Jin Song, Chu, and Wu during the Spring and Autumn periods, respectively), and the latter as the Shang minister who drowned himself, neither of these identifications is reliable. Zhu Xi's suggestion, though not definitive either, is more promising in its identification of these as ancient divinities, the 'Three Sovereigns and Five Deities' (*san huang wu di*). Here again there are various identifications, but the Three Sovereigns might refer to Fu Xi, Shennong, and Nüwa, and the Five Deities to Shaohao, Zhuanxu, Highlord Ku, Yao, and Shun. It is also possible that the Three Sovereigns refer to kings of Chu itself—see note to line 25 of 'Li sao'.

43: This line is identical with line 17 above, suggesting this song is a condensation of the opening section.

50: *Mei* means 'matchmaker' but as used in the *Elegies* seems a somewhat more capacious term, so I employ the more flexible 'messenger', though it should be understood to encompass the specific sense of a messenger carrying a marriage proposal.

66: For the 'go-between' cf. 'Li sao', line 290: 'then what need to employ a go-between?'

V. EMBRACING THE SAND

The title is ambiguous. It could refer to Qu Ping's suicide, 'embracing a stone' as he hurled himself into the Miluo River. But one might understand it more figuratively as referring to the riverbed destination of drowning, rather than to the specific suicide weapon. This understanding also leaves space for some of the potential religious implications of the act, as seen in the 'Li sao', or below in Liu Xiang's 'Nine Threnodies'. As mentioned above, Qu Yuan was worshipped after the Han dynasty as an aquatic deity, but there are clues that similar religious associations were already present in the early poems attributed to Qu Yuan.

20: As *Zhuangzi* says: 'Eradicate patterned ornaments, disperse the five tints, glue shut the eyes of Spidersight, and all the people under heaven will begin to repossess their keenness of vision. Destroy bevel and ruler, abandon compass and L-square, crush the fingers of craftsman Chui, and all the people under heaven will begin to repossess their cleverness' (see Mair, *Wandering on the Way*, 87; *Zhuangzi jishi*, 10.353). Chui was said to be a great artisan from the time of Yao or Shun.

24: Li Lou is mentioned proverbially in *Mengzi*, 4A.1, as a man of superb vision: 'Even if you had the keen eyes of Li Lou and the skill of Gongshu Zi, you could not draw squares or circles without a carpenter's square or a pair of compasses; even if you had the acute ears of Shi Kuang, you could not adjust the pitch of the five notes correctly without the six pipes; even if you knew the way of Yao and Shun, you could not rule the Empire equitably except through benevolent government.' (trans. Lau, *Mencius*, 76). Note that Mencius is reversing the point of the allusion while Qu Yuan is using it positively.

42: This line reverses line 17 above, contrasting the speaker, who is excellent both in character and outer manner, with his rivals, who are lacking in both respects.

45: A similar idiom in *Huainanzi* confirms the internal parallelism of this line: 'This is the reason why sages emphasize humaneness and embrace kindness' (Major et al., *Huainanzi*, 13.525). The whole discussion of how virtue is commemorated after death is highly relevant to 'Embracing the Sand'.

68: This line is an example of the topos of horse connoisseurship, used to represent the challenge of identifying human talent. It is repeated in the 'Nine Phases' as well. See Qian Zhongshu's discussion (*Guanzhui bian*, 945–6).

80: The text leaves it unclear what the 'model' is. I take it as referring both to the previous couplet, the principle of preferring honour over death, and also to the noble men in the previous line, nobility being defined, in part, by adherence to that same principle.

VI. YEARNING FOR A BEAUTY

This piece, with 'Regretting Past Days' and 'Grieved by the Whirlwind' below, forms an exceptional triad within the 'Nine Avowals'. The three poems all have three-character titles drawn directly from the first lines, and their rhyme schemes are irregular, suggesting that they were composed later than 'Lamenting Ying' or 'Embracing the Sand'. This particular poem addresses a key theme of the 'Li sao' and the whole Quvian tradition. The term is ambiguous in gender, not just linguistically speaking, but because of specific poetic choices that imbue it, throughout the *Elegies*, with both feminine and masculine characteristics. The 'Beauty' describes a person who is powerful, admirable, and virtuous, but all these worthy inner qualities are also represented simultaneously as corporeal, visual beauty.

14: Gaoxin is Highlord Ku, the mythical ancestor of the Shang dynasty (see 'Li sao', line 244), and the dark bird is the totem of Shang, as in *Songs* 303: 'Heaven bade the dark bird | To come down and bear the Shang, | Who dwelt in the lands of Yin so wide. | Of old God bade the warlike Tang | To partition the frontier lands . . .' Trans. Waley, *Book of Songs*, 320.

26: Zaofu was the horse-expert of King Mu of Zhou, though, as Jiang Liangfu points out, the legends about him may have arisen only in the Warring States period (see *Chongding Qu Yuan fu jiaozhu*, 4.415).

56: 'Creeping Fig' and 'Lotus Bloom' in this quatrain seem to be personifications of fragrant plants that do not refer to specific historical figures, suggesting that the fragrant plants in section IX of the 'Li sao', about which there is some controversy, can be read productively in the same fashion.

66: For Peng and Xian see 'Li sao', lines 76 and 375. That each time the term 'Peng Xian' is used in such a simple but opaque fashion suggests that even apart from the historical referent, we have here a kind of formula of Chu poetry.

VII. REGRETTING PAST DAYS

This poem is an introspective study that shares features with several other poems in the 'Nine Avowals'. It is similar to 'Rueful Remonstrance' in presenting an interior monologue with relatively little external action. Line 29, in particular, evokes the theme of expressing and unspooling one's inner thoughts to an audience from that same poem and also 'Unravelled Yearnings'. The conclusion of the poem alludes explicitly to Qu Ping's suicide, suggesting it must be a retrospective piece composed after Qu's death. Moreover, the poem reflects the increasing emphasis in the Han on the role of the courtier, and proceeds in a notably Confucian manner, focusing on the value of social harmony.

36: Baili Xi, Yi Yin, Lü Wang, and Ning Qi were all ordinary men raised to become high ministers.

40: King Fuchai of Wu failed to trust his loyal minister Wu Zixu, and ultimately Wu was conquered by Yue.

71: 'Govern at will' is literally 'govern by the heart' (*xin zhi*). The author of this poem takes a strong position against such arbitrary rulership, in favour of government by fixed laws and norms.

VIII. ODE TO THE TANGERINE

This poem is unique within the entire *Elegies* in its humble subject matter, the southern fruit tree *ju* (sourpeel tangerine). Needless to say, that is not the entire story; it becomes clear almost immediately that the subtext is praise for a certain kind of person, a Qu Yuan-like moral hero. Nonetheless, it is still not exactly obvious how this poem fits into the larger anthology. The simplest explanation of its inclusion in the anthology is that it was attributed to Qu Yuan and understood as another articulation of his ideals of virtue.

2: 'Lord and sovereign' is said in the Han commentary to be short for 'Lordly Earth and Sovereign Heaven'.

4: A proverb current in the Warring States held that north of the Huai River, the *ju* tangerine became the *chi* 'trifoliate orange', a variety with bitter fruit and white flowers.

35: The reference to Bo Yi turns the poem abruptly in a new direction, since he (with Shu Qi) is famous for refusing to serve the Zhou out of loyalty to the Shang dynasty, and instead starving to death in reclusion. In spite of all its appealing and virtuous qualities, the tangerine is doomed.

IX. GRIEVED BY THE WHIRLWIND

The final poem in the 'Nine Avowals' is a major work of over one hundred lines that bears comparison with both the 'Li sao' and 'Nine Phases' in scale, and hence provides a fittingly grand conclusion to the 'Nine Avowals'. With a main text of one hundred lines and an envoi of ten lines, the poem's structure has an unusual mathematical perfection. The central image, the whirlwind representing disaster, has been used as an image of melancholy and despair since the *Book of Songs*, 149/2: 'Not because of the whirlwind; | Not for the chariot's veering;—| But when I look to the road to Zhou | Am I sad to the core of my heart' (translation modified from Legge, *She King*, 218).

This poem and 'Ode to the Tangerine' are the only two in the 'Nine Avowals' devoted to objects, and both also conclude with homage to Bo Yi, the recluse from the end of the Shang. As different as they at first appear, then, the final two poems in the 'Nine Avowals' form a fitting coda to the set, emphasizing self-conscious literary artistry.

5: For Peng and Xian see 'Li sao', 76, 375. But praising them in terms of their 'ambitions' may suggest a different perspective on them than that of the author of the 'Li sao'.

12: 'Gorgeous patterning' (*wenzhang*) refers to all kinds of patterns and decorations, including but not limited to literary expression.

13: The speaker of *Songs* 35/2, 'Valley Wind', says, 'Who says that sowthistle is bitter? | It is sweeter than shepherd's purse' (trans. Waley, *Book of Songs*, 31). Both are common, edible plants—not worthy even to share a field with the more fragrant herbs.

16: Following Jiang Liangfu, I take 'comely person' to refer to the speaker himself here and immediately below (*Chongding Qu Yuan fu jiaozhu*, 4.443; cf. 'Li sao', line 20).

20: My translation follows the variant of 'feeling' (*gan*) for 'confusion' (*huo*). 'Lyric' here refers to the *shi* poetic genre. In later literary criticism, the *Elegies* are usually seen as the predecessors of the *fu* or rhapsody, but within this poem, at least, the *Elegies* are seen as overlapping with *shi* poetry.

52: If this poem was composed much later than the 'Li sao' itself, even its author may have been unsure of the meaning of 'Peng and Xian' in that earlier poem. Here their reference may be closer to the later understanding of a single suicidal minister, Peng Xian.

70: As mentioned in the notes above, the implications of Peng and Xian here may already be different from 'Li sao'. In particular, towards the end of this poem the speaker explicitly refers to drowning himself, and speaks of dying a martyr like Wu Zixu as well. So even though this line is almost identical to the final line of the 'Li sao', it may refer specifically to drowning oneself in protest, without the shamanistic implications of the earlier poem.

72: The term *ni* is often understood as a kind of rainbow, but instead I take it to refer to the 'fogbow', 'an arc or ring of white or weakly coloured light, regarded as being similar in form to a rainbow, caused by light shining through fog' (*OED*).

80: Mount Min is located in northern Sichuan, at the source of the Jiang.

94: These four lines describe the passage of the seasons: the heat of fiery summer, floodwaters rising in autumn, the frost and snow of winter, and finally the spring tide.

106: Shen Tudi was a retainer of the wicked Zhow, final ruler of the Shang, said to have drowned himself with a heavy stone in protest. There was some debate in the Han as to whether this kind of suicide was a valid form of political critique.

108: Hawkes understands this line also as referring solely to Shen Tudi (*Songs of the South*, 191). But Shen Tudi appears in parallel with Wu Zixu, both mentioned as analogies to the speaker's own situation.

110: This couplet is identical with 'Lamenting Ying', lines 23–4, so it may have been erroneously copied here. It is also true, however, that concluding with this powerful image of entanglement confirms the centrality and unifying force of this trope for the whole set of poems.

FAR ROAMING

'Far Roaming' begins with the familiar predicament of the frustrated minister, but then takes off in a different direction—upwards. Though originally identified as a composition by Qu Yuan, modern scholarship has questioned this attribution on numerous grounds. In particular, its references to the cult of the immortals seem to belong to the Han cultural sphere, while the poem's message of Daoist detachment and indifference to political vicissitudes is hard to relate to the passionate laments of the 'Li sao' or 'Nine Avowals'. Another striking fact, as we will see below, is that Liu Xiang himself used the same title for one of the poems in his 'Nine Threnodies'. Given the conventions of Han poetics, it seems unlikely that he would have done so if a poem by that title and attributed to Qu Yuan had already existed. Hence 'Far Roaming' may not even have been attributed to Qu Yuan until the Later Han. For a more detailed study of this poem with extensive annotation, see Kroll, 'On "Far Roaming"'. Hoshikawa divides the text, arbitrarily but effectively, into nine sections, and I follow these divisions.

23: Red Pine is the first of several immortals cited here. In contrast to the shaman heroes of the 'Li sao', these are supposed to be ordinary men who employed mystic techniques to prolong their lives and become 'transcendents' living apart from society. For a full translation and study of one of the key Six Dynasties sources on this topic, see Campany, *To Live as Long as Heaven and Earth*.

30: Fu Yue is named in *Zhuangzi* as the concluding member of a list of thirteen figures who attained the Dao. It is further asserted that he 'thereby became mister of Wuding, | grandly in possession of all under heaven; mounted upon Sagittarius, | riding upon Scorpio, | he joined the arrayed stars' (Mair, *Wandering on the Way*, 6.56). The Nascence Stars (a literal translation) refer to the Heart constellation located in the centre of the eastern quadrant of the sky, and so signifying the advent of Spring.

The appearance of Han Zhong is more puzzling. A person of this same name is mentioned in the *Shi ji* as one of the men sent by the First Emperor of Qin in search of potions of immortality (6.258). Another important source, Hong Xingzu's commentary to this line, quotes from the *Biographies of the Immortals* (a text not transmitted in complete form), identifying Han Zhong as a man of the state of Qi who was sent by the king in pursuit of potions of immortality, but imbibed them himself and thereby attained transcendence (*Chuci buzhu*, 5.164-5). Tang Bingzheng points out that it is very common for this kind of legendary figure to reappear in successive dynasties (*Chuci leigao*, 394-5).

42: This formal term 'spirit refulgent' refers simply to the sun, using a substitution that makes it loosely parallel to 'Spirit Supreme' in the 'Li sao'.

55: The *Zhuangzi* already describes an ideal, transcendent being who could 'chariot upon the transformations of the six vital breaths and thereby go wandering in infinity' (Mair, *Wandering on the Way*, 1.5). There are various identifications of these 'six vital breaths' (*liu qi*), which I render 'Six Energies' to suggest their broader connotations.

60: Nanchao has been identified as a location near the Lu River in modern Anhui province, but Hong Xingzu proposes that it is instead the resting place of the vermilion bird of the south (*Chuci buzhu*, 5.166).

62: For unified vitality, see the 'Methods of the Mind' chapter in *Guanzi*: 'What is at once with the vital force and able to bring about changes in it is called the vital essence.' See Rickett, trans. *Guanzi*, 2:60.

72: The first half of this statement is a direct quote from *Zhuangzi*: 'The ears are limited to listening, the mind is limited to tallying. The primal breath, however, responds to things vacantly' (modified from Mair, *Wandering on the Way*, 4.32). The second half follows from a principle enunciated in the same chapter: 'The Way should not be adulterated. . . . The ultimate men of the past first sought to preserve it in themselves and only after that to preserve it in others' (Mair, *Wandering on the Way*, 4.30).

81: 'Flying Font' could simply mean 'gushing springs', but it is understood by a commentator to Sima Xiangru's 'Rhapsody on the Great Man' to be a specific place located southwest of Mount Kunlun (*Shi ji*, 117.3058n.).

91: This line quotes from the opening of the tenth chapter of *Laozi*. I follow the interpretation of the Heshanggong commentary, in which the full passage reads: 'If one sustains the skysoul and earthsoul, and embraces unity, one may be without separation. If one concentrates breath, if one produces tenderness, one may resemble a little child. . .'. See Erkes, 'Ho-shang-kung's Commentary on Lao-tse', 141–2.

96: Fenglong is a celestial god, though his specific domain is disputed; since the gods of rain and thunder are mentioned explicitly below, here he must be a god of winds or clouds. Grand Tenuity is a constellation surrounding the Pole Star and forming a kind of protective barrier for it. For this whole passage, cf. Zhang Heng's celestial journey in 'Rhapsody on Contemplating the Mystery' (Knechtges, *Wen xuan*, 3:132–5).

98: The term Xunshi is obscure, but considering its prominence in the celestial pantheon here (close to the palace of the Lord of Heaven) the Han commentary identification of Venus seems plausible. The term used here, *xunshi*, literally means 'beginning of the ten-day cycle', so I translate as 'Calends Star' in parallel to the common designations of Venus as 'Morning Star' or 'Evening Star' in the West.

100: Grand Decorum is another term for the celestial court, while the mountain's name may be the same as the mountain in Liaoning province today known as Mount Yiwulü, so the protagonist is journeying from the centre of the realm to the northeast.

112: 'Curling Frond' (Goumang) is the 'attendant spirit or daemon of the east and springtime'—one of Paul Kroll's inspired renderings. See 'On "Far Roaming"', 667, note to line 112.

113: 'Supreme Illumination' (Taihao) is the sovereign deity of the east, corresponding to the Sovereign of the West in line 120 below.

116: I follow Yu Yue's emendation of 'Heaven and Earth' to 'Pool of Heaven' (the two are graphically similar). See 'Du Chuci', 12a.

120: The Han commentary distinguishes Reaper of Rushes (Rushou) as the attendant spirit (*shen*) of the West, while the Sovereign of the West

(Xihuang) is the deity (*di*) of the West. On the evolution of Goumang and Rushou in early China, see Riegel, 'Kou-mang and Ju-shou'. Though the gods mentioned here presumably had an extensive history before the *Elegies*, extant records are scanty.

126: The Mystic Warrior is the sovereign deity of the North, hence his name also refers to the northern quadrant of the heavens.

127: Civil Flourishing (Wenchang), god of writing, is also a constellation of six stars within Purple Tenuity, also corresponding to a court of the imperial palace.

146: The Spirit of Fire should be either Shennong, sovereign deity (*di*) of the South, or the Vermilion Bird. The Southern Semblances are just another term for the Nine Semblances, the mountain range where Shun was buried.

150: The goddess Fu Fei is identified as the goddess of the Luo River and also as the daughter of Fu Xi, inventor of the trigrams and writing. When all these associations were first established is uncertain.

152: The 'Nine Shao' were ancient musical pieces said to be the royal music of Shun. Since *shao* is cognate with *zhao*, 'summons', they were also seen as an ancestor to the verse form of the *Elegies* themselves (whether this had any historical basis remains unknowable). The most important reference is in the *Documents*, 'Yi Ji' chapter (see Legge, *Shoo King*, 88).

154: For the Spirit of the Xiang River, see 'Nine Songs: Lady of the Xiang River'. I reject the transposition of lines 151–2 with lines 153–4 in order to improve the rhyme scheme, which was suggested by Wen Yiduo, *Chuci jiaobu*, 82 (see also Kroll, 668, note to lines 150–60).

156: This couplet adds to the various divinities mentioned above a set of curious monsters, namely a winged dragon (wyvern), a serpent (wyrm), and a more obscure aquatic monster known as the *wangxiang* in *Zhuangzi* (translated as 'nonimagoes' by Mair; see *Wandering on the Way*, 19.181).

162: Frigid Gate is said to be a mountain in the extreme north. See Major et al., *Huainanzi*, 6.159.

164: Zhuanxu is the deity of the North, but also identified with Gaoyang, ancestor of the Chu royal lineage.

165: Wondrous Abyss ('Xuanming') is the attendant spirit of the North, corresponding to Zhuanxu. But here it is also a fitting term for the region approaching transcendence and return to the Way. See, for instance, its use in *Zhuangzi*: 'There is neither east nor west, | Beginning as he does in darkest obscurity [Xuanming], | And returning to grand perceptivity' (Mair, *Wandering on the Way*, 18.163).

167: 'Dark Frailty' is Qianying, an obscure deity identified as a 'god of creation' or a 'water deity' by Hong Xingzu, but without any corroborating sources (*Chuci buzhu*, 5.174). Commentators and translators generally accept this, even though it seems implausible that there was a belief in a divine Creator by this name that is only mentioned in a couple of texts. Instead, I take this term as parallel to Wondrous Abyss above, essentially being a descriptive appellation for the Daoist Way of perfect receptiveness.

170: The Four Margins, as above, refer to the lands within the very limits of the four directions. The Six Penumbras are the limits of the four cardinal directions plus the limits above and below.

172: For 'Mighty Chasm', the site of Daoist cosmography, see *Zhuangzi*: 'Zealot Vague was on his way east to the Mighty Chasm when he happened to meet Boreal Wind along the shores of the Eastern Sea. "Where are you going?" asked Boreal Wind. "I'm going to the Mighty Chasm." "What for?" "The Mighty Chasm is something that never fills up no matter how much water pours into it, and is never exhausted no matter how much water is drawn from it. I'm going there to wander about."' Translation modified from Mair, *Wandering on the Way*, 12.113.

178: The last six lines of the poem seem to form an independent unit, united by the rhyme and also the use of the character *wu* 'not' in all but the final line. As we have seen, the 'Li sao' and other *Elegies* employ a six-line envoi, so it seems reasonable to understand this remarkable summation as the 'Envoi' of 'Far Roaming', emphasizing a Daoist overcoming of all material obstacles and physical sensations.

DIVINATION

The poem and 'Fisherman' below both stand out within the anthology because they are narratives describing Qu Yuan in the third person. More specifically, both present a poetic dialogue between Qu Yuan and a second character not entirely sympathetic to his position. Moreover, both are written in a combination of regular and irregular verse with a few lines of prose setting the scene for the dialogue.

Qu Yuan's speech employs throughout the 'topos of the world upside-down'. He uses all kinds of examples where true excellence is ignored and the shoddy or wicked is praised. This topos grows increasingly common throughout the later *Elegies*. On the other hand, the portrayal of divination is somewhat unusual in the *Elegies*, suggesting greater scepticism than the 'Li sao'. A number of other features relate closely to issues of concern in Han intellectual debate, notably the mention of the 'Great Man', the Daoist hero who seeks out self-perfection and unity with the cosmos, just as in the 'Far Roaming'.

48: The Golden Bell is the first of the twelve pitch-pipes and hence a synecdoche for the establishment of ritual order through music. It is described as the 'guide' of the twelve pitches in Ma Rong's 'Rhapsody on the Long Flute' (see Knechtges, *Wen xuan*, 3:265).

FISHERMAN

Like 'Divination', this poem seems closely related to the 'rhapsody' (*fu*) form. Many rhapsodies from the Han are framed as fictional dialogues between historical characters, and this poem is no exception. 'Fisherman' is quoted in entirety in the *Shi ji* biography of Qu Yuan, so that Sima Qian appears to treat it as a historical episode, and it is only in the *Chuci zhangju* that it becomes a literary work attributed to Qu Yuan. But the poem also concludes with a popular song also recorded in *Mencius*. While not a definitive piece of evidence, this certainly seems to cast into question the view that it was 'authored' by Qu Yuan. Moreover, the whole piece offers a Daoist-style critique of Qu Yuan's obsessions, and again seems to belong more to the era of Han debates about Qu Yuan's political choices than to the original Chu context. Thus, as with 'Divination', the most plausible guess is that the piece belongs to the Huainan court. Whatever its origins, though, this is one of the most memorable and influential works in the *Elegies*, inspiring countless paintings of the awkward pair: sage, martyr, and poet Qu Yuan, and the humble fisherman who is willing to mock his pretensions.

5: 'Master of Three Clans' was, according to his biography, Qu Yuan's noble title, and referred to the three ruling clans of Chu, namely Zhao, Qu, and Jing.

30: This song is also preserved in *Mencius*, 4A, where Confucius remarks: 'Listen to this, my young friends. "When clear the water washes the chinstrap, when muddy it washes the feet. The water brings this difference in treatment upon itself." Only when a man invites insult will others insult him. Only when a family invites destruction will others destroy it. Only when a state invites invasion will others invade it. The *Taijia* says: "When Heaven sends down calamities, | There is hope of weathering them; | When man brings them upon himself, | There is no hope of escape"' (trans. Lau, 4A.80–1). Thus the Fisherman suggests that Qu Yuan is bringing his problems upon himself.

SUMMONS TO THE RECLUSE

This piece was composed at the court of Liu An (179–122), Prince of Huainan. Earlier pieces in the *Elegies of Chu* were studied and recited there, and courtiers also composed their own original works in a new style. The author of this piece is identified only as 'Little Mountain of Huainan', probably a kind of bibliographical label for some of the productions of this court. As we have seen, the four works 'Far Roaming', 'Divination', 'Fisherman', and 'Summons to the Recluse' all show signs of being composed or at least compiled there. 'Summons to the Recluse' reworks the form of the 'Summons to the Soul' in a secular court context, summoning a scholar back from his reclusion in the wild, embellished with the elaborate descriptive terms so typical of Han *fu* poetry.

SUMMONS TO THE SOUL

This piece is a literary fantasia framed around an actual religious ritual. The 'summons to the soul' for the most part was a funerary ritual, summoning the

soul of the deceased back in order to say farewell to it properly. But the sum-
mons could also be used for treatment of illness, and in this case the condition
of the person whose soul is at stake remains unclear. Thus in the case of this
piece one should perhaps imagine a soul on the brink of death, whose uncertain
future is precisely the issue creating drama and tension throughout the poem.

The piece as a whole contains two distinct prologues, one a sort of alterna-
tive fragment of the 'Li sao', the other a more straightforward dialogue between
the God of Heaven and a Shaman Yang; a long 'summons' text, apparently
based on at least the kind of speech made in the contemporary summons ritual;
and finally an extraordinary poetic envoi that reflects on the journey between
life and death from yet another, newly distanced perspective.

10: When *hun* occurs in isolation I translate simply as 'soul', but in special
circumstances, as here, when *hun* and *po* are distinguished, I render as
'skysoul' and 'earthsoul', since according to the traditional analysis, after
death one returns to heaven and the other to earth.

18: According to the Han commentary these lines all refer to Qu Yuan. It is
possible to understand this assertion not literally but rhetorically, though.
The passage can refer to a Quvian protagonist, whether or not the histor-
ical Qu Ping.

29: On the Shang myth of ten suns, see Sarah Allan, *The Shape of the Turtle*,
36ff.

36: These people are referred to in various classic texts, notably including
Classic of Mountains and Seas, 10: 'Lordworry Country, Sagear Country,
Tattoobrow Country, and Northyoke Country all lie south of the River
Sweetherb.' Trans. Birrell, 10.135.

40: The *fu* probably represents one of a number of venomous snakes, particu-
larly of the pit viper variety, notably the 'hundred-pacer' or 'Chinese moc-
casin' (*Deinagkistrodon acutus*), said to be so deadly that its victim cannot
walk more than a hundred paces before dying. 'Over a thousand leagues –'
is a formulaic expression, concluding three separate lines in this poem.

41: For the 'hamadryad', a synonym for the king cobra, see also 'Heavenly
Questions', #26.

48: The Sinking Sands were already mentioned in 'Li sao', line 349.

54: Yang Xiong's *Fangyan* dictionary mentions 'gourd bees', so called for
their large size. See *Fang yan jiaojian*, 11.70.

55: The 'five crops' are glutinous millet, non-glutinous millet, foxtail millet,
wheat, and wild rice (see Kroll, *Student's Dictionary*, 139).

74: The *Shanhai jing* mentions a nine-headed monster with snake's body, vas-
sal of the ancient god Gonggong, and enemy of Chu's ancestral spirit
Zhuanxu. See Birrell, *Classic of Mountains and Seas*, 17.185.

99: As in modern religious practice, these objects are all used in the summon-
ing ceremony: the baskets to receive the soul, the various threads to keep

it trapped in place. See You Guoen's perceptive comments on these lines in *Chuci lunwen ji*, 249–51.

118: 'Sunlit breezes' is an unusual expression, a poetic figure combining motion and light.

122: For 'stone-burnished' cf. *Songs* 203/1: 'But the ways of Zhou are smooth as a grindstone, | Their straightness is like an arrow; | Ways that are for gentlemen to walk | And for commoners to behold. | Full of longing I look for them; | In a flood my tears flow.' Trans. Waley, *Book of Songs*, 186.

124: *Feicui* is normally a rhyming compound referring to a single bird, the kingfisher. But commentators here follow Guo Pu's identification of *cui* as another bird with red plumage. Though impossible to identify precisely, it might be the red-necked phalarope, a migratory bird whose passages occasionally take it past China's shores. The 'equal radiance' is a common trope in the *Chuci*.

128: 'Tsatlee' is a 19th-century term for a much-desired white silk originally produced in Qili, Zhejiang (Tsatlee being the Cantonese pronunciation of this place name), which seems a fair equivalent in English for the fine white silk mentioned here.

143: The attendant ladies behave like proper Confucian advisors and offer their counsel to the king without compunction.

152: The canopies and curtains are probably both decorated with kingfisher ('halcyon') feathers, but as in line 123 above, the Han commentary provides the curious gloss that the latter is a different kind of bird, so I employ 'red-necked phalarope' for the sake of the rhetoric, while recognizing this may be a philological phantom.

174: This passage of lines 174–95 has been translated with great precision in Knechtges, 'A Literary Feast', 54. My translation borrows numerous details from this version, and Knechtges' notes should also be consulted.

177: The Han commentary identifies the 'seriously bitter' taste here as originating in 'fermented soybeans', a popular element of medieval Chinese cooking. See Huang Hsing-tsung, *Science and Civilisation in China*, Vol. 6: *Biology and Biological Technology*, Part V: *Fermentations and Food Science*, 339.

203: 'Lifting up Lotuses' appears to be an error for the more common name of the Chu song, 'Sunlit Knoll'. 'Crossing the River' is precisely the same title as the second poem of the 'Nine Avowals'. These are all Chu songs, 'new' relative to the older music of Zhou.

221: In classic musical theory there were twelve pitchpipes divided up into two groups, Yin and Yang. The six Yin pitchpipes were referred to as *lü*, and the Dalü was one of these.

230: For this whole passage on the ancient game of *liubo*, somewhat reminiscent of backgammon, see Yang Lien-sheng, 'A Note on the So-Called TLV Mirrors and the Game *Liu-po*' and 'An Additional Note on the Ancient Game Liu-po', esp. p. 129.

232: Yang Lien-sheng points out that this might refer to two teams of two players each, as depicted in an ancient mirror from the Han or Three Kingdoms era.

253: The beautiful but mysterious envoi shifts the focus to a reminiscence of a royal hunt, most likely a mythic scene of recurring, ritualistic implication. The description is curiously similar to an event recorded in the collection of historical anecdotes, *Stratagems of the Warring States*: 'Then one day the king hunted in Yunmeng. A thousand chariots with teams of four, banners and pennons darkened the sky, swamp-fires shone as rainbows do through the clouds, the bellows of buffalo and the screams of tigers echoed and shook like thunder. One maddened beast charged against the wheel of his chariot, so the king drew the bow himself and slew the creature with a single shaft. Then the king pulled a yak-tailed banner staff from its socket, impaled the trophy's head upon it, and lifting his face to the sky laughed aloud. "Ah, what pleasure I have in today's chase. A thousand autumns hence, who will share such joys with me?" ' (Crump, *Chan-Kuo Ts'e*, 228).

257: The Lu River was a tributary of the Jiang, but there is some uncertainty as to its exact location at this time. Xu Wenjing identifies it as a river in Guiyang county in the southeast corner of modern Hunan province, 300 kilometres due south of Changsha (*Guancheng shuoji*, 17.306).

272: 'Fiery radiance' refers to summer in other early texts, though here to the sun itself. For further comments on the translation of this entire passage see my study, 'The Pity of Spring'.

277: Properly the liquidambar tree or *fengxiang*, not the maple. See Wang Ping's discussion of the symbolism of the *feng* tree in this passage, in 'Sound of the Maple on the Yangzi River', 18–23.

NINE LONGINGS

With this piece we depart the shadowy world of ancient Chu for the much better-documented Han empire. Wang Bao, like Dongfang Shuo, Liu Xiang, and Wang Yi below, served in the imperial bureaucracy of the Han and left behind other extant compositions. In light of his career and surviving compositions, there is no evidence that Wang Bao shared the frustrations of a Qu Ping, and in fact the 'Nine Longings' at some points adopt a celebratory tone seemingly more appropriate for the eulogies which Wang Bao also composed. Probably these poems should be seen as one attempt at adapting the model of the earlier *Elegies* to the very different circumstances of the professional poet at a great imperial court.

I. RIGHTING THE OCCASION

This series may be distinguished from any of the preceding poems by a new note of optimism, signalled most clearly in the upbeat quality of the titles to each of the individual poems (in sharp contrast to the more traditional melancholy of the overarching title 'Nine Longings' itself). The poet discovers in a familiar situation of frustration and exile the opportunity for a journey to a better place. The Quvian protagonist has departed his own state of Chu to take refuge in a Eupatory Palace of the immortals. Only at the end does the speaker recall his sovereign and express his grief.

1: For the Pole askew, see 'Nine Avowals: Unravelled Yearnings', line 6: 'how the Pole is askew, and wanders off course'.

6: Hao and Feng were early capitals of the Zhou dynasty, founded by King Wu and King Wen respectively, and so act as synecdoche for the values of the Zhou.

7: The nine corners presumably correspond to the nine provinces of the realm as in the *Book of Documents*.

II. OPENING A ROUTE

This poem first uses the 'topos of the world upside-down' to present the parlous condition of the world, and then follows it with the celestial journey theme. The different themes are sometimes reduced to just a minimal allusion, as in the rapid two-line summary of a divination (lines 27–8).

5: The expression 'weary even in the daylight' (more literally, 'borrowing sleep') comes from *Songs* 197/2, where the original poet is lamenting that the king has been corrupted by slander.

12: The Han commentary incorrectly identifies the *xiang* here as the white elephant of the Indian divinity Samantabhadra, a Bodhisattva imported with Buddhism beginning in the later Han dynasty. In fact the chariot inlaid with ivory derives from 'Li sao', line 338: 'join chalcedony and ivory to make my chariot'.

14: The 'unflickering gleam' is identified in the Han commentary as the Cinnabar Mountain, but it could actually be any mythical place in the east, though, such as Fusang, the Sunrise Mulberry. The 'Pamir Mountains' are literally the 'Onion Range' (Congling). Whether the Pamir Mountains in Central Asia were actually the intended referent in the Han dynasty is unclear.

24: The *Annals of Lü Buwei* and *Huainanzi* mention exotic animals known as the Qiongqiong and Juxu (Knoblock and Riegel, *Annals of Lü Buwei*, 360; Major et al., *Huainanzi*, 12.447). I render the Juxu fancifully as 'chasm-spanner'.

29: The Han commentary understands this line as describing a relation between woven plants and a promise kept, but it may also borrow from the ritual usage of flowers throughout the 'Nine Songs'.

34: For the onomatopoeic description of thunder, see also 'Nine Songs: Spectre of the Mountains', line 24: 'The thunder thrashes and clashes – down the rain rushes and gushes.'

III. EXCELLENCE ENDANGERED

Many of these poems develop the same themes as the 'Far Roaming', and this piece actually uses those same two words (in line 6). But the fact that poets are

willing to use this phrase themselves suggests that they did not associate it specif-
ically with Qu Yuan, and instead saw it as a theme from a shared repertoire.

8: The 'watchtowers of Wei' represent the court, as in *Zhuangzi*: 'My person
is situated by the rivers and the sea, but my heart dwells at the court [literally
'watchtowers'] of Wei' (trans. Mair, *Wandering on the Way*, 28.292).

  According to Hao Yixing's *Erya yishu*, the Oxherd consists of three
stars and its Ox six, forming together a constellation of nine stars. See
Hao Yixing, *Erya yishu*, 8.23a.

17: The Mighty Treasure is another name for 'Chen's Treasure', a kind
of sun deity with rooster-like head and human body.

IV. ENLIGHTENING THE WORLD

Wang Bao further elaborates on the theme of escaping the corruption of the
political realm by ascending towards the celestial home of the immortals. While
the themes here can be found in the 'Li sao' itself, the emphasis is different, in
part because the journey itself occupies so little space, and also because there is
less play with the allegory of flowers and jade. As elsewhere in Wang Bao's
series, the optimism of the title contrasts with references to the Quvian trad-
ition of melancholy and self-pity.

8: The 'ram's horns' are used to describe the great Peng bird flying upon
whirlwinds at the beginning of *Zhuangzi*: 'There is also a bird named
Peng whose back is like Mount Tai and whose wings are like clouds sus-
pended in the sky. It rises upon a twisting whirlwind [twisting like ram's
horns] to a height of ninety thousand tricents, pierces the clouds and then
heads south on its journey to the distant Southern Ocean with the blue
sky touching its back' (trans. Mair, *Wandering on the Way*, 1.4–5).

18: The White Maiden is a musician whose zither-playing was so sorrowful
that Fu Xi broke the fifty-stringed zither into a twenty-five-stringed one
(*Shi ji*, 12.472; also mentioned in Li Shangyin's great poem, 'The
Emblazoned Zither'). The identity of the royal consort is unclear. See Yu
Yue, 'Chuci renming kao', 10a/b.

24: Zhurong is the god of the South, and Refulgent Clarity (Zhaoming) an
appellation for the accompanying Spirit of Fire (the element associated
with the south).

30: The 'West Pleasance' is the imperial hunting park west of the capital. For
the hills compared to carriages, cf. 'Nine Avowals: Unravelled Yearnings',
lines 71–2: 'Boulders square as chariots towering | Thwart my desire –'.

V. HONOURING VIRTUE

At first Wang Bao ponders mortality, transience, and Qu Ping himself, but the
poem then takes a surprising turn by ending with an ecstatic, divine encounter
in the manner of the 'Nine Songs'. In that sense this poem marks an important
stage in the development from the earlier *Elegies* to the later tradition of imperial

poetry. Its sober reflections on transience and ageing somehow combine with the theme of the divine encounter in a way that can make sense only in the context of the *Elegies*.

VI. GUARDING MERIT

At this point the various alternatives presented in the earlier pieces seem to have failed, leaving Wang Bao in a state of desolation conveyed by the autumnal imagery of the opening, following the model of the 'Nine Phases'.

6: Chen Zhi shows in 'A Study of the Bird Cult of the Shang People' that the 'dark bird' was a totemic symbol of the Shang people, later misidentified as a swallow. Here it might refer to the swallow departing for the winter, but has larger mythic resonance as well. For the 'spirit mound', cf. the 'Mound of Gao' in 'Li sao', line 216.

VII. LONGING FOR LOYALTY

In spite of its title, this poem is again closely related to the 'Far Roaming', describing a spirit journey through the heavens. This poem is distinguished by its neat structure with three distinct divisions. Han poets compensated for a lack of innovation in material by increased attention to form and concise deployment of vivid contrasts.

1: The nine stages of divinity refer to the nine layers of Heaven.

3: The 'mound of power' might be a variant of the Mound of Gao as in the previous poem, namely a royal tomb also symbolic of the state.

11: The Five Planets, representing the Five Phases of Han cosmology, are identified as Jupiter, Mars, Venus, Mercury, and Saturn in *Han shu*, 26.1305.

16: The Mystic Warrior is the god associated with the Northern Quadrant of the heavens, as well as with the element of water. 'Water's source' (*shuimu*) is identified in the Han commentary as an aquatic deity, but this seems an inference from context. The term is obscure, though one is tempted to adopt its later meaning of 'jellyfish'.

17: Floriate Canopy is a constellation of seven stars in Cassiopeia close to the Pole Star, and so called because it acts as a protective canopy for the emperor.

20: The Treasury and Tower are a double constellation comprising ten stars in the eastern quadrant, overlapping in part with the Centaur. The Gourd is a northern constellation of five stars.

25: This line quotes directly from *Songs* 26/4: 'In the still of night I brood upon it; | In the waking hours I rend my breast.' Trans. Waley, *Book of Songs*, 24.

VIII. CULTIVATING DELIGHT

This poem elaborates on the allegory of middle age so central to the 'Li sao'. The protagonist is tired by his journey and facing a mid-life crisis. The ritually sanctioned gesture of respect at the end, 'bowing over the crossbar', is a revealing example of what could be termed the 'Confucianization' of the *Elegies*. Much as they strive to imitate Qu Yuan's model, the bureaucrat-poets of the Han struggle to project the same sense of aristocratic aplomb.

30: 'Bowing over the crossbar' (of a carriage) was a modest gesture of respect. See Legge, *Lî Kî*, 90.

IX. UPROOTING AND INSIGHT

The title of this final poem is highly unusual and open to various interpretations, but the envoi suggests an interpretation: 'Rotting tree stumps are cleared away – so that eupatory and angelica become visible.' In other words, the 'uprooting' of the decayed tree stumps clears the way for the aromatic herbs to show themselves, and thus this poem ends on an unusually optimistic note. The theme of 'uprooting' is also established from the beginning of the poem with the topos of the world upside-down, as we see a wide array of images representing the confounded, inverted situation of the contemporary world. One could compare the role of the envoi in the 'Li sao' or 'Nine Avowals: Unravelled Yearnings'.

6: 'Sui's pearls and He's jade' are the pearls of the Marquis of Sui and the jade of Master He, symbols of hidden talent.

22: 'Bend in the Hillside' is the title of *Songs* 252, a celebratory and auspicious verse: 'Through a bend in the hillside | A gust of wind came from the south. | All happiness to our lord. | We come to sport, we come to sing, | To spread his fame.' Trans. Waley, *Book of Songs*, 254.

35: The Four Toadies are probably four ancient tribes, each descended from a good-for-nothing character (*Shi ji*, 1.36): Hundun, Qiongqi, Tuwu, and Taotie. Alternatively they might be the four villains mentioned in the *Documents* (Legge, *Shoo King*, 39–40): Gonggong, Huandou, Sanmiao, and Gun. In either case they refer to four enemies expelled by Shun, and thus preparing the way for the rule of Yu.

SEVEN REMONSTRANCES

This set of poems is attributed to Dongfang Shuo, a successful writer and prominent wit at the court of Emperor Wu (r. 140–87 BCE). It follows the piece by Wang Bao which must have been composed later, but then there is not necessarily any expectation that these poems are arranged in chronological order. Dongfang Shuo's most famous extant composition, 'Replying to a Guest's Objections', is a lively composition in which an anonymous interlocutor challenges Dongfang, asking him why talented scholars can achieve no more than a modest official post in government. Dongfang responds by explaining that it is precisely because the realm is prosperous and at peace that there are fewer opportunities for scholars to be influential in politics. In that dialogue, Dongfang adopts a cheerful tone of acceptance, recognizing that changing circumstances require the scholar to adapt as necessary. The 'Seven Remonstrances' are the mirror image of this complacency, with Dongfang here borrowing Quvian tropes and images to express frustration with the identical situation. In spite of the disparity of content, one does get an inkling of humour. For instance, the first poem opens with a memorable depiction of Qu Yuan as a sort of country bumpkin incapable of dealing with sophisticated courtiers.

I. ON FIRST BEING EXILED

Dongfang Shuo here presents a more balanced take on the Qu Yuan legend than can be found in other early accounts, a portrait of a plain-spoken rustic ill-suited to court manners and intrigue. This is by no means a critical assessment overall, however, as the poem goes on to praise Qu Yuan's virtue, initially by comparing him with bamboo.

6: Apparently imputing a modesty to Qu Yuan that is rarely seen in the works attributed to him.

38: This couplet is reminiscent of the seminal couplet in 'Far Roaming', lines 11–12: 'Those who have gone before I cannot equal – | of those yet to come I can learn nothing.'

39: This line is repeated as a chorus in two different *Songs* poems, 65 and 121.

II. DROWNING IN THE RIVER

This poem is one of the longest in Dongfang Shuo's suite, and continues to relate Qu Yuan's life in the third person. It can be read as a more coherent and historical-minded account than many of the other *Elegies*. At the same time, the poet does attempt some bold new similes, like that of wildfire spreading amid the drifting fleabane in line 68.

10: This line seems to refer to the ironic story recounted in the 'Five Vermin' chapter of *Han Fei zi*, in which the exemplary and virtuous governance of King Yan of Xu led to the downfall of his state. The lesson is that 'benevolence and righteousness once serviceable in olden times are not so at present'. See Liao, *The Complete Works of Han Fei tzŭ*, 2:278–9.

18: Under the benevolent regime of the early Zhou, the worthy advisors who had previously secluded themselves were able to attain their due reputation. This line marks the conclusion of this section, even though the same rhyme continues into the following lines.

24: According to a proverb, at the salted-fish shop everything assimilates the same stench.

30: At his best Dongfang Shuo seems to be able to point out the ironies of history in a way that is new in the *Elegies*, as here where he points out the bright side of the legacy of Bo Yi and Shu Qi, who have garnered much admiration since their miserable deaths by starvation.

44: As above, Wu Zixu was not buried because instead the King of Wu had his corpse tied to leather balloons so that it would float in the Yangtze River.

55: The 'square-set ship' was said to be ridden only by grandees, not ordinary gentry.

58: The Han commentary identifies 'Master Shen' as Wu Zixu, but a simpler interpretation would be Shen Tudi, said to have drowned himself in protest at the tyrannical rule of Zhow.

78: This line again seems to offer an implicit criticism of Qu Yuan, for committing suicide rather than finding an alternative beyond Chu. 'To the east' might refer to travelling to another state in pursuit of a wiser employer.

80: This couplet may be noted as an early gloss on the title of the fifth poem in 'Nine Avowals: Embracing the Sand'.

III. INDIGNANT AT THE WORLD

This poem is a lengthy but coherent treatment of the great theme of the world out of joint. From the title to the introductory section proclaiming the theme, to the various metaphors and historical allusions arrayed throughout, to the powerful conclusion, it is a restatement of the Qu Yuan story as it increasingly became understood in the Han: the courtier too good for this world who was forced to drown himself.

11: This is a paraphrase of the *Shijing* 203/1: 'But the ways of Zhou are smooth as a grindstone, | Their straightness is like an arrow; | Ways that are for gentlemen to walk | And for commoners to behold.' Trans. Waley, *Book of Songs*, 186.

16: According to the Han commentary, these are Yu, Ji (Lord Millet), Xie, Gaoyao, Bo Yi, Chui, Yi, and Kui, the eight worthy ministers from the age of Yao and Shun. But Yu Yue proposed instead that the term refers to the eight schools of Confucius's followers mentioned in chapter 50 of *Han Fei zi*. See Liao, *The Complete Works of Han Fei tzǔ*, 2:298.

22: This is a typical example of the topos of the world upside-down, as applied to the female concubines and attendants of the Emperor: Xi Shi was a famous beauty and 'Homely Crone' her antithesis.

36: This couplet seems out of place and the explanation of the Han commentary is not much help. But a story recorded much later (in a compilation by Yin Yun of the Liang dynasty) tells of Confucius meeting two silkworm-tending maidens who offer him a riddle that turns out to hold the key to escape from imprisonment and starvation in Chen. Though there is no way to tell if Dongfang Shuo knew the story in this same form, the basic plot in both cases seems to be Confucius encountering maidens who appear ordinary but turn out, like the great ministers of yore, to have unappreciated talents. See *Han Wei Liuchao biji xiaoshuo daguan*, 1023.

44: Kings Li (2r. 758–741 BCE) and Wu (r. 741–690 BCE) of Chu both failed to see that Master He's stone concealed priceless jade.

IV. RESENTFUL THOUGHTS

The Han *Elegies* often reflect a sense of increasing constraints on the poet or official, who no longer has any real alternative outside the imperial court. The extreme concision of this poem compared to the earlier *Elegies* has a formal parallel to its own message of self-confinement.

V. MOURNING MY PLIGHT

This poem at first seems to be aiming for the transcendence of a 'Far Roaming', but ultimately the poet remains content with the humble life of a 'recluse' who voluntarily rejects the political life of the capital to live in solitude. This was an ideal that became well established during the Han dynasty and continued to be an important model for the literati of imperial China.

6: This line is identical to 'Nine Avowals: Grieved by the Whirlwind', line 41.

10: Here the Pool of Affinity, previously seen as a mythological pond full of water for the hero's steed in 'Li sao', line 193, appears instead in its astronomical guise, where it is a small constellation of three stars just south of the 'Heavenly Lake' (Tianhuang).

21: For this proverb see 'Nine Avowals: Lamenting Ying', line 64.

29: 'Mount Heng' refers to the northern Marchmount in Hebei rather than the southern one in Hunan. Riding on the whirlwind, the poet is free to journey to every corner of the realm.

32: A proverb also quoted in 'Nine Avowals: Rueful Remonstrance', line 51.

45: Han Zhong is the immortal also mentioned in 'Far Roaming', line 30. But note that there he already inhabits the stellar regions, whereas here he seems to be a recluse abiding at Mount Guiji (just south of modern Shaoxing, Zhejiang province).

59: The Eight Mainstays support the four corners of the cosmos and farthest extremes of the four directions. Cf. 'Heavenly Questions', #5.

VI. LAMENTING MY FATE

This poem's title is very similar to that of an independent poem in the *Elegies*, 'Lamenting Time's Fate' (see below). Both reflect a theme prominent in writings by former Han court officials, that of the 'scholar's frustration', as it was memorably described by Hellmut Wilhelm. Once the subject matter is understood, we can appreciate a poem like this as a new rendition of a familiar theme.

13: 'Wondrous lodge' has a Daoist inflection and implies a condition of being hidden and safe from worldly dangers. *Xuan* in particular does not just mean 'dark', 'obscure', but also 'profound' or even 'wondrous', as in the first chapter of the *Laozi*, which states: 'Wonder upon wonder, | The gate to all marvels'.

23: See 'Li sao', line 323, and section IX in general.

31: This is a difficult line, but the gist is that the speaker reflects on the heroes and sages of the past and compares them to the inferior men of his own day.

33: This is a direct quotation of 'Li sao', line 129.

VII. UNWISE COUNSEL

The concluding poem of this series focuses strictly on the 'topos of the world upside-down', while making it clear that the topos is a traditional one by opening with a quotation of 'Nine Avowals: Crossing the River'. Unpromising and derivative as the topic might seem at first, the poem elaborates its theme in an unusually fluent way, concluding with a rhetorical question of some power.

1: This line directly quotes 'Li sao', line 85.

40: For the important but somewhat elusive institution of the Hall of Light (Mingtang), see Maspero's classic study, 'Le Ming-t'ang et la crise religieuse chinoise avant les Han'.

41: The vagueness of this praise for Peng and Xian suggests to me that even Wang Bao had little idea of who they were or in what respect they 'had found their pleasure and delight'.

58: This is a paraphrase of the *Huainanzi* (see Major et al., *Huainanzi*, 6.220) and a statement of the resonance theory that became dominant in the Han dynasty. Although these poems quote directly from the 'Li sao', then, they also introduce original notions.

ENVOI

This poem starts out with a literal quotation from the 'Li sao' and uses it as the starting point for a full-throated statement of regret. Rather than the indecision and ambivalence that characterize the 'Li sao' itself, however, this poem starts from a position of futility. The poet responds to the situation constructively, though, by the turning to the model of Daoist teaching, with a prominent allusion to the *Huainanzi*, and an explicit reference to Liezi (Master Lie), the Daoist sage to whom another important collection by that name is attributed.

1: The poem opens with a direct quotation of 'Nine Avowals: Crossing the River', line 49.

4: Floriate Pond is said to be another site on Mount Kunlun.

6: The 'Litheloined' (Yaoniao) is a famous steed, here contrasted with the awkward camel.

14: The Nine Tripods symbolizing Zhou authority were said to have been sunk in the Si River and lost permanently, an event that symbolized the decline of Zhou authority.

NINE THRENODIES

The 'Nine Threnodies' are distinctive within the entire anthology in that they do not merely imitate the Quvian model, but instead are self-conscious, intricately elaborated poems composed in the refined, aristocratic, and confident voice of their author Liu Xiang.

The title of this set is distinctive. *Tan* means either a lament, or a sigh. It recurs in each poem as the subtitle of the epilogue. This is another innovation that distinguishes the series from any preceding works in the anthology, which creates an intriguing self-similarity in the poems (each one is a *tan* which contains another *tan* inside it). The rendering 'threnody' suggests the artificiality and conscious reflection on tradition that are implicit in the source text.

The 'Nine Threnodies' are composed carefully in a coherent sequence, unlike many of the other poem series in the *Elegies*. Roughly speaking, the first three establish the context, following the model of the 'Li sao'. The third Threnody in particular, with its vivid images drawn from the *Changes*, *Analects*, and *Songs*, deserves recognition as an ambitious Han poem of personal experience, drawing simultaneously on Han scholasticism and on the fountainhead of sorrow, the *Elegies*. The next three poems draw more on the 'Nine Avowals', describing the poet's sense of confusion and exile. Finally, the last three poems are the most ambitious, ranging through reflections on history to celestial journeys that roam in directions exceeding the limits of the other *Elegies*. For more on Liu Xiang and these poems, see my article 'Roaming the Infinite'.

I. FACING ANARCHY

The first of the Threnodies is an encapsulation of the whole series. It loosely follows the 'Li sao' with its discussion of Qu Yuan's parentage. The poem sums up the traditional themes of the slandered hero and even his voyage across the cosmos. But at the end, aquatic imagery which had been present earlier abruptly comes to the fore, with the 'Threnody' coda departing entirely from the traditional themes and instead describing a tempest. The poem proper concludes with a moving contrast of body perishing and soul grieving, in tandem with one another.

1: Boyong is the same 'parent' of Qu Yuan named in the 'Li sao'. There has long been debate over whether the term refers to Qu's father or remote ancestor. As discussed above, I incline to the traditional view that it refers simply to Qu Yuan's father (though certainly not excluding mythic resonances behind that). One piece of evidence for the alternative interpretation is this line, which might also be rendered 'That *final* scion of his majesty Boyong'. But the term *mo zhou*, though it can mean 'final scion', is also a common expression in Han texts for descendants, and does not necessarily imply remoteness. In particular, *mo* originally means simply 'branch' (in contradistinction to *ben*, 'root'), and so the compound can simply mean 'progeny' (for an example see Cutter, 'Saying Goodbye', 86).

6: These lines reference the corresponding lines 5–6 in the opening of 'Li sao'.

8: The trope of illumination equal to the celestial bodies is not just a figure of speech but has a profound religious significance in early China. Cf. 'Nine Avowals: Crossing the River', lines 11–12.

9: Cf. 'Far Roaming', line 58: 'Letting essential energies enter and filthy impurities depart.'

20: This line is a quotation from the opening of 'Fisherman'.

29: 'Mound of Gao' is an allusion to 'Li sao', line 216.

42: The Han commentary identifies 'wondrous rocks' (*xuanshi*) as the name of a mountain, but it is not known from other sources and is presumably chosen solely for its evocative quality. Dongting is the great lake in Chu into which the Xiang River feeds, as in 'Lady of the Xiang' in the 'Nine Songs'.

44: Stonewall is identified as one of the peaks of Nine Semblances, the burial place of Shun, according to a gazetteer (quoted in *Taiping yulan*, 41.91a, and cited by Huang Linggeng, *Chuci zhangju shuzheng*, 13.2416). Unlike the journeys in the 'Li sao' it does not seem that the protagonist is covering much distance here.

48: The elegant echoes of the 'Nine Songs' in this quatrain show how it was possible for later poets to borrow from that tradition of magical symbolism. This quatrain is critical in order to convey that the protagonist's journey away from the capital is not just a physical one but also a journey towards spiritual powers beyond the ken of the court.

52: This is a variation of 'Nine Avowals: Unravelled Yearnings', line 58: 'My soul each evening travels back there nine times'. The 'viscera' are used frequently in Chinese poetry where we might say 'heart' in English (equally grotesque if one thinks too closely about the anatomical implications).

II. DEPARTING THIS WORLD

Where the first Threnody emphasized the unfortunate circumstances met by Qu Yuan, this one emphasizes his response. As with the first poem in the series, the title 'Departing This World' (Li shi) can be understood as a gloss on the enigmatic compound 'Li sao', emphasizing the theme of the cosmic journey away from Chu.

8: The attendant spirits of the four seasons (and also of the four directions) are Goumang for spring/south; Rushou for autumn/west; Xuanming for winter/north; and Zhurong for summer/east.

14: These are the same names as given in the 'Li sao', but Liu Xing specifies the manner in which the names are obtained: two different types of divination, first by reading the cracks in the tortoise plastron, second by the hexagrams of the *Changes*. According to the Han commentary, the phrase 'Spirit Harmony' is coined according to the hexagram Kun for earth.

31: See *Book of Documents*, 'Great Plan' chapter: 'Without deflection, without partiality, | Broad and long is the royal path' (Legge, *Shoo King*, 331). One of Liu Xiang's major works was a treatise on the 'Great Plan' elaborating on the correlations of the cosmos as a guide for rulership. See Cheng Sudong, 'Liudong de wenben: Liu Xiang "Hongfan wuxing zhuanlun" yiwen kaobian'.

42: There is a strange ambiguity in this line, which at first seems to affirm the view that Peng Xian was a courtier who drowned himself, until one notices the usage of the verb 'roam', with its powerful Daoist implications. The way that Liu Xiang casually refers to the canonical 'nine years' ought to cast into doubt interpretations of 'Lamenting Ying', line 46, that attempt to identify exactly what year Qu Yuan composed it.

49: The 'tributary' (*tuo*) is said to be either an alternative name for the Jiang or perhaps a tributary of it. It is mentioned in *Songs* 22/3 where it is distinguished from the Jiang (but then identified with it in the Mao commentary).

60: One of the basic devices of Liu Xiang in these poems is a neat division of the self into its various components: here emotional, spiritual, mental, and soul-like. These are all overlapping too, of course, but there is still a fundamental divide between the emotional, mental components which are mired in place, in contrast to the spirit/soul which is free to wander further off.

65: This line refers us back to 'Nine Avowals: Lamenting Ying'.

III. RESENTFUL THOUGHTS

This poem concludes the first triad of the 'Nine Threnodies' with an introspective piece focusing on the plight of the frustrated courtier. It is distinguished by its panoply of literary techniques, some highly unusual within the *Elegies*. In particular, the poem employs a wide range of images from pre-Qin classics such as the *Book of Changes* and *Analects*.

6: For the withered poplar, see *Changes*, hexagram #28, 'Preponderance of the Great': 'A dry poplar sprouts at the root. An older man takes a young wife. Everything furthers' (trans. Wilhelm-Baynes, *I Ching*, 111).

8: For the high ramparts, see *Changes*, hexagram #40, 'Deliverance': 'The prince shoots at a hawk on a high wall. He kills it. Everything furthers' (trans. Wilhelm-Baynes, *I Ching*, 157). Like the poplar in the previous couplet, this is a positive image in the original source. The Han commentary identifies the pigeon as a symbol of slanderous men, but I prefer to understand the pigeon calling as another figure for the poet's creative power.

11: For the road to Zhou see preface to 'Nine Avowals: Grieved by the Whirlwind', above, but also *Songs* 203/2: 'Slight and elegant gentlemen, | Walk along that road to Zhou. | Their going and coming, | Makes my heart ache' (trans. Legge, *She King*, 354). The 'road to Zhou' itself suggests longing for the restoration of Zhou order.

14: See *Book of Changes*, hexagram #22, 'Grace': 'Grace in hills and gardens. The roll of silk is meagre and small' (trans. Wilhelm-Baynes, *I Ching*, 93). Exactly as in the *Changes*, the idea is that the roll of silk is not very impressive, but its pristine quality represents the honesty and truth of the speaker's feeling.

16: This line is another example of the 'topos of celestial radiance'. The 'patterning' *wen* is a prominent word in Chinese thought. It refers to external ornament simultaneously correlated with internal excellence and virtue.

20: The key to this quatrain is the parallelism of the subjects in each line, together forming a coherent thought linking all four of them.

22: 'Suffer blame' or *li you* is a phrase very similar to the title of the 'Li sao'. It occurs once in the 'Li sao' itself and twice within these 'Nine Threnodies', and may be considered an encapsulation of the 'Li sao' theme. The 'jade portal' is a generic term for the gate of the royal capital.

24: Guan Longpang was a minister executed by Jie, final emperor of the Xia dynasty. But note that the two components of 'Longpang' occur in reverse (pronounced 'Fenglong') as the name of a mountain in 'Nine Threnodies' 1/49 above, in the trope of antonomasia.

30: These black (or 'blue') flies appear in *Songs* 219 as a figure for slanderous men. Lady Li slandered Shensheng, the heir to Duke Xian of Jin, so that he was exiled and committed suicide.

35: 'Propriety' is literally just 'violating the face', a usage consistent with the modern Chinese use of 'face' (*mianzi*).

38: This quatrain and the succeeding one return to the topos of the world upside-down. Selinea, osmanthus, and ginger-lily are fragrant plants much appreciated throughout the *Elegies*. The second one, though, has the equally fragrant lovage root being watered from a ditch inadequate to its high quality. This passage is difficult and may have suffered textual corruption.

42: Tangxi and Gan Jiang are two famous swords of antiquity from Chu and Wu respectively. Cf. *Analects* 17/4: 'The Master, having come to Wu Cheng, heard there the sound of stringed instruments and singing. Well pleased and smiling, he said, "Why use an ox knife to kill a fowl?"' (Legge, *Confucian Analects*, 319).

44: The leopard hide derives from *Analects*, 12/8, in which Zigong comments that external patterning (*wen*) is related to internal substance (*zhi*), while the 'hairless hide' of the tiger or leopard is worth as much as that of a dog or sheep. Similarly here, the superficial people are using a precious hide in the same way they would use an ordinary one. The 'precious jade of Master He from Jing' (in Chu) is proverbial enough that it can be referred to by various more compressed formulations. Here the text gives just 'Jing-He' and for convenience I have clarified it in the translation.

53: *Jianjian* is the sound of a carriage in *Songs* 73/1: 'I brought my great carriage that thunders | And a coat downy as rush-wool. | It was not that I did not love you, | But I feared that you had lost heart' (trans. Waley, *Book of Songs*, 62). Its Old Chinese pronunciation *$g(r)âm$? is rather close to the equally onomatopoeic 'rumble'.

64: In this poem the various references to Chu rivers seem to imply enjoyment of the journey rather than an anticipation of suicide. Note how the penultimate line prepares for the opening of the succeeding poem.

IV. FARAWAY DEPARTURE

This poem is rich in intertextual echoes of 'Nine Avowals: Lamenting Ying', detailing the poet's journey southward. However, even in this case, the religious valence of the poem is somewhat deeper than in any of the 'Nine Avowals', as the poem opens by referring to a whole pantheon of divine allies. Indeed, it is not only the 'Li sao' or 'Nine Songs' that are imbued with religious elements; a sense of the divine recurs periodically throughout the *Elegies*, and particularly within these Threnodies.

1: For this line the commentary cites *Songs* 40/1, where *yinyin* is said to mean sorrowful rather than concealed. There is a natural semantic transition between these senses, though, parallel to the relationship among Latin *angustus* 'narrow' / English *anxiety* / German *Angst*.

4: One cannot help but think of *Songs* 26/2: 'My heart is not a stone, | It cannot be rolled about'.

8: The Eight Spirits may be the spirits of the eight cardinal directions (north, northwest, west, etc.). According to the Han commentary the Nine Qi are the nine stars of the Northern Dipper. But this constellation only has seven stars (see Schlegel, *Uranographie Chinoise*, 502–6). More likely, the term refers here to nine gods associated with the Northern Dipper, as in 'Nine Threnodies: Far Roaming', line 27 below. For the Six Ancestral Powers see 'Nine Avowals', 1/6.

10: For the 'Five Elemental Deities' see 'Nine Avowals', 1/5.

12: Cf. 'Li sao', line 141. More generally, throughout the *Elegies*, the gods are encountered and represented via various intermediaries, whether shamans, matchmakers, spirit mediums, or others.

14: With Supreme Unity, Sovereign Earth was one of the key deities to whom sacrifices were offered in the Former Han.

18: The simurgh (*junyi*), which sometimes also refers to an actual bird, the golden pheasant, is a totem of the Yellow Emperor.

19: 'Pristine Spirit' (*qingling*) is a Daoist term probably referring to the heavens.

26: For 'resplendent begetter' see 'Li sao', 2.

31: For 'Lord Yang' see 'Nine Avowals: Lamenting Ying', line 21.

44: For these place names see 'Nine Avowals: Lamenting Ying', lines 16 and 33. Whereas the Han commentary had identified 'Dragongate' as a place in eastern Chu, here it seems to be situated on the Yellow River, closer to its location in the *Documents*. The 'great mound' may be the same as the 'Mound of Gao', burial place of Chu ancestors.

60: Liu Xiang is the only author in the *Elegies* to employ the compound *saosao*, '*sao*-like sorrow'. It has been glossed as meaning simply 'sorrowful' but in my view is also a self-conscious allusion to the 'Li sao', implying 'sorrowful in the manner of the "Li sao"'. 'Undisentangleable' (*bu shi*) is a kind of formula that occurs as the end of a line three times in the 'Nine Avowals'.

V. CHERISHING HEROES

Based on its title and opening, we should understand this as a poem essentially and primarily about reading the 'Li sao'. That is, here in the central poem of the series of 'Nine Threnodies', Liu Xiang highlights the inspirational role of the 'Li sao' itself for his composition. It is not the model, but the subject matter itself. The main poem concludes with the hero gazing back towards Chu and wondering who will be able to revive the state.

4: The driver's reaction highlights the fact that they are journeying far away from the capital, so the driver is the poet's only companion.

12: This line is a variation of 'Nine Avowals: Crossing the River', line 4.

19: Cf. *Songs* 148/2: 'In the lowlands is the goat's-peach; | Very delicate are its boughs. | Oh, soft and tender, | Glad I am that you have no home.' Trans. Waley, *Book of Songs*, 114.

25: The recluses Xu You and Bo Yi, not of much importance in the earlier *Elegies* as the cult of reclusion was still developing.

30: As the commentary points out, all these figures have previously appeared in the 'Nine Avowals'. The received text has Shenxu of Wu rather than Zixu, probably an error. Wu Zixu (originally of Chu but defecting to Wu) and his friend Shen Baoxu of Chu are often confused. Wu Zixu asked King Fuchai to remove his eyes and place them on the city gates so he could watch even after his own death when Wu was finally conquered by Yue.

50: These lines follow the 'Nine Songs' closely.

51: For the Mound of Gao see 'Li sao', line 216, and 'Nine Threnodies: Facing Anarchy', line 29 above.

53: For the metaphorical usage of 'ridgepole' (*dong*) as an important person for the state, see *Zuo zhuan*, Xiang 31: 'You sire, are the ridgepole for the domain of Zheng. If the ridgepole breaks and the rafters collapse, I will be crushed.' Trans. modified from Durrant et al., *Zuo Tradition*, 1289.

65: The reduplicative *yuanyuan* 'distressed and desolate' is repeated in the first line of the following poem, employing the figure of anadiplosis.

VI. MELANCHOLY AND SUFFERING

As in 'Nine Avowals: Lamenting Ying', Liu Xiang here claims to have been exiled for nine years. In neither case should we attempt to identify the specific dates: nine years is the appropriate length of an exile just as nine is the correct number of songs for a suite. Just as in that poem, the speaker here gazes back towards Ying from some place nearby. Summing up the content of this poem and the preceding ones, the poet even refers explicitly to this key source text, the 'Nine Avowals', in line 34 of this poem.

2: If referring to Qu Yuan's own biography as understood in the Han dynasty, this line would presumably be lamenting the imprisonment of King Huai by Qin.

17: One of the tunes played by Music Master Kuang summoned down sixteen dark cranes. Their responding calls form a model of the harmonious resonance between sovereign and vassal.

21: The Three Birds are the messengers of the Spirit Mother of the West, who lives on Mount Triperil.

31: The reed-organ figures in *Songs* 161/1: 'I have a lucky guest. | Let me play my zither, blow my reed-organ, | Blow my reed-organ, trill their tongues, | Take up the baskets of offerings' (trans. Waley, *Book of Songs*, 133) and elsewhere as a figure of conviviality.

41: The image of the kudzu vines creeping over the earth can be found in *Songs* 71, but it is adapted here to suit the topos of the world upside-down.

46: For the Shao music of Lord Shun see 'Li sao', line 363, and for the 'Frenzied Chu' dance see 'Summons to the Soul', line 219.

48: The ancient symbols of imperial power, the Nine Tripods, said to have been forged by Yu of Xia, were sunk into the Si River under King Xian of Zhou (368–321 BCE). Precisely the same imagery is opposed in a couplet of Jia Yi's 'Lamenting Qu Yuan'. See Watson, *Records of the Grand Historian, Han Dynasty I*, 446.

56: The description of crying is almost a quotation from *Songs* 58/2: 'I climbed that high wall | To catch a glimpse of Fu-guan, | And when I could not see Fu-guan | My tears fell flood on flood.' Trans. Waley, *Book of Songs*, 50.

64: Cf. 'Lamenting Ying', lines 21–2: 'Riding upon the swelling, surging waves of Lord Yang – | Swept away all at once, where will I moor next?' The poets of the *Elegies* are profoundly averse to 'going with the flow'.

68: The 'carriage driver' (*pufu*) is a key motif of the *Elegies* because of the conclusion to the 'Li sao', where his sadness indicates the poet's exhaustion from long travelling. But it can be traced even further back to *Songs* 168 as well: 'We bring out our carts | On to those pasture-grounds. | From where the Son of Heaven is | Orders have come that we are to be here. | The grooms are told | To get the carts loaded up. | The king's service brings many hardships; | It makes swift calls upon us.' Trans. Waley, *Book of Songs*, 141.

VII. LAMENTING MY DESTINY

This poem begins by telling us more about the 'resplendent begetter' of the 'Li sao'—in that poem probably the poet's father, but perhaps a more remote ancestor. In this case it is impossible to tell precisely whom Liu Xiang has in mind, but he seems to be referring obliquely to the distinguished early emperors of the Han, whether the founder Gaozu, or perhaps Emperor Wu. The poem then contrasts the righteous rule of past sages with the parlous state of the present.

2: These lines reference the opening of the 'Li sao', but then turn in a different direction to describe the period when the poet's father (or ancestor?) ruled.

14: Qu Yuan seeks to meet the goddess Fu Fei at 'Li sao', 222. The conjunction of the Yi and Luo rivers was next to Luoyang. According to one legend, Fu Fei, daughter of Fu Xi, was said to have drowned in the Luo River.

16: Lü Shang and Guan Zhong are cited as models of ministerial excellence.

19: Yu Yue explains that *sanmiao* here does not mean the Sanmiao people from the *Documents*, but rather 'descendants of the three [villains]', namely Hundun, Qiongqi, and Taotie. See *Zuo zhuan*, Duke Wen, 18.7c (*Zuo Tradition*, 575); Yu Yue, 'Chuci renming kao', 5a.

24: Song Wan was guilty of regicide, killing Lord Min in the Meng Marsh (*Zuozhuan*, Duke Zhuang, year 12; Durrant et al., *Zuo Tradition*, 169). The Duke of Zhou and the Duke of Shao were worthy confederates of the founder of the Zhou, King Wu. According to the *Documents*, the Duke of Zhou did indeed spend two years in the east after being slandered by two courtiers. See 'The Metal-Bound Coffer', in Legge, *Shoo King*, 358–9.

28: The 'lady of Cai' was faithful to her husband and refused to remarry even after he contracted a serious illness. She is praised in Liu Xiang's own *Biographies of Exemplary Women*, ch. 4. The savage lady may refer to the second wife of Duke Xian of Jin, Lady Li, who slandered her stepson Shensheng. She was originally from a foreign tribe (the Rong). Her biography is in Kinney, *Exemplary Women of Early China*, 71.

30: Qing Ji was the half-brother of King Helu of Wu who objected to the king's immorality, saying, 'The king of Wu is thoroughly unprincipled.' King Helu sought persistently to have him killed but failed each time. Even the king's clever servant Yao Li failed. See *Annals of Lü Buwei*, 11.248–9. Chen Buzhan was a nobleman of Qi. He attempted to save his lord, Duke Zhuang of Qi, from an assassin, but was so terrified he dropped his spoon while eating, and fell off the carriage. He was said to possess a humane sort of bravery (but not a martial one). See Liu Xiang's own *Xin xu jiaoshi*, 8.1048–53.

31: For Bo Ya's musical instrument 'Sounding Bell', see Wang Bao's 'Eulogy on the Supreme Ruler Obtaining a Worthy Vassal', *Han shu*, 64B.2826. It might be one of the traditional sets of chimes, or alternatively the name of a zither, since Bo Ya is usually associated with this instrument.

33: Cf. 'Nine Avowals: Embracing the Sand', line 29: 'Blending indiscriminately jade and pebbles'.

39: *Songs* 184 describes a crane crunkling in this 'ninefold marsh', a place of exile for the virtuous. In the first stanza: 'When a crane cries at the Nine Swamps | Its voice is heard in the wild. | A fish can plunge deep into the pool | Or rest upon the shoals.' Trans. Waley, *Book of Songs*, 158.

42: Thorny limebush (*Citrus trifoliata*) and wild jujube (*Zizyphus jujuba*) are frequently used to represent petty or corrupt men.

64: Cf. 'Nine Threnodies: Resentful Thoughts', line 55, above.

VIII. YEARNING FOR ANTIQUITY

In spite of its title, much of this poem is dedicated to the introspective melancholy of the protagonist. Beginning with a gloomy landscape scene, he then describes his own personal situation in a memorable quatrain that proceeds from the state of his hair, to that of his body, on to his displaced soul, only to conclude finally with the tears he weeps—a miniature road-map to the components of Chinese poetry.

36: 'Nine Avowals: Unravelled Yearnings', line 33, also mentioned the Three and Five, a cryptic term for revered rulers of the past. The 'Great Plan' chapter of the *Documents* was of special importance to Liu Xiang, forming part of the topic of a treatise he compiled on historical omens.

46: Wu Huo was a strong man and loyal servant of King Wu of Qin. He is mentioned in *Mencius* (Lau, 6B.134) and normally seen as a positive figure, but Liu Xiang seems to view him negatively, perhaps because he is known for his strength rather than for his virtue. The Duke of Yan was King Wu of Zhou's aide, Duke Shao, later enfeoffed with the state of Yan.

48: Kuai Kui was the unfilial son of Duke Ling of Wei. The Pure Chamber is identified by the Han commentary as the Pure Temple dedicated to the ancestors, as in *Songs* 266: 'Ah! solemn is the ancestral temple in its pure stillness. | Reverent and harmonious were the distinguished assistants; | Great was the number of the officers:– | All assiduous followers of the virtue of King Wen.' Trans. Legge, *She King*, 569.

Gaoyao was the ideal minister to Shun, so this couplet is anachronistic: this is one of many historical allusions, some conceivably having contemporary significance as well.

IX. FAR ROAMING

Liu Xiang's 'Nine Threnodies: Far Roaming' shares its title with the 'Far Roaming' attributed to Qu Yuan (VI, above). As discussed in the preface to that poem, though, there is evidence that it was composed not by Qu Yuan but by a Han poet. In fact, the existence of this second poem under the same title is powerful evidence to that effect; for if Liu Xiang had known a poem by Qu Yuan under this title, it is unlikely he would have composed his own poem under the same heading. Liu Xiang's poem is a much more concise treatment of a similar theme, with less invocation of Daoist themes (including concepts borrowed from *Laozi*, and specific discussion of methods for achieving immortality). It shares, though, the triumphant conclusion of the other poem.

16: The Nine Shores represent the Nine Extremities of the oceans. The Four Spirits are perhaps the unicorn, phoenix, tortoise, and dragon (Huang Linggeng, *Chuci zhangju shuzheng*, 13.2627).

19: The Boundless Capital is Duguang, also written in reverse as Guangdu. It has further been identified with Chengdu (see Knechtges, *Wen xuan*, 3:116, note to line 151). See *Classic of Mountains and Seas*: 'To the southwest of there, along the River Black is the Wilderness of the Boundless Capital. Sovereign Millet [Hou Ji] lies buried on it. Here there are waxy beans, swelling rice, rich millet, and full-seeded millet, and this is where the hundred grains grow naturally in the wild' (trans. Birrell, 18.191–2).

22: Jade Balance is the fifth star in the Northern Dipper (see Schlegel, *Uranographie chinoise*, 503). Regarding the two lodges, see *Chuci zhangju shuzheng*, 13.2631.

24: Ending at Sunrise Mulberry in the east, Liu Xiang concludes the journey by reversing the orthodox cosmological order, of East–South–West–North. Han poetry often follows this order strictly, so it is unclear why Liu Xiang reverses it here. See Knechtges, 'Journey to Morality', 170.

40: The 'mystic spirit' is said by Huang Linggeng to be Zhuanxu, but Zhuanxu appears by name in the following stanza, so the precise divinity intended here is uncertain.

44: Zhuanxu is the mythic ancestor of Chu and sovereign deity of the north (also known by the title of Gaoyang as Qu Yuan's revered Chu ancestor), while Wondrous Abyss is the attendant spirit of the north, as in 'Far Roaming', line 165. Kongsang is identified by commentators as a mountain, or simply as a 'hollow mulberry', but may be instead the habitation of transcendents far beyond mortal lands (see Glossary).

47: For the willow boat, see *Songs* 176/4.

50: The Yuan and the Xiang are Chu rivers, passing through modern Hunan and Hubei provinces.

60: As with 'Nine Threnodies' IV, Liu Xiang concludes with the reduplicative compound *saosao*, a striking choice which I take to be an allusion to the 'Li sao', even while it also has a surface meaning of 'sorrowful'.

73: 'Roaming the Infinite' (*you wuqiong*) appears in the first chapter of *Zhuangzi*: 'Supposing there were someone who could ride upon the truth of heaven and earth, who could chariot upon the transformations of the six vital breaths and thereby go wandering in infinity [roaming the Infinite], what would he have to rely on?' See Mair, *Wandering on the Way*, 1.5.

LAMENTING TIME'S FATE

Zhuang Ji (2nd c. BCE; a.k.a. Yan Ji because of a taboo on Zhuang during the reign of Emperor Ming, 57–75 CE) was another prominent writer of the Former Han like Dongfang Shuo, but this is his only extant work. The topic of the poem, as Hellmut Wilhelm showed in his classic article on 'The Scholar's Frustration', became a popular topic for Han writers of *fu* poetry. Han writers lamented that they had been born in the wrong time precisely because the Han was a strong, unified empire, which ironically gave less scope to the wise minister than had the competitive and rapidly changing environment of the Warring States.

The four lines 129–32 are particularly noteworthy for how they look back on Qu Yuan as a remote figure of the past to be mentioned together with Wu Zixu; emphasizing their primary virtues, moreover, as 'loyalty and fidelity'. Throughout the history of imperial China this would continue to be a matter of debate: did Qu Yuan really exemplify loyalty, even though he abandoned the state of Chu? Yang Xiong, for one, objected to Qu Yuan's suicide, and it is worth comparing the 'Li sao' itself to see what virtues are emphasized in that poem. The crystallization of the cult of loyalty in the Han would have far-reaching consequences for Chinese culture throughout the imperial era, and after. On the other hand, the conclusion of this poem ends up being surprisingly similar to 'Far Roaming', with the poet abandoning the corruption of politics for Daoist self-refinement. The language of 'purity' emphasizes the hero's decisions to escape from his worldly troubles entirely. By the end of the poem his sole concern is with prolonging his life.

1: One of the major topics of the *Elegies* composed in the Han is precisely the inferiority of the poets themselves to their great predecessor Qu Yuan.

4: This couplet is very similar to the famous lines 11–12 of 'Far Roaming' above.

18: Mount Concentration (Zhongshan) is referred to in the *Shanhai jing*: 'So the Yellow Lord [Huangdi] took some lustrous jade blossoms from Mount Secret [Mishan] and threw them against the south face of Mount Concentration' (translation modified from Birrell, *Classic of Mountains and Seas*, 2.21).

42: Compare the opening of 'Nine Avowals: Crossing the River'.

47: As often in the *Elegies*, the language of carpentry is borrowed for metaphors of governance.

66: Long Lian and Meng Ju were women famous for their ugliness and virtue, respectively.

87: Guan Zhong and Yan Ying were famously wise counsellors of the state of Qi, both of whom were immortalized in books purporting to transmit their wisdom (*Guanzi* and *Yanzi chunqiu*, respectively).

102: This line employs two bold metaphors for the life of the recluse, making his very clothes and home out of the natural landscape.

104: The latter line is nearly identical with one in 'Nine Avowals: Crossing the Jiang'.

113: The term used for the langur monkey here, the *xiaoyang*, has been identified with the 'spectre of the mountains' in the 'Nine Songs' as well (see *Chuci buzhu*, 2.82).

130: That Qu Yuan drowned himself in the Miluo River is a commonplace established in the *Shi ji* biography and much repeated thereafter, but it is rarely stated in the *Elegies* themselves. Needless to say, it would be odd for Qu Yuan himself to refer to his suicide in the past tense, but it is also unusual in the poems of Song Yu, Liu Xiang, etc. Though the 'Nine Threnodies' do mention the river, they do not state explicitly that it was the site of Qu Yuan's drowning.

RUEFUL OATH

Jia Yi (*c*.200–168 BCE) was a talented scholar promoted at a young age by Emperor Wen, who was later opposed by his older colleagues at court and demoted to the position of grand tutor for the King of Changsha (in modern Hunan). Jia Yi returned to the capital as grand tutor to prince Liu Yi in 172, but when the prince died in an accident in 169, Jia Yi was overcome with grief and followed his prince the year after. In spite of his short life, Jia Yi was a prolific writer of poetry and prose, and himself recognized the parallel between his life and that of Qu Yuan, in his famous 'Rhapsody of Lament for Qu Yuan' (for a translation see Watson, *Records of the Grand Historian: Han Dynasty I*, 445–7). He also composed the memorable 'Rhapsody on the Houlet', a philosophical poem reflecting on the vicissitudes of life from a Daoist perspective (for translations see Watson, *Records of the Grand Historian: Han Dynasty I*, 447–50, and also Knechtges, *Wen xuan*, 3:41–9). If this poem is authentic it would be one of the earliest Han-period *Elegies*. If not composed by Jia Yi himself, it seems to belong to the same cultural context in the Former Han, when scholars were consciously comparing themselves to Qu Yuan and reflecting on the injustices of their disordered age.

8: 'Midnight mists' were supposedly part of the diet of a Daoist practitioner, as we have seen above in 'Far Roaming', line 55.

12: The Vermilion Bird is the attendant spirit of the south, and the Azure Dragon and White Tiger of east and west, respectively. The hero has started out in the north in the previous quatrain.

20: Cf. 'Nine Avowals: Lamenting Ying', line 36.

21: The *hu* bird is sometimes identified with the swan, but then the colour would be hard to explain. It may in fact be a mythical bird more akin to the gargantuan *peng* bird than any ordinary fowl. It symbolizes the talented hero capable of crossing vast distances and achieving greatness.

27: The significance of Shaoyuan is unclear.

30: The 'pure tone of Shang' is one of the five notes of the traditional Chinese scale, associated with feelings of remoteness, longing, and a bracing autumn chill (as in 'Nine Phases' above).

58: Lai Ge seems to be an alternative name for Lei Kai, corrupt vassal of the last ruler of Shang, Zhow, while Sire Mei was an honest advisor who was punished for his honesty. See 'Heavenly Questions', quatrain 75.

68: Though this passage is not identified explicitly as a *luan* envoi the three-word exclamation, 'It is done, alas!' recalls the opening of the 'Li sao' envoi.

76: This expression is nearly identical to a couplet in Jia Yi's 'Lament for Qu Yuan'. See Watson, *Records of the Grand History: Han Dynasty I*, 446.

GREATER SUMMONS

We know even less of the origins of 'Greater Summons' than the other poems in the anthology, since the earliest attributions were divided between either Qu Yuan or Jing Cuo; but Jing Cuo is the name for an epigone of Qu Yuan, like

Song Yu, of whom little is known. Based on its content, though, the poem seems to be in the vein of 'Summons to the Soul' but likely composed later. Like the 'Nine Phases', it is distinctly eulogistic, concluding with praise for a benevolent regime.

Unlike 'Summons to the Soul', this poem lacks a framing narrative, consisting solely of the summons itself. While mostly following the same pattern as the main text of 'Summons to the Soul', the 'Greater Summons' concludes with a fascinating, rhapsodic invocation in praise of a wise government. Immediately following the description of the beauties of the attendant ladies and palace gardens, it comes as something of a non sequitur; but this political turn within a poem that is otherwise devoted mainly to superstitious fears and sensuous pleasures actually reflects one of the basic principles of the *Elegies*: aesthetic admiration and erotic desire are conceived of as parallels and forerunners of the mature relationships of political harmony. By virtue of its more explicit political framework is this 'Summons' greater than its model.

25: The 'short-bodied fox' is another name for the 'sand-spitter' mentioned below (see Kroll, *Student's Dictionary*, 573). I render the obscure 'short-bodied fox' freely as 'newt-fox' to suggest its amphibious habitat.

58: For the following difficult passage I have consulted Knechtges, 'A Literary Feast', 56–7.

66: The precise nature of *lao* 'yoghurt' is unclear—for more information see Huang Hsing-tsung, *Science and Civilisation in China*, vol. 6, part 5, 252.

84: The 'pure' (i.e. strained of impurities) 'wine' (really another kind of ale) is described as *chu*, with an interesting ambiguity: it can be either a proper noun (the kingdom of Chu) or an adjective also describing the 'pure' or 'refreshing' quality of the libation. See Jiang Liangfu's thorough discussion in *Er Zhao jiaozhu*, 689.

90: Fu Xi is the ancient culture-hero said to have invented the zithern, as well as the eight trigrams, etc. 'Propitious Phases' may refer to the same music as the 'Nine Phases'. 'Shang Harmonies' has also been identified with the 'Li sao', but Jao Tsung-i cast doubt on this theory ('"Li sao" *laoshang* bian', appendix 1 to *Chuci yu ciqu yinyue*), and indeed the two terms are not phonologically close.

91: The Chu song 'Sunlit Knoll' is also mentioned in 'Summons to the Soul', line 203.

94: The more obvious interpretation of 'Sky Mulberry' is as a mythical place name, but in the context of the various musical performances in this passage, the Han commentary's identification as the name of a famous zither seems superior.

99: According to Hong Xingzu, the 'four superior' refers to the four distinctive modes of music, namely the ocarina of Dai, Qin, Zheng, and Wei; the 'Jiabian' of Fu Xi; the 'Laoshang' of Chu (see note to line 90 above); and the panpipes of Zhao (*Chuci buzhu*, 10.221).

124: An elegant visual simile based on an object of foreign import, S-shaped belt hooks. See Maenchen-Helfen, 'Are Chinese *hsi-p'i* and *kuo-lo* IE Loan Words?'

126: This line relates the piece to the psychological preoccupations of the other *Elegies*.

134: The Han commentary cites *Songs* 217/3: 'Enjoy wine to-night; | Our lord holds feast' (trans. Waley, *Book of Songs*, 205).

147: For the 'winding rooms' see also Wang Yanshou's 'Rhapsody on the Hall of Numinous Brilliance in Lu', line 68 (trans. Knechtges, *Wen xuan*, 2:269).

165: For this passage, Huang Linggeng compares the instructions on preserving the utmost health in the *Ten Questions* (Shi wen) text excavated from Mawangdui (*Chuci zhangju shuzheng*, 2807).

175: The 'Lord of the Three Jade Discs' may have been an actual title from Chu.

183: I follow Jiang Liangfu's suggestion that *mei* implies specifically *mei zheng* 'ruling in harmony', in more pedestrian terms 'fair government', as in the envoi of the 'Li sao'. See *Er Zhao jiaozhu*, 725.

211: The 'Three Excellencies' were three key positions in the government bureaucracy whose specific titles and functions evolved over time. See Bielenstein, *Bureaucracy of Han Times*, 7–11.

212: Jiang Liangfu points out that 'ascending and descending' had a special ceremonial significance in Warring States texts, so this line implies specifically that the Three Excellencies are acting with propriety at the court. See *Er Zhao jiaozhu*, 736.

214: I take the 'nine dignitaries' as a general term for the noble officers of the court. The Han commentary's suggestion that it is an extension of the 'Three Excellencies' above seems like a wild guess.

220: As with the 'Li sao', this poem concludes with a cryptic term that seems to be the key to the meaning of the entire poem (somewhat like 'Rosebud' in *Citizen Kane*), but unfortunately is obscure to us. The Han commentary identifies the 'Three Kings' as Yu, Tang, and King Wen, but it could also be three ancestral rulers of Chu. The referent may be the same as for the 'Three Sovereigns' of 'Li sao', line 25.

NINE YEARNINGS

These poems, attributed to the compiler of the earliest surviving text of the anthology, present a historical enigma. Not only would it have been unusual to include one's own work in an anthology of classic compositions, but the commentary to these poems includes obvious blunders that make it inconceivable that the author and commentator are the same person. Nonetheless we can appreciate the 'Nine Yearnings', not so much as an original poetic composition in the sense we might take for granted, but rather in a postmodern vein as compositions playing with the themes of the earlier *Elegies*; as in the second poem of the series, with its long catalogue of animals from the natural world, concluding in a comic vein with a variety of insects pestering the protagonist as they crawl and flitter around him.

The 'Nine Yearnings', carefully examined, reflect a number of distinctive trends in the Later Han, notably including what might be termed the 'Confucianization' of the *Elegies*, with frequent references to the texts explicitly concerned with Confucius himself, in particular the *Analects*. The position of the 'Nine Yearnings' at the end of the long tradition compiled into the *Elegies* suggests that in some sense they mark the terminus of a rich legacy from early China. In fact, though, the story did not end here; in various guises, often inverted and transformed, the *Elegies* would remain a potent source of inspiration for millennia to come.

I. SUFFERING BLAME

The title of this poem may be a gloss on 'Li sao', since 'suffering blame' is one of the possible interpretations of that challenging title. On the other hand, the poem's opening seems closer to the 'Nine Phases', with its synonymous exclamations of woe. As with many of the *Elegies*, the poem presents one possible interpretation of the 'Li sao' as a poem essentially about 'misery and woe'.

Though the poem draws on diverse sources from throughout the *Elegies*, it also contains original touches. The animal metaphors in lines 24–5 are novel and memorable, and the dense collocation of historical allusions in lines 18–21 deals with historical materials in a novel manner—too novel for some readers, as the *Chuci zhangju* commentary misinterprets 'Ding' in line 19. From context this is clearly the name of an ancient, model ruler, but the commentary glosses it as a common verb. This shows that Wang Yi could not have been the author or compiler of the entire commentary.

13: The Six Evils are untimely death, illness, melancholy, poverty, ugliness, and frailty, as named in the *Book of Documents*, 'Hong fan' (Great Plan) chapter (Legge, *Shoo King*, 343), important throughout the Han *Elegies*.

20: Ding refers to King Wu Ding of the Shang and Wen to the founding King Wen of the Zhou. King Ping of Chu was the foolish, easily misled king who had Wu Zixu's father and brother killed; King Fuchai was the final king of Wu, whose errors led to its conquest by Yue.

22: Parallel to the four sovereigns above, four ministers are named here. Lü refers to Lü Wang, advisor to King Wen of Zhou, and Fu to Fu Yue, advisor to King Wu Ding of Shang. The chronological order of these two names is reversed, and Huang Linggeng speculates the order is changed to fit the order of the four tones (*Chuci zhangju shuzheng*, 17.2844). Ji refers to the Chu minister Fei Wuji, and Pi to the Wu minister Bo Pi. Lü Wang and Fu Yue helped to establish Shang and Zhou; Fei Wuji and Bo Pi were responsible for the downfalls of Kings Ping and Fuchai, respectively.

35: This line is nearly identical with 'Far Roaming', line 8: 'my lone soul distressed and bereft until the dawn.'

II. INDIGNANT AT THE SOVEREIGN

This title suggests that the frustration of the earlier *Elegies* here has crystallized into unmitigated negativity. With regard to its specific style, though, this is one of the few Han *Elegies* to introduce new fauna into its poetic lexicon, with the poet showing a new concern for the insects that have joined him in his isolation.

14: The Jade Dipper, i.e. the Great Dipper of Heaven, refers to the ruling principles and specifically to the virtuous counsellors whom the ruler ought to seek out and prize. The Pivot is the first star of the dipper, opposite from its Handle. This term is unconventional but readily understood.

17: Qiu Mu was a minister of Song during the Spring and Autumn period. He was killed by usurpers in 682 BCE just after his own lord, Duke Min. Xun Xi was a minister of Jin who committed suicide in 651 after his duke was killed by usurpers.

18: Peng is Peng Xian (the Shang minister possibly invented in the Han commentary to the *Elegies*) or Peng Keng, and Wu is Wu Guang. Tang offered the throne to Wu Guang but he refused and drowned himself in protest.

22: These represent the four stars comprising the bowl of the Dipper.

24: The Fire Star Antares signals the onset of autumn, as in *Songs* 154/1: 'In the seventh month the Fire ebbs; | In the ninth month I hand out the coats' (trans. Waley, *Book of Songs*, 120). The braces and buttresses are six stars in Boötes aligned with the handle of the Dipper.

III. DETESTING THE AGE

This poem opens tentatively with the 'Nine Songs' theme, but then imitates the 'Li sao' instead, including a dialogue with a deity. The dialogue with the deity is one of the most important features of the 'Li sao', often ignored in later imitations. On the other hand, the content of the deity's speech reflects centuries of Han Confucian scholarship, as seen immediately by the reference to the two key Confucian virtues of 'humaneness and dutifulness' (*ren yi*).

6: Neither of the birds here is easily identified. Both seem to be the avian equivalents of the 'petty man'.

11: Cf. 'Li sao', lines 343–4: 'Lifting up clouds and coronas that block out the sun – | I sound jade chimes with a jingle and jangle.'

19: Supreme Illumination (Taihao) is another title for Fu Xi.

22: Both Bin and Qi are places in the ancient homeland of the Zhou, in modern Shaanxi province.

28: The Long mountains, as well as the more picturesque-sounding Cinnamon Car and Heli River, are all located in the far west (modern Gansu province). See He Jianxun, *Chuci xingu*, 377.

IV. CONDOLING WITH THE SOVEREIGN

As previously, the mood seems to have turned to one of futility. The main interest of this poem is metrical, in the transition from rapid-fire tetrasyllabic verse to *sao*-style lines in the second half. The sense of oppression in the first half modulates into a more capacious realm of interiority.

10: Sweet cicely looks not unlike the other fragrant plants and is much used medicinally, but its fruit contains tiny barbs that stick to clothing, so it is a fine symbol for the petty men, in contrast to the sweet-smelling liquorice root.

22: Confucius had called himself 'the man of east, west, north, and south' (wanderer without fixed abode). See Legge, *Lî Kî*, 2.123.

25: Cf. 'Li sao', line 368: 'Idly gyring to and fro, I gaze back and advance no farther.'

V. ENCOUNTERING DISASTER

Like some of the 'Nine Threnodies', this one too starts out by describing Qu Yuan in the third person. The protagonist is not Qu Yuan but a Quvian character with whom the poet identifies.

5: See *Songs* 80/1, praising an official who serves his lord faithfully: 'His furs of lamb's wool so glossy! | Truly he is steadfast and tough. | That great gentleman | Would give his life rather than fail his lord.' Trans. Waley, *Book of Songs*, 68.

10: With its red body and golden crest, the 'golden pheasant' (*junyi*) was a much-admired bird compared to the phoenix (see Kroll, *Student's Dictionary*, 234).

18: Riverdrum refers to the Oxherd constellation opposite the Milky Way from the Weaving Woman.

20: Triaster and Heart are corresponding constellations at opposite ends of the sky, west and east respectively.

23: 'Mullet's Mouth' (*juzi*) is another term for the Wall asterism in the northern quadrant of the sky, corresponding to part of Pegasus. See Schlegel, *Uranographie chinoise*, 302–4.

30: Yan and Ying are the principal cities of Chu (located at modern Yicheng and Guangling, respectively, in Hubei). Yan briefly served as the capital as well: see Jiang Liangfu, 'Chu Ying du kao', 231–3.

VI. MOURNING DISORDER

Its simplicity and focus on signs of disorder in the world at large (rather than the condition of the protagonist) makes this poem one of the more effective treatments of its theme in the *Elegies*.

5: Both Hua Du and Song Wan killed their own sovereigns. For Hua Du, see *Zuo zhuan*, Huan 2: 'Huafu Du of Song attacked the Kong house, killing

Kongfu and seizing his wife. The lord was angry, and Huafu Du was filled with fear. As a result he assassinated Lord Shang. The noble man considered that Du first had a heart in which there was no place for his ruler and only afterward was stirred to his evil act.' See Durrant et al., *Zuo Tradition*, 75. Song Wan was guilty of regicide, killing Lord Min in the Meng Marsh (*Zuo zhuan*, Duke Zhuang, year 12; Durrant et al., *Zuo Tradition*, 169).

8: The white dragon and numinous tortoise are images of victimization with long pedigrees. For the former, see the preface to 'Nine Songs: Sire of the Yellow River', above; for the latter, see *Zhuangzi*, in which a sacred white tortoise is captured and killed in an attempt to see the future (Mair, *Wandering on the Way*, 272).

10: Zou Yan was an important third-century BCE thinker whose ideas anticipated much of Han cosmology. He is said to have been slandered by contemporaries and imprisoned by the King of Yan. Confucius found himself desperate and on the edge of starvation while looking for work between Chen and Cai.

24: 'Oat-grass' and 'wool-grass' are both common wild grasses (*Miscanthus sinensis* and *Scirpus cyperimus*, respectively).

42: The 'great illumination' is the sun, but also, by extension, the representative of supreme virtue, the sovereign.

VII. GRIEVING FOR THE AGE

The key to an appreciation of the 'Nine Yearnings' is recognition of the playful literary flourishes that appear here and there within the series. For instance, this poem opens with an apparently unnecessary description of a pleasant summer scene, and in general the poem is oddly idyllic in comparison with the preceding poems, as one-third through, the poet declares his intention to forget about political frustrations and instead enjoy himself on a mystical journey.

5: 'Blue rocket' or 'wolf's bane' are common names for the toxic plant aconite. Sowthistle is also reputed for its bitterness.

6: Cf. 'Li sao', lines 51–2, 'Marking plots for the peony and gooseneck – combining there asarum and fragrant angelica.'

14: This line refers to a mildly controversial aspect of Baili Xi's legend. Originally a vassal of the state of Yu, he had himself traded to the state of Qin, where he eventually became an important minister. See the explanation for why this was a noble deed in *Mencius* (Lau, 5A.109–10).

26: The seeming paradox of 'attaining non-action' is familiar from Daoist thought.

28: The Mystic Warrior, attendant spirit of the north, is said to be half-snake, half-tortoise.

36: The Jade Stair is the same constellation known as Purple Tenuity, guarding the Dipper on its northwest side.

38: The White Maiden and the Huntress seem to be two celestial goddesses. See Yu Yue, 'Chuci renming kao', 16a.

VIII. LAMENTING THE TURNING YEAR

Following the more optimistic summer poem preceding, Wang Yi here turns to a more melancholy subject matter, with the new season identified already in the first line as autumn. The opening is indeed closely parallel to that of the previous poem. This poem is particularly rich in symbolism relating to the topos of the world upside-down, and concludes with the poet snowed in and lacking any route onward—preparing the reader for the final poem of the series.

16: Huang Linggeng suggests, plausibly, that this, the sword 'Inksun' (Moyang), is simply a phonetic variant of Mo Ye, one member of the swordsmith couple who produced Supreme Buttress (*Chuci zhangju shuzheng*, 17.2939).

19: The Han commentary identifies these scorpions as flatterers. Cf. *Songs* 225, in which women's elaborately done-up hair is compared to a scorpion's tail.

IX. FURTHERING MY INTENT

This poem's title asserts the proper role of poetry as not just a means of 'expression' but a discipline of virtue (in contrast to the maxim of the 'Great Preface' to the *Book of Songs*, 'poetry articulates intentions'). In contrast to the title, though, the poet's deliberations and reflections through the series seem to have allowed him to approach transcendence, as the main subject of this poem is actually wandering among the stars.

20: For Yan and Ying see 'Nine Yearnings', 5/30 above. According to the Han commentary, 'circuitous springs' represents the Milky Way.

23: The Bright and Dark (literally 'dark and yellow') refer to Heaven and Earth.

29: 'The Fork-net of Heaven' is a constellation corresponding to eight stars in the head of Taurus.

34: Here the hero approaches Heaven's equivalent of the imperial court, suggesting proximity to imperial power as well. Grand Tenuity is one of the three barriers around the Dipper, consisting of ten stars between Virgo and Leo. The Three Platforms or Three Eminences comprise three pairs of stars within Ursa Major.

ENVOI

The envoi to Wang Yi's suite of poems is similar in form to that of Wang Bao's 'Nine Longings', just a few, dense lines long. Though they may owe their inspiration to the 'Li sao' itself, the effect is very different. Among other things, this envoi does not recapitulate a journey, but makes a dramatically different statement from the poems that precede. The anthology thus concludes happily on a note of fantasy, reasserting the ideal in spite of bitter reality.

2: The Three Luminosities are Sun, Moon, and Stars.

4: The Trigger and the Transverse are the third and fifth stars in the Great Dipper.

GLOSSARY/INDEX

All index entries refer to poems in the *Elegies* either by line number, or by number of poem within a suite followed by a forward slash and then line number. In the case of 'Heavenly Questions', the # sign is followed by the number of the quatrain, rather than the line.

FLORA AND FAUNA

This list has been compiled with help from Pan Fuh-Jiunn's *Chuci zhiwu tujian*, Kroll's *Student's Dictionary*, and other sources. It omits a few common terms that need no comment (e.g. 'dragon'). Scientific names are meant to be illustrative rather than determinative.

angelica (*bai zhi* 白芷, *chai* 茝, etc.) The single flower most consistently representing the virtuous courtier throughout the *Elegies*, a perennial shrub with small white flowers and extremely aromatic plants and leaves. *Angelica dahurica.*
'Li sao', 11, 28, 52, 69, 82, 307; 'Nine Songs', 4/9, 4/24, 4/29; 'Nine Avowals', 6/35, 9/14; 'Summons to the Soul', 253; 'Nine Longings', 1/9, 3/5, 9/34; 'Seven Remonstrances', 2/18, 2/23, 3/9; 'Nine Threnodies', 1/27, 3/39, 5/14, 7/37, 9/53; 'Greater Summons', 153; 'Nine Yearnings', 1/6, 7/6.

asarum (*heng* 衡 or *du heng* 杜衡) Known for its root whose fragrance resembles ginger, it has broad, flat leaves said in Chinese to resemble horse's hoofs (hence its modern name *mati xiang*). *Asarum forbesii.*
'Li sao', 52; 'Nine Songs', 4/30, 9/7; 'Nine Avowals', 9/43; 'Seven Remonstrances', 3/9; 'Nine Threnodies', 1/27; 'Nine Yearnings', 7/6.

blackberry lily (*she gan* 射干) A fragrant plant also known as the 'leopard lily' for its orange leaves spotted with red. *Belamcanda chinensis.*
'Nine Threnodies', 7/43.

blue rocket (*jin* 菫) This term refers to the genus *Aconitum*, whose plants belong to the buttercup family and bear appealing hood-shaped blue flowers, but are actually extremely poisonous. Also known as 'wolf's bane' in English.
'Nine Yearnings', 7/5.

bulrush (*fan* 蘋 or *baifan* 白蘋) An aquatic reed perhaps part of the *Scirpus* family; not well identified.
'Nine Songs', 4/5; 'Nine Avowals', 9/43; 'Summons to the Recluse', 24.

calamus (*sun* 蓀 or *quan* 荃) This key term in the *Elegies* originally referred to a specific plant but is typically personified in the poems. Its common name can also be given as sweet sedge or sweet flag. Its modern Chinese name *changpu* is homophonous with an ancient goddess, Chang Pu, mother of Chu ancestor Gaoyang. Calamus thus seems to have had special significance for ancient Chu ritual.
'Li sao', 39, 308; 'Nine Songs', 3/12, 4/21, 6/6, 6/28; 'Nine Avowals', 4/7, 4/26, 4/32; 'Nine Threnodies', 5/20, 7/43.

caltrop (*ci* 蒺) A weed known for its hard, spiny fruits. *Tribulus terrestris.*
'Li sao', 135.

carpetgrass (*lü* 菉) A weedlike grass that inhabits wet and marshy areas. *Arthraxon hispidus*.

'Li sao', 135; 'Summons to the Soul', 253.

catalpa (*zi* 梓 or *qiu* 楸) A genus of trees with pale clusters of flowers, but also fine wood used for musical instruments.

'Nine Avowals', 3/13; 'Summons to the Soul', 239.

chasm-spanner (*juxu* 距虛) A fantastic animal.

'Nine Longings', 2/24.

chrysanthemum (*ju* 菊) Celebrated for its autumn and winter blooms. Though today we are familiar with the cultivated varieties, the wild plant was small with small yellow flowers, frequently used in medicine or for flavouring beverages. *Chrysanthemum sinense*.

'Li sao', 66; 'Nine Songs', 11/4; 'Nine Avowals', 1/83.

cinnamon tree (*gui shu* 桂樹) The term *gui* can refer to at least two different plants (see also **osmanthus**). When a fragrant tree is specified, rather than a flowering bush, the referent is likely to be the sweet-smelling cinnamon tree. *Cinnamonum cassia*.

'Far Roaming', 88; 'Seven Remonstrances', 5/64; 'Greater Summons', 153.

cocklebur (*shi* 菋 or *xi'er* 枲耳) An invasive weed with spiny green fruits. *Xanthium sibiricum*.

'Li sao', 135; 'Nine Yearnings', 8/14.

coco-grass (*suo* 莎) Also called nut grass or nut sedge; a fast-growing and bitter but edible grass. *Cyperus rotundus*.

'Summons to the Recluse', 23.

cogongrass (*mao* 茅) A very hardy and rapidly spreading grass. *Imperata cylindrica*.

'Li sao', 308.

coltsfoot (*kuandong* 款冬) Perennial whose dandelion-like blossoms bloom and fade before leaves have grown. *Tussilago farfara*.

'Nine Longings', 9/3.

creeping fig (*bili* 薜荔) Trailing vine frequently used in medicine. Its small fruits are barely edible. *Ficus pumila*.

'Li sao', 70; 'Nine Songs', 3/11, 3/21, 4/25, 9/2; 'Nine Avowals', 6/53; 'Nine Threnodies', 1/47, 5/49.

demoiselle crane (*kun he* 鵾鶴 or *kun ji* 鵾雞) Sometimes identified as a variety of stork, but this is unlikely considering its loud, mournful call, since storks are mute. The term should thus refer to another variety of fowl such as the demoiselle crane, known for its trumpet-like call. The demoiselle crane migrates across Eurasia and is known as the *koonj* in Northern India, so this might even be a loan word.

'Nine Phases', 18; 'Seven Remonstrances', 5/67; 'Greater Summons', 159.

elaphure (*mi* 麋) Père David's deer, a species native to premodern China but now extinct in the wild. Though closely related to the common deer, this is a distinct species whose common name in Chinese is the 'four unlike' because it shares features of, and yet is not the same as, any of the four common species of deer, cow, camel, and horse. *Elaphurus davidianus*.

'Nine Songs', 4/13; 'Seven Remonstrances', 1/22.

eupatory (*lan* 蘭) Like the angelica, this is one of the plants most commonly used throughout the *Elegies* to represent the protagonist's own inherited virtue and excellence. The term *lan* after the Song dynasty refers primarily to the orchid, but in early China is instead the thoroughwort (*Eupatorium chinense*), a perennial in the aster family named for its perfoliate leaves. Unlike the orchid, it has unprepossessing white or purple flowers in clusters. Since ancient times, though, it has been prized throughout Eurasia for its medicinal properties. For the English translation, I use the old anglicization of the genus name, meaning 'well-sired'. The genus is named after Mithridates VI Eupator, King of Pontus, famous master of potions, poisons, and languages, who is said to have used the *Eupatorium* as part of a herbal concoction (see Adrienne Mayor, *The Poison King: The Life and Legend of Mithridates*). Mithridates' medicinal powers are celebrated in the eponymous poem by Emerson: 'Hemlock for my sherbet cull me, | And the prussic juice to lull me . . .'

'Li sao', 12, 49, 109, 210, 272, 307, 313, 323; 'Nine Songs', 1/7, 2/1, 3/19, 4/9, 4/23, 6/1, 6/7, 11/4; 'Nine Avowals', 9/14; 'Summons to the Soul', 132, 168, 242, 245, 263; 'Nine Longings', 1/8, 5/3, 6/17, 9/34; 'Seven Remonstrances', 2/18, 6/23; 'Nine Threnodies', 1/27, 5/15, 9/53; 'Greater Summons', 153; 'Nine Yearnings', 4/32.

fagara (*jiao* 椒) The Sichuan pepper, familiar from Sichuan cuisine today for its numbing-hot taste. One of the most admired plants in the *Elegies*, presumably because its unprepossessing appearance conceals a powerful and appealing flavour. *Zanthoxylum bungeanum*.

'Li sao', 27, 110, 276, 280, 317, 323; 'Nine Songs', 1/8, 4/22; 'Nine Avowals', 1/82, 9/22; 'Seven Remonstrances', 5/66, 6/23; 'Nine Threnodies', 1/21, 5/11; 'Nine Yearnings', 8/13.

fleabane (*peng* 蓬) Though possessing medicinal properties, this perennial is better known in Chinese lore for its wild-looking, bristly appearance, and its fast-spreading roots which have made it a prominent symbol of the rootless, homeless refugee. Perhaps *Erigeron acer*.

'Seven Remonstrances', 2/68, 3/7, 7/44; 'Lamenting Time's Fate', 90.

ginger (*ranghe* 蘘荷, *poju* 尊苴) The myoga ginger. Frequently used in East Asian cuisines today, for Liu Xiang it was a common and vulgar herb. *Zanziber mioga*.

'Nine Threnodies', 7/44; 'Greater Summons', 68.

ginger lily (*duruo* 杜若) A variety of ginger. A perennial with white flowers whose root is used medicinally. *Alpinia officinarum*.

'Nine Songs', 3/35, 4/37, 9/21; 'Nine Avowals', 7/58, 9/22; 'Seven Remonstrances', 5/63; 'Nine Threnodies', 5/11; 'Nine Yearnings', 4/32.

golden crane (*huanghu* 黃鵠) The *hu* bird is sometimes identified with the swan, but then the colour would be hard to explain. It may in fact be a mythical bird more akin to the gargantuan *peng* bird than any ordinary fowl. It symbolizes the talented hero capable of crossing vast distances and achieving greatness.

'Far Roaming', 40; 'Rueful Oath', 21, 35, 39.

gooseneck (*jieju* 接輿) Identified by Pan Fuh-Jiunn as *Lysimachia clethroides* or 'gooseneck loosestrife', a tall, elongated plant with small white flowers. Hawkes translated creatively as 'cart-halt'.

'Li sao', 51, 324.

halcyon kingfisher (*feicui* 翡翠) The bird or its turquoise plumes often employed in royal decoration.

'Nine Songs', 6/25; 'Summons to the Soul', 124, 152; 'Greater Summons', 162.

hamadryad (*hui* 虺) Properly speaking this Chinese term refers to a hydra-like monster with nine heads, but I use this synonym for 'king cobra' as a suggestive equivalent.

'Heavenly Questions', #26.

hooters and howlets (*chixiao* 鴟鴞) Owls were often regarded as birds of ill omen in early China because of their loud shrieking, and so I translate accordingly. But this same term *chixiao* sometimes may refer to a different bird: see **wren**.

'Seven Remonstrances', 1/28, 3/5, 4/13; 'Nine Threnodies', 6/42.

hyssop (*huo* 藿 or *huoxiang* 藿香) A perennial with vertical clusters of purple flowers. Though it has medicinal uses, it is mentioned only once in the *Elegies* and treated as a common weed there. *Agastache rugosus*.

'Nine Threnodies', 7/44.

knotweed (*pian* 萹) A common and hardy weed. *Polygonum aviculare*.

'Nine Avowals', 6/39; 'Seven Remonstrances', 3/24.

kudzu (*ge* 葛) The hardy creeping vine of the genus *Pueraria*.

'Nine Songs', 9/18; 'Nine Threnodies', 6/41.

lady-lichen (*nü luo* 女羅) 'Lady lichen' trails down from tree trunks and branches in long clumps resembling human hair. A species of *Usnea*.

'Nine Songs', 9/2.

liquorice root (*gaoben* 藁本) Herb similar to lovage, with umbrels of tiny white flowers. The stems are fragrant and the leaves can be consumed medicinally. *Ligusticum sinense*.

'Nine Threnodies', 3/38; 'Nine Yearnings', 4/10.

lotus (*he* 荷) The water-blooming lotus is one of the most celebrated of Asian flowers, but was not so pre-eminent in China before the arrival of Buddhism. It appears occasionally but not ubiquitously in the *Elegies*.

'Li sao', 113; 'Nine Phases', 193; 'Nine Songs', 3/22, 4/20, 4/29, 6/15, 8/3; 'Nine Avowals', 6/55; 'Summons to the Soul', 160; 'Nine Longings', 5/20; 'Nine Threnodies', 1/45.

magnolia (*mulan* 木蘭, *xinyi* 辛夷) The familiar flowering tree. In Chinese, though, its name contains the keyword *lan* 'eupatory' and it is regarded as a related species with parallel connotations.

'Li sao', 15, 65; 'Nine Songs', 4/24, 9/6; 'Nine Avowals', 1/81, 2/52; 'Nine Longings', 5/6; 'Seven Remonstrances', 5/66; 'Nine Threnodies', 5/20, 6/42.

mallotus (*qiu* 楸) Flowering shrub with edible leaves and fruits known for their pharmaceutical properties, including antacid and anthelmintic ones. *Mallotus japonicus*.

'Nine Phases', 44; 'Nine Avowals', 3/13.

melilotus See **sweet clover**.

moccasins and pit vipers (*fushe* 蝮蛇) Venomous snakes.

'Summons to the Soul', 39.

mugwort (*ai* 艾) A common, toxic herb that is a variety of artemisia.

'Li sao', 271, 310.

mystic mushroom (*ling zhi* 靈芝) A type of mushroom thought to have magical properties, instilling long life or helping to communicate with the divine. *Ganoderma lucidum*.

'Nine Songs', 9/17; 'Nine Longings', 2/16; 'Seven Remonstrances', 8/9; 'Nine Yearnings', 3/32.

oreorchis (*shilan* 石蘭) The *Oreorchis patens* is a variety of orchid whose flowers have an inverted-bell shape. It grows commonly on hills and ravines. Pan Fuh-Jiunn identifies *shilan* 石蘭 as the *Dendrobium nobile* orchid. More likely, though, it is the *shanlan* 山蘭 or *Oreorchis patens*, a variety of orchid native to Asia that resembles eupatory.

'Nine Songs', 4/28, 9/7.

osmanthus (*gui* 桂) Genus of aromatic shrubs whose leaves are nowadays frequently used to infuse both tea and wine. It is another modest plant prized mainly for its invisible aroma, and hence a fitting symbol for the virtuous nobleman.

'Li sao', 27, 71; 'Nine Songs', 1/8, 3/19, 4/23, 5/23, 7/22, 9/6; 'Summons to the Recluse', 1, 6, 31; 'Nine Longings', 1/11, 1/15, 9/21; 'Seven Remonstrances', 3/23, 5/56, 5/63; 'Nine Threnodies', 1/21, 5/19, 6/41; 'Nine Yearnings', 9/3.

parasol tree (*wutong* 梧桐) The Chinese parasol tree derives its English name from its singularly large and shade-giving leaves. Its wood is used in making musical instruments, and it becomes much more prominent in medieval poetry. *Firmiana simplex*.

'Nine Phases', 44.

peony (*liuyi* 留夷) The familiar plant with large, fragrant blossoms. In ancient China often used for flavouring food.

'Li sao', 51.

phalarope (*cui* 翠) Unidentified, but perhaps the red-necked phalarope, a migratory bird whose passages occasionally take it past China's shores.

'Summons to the Soul', 124, 152 (see notes).

pigweed (*jili* 蒺藜) An extremely fast-growing weed, the *Chenopodium album*. The term 'pigweed' is used to refer to a number of different kinds of weeds which are nutritious, and so useful in animal fodder, but otherwise not particularly distinguished.

'Seven Remonstrances', 4/10; 'Nine Threnodies', 7/44, 8/42.

pomelo (*you* 柚) Grapefruit-like citrus fruit with yellow-green peel.

'Seven Remonstrances', 1/29, 5/65, 8/11.

pony aster (*malan* 馬蘭) Shrub with clusters of small purple flowers. But its evocative Chinese name 'horse *lan*' demands a more literal translation, hence my 'pony aster'. It resembles the *lan* 'eupatory' but is apparently considered more common and base. *Aster trinervius*.

'Seven Remonstrances', 3/8.

prickly ash (*shi* 樧) A flavourful plant like the 'fagara' with which it is paired. In context it seems to have a neutral or ambivalent status. *Zanthoxylum ailanthoides*.

'Li sao', 318.

privet (*zhen* 楨) Shrub with small white flowers. *Ligustrum lucidum*.

'Seven Remonstrances', 5/66.

raccoon-dog (*li* 狸) Tree-climbing, carnivorous quadruped related to the fox. Familiar in Japanese culture as the *tanuki*.

'Nine Songs', 9/5.

river lovage (*jiang li* 江離, also *xiongqiong* 芎藭) *Ligusticum chuanxiong*. A very popular aromatic herb particularly associated with the Yangtze River region (hence its name). Since it is native to China, it lacks an appropriate common name in English, and instead is rendered as 'lovage' (*Levisticum officinale*), a fragrant herb also in the parsley family, whose name is a contraction of 'love-ache' and hence shares the connotations of romantic longing particularly relevant to the *Elegies*.

'Li sao', 11, 324; 'Nine Avowals', 1/83; 'Nine Longings', 5/5; 'Seven Remonstrances', 4/9; 'Nine Threnodies', 5/10, 7/37.

rosemallow (*furong* 芙蓉) *Furong* often refers to lotus blossoms, but in the 'Li sao' is used in contradistinction to them and so probably refers to the *Hibiscus mutabilis*. See Kroll, *Student's Dictionary*, 120.

'Li sao', 114.

safflower (*nianzhi* 撚支) Unlike many of the flowers mentioned in the earlier *Elegies*, it is distinguished for visual and not olfactory properties, namely its use in purple dye and cosmetics. The name is written using various Chinese characters but is surely a transcription of a foreign word of unknown origin. *Carthamus tinctorius*. See Laufer, *Sino-Iranica*, 324–8.

'Nine Threnodies', 5/50.

sand-spitter (*yu* 蜮) An obscure aquatic or amphibious animal, native to the south and rather threatening.

'Greater Summons', 28.

selinea (*miwu* 糜蕪) Also known as hemlock-parsley. A tall perennial with prominent umbels of white flowers. Conflated in some sources with 'river lovage'. *Conioselinum chinense*.

'Nine Songs', 6/1; 'Nine Threnodies', 3/37.

serpent eagle (*zhen* 鴆) Powerful and venomous bird.

'Li sao', 237.

shepherd's purse (*ji* 薺) A low-lying, flavourful but bitter herb, today used as dumpling filler. *Capsella bursa-pastoris*.

'Nine Avowals', 9/13.

shrike (*tijue* 鶗鴂) Carnivorous, medium-sized bird whose call announces the onset of autumn.

'Li sao', 299.

simurgh (*luan* 鸞) Ancient China was rich in bird symbolism, so in addition to 'phoenix', the legendary Iranian simurgh, a giant bird of prey, provides a loose equivalent for the auspicious, mythical *luan*.

'Nine Avowals', 2/48, 5/27; 'Far Roaming', 150; 'Seven Remonstrances', 8/1; 'Nine Threnodies', 4/18, 9/29; 'Lamenting Time's Fate', 121; 'Rueful Oath', 69; 'Greater Summons', 158.

slough grass (*sumu* 宿莽 or *mu* 莽) This perennial grass is often found in marshy areas. Its name literally means 'the dormant [or enduring]', and so it is symbolic of the steadfastness of the hero. *Beckmannia syzigachne*.

'Li sao', 16; 'Nine Avowals', 6/36.

snowparsley (*sheng* 繩) Resembles some of the more common fragrant herbs in the *Elegies*, having small umbels of white flowers, and is used widely in Chinese medicine. *Cnidium monnieri*.

'Li sao', 72.

soma (*shuma* 疏麻; *xihua* 枲華) Ritual herbs of uncertain identity, perhaps related to the Vedic *soma*.
    'Nine Songs', 5/17; 'Heavenly Questions', #27.

sowthistle (*tu* 荼) A notably bitter herb. *Sonchus oleracheus*.
    'Nine Avowals', 9/13; 'Nine Yearnings', 7/5.

spirax (*qiu* 虯) Variety of dragon distinguished by its coiled form. See Kroll, *Student's Dictionary*, 374.
    'Nine Avowals', 2/8; 'Nine Longings', 2/11.

stoneseed (*zi* 紫) Also known as purple gromwell, a small herb with noted medicinal properties. *Lithospermum erythrorhizon*.
    'Nine Songs', 4/21.

sweet cicely (*jiru* 蘪蕪) One of several common names for the *Osmorhiza aristata*. A herb whose fruits contain tiny barbs that attach to clothing.
    'Nine Yearnings', 4/9.

sweet clover (*hui* 蕙) The *Melilotus indicus* or melilotus, a fragrant herb. Pan Fuh-Jiunn argues that this is 'basil', but admits the objection (made by a number of scholars, notably Laufer, *Sino-Iranica*, 588) that basil was not imported to China till a later period. Alternatively, it may be identified as the fragrant patchouli, member of the mint family (see Li Hui-lin, *Nan-fang ts'ao-mu chuang*, 75). Along with eupatory and osmanthus, one of the most highly prized herbs of the *Elegies*.
    'Li sao', 50, 71, 81, 179, 308; 'Nine Phases', 73, 77; 'Nine Songs', 1/7, 4/26, 6/15; 'Nine Avowals', 1/81, 7/58, 9/1; 'Nine Longings', 1/11, 2/29; 'Seven Remonstrances', 2/23; 'Nine Threnodies', 1/27, 5/9, 5/15, 5/20, 7/43.

sweet pear (*gantang* 甘棠) Technically the 'birchleaf pear'. Its 'sweet' aspect probably refers to the fragrance of its white flowers rather than to the fruit itself, which is small and not particularly tasty. *Pyrus betulaefolia*.
    'Nine Threnodies', 8/41.

tangerine (*ju* 橘) More precisely, the 'sourpeel tangerine' native to the south. *Citrus reticulata*.
    'Nine Avowals', 8/2; 'Seven Remonstrances', 1/29, 5/65, 8/11.

thorny limebush (*zhi* 枳) Citrus tree with small and unappealing fruit. *Citrus trifoliata*.
    'Nine Threnodies', 7/42.

tricolour bloom See **mystic mushroom**.

unicorn (*qilin* 麒麟) Actually more like a griffin, but the equivalence is standard and both share auspicious connotations (unlike the misleading 'dragon').
    'Nine Threnodies', 7/39; 'Rueful Oath', 75.

water chestnut (*ji* 芰, *jihe* 芰荷) More familiar to us as the oblong fruits used in Chinese cuisines, the emphasis in the *Elegies* is more on the broad leaves spreading lotus-like over the surface of ponds and lakes. The compound *jihe* could refer just to water chestnut, or to water chestnut and lotus together. *Trapa bispinosa*.
    'Li sao', 113; 'Summons to the Soul', 161; 'Nine Threnodies', 1/45.

water mallow (*pingfeng* 屏風) The watershield, a water plant with unusual purple flowers emerging from purple stems. *Brasenia schreberi*.
    'Summons to the Soul', 162.

waterclover (*pin* 蘋) Genus *Marsilea* of aquatic ferns, known for clusters of four leaflets floating on the water's surface.
'Nine Songs', 4/7; 'Summons to the Soul', 253.

wormwood (*xiao* 蕭 or *ai* 艾) A shrub with strong aroma, regarded in the *Elegies* as a disreputable weed. *Artemisia dubia*.
'Li sao', 310; 'Seven Remonstrances', 3/7; 'Greater Summons', 69.

wren (*chixiao* 鴟鴞) This term normally refers to the owl in later texts, but in *Songs* 155, the Mao commentary glosses it instead as *ningjue* 'wren'. The diminutive wren is fitting for many contexts in which the term *chixiao* appears in the *Elegies*, particularly when representing 'petty men'. Cf. discussion of *Songs* 155 in Huang Kuan-yun, 'Poetry, "The Metal-Bound Coffer", and the Duke of Zhou'.
'Rueful Oath', 36; 'Nine Yearnings', 9/6.

PROPER NAMES

Compiled with assistance from Jiang Liangfu's *Chuci tonggu* (Vol. 2) and Yu Yue's 'Chuci renming kao'. Some very common place names or problematic terms are omitted.

Anqi Sheng 安期生 An immortal said to live across the oceans at Mount Penglai.
'Nine Yearnings', 7/34.

Ao 澆 Legendary figure of herculean strength and son of Han Zhuo. His physical strength was not matched by equivalent strength of will—indulging in adultery with Lady Tangent, he was murdered by Shaokang. See also **Han Zhuo**.
'Li sao', 153; 'Heavenly Questions', #44, #46.

Archer Yih See **Yih, the Archer**.

Azure Dragon (Canglong 蒼龍) Attendant deity of the west.
'Nine Phases', 248; 'Nine Threnodies', 4/15; 'Rueful Oath', 11.

Baili Xi 百里奚 A grandee of the state of Yu during the Spring and Autumn era. When Yu was conquered by Jin, Baili Xi was sent as a slave accompanying the daughter of Duke Xian of Jin when she was married into Qin. He fled to Chu, but was ransomed back by Duke Mu of Qin (r. 659–621 BCE), who had heard of his reputation for talent and wanted to employ him.
'Nine Avowals', 7/33; 'Nine Yearnings', 7/14.

Bao Si 褒姒 Concubine of King You of Zhou (r. 781–771 BCE), said to have caused the downfall of the Western Zhou.
'Heavenly Questions', #71.

Bi Gan 比干 (11th c. BCE) Bi Gan was a minister to the wicked final King of the Shang Dynasty, Zhow. When he valiantly protested at Zhow's decadence, Zhow had him killed. According to another version of the story, Zhow cut him open and looked at his heart. See *Shi ji*, 3.108.
'Heavenly Questions', #74; 'Nine Avowals', 2/44; 'Seven Remonstrances', 2/14, 3/39, 4/4; 'Rueful Oath', 61; 'Nine Threnodies', 3/24, 5/30; 'Nine Yearnings', 8/26.

Blackwater (Heishui 黑水) River in the remote west.
'Heavenly Questions', #28.

Bo Chang 伯昌 See **Wen, King of Zhou**.

Bo Pi 伯嚭 Minister to King Fuchai of Wu, and like Wu Zixu a refugee from Chu.
'Nine Yearnings', 1/22.

Bo Ya 伯牙 According to legend, Bo Ya was a master of the zither, and his friend Zhong Ziqi was a perceptive listener who could understand exactly what Bo Ya had in mind in each tune. See the 'Questions of Tang' chapter in *Liezi* (Graham, *Book of Lieh-tzŭ*, 109–10). After Zhong Ziqi died, though, Bo Ya destroyed his instrument because he knew he would never find such a sympathetic audience again (see Knoblock and Riegel, trans., *Annals of Lü Buwei*, 14.308).
'Seven Remonstrances', 7/49; 'Nine Threnodies', 7/31.

Bo Yi 伯夷 A loyalist to the fallen Shang dynasty, who refused to eat 'the millet of Zhou' (to accept a position under the Zhou after its conquest of Shang), and instead starved to death. An iconic figure of loyalty and protest who resembles Qu Yuan while also differing in important ways. In later texts he is always paired with his brother Shu Qi, but in the *Elegies* Bo Yi is often singled out for praise.
'Heavenly Questions', #89; 'Nine Avowals', 8/35, 9/98; 'Seven Remonstrances', 2/28; 'Nine Threnodies', 5/25, 8/57; 'Lamenting Time's Fate', 149.

Bole 伯樂 Eminent horse-trainer who appears in the *Elegies* as an excellent judge of equine talent, a figure for the ideal ruler who has equally fine perception of human talent. Also known as Sun Yang.
'Nine Phases', 235; 'Nine Avowals', 5/67; 'Seven Remonstrances', 3/30.

Boundless Capital (Duguang 都廣 or Guangdu 廣都) A southern city, perhaps Chengdu.
'Nine Threnodies', 9/19.

Boyong 伯庸 Qu Yuan's father or perhaps more remote ancestor in the 'Li sao'.
'Li sao', 2; 'Nine Threnodies', 1/1.

Bozhong 嶓冢, **Mount** Located on the western frontier of Chu territory (in present-day Ningqiang 寧強 county, Shaanxi). According to the *Classic of Mountains and Seas*, at least: 'The River Han rises here and flows southeast to empty into the River Flood. . . . Among the animals here are numerous rhinoceros of two kinds, and black bears and brown bears' (trans. Birrell, 2.15–16).
'Nine Avowals', 6/29.

Broken Mountain (Buzhou shan 不周山) Broken Mountain is the site of the famous battle of Gong Gong and Zhuanxu which threw the universe off balance, creating a gap to the southeast. See Birrell, *Chinese Mythology*, 97–8.
'Li sao', 355; 'Lamenting Time's Fate', 45.

Calamus, Lord See calamus under *Flora and Fauna*.

Calends Star (Xunshi 旬始) Identified as the planet Venus, while the name literally means 'beginning of the ten-day cycle', so I translate as 'Calends Star' in parallel to the common designations of Venus as 'Morning Star' or 'Evening Star'.
'Far Roaming', 98.

Canglang 滄浪, **River** The Han River, in modern Hubei province.
'Fisherman', 33.

Cave of Winds (Fengxue 風穴) Mythological location and final roosting place of the phoenix, according to *Huainanzi* (Major et al., trans., 6.222).
'Nine Avowals', 9/77.

Cenyang 涔陽 Place located approximately 50 kilometres south of Chu's capital at Ying, on the north side of the Cen River.
'Nine Songs', 3/13.

Chalcedony Gleam (Yaoguang 瑤光) The auspicious seventh star in the Dipper.
'Nine Longings', 2/26; 'Nine Threnodies', 9/32.

Chalcedony Terrace (Yaotai 瑤臺) A site in Chu used specifically for wedding ritual (Jiang Liangfu, *Chuci tonggu*, 2:768–9).
'Li sao', 235.

Chang 昌, **Prince** See Wen, King of Zhou.

Chang'e 嫦娥 Divine maiden who stole the elixir of immortality from Archer Yih and then fled to live in the moon.
'Heavenly Questions', #40.

Chen Buzhan 陳不占 Chen Buzhan was a nobleman of Qi. He attempted to save his lord, Duke Zhuang of Qi, from an assassin, but was so terrified he dropped his spoon while eating, and fell off the carriage. He was said to possess a humane sort of bravery (but not a martial one). See Liu Xiang, *Xin xu jiaoshi*, 8.1048–53.
'Nine Threnodies', 7/30.

Cheng Tang 成湯 See Tang.

Chui, the Artful (Qiao Chui 巧倕) Legendary artisan from remote antiquity, the time of Yao or Shun.
'Nine Avowals', 5/19; 'Seven Remonstrances', 7/42.

Cinnabar Hill (Danqiu 丹丘) Habitation of the transcendents, whose potions of long life frequently employ cinnabar.
'Far Roaming', 77.

Cinnabar River (Dan shui 丹水) Probably the same as the 'River Scarlet'.
'Rueful Oath', 19.

Civil Flourishing (Wenchang 文昌) God of writing and scholarship and also a constellation within Purple Tenuity, corresponding to a court of the imperial palace.
'Far Roaming', 127.

Cloud Carried (Chengyun 承雲) Musical piece for celestial performance.
'Far Roaming', 151.

Concentration, Mount (Zhong shan 鍾山) Mountain associated with the Yellow Emperor.
'Lamenting Time's Fate', 18.

Crooked Bank (Wangzhu 枉陼) Located along the Yuan River, south of modern Changde, Hunan.
'Nine Avowals', 2/23.

Crossing the River (Shejiang 涉江) Chu musical piece.
'Summons to the Soul', 202.

Curling Frond (Goumang 勾芒) The attendant spirit of the east.
'Far Roaming', 112.

Da Ji 妲己 Concubine of Zhow.
'Heavenly Questions', #79.

Dai 代 Ancient kingdom located in region of modern Hebei and Shanxi.
'Greater Summons', 41.

Dan 旦. See Zhou, Duke of.

Dark Frailty (Qianying 黔嬴) Daoist deity of receptiveness.
'Far Roaming', 167.

Darkslope (Youling 幽陵) Youzhou, the northern province corresponding roughly to modern Hebei and Liaoning.
'Greater Summons', 193.

Dawnsong (Zhaoge 朝歌) Capital of the final emperor, Zhow, of Shang.
'Nine Avowals', 7/35.

Desperation Rock (Qiongshi 窮石) A mountain in the far west.
'Li sao', 227; 'Heavenly Questions', #38.

Dimming Wood 若木 Mythical tree located in the far west, representing the sunset.
'Li sao', 195; 'Nine Avowals', 9/35.

Dongting 洞庭, **Lake** The central geographical feature of Chu and confluence of multiple rivers.
'Nine Songs', 3/10, 4/4; 'Nine Avowals', 3/26; 'Nine Threnodies', 1/42.

Dragongate (Longmen 龍門) Dragongate is said in the Han commentary to be the eastern gate of Chu. But this is obviously just inferred from the context of the previous line. It is worth noting, then, that another Dragongate located on the western reaches of the Yellow River appears in the *Documents* (Legge, *Shoo King*, 127).
'Nine Avowals', 3/33; 'Nine Threnodies', 4/43.

Dragonmeet, Mount (Fenglong 逢龍) A mythical mountain mentioned by Liu Xiang.
'Nine Threnodies', 1/49.

Du Ao 堵敖 (a.k.a. Zhuang Ao 莊敖, Xiong Jian 熊囏, r. 676–675 BCE) Early ruler of Chu, killed and replaced by his younger brother Xiong Hun, who reigned as King Wen (r. 674–626 BCE).
'Heavenly Questions', #95.

E 鄂, **Islet of** Today known as Echeng in Hubei province, a little further down the Yangtze River than modern Wuhan.
'Nine Avowals', 2/15.

Earthking (Tubo 土伯) Hades.
'Summons to the Soul', 85.

Eminent Hill (*chongshan* 崇山) Said to be the destination where Shun exiled the villain Huandou.
'Nine Threnodies', 9/45.

Fathomless Abyss (Yu yuan 虞淵) Said to be the place where the sun sets.
'Nine Threnodies', 40.

Fei Wuji 費無忌 The treacherous tutor to the heir of King Ping of Chu (r. 528–516 BCE). He slandered Wu Zixu's father Wu She, eventually leading to the executions of Wu She and his older son Shang, and Wu Zixu's flight to the state of Wu.
'Nine Yearnings', 1/22.

Feng 鄷 Early capital of the Zhou under King Wen, located in Hu county, Shaanxi.
'Nine Longings', 1/6.

Fenglong 豐隆 God of clouds. Sometimes identified as Master of Thunder instead.
'Li sao', 221; 'Nine Avowals', 6/10; 'Far Roaming', 95.

Floriate Canopy (Huagai 華蓋) A constellation of seven stars in Cassiopeia close to the Pole Star, and so called because it acts as a protective canopy for the emperor.

'Nine Longings', 7/18.

Floriate Pond (Huachi 華池) Said to be a site on remote Mount Kunlun.

'Seven Remonstrances', 8/4.

Flying Font (Feiquan 飛泉) Understood by a commentator to Sima Xiangru's 'Rhapsody on the Great Man' to be located southwest of Mount Kunlun (*Shi ji*, 117.3058n.).

'Far Roaming', 81; 'Nine Longings', 2/15.

Flying Lian (Feilian 飛廉) God of winds. Depicted with cervine body and bird-like head.

'Li sao', 198; 'Nine Phases', 250; 'Far Roaming', 114, 117; 'Nine Yearnings', 1/12.

Frenzied Chu (Ji Chu 激楚) A wild Chu dance.

'Summons to the Soul', 219, 228; 'Nine Threnodies', 6/46.

Frigid Gate (Hanmen 寒門) Said to be a mountain in the extreme north. See Major et al., *Huainanzi*, 6.159.

'Far Roaming', 162.

Fu Fei 宓妃 Goddess of the Luo River. Also said to be the daughter of Fu Xi.

'Li sao', 222; 'Far Roaming', 150; 'Nine Threnodies', 7/14.

Fu Xi 伏羲 (a.k.a. Taihao 太皓, Supreme Illumination) Ancient divinity said to be inventor of the trigrams and writing. In the Han also considered the sovereign deity of the East.

'Far Roaming', 113; 'Nine Yearnings', 3/14; 'Lamenting Time's Fate', 47; 'Greater Summons', 89; 'Nine Yearnings', 3/14, 3/19.

Fu Yue 傅說 Minister to Wu Ding, ancestral king of Shang, but also said to have achieved immortality.

'Li sao', 291; 'Far Roaming', 29; 'Nine Longings', 1/21; 'Nine Yearnings', 9/27.

Fuchai 夫差 (r. 495–473 BCE) Final king of Wu, he heeded slander and sentenced Wu Zixu to death; not long after, Wu was conquered by its long-time rival Yue.

'Nine Avowals', 7/39; 'Nine Yearnings', 1/20.

Gan Jiang 干將 Famous swordsmith of the King of Wu; also refers to the precious sword forged by him.

'Nine Longings', 2/22; 'Nine Threnodies', 3/42.

Gao, Mound of (Gaoqiu 高丘) Though *gaoqiu* can just mean 'High Hill', Huang Linggeng argues that it is actually the burial mound of Gaoyang, Chu ancestor (see *Chuci zhangju shuzheng*, 1.376).

'Li sao', 216; 'Seven Remonstrances', 6/39; 'Nine Threnodies', 1/29, 5/51, 8/63.

Gaoxin 高辛 See **Highlord Ku**.

Gaoyang 高陽 Founding ancestor of the state of Chu, also one of the Five Gods, associated with antiquity.

'Li sao', 1; 'Far Roaming', 49, 164; 'Seven Remonstrances', 3/13; 'Nine Threnodies', 1/3, 9/43.

Gaoyao 咎繇 Wise minister to Shun.

'Li sao', 288; 'Nine Longings', 8/28; 'Nine Avowals', 1/8; 'Nine Threnodies', 2/12, 7/20, 8/48; 'Nine Yearnings', 1/11.

Golden Bell (Huangzhong 黃鐘) First of the twelve pitch-pipes.

'Divination', 47.

Gong, Earl of (Gong Bo 共伯, personal name He 和, r. 841–828 BCE) Ruled in place of incompetent King Li of Zhou.

'Heavenly Questions', #88.

Gossamer Maid (Xian'e 纖阿) Otherwise unknown, she is also mentioned in Sima Xiangru's 'Rhapsody on Sir Vacuous', where the Fu Qian commentary explains that she jumped on the moon and rode it into the sky (see *Shi ji*, 117.3009n.; Knechtges, *Wen xuan*, 2:63). The Han commentary incorrectly identifies her as an expert rider.

'Nine Threnodies', 8/59.

Grand Decorum (Taiyi 太儀) Epithet for the celestial court.

'Far Roaming', 99.

Grand Tenuity (Taiwei 太微) One of the three barriers around the Dipper, consisting of ten stars between Virgo and Leo.

'Far Roaming', 96; 'Nine Yearnings', 9/33.

Great Gourd (*paogua* 匏瓜) A northern constellation of five stars.

'Nine Longings', 7/20.

Great Man (Daren 大人) A Daoist hero who roams freely throughout the universe.

'Divination', 18.

Great Pitch (Da lü 大呂) One of the six Yin pitchpipes, corresponding to the tone of Yu, and representing ritual harmony.

'Summons to the Soul', 221.

Great Plan (Hongfan 洪範) Chapter of the *Documents* presenting principles and models of governance.

'Nine Threnodies', 8/36.

Guan Longpang 關龍逄 An honest minister under the rule of wicked Jie, mentioned in conjunction with Bi Gan in *Zhuangzi* (Mair, *Wandering on the Way*, 4.31).

'Nine Threnodies', 3/23.

Guan Shuxian 管叔鮮 Younger brother to King Wu of Zhou who rebelled against his successor, King Zheng, and was defeated by the Duke of Zhou.

'Heavenly Questions', #83.

Guan Zhong 管仲 A.k.a. Guan Yiwu. Gifted advisor to Duke Huan of Qi whose final advice went unheeded.

'Heavenly Questions', #72; 'Seven Remonstrances', 2/6; 'Nine Threnodies', 7/16; 'Lamenting Time's Fate', 87; 'Nine Yearnings', 7/13.

Guang 光 See Helu.

Guiji 會稽, **Mount** Nowadays more commonly known as Censer Peak, the famous mountain just south of modern Shaoxing, Zhejiang province. One of the landmarks outside of Chu proper which appears only in poems dating to the Han.

'Seven Remonstrances', 5/44; 'Nine Threnodies', 9/47.

Gun 鯀 Mythical hero, father of Yu. By some accounts an aquatic deity with piscine body. Gun was appointed to deal with a flood, but upon failure was exiled by Shun to Mount Plume where he died. For more on Gun, see Lewis, *The Flood Myths of Early China*, 60–4 and 102–6.

'Li sao', 131; 'Heavenly Questions', #12–15, #38–39; 'Nine Avowals', 1/64.

Hairuo 海若 See **Ocean Eminence.**

Hall of Light (Mingtang 明堂) Ceremonial hall for worship of sun and moon.

'Seven Remonstrances', 7/40, 8/13.

Han 漢, **River** Major tributary meeting the Yangtze River at modern Wuhan.

'Nine Threnodies', 8/55; 'Nine Yearnings', 3/1, 3/35.

Han Xin 韓信 (?–196) General who led many of Liu Bang's campaigns to establish the Han dynasty. Ultimately slandered by Empress Lü and executed.

'Nine Threnodies', 7/35.

Han Zhong 韓眾 Sent to find potions of immortality under the reign of the First Emperor of Qin. See *Shi ji*, 6.252.

'Far Roaming', 30; 'Seven Remonstrances', 5/45.

Han Zhuo 寒浞 (Xia era) Served as the prime minister of Archer Yih, but then murdered him, cooked up his remains and attempted to serve them to Yih's own son for dinner. When Yih's son refused, he killed him as well and usurped the throne of the Xia. He had a son Ao known for his Herculean strength. Finally Han Zhuo was killed by Mi, who installed Shaokang as the new sovereign. This bloody tale of betrayal and necrophagy, with its fascinating echoes of the House of Atreus, seems to have exceeded the bounds of good taste as conceived in the Han dynasty, and so is not found in the *Shi ji* itself, but in another early history which is not fully extant, the *Diwang shiji* (3.24, also quoted in the commentary to *Shi ji*, 2.86).

'Li sao', 152; 'Heavenly Questions', #37.

Hanging Garden (Xuanpu 懸圃, also written 'Wonder Garden') Hanging Garden was said to be one of three peaks at Kunlun.

'Li sao', 186; 'Heavenly Questions', #21; 'Nine Longings', 2/25; 'Lamenting Time's Fate', 17.

Hao 鄗 Early capital of the Zhou under King Wu, located near modern Xi'an.

'Nine Longings', 1/6.

He of Jing, Master 荊和氏 Having a precious jade, he offered it to the Duke of Jing, but the Duke did not believe in its value and instead had one of his legs cut off. Offering it again, he lost another leg. Finally on the third opportunity the Duke discovered the jade's value.

'Nine Longings', 9/6; 'Seven Remonstrances', 3/41, 7/51; 'Nine Threnodies', 3/44, 5/28.

Heaven's Ford (Tianjin 天津) The constellation known in the West as Cygnus, which lies across the Milky Way.

'Li sao', 345.

Heli 合黎, **River** River in the far west near Mount Kunlun.

'Nine Yearnings', 3/28.

Helu 闔廬, King of Wu (also known as Helü 闔閭, personal name Guang 光, r. 514–496 BCE) Ruler of Wu at the time of its great contest with the neighbouring state of Yue, he led Wu to its ruin under the rule of his son, Fuchai.

'Heavenly Questions', #86, #93.

Heng 恆, **Mount** The northern Marchmount in modern Hebei province.

'Seven Remonstrances', 5/29.

High Lord (*di* 帝) The term *di* is notoriously problematic, particularly because its meaning shifted dramatically over the course of the first millennium BCE. Though it originally seems to have referred to either one or a set of supreme gods, the First Emperor of Qin adopted it as his title, 'Emperor'. The intentionally vague 'High Lord' is aimed to capture the weight but also ambiguity of this special term.

'Li sao', 1, 207; 'Nine Songs', 2/7, 4/1; 'Heavenly Questions', #13, #34, #35, #76, #80; 'Far Roaming', 97; 'Summons to the Soul', 7, 79.

Highlord Ku (Di Ku 帝嚳) Mythological ancestor of the Shang dynasty, identified by Sima Qian as the great-grandson of the Yellow Emperor. Allan notes that he has been identified with another remote ancestor, Di Jun, and with Shun (*Shape of the Turtle*, 34).

'Li sao', 244; 'Heavenly Questions', #55; 'Nine Avowals', 6/13.

Homely Crone (Momu 嫫母) The fourth concubine of the Yellow Emperor in remote antiquity, famed for her ugliness.

'Nine Avowals', 7/60; 'Seven Remonstrances', 3/22.

Honing God (Li shen 厲神) Apparently a god with power over the returning souls of those who died violently.

'Nine Avowals', 47.

Horn Portal (Jiaoxiu 角宿) The first of seven constellations composing the Dark Dragon, the eastern quadrant of the sky.

'Heavenly Questions', #11.

Hou Ji 后稷 Ancestor of the Zhou people, born according to *Songs* 245 out of the footprint of the goddess Jiang Yuan. See Kinney, *Exemplary Women of Early China*, 3–4.

'Heavenly Questions', #76; 'Nine Yearnings', 10/5.

Hou Xin 后辛 See **Zhow**.

Hua Du 華都 Vassal of the state of Song who killed his own lord.

'Nine Yearnings', 6/5.

Huai 淮, **River** Not mentioned in the first few poems of the anthology, its appearance suggests the broader geographical perspective of the Han.

'Nine Avowals', 9/103; 'Nine Longings', 5/13; 'Nine Threnodies', 6/47.

Huai 懷, **King of Chu** (r. 328–299 BCE) Ill-fated ruler who died in captivity of Qin.

'Nine Threnodies', 1/4.

Huan, Duke of Qi 齊桓公 (r. 685–643 BCE) One of the Five Hegemons, famous leaders of the Spring and Autumn period. In the *Elegies* appreciated for employing Ning Qi and other talented men.

'Li sao', 296; 'Nine Phases', 234; 'Heavenly Questions', #72; 'Nine Avowals', 7/37; 'Seven Remonstrances', 2/5, 3/34; 'Nine Yearnings', 7/15.

Huangzhi 黃支 A country said to be located at the southern Pole, perhaps related to Jiaozhi.

'Nine Yearnings', 7/24.

Jade Balance (Yuheng 玉衡) The fifth star in the Dipper.

'Nine Threnodies', 9/21.

Jade Stair (Yutai 玉臺) Also known as Purple Tenuity, this constellation guards the Dipper on its northwest flank.

'Nine Yearnings', 7/36.

Ji, Master (Jizi 箕子) Virtuous minister to the final king of Shang, Zhow. In order to protect himself he feigned madness and so survived, unlike Sire Mei. Important as one of the historic models among which Qu Yuan finds himself striving to choose. For more on these issues see Schneider, *A Madman of Ch'u*.

'Heavenly Questions', #75; 'Seven Remonstrances', 2/20; 'Rueful Oath', 62.

Jian Di 簡狄 Later identified as a concubine of Di Ku, Jian Di may originally have been a tutelary goddess of the Shang people. She was said to be of the Yousong clan, and gave birth to Shang ancestor Xie. For the version of her life as understood and rationalized by Han scholars, see Kinney, *Biographies of Exemplary Women*, 4–5.

'Heavenly Questions', #55.

Jiang 江 The Yangtze River, traditionally just called Jiang, 'the River', perhaps a loan word from the Austroasiatic term.

'Nine Songs', 3/6, 3/14, 3/33, 4/35; 'Nine Avowals', 2/14, 3/6, 3/26, 3/35, 3/43, 6/34, 9/103; 'Summons to the Soul', 264; 'Seven Remonstrances', 3/65, 6/32; 'Nine Threnodies', 1/37, 2/55, 3/52, 4/30, 5/55, 6/47, 8/26; 'Nine Yearnings', 3/35.

Jiaozhi 交阯 A kingdom in northern Vietnam, later sometimes used to refer to Vietnam as a whole. In Vietnamese pronounced Giao Chi.

'Greater Summons', 194.

Jie 桀 Tyrannical ruler of the Xia who led to the fall of the dynasty. Among other misdeeds, known for jailing Tang.

'Li sao', 31, 157; 'Heavenly Questions', #47, #53.

Jiezi Tui 介子推 Once a loyal retainer of Duke Wen of Jin, he later was ignored and went to live in mountain reclusion with his mother. When Duke Wen repented and sought him out, he discovered Tui was hiding in the mountains and attempted to smoke him out. Tui refused to come down from the mountain, and held onto a tree until he was burnt to death (see *Zhuangzi jishi*, 29.998). But note that this morbid account of his death does not appear in the *Shi ji* biography (*Shi ji*, 39.1662).

'Nine Avowals', 7/41–4, 9/97; 'Seven Remonstrances', 4/5; 'Nine Threnodies', 5/26.

Jili 季釐 One of Shun's sons.

'Heavenly Questions', #52.

Jing 荊 Geographical term short for Jingzhou 荊州, roughly equivalent with the territory of Chu itself.

'Heavenly Questions', #93.

Jizhou 冀州 Jizhou is traditionally one of the Nine Provinces of China, but in the 'Nine Songs' seems to be used to refer to the Central States in general (since it is opposed to the 'Four Oceans' surrounding the world in the next line).

'Nine Songs', 2/11.

Kuai Kui 蒯聵 The unfilial son of Duke Ling of Wei (r. 543–493 BCE).

'Nine Threnodies', 8/47.

Kuang, Music-Master (Shi Kuang 師曠) Famous music master to Duke Ping of Jin (r. 557–532 BCE). For the tale of his performance, the enjoyment of which ultimately led to Duke Ping's death, see Liao, *The Complete Works of Han Fei tzǔ*, 1:74–8.

'Nine Threnodies', 2/11.

Kunlun 崑崙, **Mount** Mythological mountain at the centre of the world or *axis mundi*. Chūbachi Masakazu has argued that the mountain sits atop a system of rivers and waterways, including the 'Yellow Springs' (the underworld).

'Li sao', 341; 'Nine Songs', 8/5; 'Heavenly Questions', #21; 'Nine Avowals', 2/10, 9/79; 'Nine Threnodies', 9/9; 'Lamenting Time's Fate', 17; 'Rueful Oath', 16; 'Nine Yearnings', 3/29.

Lady Xu the Shamaness (Nüxu 女嬃) The Han commentary claims that Nüxu is Qu Yuan's sister, but in fact this is just an honorific term for a female shaman in ancient Chu. See *Han shu*, 63.2761; Huang Linggeng, *Chuci zhangju shuzheng*, 1.249–50.

'Li sao', 129; 'Seven Remonstrances', 6/33.

Lai Ge 來革 Toady to Zhow. Probably a graphic variant of Lei Kai.

'Rueful Oath', 58.

Lei Kai 雷開 Toady to Zhow.

'Heavenly Questions', #74.

Li 厲, **King of Chu** (r. 757–741 BCE) Said to be one of the kings of Chu who ignored Master He's jade.

'Seven Remonstrances', 3/33.

Li, Lady of Jin (Jin Li ji 晉驪姬) Lady Li slandered the rightful heir to Jin, so that he was exiled and committed suicide. See also **Shensheng**.

'Seven Remonstrances', 2/7; 'Nine Threnodies', 3/30.

Li 醴, **River** Flows due east into Lake Dongting.

'Nine Songs', 3/34, 4/36.

Li Lou 離婁 Man famous for superb vision.

'Nine Avowals', 5/23.

Lie, Master (Liezi 列子) Sage-immortal to whom an eponymous Daoist compilation is attributed.

'Seven Remonstrances', 7/63.

Litheloined (Yaoniao 要褭) A famous horse.

'Seven Remonstrances', 8/5.

Long Lian 隴廉 Woman proverbial for her ugliness.

'Lamenting Time's Fate', 66.

Long 隆, **Mountains** Mountain range in the far west, i.e. modern Gansu province.

'Nine Yearnings', 3/27.

Lord of Winds See **Flying Lian**.

Lu 廬, **River** Tributary of the Jiang.

'Summons to the Soul', 254.

Luo 雒, **River** Tributary of the Yellow River originating in Shaanxi.

'Heavenly Questions', #35; 'Nine Threnodies', 7/14.

Lü Wang 呂望 Hero known by a number of other aliases, such as Lü Shang (probably his original name) and Taigong Wang. Distinguished counsellor to the early Zhou kings who helped to overthrow the Shang, he had once worked as a butcher at the Shang capital Dawnsong.

'Li sao', 293; 'Nine Phases', 109; 'Heavenly Questions', #81; 'Nine Avowals', 7/35; 'Seven Remonstrances', 2/12, 3/31; 'Nine Threnodies', 7/16; 'Lamenting Time's Fate', 151; 'Nine Yearnings', 1/21.

Many-Crowned Mountain (Wanshou 萬首) Mountain of the immortals.
'Nine Longings', 8/18.

Many-Faceted Majesty 重華 Epithet of **Shun**.

Marchmount (Yue 嶽) The five sacred mountains of China, each with its own distinguished history, so as to 'mark' (of which 'march' is an archaic form) out a spiritual landscape: Mount Song in the centre, Mount Tai in the east, Mount Heng in the south, Mount Hua in the west, and Mount Heng (again, but with a different graph) in the north.
'Heavenly Questions', #52; 'Nine Threnodies', 4/7.

Master of Rains (Yushi 雨師) See **Pingyi**.

Master of Three Clans (Sanlü dafu 三閭大夫) Qu Yuan's noble title in Chu, perhaps having to do with records of the three ruling clans of Chu: Zhao, Qu, and Jing.
'Fisherman', 7.

Master of Thunder (Leishi 雷師) Celestial deity entrusted with command of thunder.
'Li sao', 200; 'Nine Phases', 249; 'Far Roaming', 132.

Meng 夢 See **Shou Meng**.

Meng 蒙, **Mount** Probably the same as Mount Min 岷, figuring in the legend of Jie. The mountain, if a real place is indicated, was located 100 kilometres west of Chengdu, and also marks the source of the Jiang.
'Heavenly Questions', #47; 'Nine Avowals', 9/80.

Meng Ju 孟娵 Virtuous woman otherwise unknown.
'Lamenting Time's Fate', 66.

Mighty Chasm (Dahuo 大壑) Place of infinite depths.
'Far Roaming', 172.

Mighty Treasure (Jubao 鉅寶) Sun deity with rooster-like head and human body.
'Nine Longings', 3/17.

Miluo 汨羅, **River** Said to be location of Qu Yuan's drowning. Tributary of the Xiang.
'Seven Remonstrances', 6/9; 'Nine Threnodies', 2/44, 4/28; 'Lamenting Time's Fate', 130; 'Nine Yearnings', 5/2.

Min 岷, **Mount** See **Meng, Mount**.

Mingtiao 明條 Place north of modern Anyi in Shanxi province, where Jie was exiled by Tang.
'Heavenly Questions', #54.

Moxi 妹嬉, **Lady** Consort of Jie.
'Heavenly Questions', #47.

Mu 穆, **Duke of Qin** (r. 659–621 BCE) One of the Five Hegemons, outstanding monarchs of the Spring and Autumn period, but significant in the *Elegies* as the patron of Baili Xi.
'Nine Avowals', 7/37; 'Nine Yearnings', 7/15.

Mu, King of Zhou (Zhou Mu wang 周穆王) Seventh King of Zhou, son of King Zhao, whose western journeys are recorded in the apocryphal *Biography of Prince Mu*.
'Heavenly Questions', #70.

Mulberry Door (Sang Hu 桑扈) One of a trio of eccentrics mentioned in *Zhuangzi*. After he died, his friends sang around his body without giving him a proper ritual burial. See Mair, *Wandering on the Way*, 6.60.

    'Nine Avowals', 2/40.

Mullet's Mouth (*juzi* 娵觜) The Wall asterism in the northern quadrant of the sky, corresponding to part of Pegasus.

    'Nine Yearnings', 5/23.

Murky Strand (Mengsi 蒙汜) Setting place of the sun.

    'Heavenly Questions', #8.

Mystic Base (Xuanzhi 玄趾) Perhaps a mountain near Mount Triperil.

    'Heavenly Questions', #28.

Mystic Warrior (Xuanwu 玄武) Attendant deity of the North, often portrayed as half-snake, half-tortoise.

    'Far Roaming', 126; 'Nine Longings', 7/15; 'Nine Yearnings', 7/28.

Nine Phases (Jiu bian 九辯) Royal music of Xia, but also title appropriate for a piece in the *Elegies*.

    'Li sao', 145; 'Heavenly Questions', #34.

Nine Rivers (Jiu he 九河) Chūbachi Masakazu argues convincingly that these are not the nine branches of the Yellow Rivers but rather the nine rivers of the aquatic realm surrounding Mount Kunlun (*Chūgoku no saishi to bungaku*, 20–2).

    'Nine Songs', 6/19, 8/1.

Nine Semblances (Jiu yi 九疑) A mountain range and the burial place of Shun, but also a group of deities. D'Hervey helpfully observes that these mountains often described as 'Nine Doubts' can be understood in the reverse sense as well. See *Le Li-sao*, 51 n. 95.

    'Li sao', 282; 'Nine Songs', 4/33; 'Far Roaming', 146; 'Nine Longings', 8/16.

Nine Shao (Jiu shao 九韶) Royal music of Shun, perhaps equivalent with 'Nine Summons'.

    'Li sao', 363; 'Far Roaming', 152; 'Nine Threnodies', 6/45.

Nine Songs (Jiu ge 九歌) Royal music of ancient Xia dynasty.

    'Li sao', 363; 'Heavenly Questions', #34.

Nine Sons (Jiu zi 九子) Tail constellation in the eastern quadrant of the sky, and part of the myth involving Lady Tangent.

    'Heavenly Questions', #10.

Ning Qi 甯戚 (Spring and Autumn period) Ning Qi was singing to himself as he fed his oxen when he was overheard by Duke Huan of Qi, who then employed him as a minister. A common figure for talent appreciated and raised to an appropriate position.

    'Li sao', 295; 'Nine Phases', 233; 'Nine Avowals', 7/36; 'Seven Remonstrances', 3/33.

North Lodge (Beigu 北姑) Location undetermined.

    'Nine Avowals', 4/76.

Nü Wa 女媧 Ancient goddess who figures in numerous important myths, including of fashioning humanity, of restoring heaven after it was damaged by the battle of Gong Gong and Zhuanxu, and of changing her own form. In some accounts she has the body of a snake and is the consort of Fu Xi.

    'Heavenly Questions', #50.

Nymph Lü (Lü ju 閭娵) A beautiful concubine of the King of Liang, Wei Ying (r. 370–319 BCE).
'Seven Remonstrances', 3/50.

Ocean Eminence 海若 Oceanic deity of whom little is otherwise known.
'Far Roaming', 154.

Palace of Long Life (*shou gong* 壽宮) Perhaps equivalent to **Palace of the Spring**.
'Nine Songs', 2/5.

Palace of the Spring (Chungong 春宮) Palace of the immortals in Heaven.
'Li sao', 217.

Pamir Mountains (Congling 蔥嶺) Literally 'onion range', the modern translation of this mountain range in central Asia just beyond Xinjiang. Perhaps originally not specifying a particular mountain range.
'Nine Longings', 2/13, 7/10.

Pawlonia Sheet (Ban tong 板桐) Peak on Mount Kunlun.
'Lamenting Time's Fate', 20.

Peng and Xian 彭咸 'Peng Xian' was identified by the Han commentary as a Shang-dynasty nobleman who suffered a fate similar to that of Qu Yuan's, drowning himself out of frustration, but there seems to be no early evidence for such a claim (as Dai Zhen already observed in *Qu Yuan fu Dai shi zhu*, 1.4b). Another possibility is that Peng Xian is related to 'Old Peng' or Peng Keng, celebrated in the *Analects* for his longevity. But Peng and Xian were most likely two ancient shaman heroes, Wu Peng and Wu Xian.
'Li sao', 76, 372; 'Nine Avowals', 4/34, 6/66, 9/5, 9/52, 9/70; 'Seven Remonstrances', 7/41; 'Nine Threnodies', 2/42.

Peng Keng 彭鏗 The extremely long-lived minister said to have cooked a pheasant soup for Yao, and possibly one member of the pair 'Peng and Xian'.
'Heavenly Questions', #87; 'Nine Yearnings', 2/18.

Penglai 蓬萊, **Mount** Mystic home of the immortals.
'Nine Yearnings', 7/34.

Ping 平, **King of Chu** (r. 528–516 BCE) Easily misled ruler who drove Wu Zixu out of Chu.
'Nine Yearnings', 1/20.

Pingyi 萍翳 (or Fengyi 馮夷) God of Rain, or an unspecified water god. The name of this god is written several different ways. Jiang Liangfu argues that Pingyi and Fengyi are different (*Chuci tonggu*, 1:241–4), but their phonological similarity makes this hard to accept.
'Heavenly Questions', #42; 'Far Roaming', 131, 154.

Plainspoken Paragon (Jianxiu 謇修) According to the Han commentary, Plainspoken Paragon (Jianxiu) was an advisor of Fu Xi.
'Li sao', 224.

Platform of Mulberries (Taisang 台桑) Uncertain, but the site of Yu's romance with the lady of Mount Soil.
'Heavenly Questions', #30.

Pleasance of Jasper (Yao zhi pu 瑤之圃) Hunting park of Shun in the realm of immortals.
'Nine Avowals', 2/9.

Plucking Water Chestnuts (Cai ling 采薆) Chu musical piece.
'Summons to the Soul', 202.

Plume, Mount (Yushan 羽山) Mythical mountain of uncertain location, known as the site of Gun's exile.
'Li sao', 132; 'Heavenly Questions', #14.

Pool of Affinity 咸池 Also 'Pool of Heaven'. 'Affinity' is suggested by this word's use in hexagram #31 of the *Book of Changes* to mean 'mutual resonance'. Like *ling* 'spirit', *xian* is a keyword in the 'Li sao' and in early mythology in general. Also the name of a musical piece.
'Li sao', 193; 'Nine Songs', 6/21; 'Far Roaming', 116, 151; 'Seven Remonstrances', 5/10; 'Nine Threnodies', 9/22; 'Nine Yearnings', 3/18.

Pool of Heaven See Pool of Affinity.

Prospect Shu (Wangshu 望舒) Charioteer of the moon.
'Li sao', 197.

Pure Fox (Chun Hu 純狐) Wife of Archer Yih, whom she conspired with Han Zhuo to murder.
'Heavenly Questions', #37.

Qi 啟 The son and heir of the ancient ruler Yu of the Xia dynasty. Said to have journeyed to Heaven to bring back celestial music; later said to have enjoyed a debauched lifestyle on the throne.
'Li sao', 145; 'Heaven Questioned', 32–4.

Qi, Mount (Qi 岐 or 歧, literally 'forking path' or my 'Tangent' in the name of Lady Tangent above) A sacred site in the founding myth of the Zhou, as the place where Gugong Danfu and Jiang Yuan come to settle in *Songs* 237. Perhaps an alternative *axis mundi* to Mount Kunlun.
'Heavenly Questions', #78–9.

Qian 鍼: Younger brother of Duke of Qin (r. 604–577 BCE).
'Heavenly Questions', #90.

Qiao, Prince (Wangzi Qiao 王子喬) Historically prince and heir apparent to King Ling of Chu, he is said to have risen to immortality upon a crane. During the Han he became a cult figure, with at least one temple dedicated to him in the Later Han (Campany, *Strange Writing*, 193–5). Devotion to Prince Qiao seems to reflect the proto-Daoist cult of the immortals, which was to a large extent separate from ancient Chu religion.
'Far Roaming', 54ff.; 'Nine Threnodies', 5/23, 9/5; 'Lamenting Time's Fate', 112; 'Rueful Oath', 28.

Qing Ji 慶忌 Virtuous half-brother of King Helu of Wu.
'Nine Threnodies', 7/29.

Qiu Mu 仇牧 Minister of the state of Song during the Spring and Autumn period. He was killed by usurpers in 682 BCE just after his lord, Duke Min 閔.
'Nine Yearnings', 2/17.

Qu Yuan 屈原 (*fl.* 300 BCE) Chu nobleman, unsuccessful politician, and revered poet.
'Nine Longings', 5/10; 'Seven Remonstrances', 1/1, 2/76; 'Nine Threnodies', 1/2, 5/1; 'Lamenting Time's Fate', 130; 'Nine Yearnings', 5/1.

Reaper of Rushes (Rushou 蓐收) Attendant spirit (*shen*) of the West.
'Far Roaming', 120.

Red Pine 赤松 Said to have been Rain Master in remote antiquity, under the reign of Shennong 神農, inventor of agriculture, before he ascended to immortality.

'Far Roaming', 23; 'Lamenting Time's Fate', 111; 'Rueful Oath', 28.

Refulgent Clarity (Zhaoming 昭明) See **Spirit of Fire**.

Responsive Dragon (Yinglong 應龍) Mythological figure of whom not much is known.

'Heavenly Questions', #17.

Righteous Principle (Zhengze 正則) Qu Yuan's personal name according to the 'Li sao'. Alternatively, a fictional name for the composite protagonist of the poem.

'Li sao', 7; 'Nine Threnodies', 2/13.

River See **Jiang**.

Sao 騷 By analogy with its use in the title of the 'Li sao', used as the name of the poetic genre that developed out of that poem, including the entire *Elegies* and also a fair amount of later poetry. Also used exceptionally in an adverbial fashion in the poetry of Liu Xiang.

'Nine Threnodies', 4/60, 8/7, 9/60.

Scarlet, River (Chishui 赤水) The River Scarlet appears in *Classic of Mountains and Seas*, where it is said to be rich in white jade and cinnabar (e.g. *Shanhai jing jiaozhu*, 1.7; Birrell, *Classic of Mountains and Seas*, 5). Thus it may be the same as the 'Cinnabar River' as well.

'Li sao', 350; 'Rueful Oath, 19.

Shaman Xian (巫咸) Divinized shaman ancestor. Perhaps one half of 'Peng and Xian'.

'Li sao', 279.

Shaman Yang (Wuyang 巫陽) Character in 'Summons to the Soul', also the name of an ancestral shaman.

'Summons to the Soul', 7, 12, 18.

Shang 商 Second-millennium BCE dynasty preceding the Zhou. Heavily documented by the fascinating but obscure oracle-bone inscriptions (see e.g. 'Wang Hai'). Some evidence suggests that Chu inherited an important cultural legacy from Shang, e.g. bird totemism. Also the name of one note of the pentatonic scale.

'Li sao', 160; 'Heavenly Questions', #67, #78–80, #82; 'Rueful Oath', 30; 'Greater Summons', 90.

Shangjia Wei 上甲微 Remote ancestor of the Shang, son of Wang Hai.

'Heavenly Questions', #60.

Shao 韶 See **Nine Shao**.

Shao, Duke 邵公 Personal name Shi 奭, a.k.a. Duke of Yan 燕 where he was enfeoffed. Along with the Duke of Zhou, Dan, one of the two principal ministers in the early Zhou, charged with control of the western kingdoms.

'Nine Threnodies', 7/24, 8/46; 'Nine Yearnings', 6/6.

Shaokang 少康 Hero of Xia and model ruler who killed Ao, overturning the Han Zhuo family. *Zuozhuan*, Duke Ai, Year 1, reports his story in a speech attributed to Wu Zixu: 'In former times, Ao of Youguo killed the ruler of Zhenguan and attacked Zhenxun, then extinguished Xiang, Lord of Xia. The lady Min, who was pregnant, escaped through a culvert in the walls and returned to Reng. There she bore Shaokang, who became director of herdsmen for Reng. Hating

Ao, Shaokang was able to defend himself against him. When Ao sent Jiao to seek him out, he fled to Yu and served there as director of cooks, thus ridding himself of his trouble. Si of Yu thereupon married his two daughters to him and established him in the settlement Lun, where he ruled over one hundred square *li* of land and a population of five hundred.' See Durrant et al., *Zuo Tradition*, 1835.
'Li sao', 247; 'Heavenly Questions', #44–6.

Shen Baoxu 申包胥 A loyal patriot of Chu who, after saving it from the armies of Wu, refused any reward from King Zhao 昭, and instead went into reclusion at the Five Lakes. Sometimes confused with his compatriot Wu Zixu.
'Nine Phases', 141; 'Nine Threnodies', 9/48.

Shen Tudi 申徒狄 An honest retainer of the wicked Zhow, final ruler of the Shang. Shen is said to have drowned himself with a heavy stone in protest at Zhow's corruption.
'Nine Avowals', 9/106; 'Seven Remonstrances', 2/58; 'Nine Threnodies', 5/24.

Shensheng 申生 (d. 656 BCE) Son of Duke Xian 獻 of the state of Jin 晉. Slandered by Duke Xian's concubine Lady Li, he committed suicide. After Duke Xian 獻 of Jin (d. 651 BCE) was led astray by his new concubine from Li 驪, he abused his loyal and faithful son Shensheng who ought to have been his heir (*Shi ji* 39.1641–6).
'Nine Avowals', 1/61; 'Seven Remonstrances', 2/8; 'Nine Threnodies', 5/27.

Shi Yan 師延 See **Yan, Music-Master**.

Shou Meng 壽夢 (?–561) Grandfather of the famous King of Wu, Helu 闔廬, originally Sir Guang 光. The succession was contested among Shou Meng's grandsons, and Helu ultimately won the throne by murdering his cousin in cold blood, using a dagger concealed inside a fish (see *Shi ji*, 31.1463).
'Heavenly Questions', #86.

Shu Qi 叔齊 With Bo Yi, one of two Shang loyalists who starved to death rather than serve the Zhou. See also **Bo Yi**.
'Heavenly Questions', #89; 'Seven Remonstrances', 2/28.

Shun 舜 Shun was the virtuous sage-king who succeeded Yao, even though he was not his son or blood heir. For a full treatment of the various different representations of Yao and Shun, see Allan, *The Heir and the Sage*.
'Li sao', 29, 144, 161, 287; 'Nine Phases', 185, 213; 'Heavenly Questions', #48, #51–2; 'Nine Avowals', 2/9, 3/53, 5/47, 5/51; 'Nine Longings', 8/27, 9/36; 'Seven Remonstrances', 1/17, 2/3, 3/14; 'Nine Threnodies', 9/46; 'Lamenting Time's Fate', 48.

Silver Pillar (Cangwu 蒼梧) Silver Pillar is a free translation of the place name Cangwu. Though the name of a mountain in modern Hunan, this was identified as the burial place of Shun.
'Li sao', 185; 'Nine Threnodies', 1/43, 9/46.

Sinking Sands (Liusha 流沙) Sinking Sands 流沙 is conceived as a specific place west of Dunhuang, as mentioned in the *Classic of Mountains and Seas*: 'The Flowing Sands rise on Mount Bell, then course westwards, and run on southwards through the Waste of Offspringline, and then the sands go southwest to enter the sea by the mountains of the River Black' (Birrell, 139; *Shanhai jing jiaozhu*, 11.256).
'Li sao', 349; 'Summons to the Soul', 48.

Sire Mei (Mei Bo 梅伯) Nobleman of Shang punished hideously by the wicked Zhow. Mentioned in a number of early texts (such as *Huainanzi*, 17.699), but only ever in this context.

'Heavenly Questions', #75; 'Rueful Oath', 57.

Sire of Might (Boqiang 伯強) Perhaps a divinity for those who died by violence.

'Heavenly Questions', #10.

Sire of the Yellow River (Hebo 河伯) Both god of the Yellow River and possibly also the name of an ancient tribe competing with the Xia.

'Heavenly Questions', #35; 'Nine Longings', 5/25.

Sky Mulberry (Kongsang 空桑) Often identified simply as a 'hollow mulberry tree', but in early texts apparently a celestial mountain (see Chūbachi, *Chūgoku no saishi to bungaku*, 34). Also the name of a zither.

'Nine Songs', 5/6; 'Nine Threnodies', 9/44; 'Greater Summons', 94.

Skywind (Langfeng 閬風) Said to be a peak on Mount Kunlun.

'Li sao', 214; 'Lamenting Time's Fate', 20.

Soil, Mount (Tushan 鎽山) The lady of Tushan was the consort of Xia Yu and mother of Qi. See Kinney, *Exemplary Women of Early China*, 5–6.

'Heavenly Questions', #30.

Song Wan 宋萬 Actually named Chang Wan, but identified as Song Wan because he was a man from the state of Song. Song Wan was guilty of regicide, killing Lord Min in the Meng Marsh after he had been disrespected by him (see *Zuo zhuan*, Duke Zhuang, year 12.1; Durrant et al., *Zuo Tradition*, 169).

'Nine Yearnings', 6/5, 7/23.

Songs (or *Book of Songs*, *Shijing* 詩經) The great anthology of 305 poems.

'Nine Phases', 153.

Southern Nest (Nanchao 南巢) Resting place of the Vermilion Bird.

'Far Roaming', 60.

Stonewall (Shicheng 石城) One of the peaks of Mount Kunlun.

'Nine Threnodies', 1/44.

Southern Semblances See **Nine Semblances**.

Sovereign of the West (Xihuang 西皇) Identified in the Han commentary (not necessarily accurately) as Shaohao Zhi, ancestor of the Shang people and associated with a divine bird or phoenix. According to Sima Qian, Shaohao was son of the Yellow Emperor.

'Li sao', 352.

Spirit Aura (Lingfen 靈氛) Probably the same as Wu Fen, legendary shaman mentioned as one of ten who inhabit a magical mountain in the *Classic of Mountains and Seas* (Birrell, 16.174).

'Li sao', 258, 277, 333.

Spirit of Fire (Yanshen 炎神) Deity accompanying Zhurong, sovereign deity of the South. A.k.a. 'Refulgent Clarity'.

'Far Roaming', 145; 'Nine Longings', 4/24.

Spirit of the Xiang River (Xiangling 湘靈) Goddess of the Xiang as in 'Nine Songs'.

'Far Roaming', 153.

Spirit Harmony (Lingjun 靈均) Qu Yuan's (or a fictional protagonist's) style name (*zi*) according to the 'Li sao'.

'Li sao', 8; 'Nine Threnodies', 2/14.

Spirit Huai (Linghuai 靈懷) Portmanteau of 'King Huai' and 'Spirit Paragon'.

'Nine Threnodies', 2/1–5.

Spirit Paragon (Lingxiu 靈脩) The object of Qu Yuan's admiration and resentment in the 'Li sao'. Apparently a pseudonym for King Huai of Chu; alternatively, a fictional character based on the sovereign. Sometimes represented as a love object, but also (1) a kind of shaman or religious character, as indicated by the term 'spirit' (*ling*), which can mean either spiritual power, divinity, or the shaman assuming a divine persona; and (2) a moral paragon, as indicated by the second term in the name, *xiu*, likewise a keyword throughout the *Elegies*, referring both to 'adornment' and 'refinement' and the ultimate goal of moral improvement, the sagely ideal. A complex term whose meaning can only be elicited gradually by careful and repeated reading of the entire 'Li sao' and 'Nine Songs'.

'Li sao', 44, 48, 85. 'Nine Songs', 9/15; 'Seven Remonstrances', 6/28, 7/1; 'Nine Threnodies', 1/19, 8/30.

Stellar Yang (Chenyang 辰陽) Located near modern Chenxi county in Hunan province, on the Chen River which feeds into the Yuan.

'Nine Avowals', 2/24.

Sui, Marquis (Suihou 隨侯) The pearls of the Marquis of Sui are a common symbol of unappreciated talent in later poetry.

'Nine Longings', 9/6.

Sun Yang 孫陽 See **Bole**.

Sunlit Knoll (Yang e 陽阿) Chu musical piece.

'Summons to the Soul', 203; 'Greater Summons', 91.

Sunny Vale (Yanggu 湯谷, also written 暘谷) Mentioned in numerous early texts as the starting point of the sun's journey. It may be an alliterative compound: **lang-lok*.

'Heavenly Questions', #8; 'Far Roaming', 79; 'Nine Threnodies', 9/22; 'Greater Summons', 19.

Sunrise Mulberry (*fusang* 扶桑) The mythical tree in the far east where the sun rises. The mulberry tree is prominent throughout early Chinese mythology and religion, symbolic of creativity and fertility.

'Li sao', 194; 'Nine Songs', 7/2; 'Lamenting Time's Fate', 44.

Supreme Buttress (Taie 太阿) The famous sword said to have been forged by the legendary married swordsmiths, Gan Jiang and Mo Ye.

'Nine Longings', 9/8; 'Seven Remonstrances', 8/8.

Supreme Illumination (Taihao 太皓) See **Fu Xi**.

Supreme Unity (Taiyi 太一) Either a philosophical concept of absolute oneness, or a powerful deity.

'Nine Longings', 3/11; 'Nine Threnodies', 4/12; 'Rueful Oath', 10; 'Nine Yearnings', 7/36.

Tai, Lord 太公 See **Lü Wang**.

Tai 泰, **Mount** The Eastern Marchmount, a sacred mountain located in modern Shandong province.

'Nine Longings', 3/7; 'Seven Remonstrances', 7/3.

Taihao 太皞 See **Fu Xi**.

Tang-Yao 唐堯 See **Yao**.

Tang 湯 (also Cheng Tang 成湯) Founding emperor of Shang. See 'Li sao', 287; 'Heavenly Questions', #47, #62–64 #85; 'Nine Avowals', 5/51, 7/37; 'Seven Remonstrances', 'Lamenting Time's Fate', 50.

Tangent, Lady (Nüqi 女歧) Somewhat fanciful translation for the celestial goddess and also sister-in-law of Ao with whom he committed adultery (perhaps different figures, but it is nonetheless significant they share a name and hence a mythical archetype).
'Heavenly Questions', #10, #45.

Tangxi 棠谿 Famous sword of Chu.
'Nine Threnodies', 3/41.

Torch Dragon (Zhulong 燭龍) See *Classic of Mountains and Seas*: 'There is a god-human here with a human face and a snake's body, and he is scarlet. He has vertical eyes that are in a straight seam. When this deity closes his eyes, there is darkness. When the deity looks with his eyes, there is light. He neither eats, nor sleeps, nor breathes. The wind and the rain are at his beck and call. This deity shines his torch over the ninefold darkness. This deity is Torch Dragon' (Birrell, *Classic of Mountains and Seas*, 17.188).
'Heavenly Questions', #23; 'Greater Summons', 40.

Tarryhere, Mount (Yanzi 崦嵫) Mountain said to be location where the sun sets.
'Li sao', 190.

Three Platforms (Sanjie 三階) Three pairs of stars within Ursa Major.
'Nine Yearnings', 9/34.

Three Sovereigns (Sanhou 三后) Three ancient rulers of uncertain identity.
'Li sao', 25.

Tiao 條 See **Mingtiao**.

Tiered Palisade (Cengcheng 增城) A site on Mount Kunlun.
'Heavenly Questions', #21.

Treasury and Tower (*kulou* 庫樓) Double constellation overlapping in part with the Western constellation Centaur.
'Nine Longings', 7/19.

Triaster and Heart (*shen chen* 參辰) Two opposing constellations (roughly Orion and Scorpio) at the west and east of the sky, respectively.
'Nine Yearnings', 5/20.

Trigger and Transverse (Ji Heng 機衡) The third and fifth stars in the Dipper.
'Nine Yearnings', 10/4.

Triperil, Mount (Sanwei shan 三危山) Today the name of a specific mountain range in Dunhuang, Gansu province, but in the *Elegies* simply a remote mountain in the west.
'Heavenly Questions', #28; 'Nine Threnodies', 9/15.

Tui, Sir See **Jiezi Tui**.

Twinkling Indicator (Zhaoyao 招搖) The star at the end of the handle of the Great Dipper.
'Nine Threnodies', 1/10.

Vermilion Bird (Zhuque 朱雀) Attendant deity of the south.
'Nine Phases', 247; 'Nine Threnodies', 4/18; 'Rueful Oath', 9.

Wang Hai 王亥 Remote Shang ancestor, identified in *Shi ji* as Wang Zhen (*Shi ji*, 3.92), shown by Wang Guowei to be identical with the figure worshipped in the oracle-bone inscriptions as Wang Hai. See Wang Guowei, 'Yin buci zhong suo jian xiangong xianwang kao'.
'Heavenly Questions', #56.

Wang Heng 王恆 Remote Shang ancestor and younger brother of Wang Hai.
'Heavenly Questions', #59.

Wang Liang 王良 A famous charioteer from the state of Jin, later also represented astrologically (see Knechtges, *Wen xuan*, 3:123). Possibly the same as Bole. See Yu Yue, 'Chuci renming kao', 8a.
'Seven Remonstrances', 7/22.

Wang, Master (Shi Wang 師望) See **Lü Wang**.

Wang Ming 王冥 Remote Shang ancestor, father of Wang Hai. His personal name is written as Ji in the *Elegies*.
'Heavenly Questions', #56, #59.

Weakwater (Ruoshui 弱水) Weakwater is a river whose source is said to be near Mount Kunlun. A similar term is identified as the habitation of Changyi, Chu ancestor and progenitor of Zhuanxu. See *Classic of Mountains and Seas*, 18: 'Radiant Thought [Changyi] came down on earth to settle by the River Accord [Ruoshui], and he gave birth to Fence Flow [Hanliu]' (Birrell, 191).
'Nine Longings', 8/9; 'Lamenting Time's Fate', 21.

Weaving Girl 織女 The star Vega, said to be separated from the Oxherd by the Milky Way, except for on the evening of the seventh day of the seventh month (*qi xi*), when the two are briefly reunited. The Weaving Girl is already described in *Songs* 203/6.
'Nine Yearnings', 9/28.

Wei 微 See **Shangjia Wei**.

Wei Basin (Weipan 渭盤) Located on the Wei River flowing from Mount Tarryhere in the far West.
'Li sao', 228.

Wen 文, **Duke of Jin** (r. 636–628 BCE) One of the Five Hegemons, and patron of Jiezi Tui.
'Nine Avowals', 7/42.

Wen 文, **King of Jing** 荊 (r. 689–677 BCE) King of Chu (for which Jing is an alternative name) who destroyed the state of Xu, according to a legend which may not be historical. See Tang Bingzheng et al., *Chuci jinzhu*, 293.
'Seven Remonstrances', 2/10.

Wen 文, **King of Zhou** Personal name Chang and 'Prince of the West' (Xibo). Revered as founding ruler of the Zhou after his son, King Wu, completed the conquest of the Shang.
'Li sao', 294; 'Heavenly Questions', #78, #80–1; 'Seven Remonstrances', 3/32; 'Lamenting Time's Fate', 151; 'Nine Yearnings', 1/19, 3/22.

Wen, Sir (Ziwen 子文) Chief minister of Chu from 664 to 637 BCE. Born of an adulterous liaison.
'Heavenly Questions', #94.

West, Prince of the (Xibo 西伯) See **Wen, King of Zhou**.

West Pleasance (Xiyu 西囿 Imperial hunting park west of the capital.
'Nine Longings', 4/29.

White Maiden (Sunü 素女) Talented zither-player of antiquity.
  'Nine Longings', 4/17; 'Nine Yearnings', 7/37.

White Tiger (Bai hu 白虎) Attendant deity of the west.
  'Rueful Oath', 12.

Whitewater (Baishui 白水) Mythical river in the west.
  'Li sao', 213; 'Nine Threnodies', 8/51.

Wolf of Heaven (Tianlang 天狼) A single red star southeast of the Well constellation. Schlegel finds its significance in that the wolf's trail was particularly easy to mark out, according to Chinese hunting lore. Similarly, the Wolf rose early in the evening after the first month of summer, late April or May in the Western calendar (*Uranographie chinoise*, 430–2).
  'Nine Songs', 7/20.

Wondrous Abyss (Xuanming 玄冥) Attendant spirit of the north.
  'Far Roaming', 165; 'Nine Threnodies', 9/44.

Wu 武, **King of Chu** (r. 740–690 BCE) Said to be one of the kings of Chu who failed to appreciate the value of Master He's jade.
  'Seven Remonstrances', 3/33.

Wu 武, **King of Zhou** Personal name Fa 發, he defeated the final ruler of the Shang, Zhow, at Muye to establish the authority of the Zhou. Established the Zhou capital at Haojing (southwest of modern Xi'an).
  'Heavenly Questions', #68, #82; 'Nine Avowals', 7/37.

Wu Ding 武丁 Admirable Shang king.
  'Li sao', 292; 'Nine Yearnings', 1/19.

Wu Guang 務光 ('Oblivious to Glory') Appears in *Zhuangzi* as an advisor to Tang, founder of the Shang dynasty. Tang seeks to abdicate in favour of his worthy advisor, but Oblivious to Glory declines, and drowns himself in the Lu River instead. See Mair, *Wandering on the Way*, 28.294–5.
  'Lamenting Time's Fate', 97; 'Nine Yearnings', 2/18.

Wu Huo 烏獲 Strong man and loyal servant of King Wu of Qin.
  'Nine Threnodies', 8/45.

Wu, Sir See Wu Zixu.

Wu Zixu 伍子胥 Personal name Yun, a native of Chu. Following slanderous counsel, the King of Chu had his father and older brother murdered. Wu Zixu fled to the state of Wu, where he served effectively and succeeded in a major expedition against Chu, achieving vengeance. But he was again betrayed in Wu and killed himself on the command of the King. See *Shi ji*, 66.2171–80, and the survey of early historical representations of Wu in Milburn, *Cherishing Antiquity*, 80–93.
  'Nine Avowals', 2/43, 7/40, 9/104; 'Nine Longings', 5/9; 'Seven Remonstrances', 2/44, 3/40, 4/3; 'Nine Threnodies', 5/29; 'Lamenting Time's Fate', 129; 'Nine Yearnings', 8/25.

Xi Shi 西施 A beauty of the Yue state from the Spring and Autumn period. Given to the King of Wu as a present, her charms distracted him from governance and Wu was soon defeated by Yue.
  'Nine Avowals', 7/61; 'Seven Remonstrances', 3/21; 'Nine Threnodies', 8/43.

Xia 夏 Ancient dynasty preceding the Shang. Its precise historical dates and circumstances are still controversial. It is also important to note that views of Xia history evolved during the period reflected in the *Elegies*; Han scholars had a distinct sense of dynastic succession that had coalesced gradually and may not have been shared by Qu Yuan.

'Li sao', 146; 'Heavenly Questions', #35.

Xia 夏, **River** Located in central Chu, it splits off from the Yangtze River near Ying, and flows eastward to rejoin it at Xia (modern Wuhan City).

'Nine Avowals', 3/6, 3/43, 6/34; 'Nine Threnodies', 4/44.

Xia Cove (Xiapu 夏浦) Where the Xia River rejoins the Yangtze near modern Wuhan.

'Nine Avowals', 3/31.

Xian 獻, **Duke of Jin** 晉 (d. 651 BCE) Ruler beguiled by concubine, Lady Li.

'Seven Remonstrances', 2/7.

Xian, Shaman (Wu Xian 巫咸) Shaman Xian is a heroic shaman of antiquity of whom little is known. He appears also in the *Classic of Mountains and Seas*. He may be one member of the pair 'Peng and Xian'.

'Li sao', 279.

Xiang 象 Younger half-brother of Shun.

'Heavenly Questions', #51.

Xiang 湘, **River** Fundamental to ancient Chu geography, both spatial and spiritual. Flows north across the territory of modern Hunan province, past Mount Heng (the Southern Marchmount), to empty into Lake Dongting.

'Li sao', 143; 'Nine Songs', 3/5; 'Nine Avowals', 2/14, 5/61, 7/23; 'Fisherman', 27; 'Nine Longings', 5/10; 'Seven Remonstrances', 2/77, 6/8, 6/9; 'Nine Threnodies', 1/37, 2/54, 3/52, 3/64, 4/30, 4/45, 5/55, 8/20, 9/50; 'Nine Yearnings', 5/2.

Xie 契 Primordial ancestor of the Shang people.

'Nine Yearnings', 10/5.

Xihe 羲和 Charioteer of the sun, usually identified as female in ancient myth, but sometimes also seen as a male official. According to the *Classic of Mountains and Seas*, 'Beyond the southeast sea, along the banks of the River Sweet there is the Country of Xihe. There is a girl here. Her name is Xihe. She is just now giving the sun a bathe in Sweet Gulf. Xihe is the wife of the Great God Jun. She gave birth to the ten sons' (Birrell, *Classic of Mountains and Seas*, 15.170).

'Li sao', 189; 'Heavenly Questions', #23.

Xiong Jian 熊囏 (r. 674–672 BCE) An early ruler of Chu.

Xiu Ji 脩己 Wife of Gun.

'Heavenly Questions', #39.

Xu Cove (Xupu 溆浦) Located in modern Hunan province roughly 50 kilometres east of Stellar Yang, on the Yuan River further upstream than Crooked Bank.

'Nine Avowals', 2/27.

Xu You 許由 Mythic recluse said to have been offered rule by Yao, but who rejected it.

'Nine Threnodies', 5/25.

Xuanyuan 軒轅 See **Yellow Emperor**.

Xun Xi 荀息 Minister of Jin who committed suicide in 651 BCE after his duke was killed by usurpers.

'Nine Yearnings', 2/17.

Yan 偃, **King of Xu** 徐 (10th c. BCE) Benevolent but ill-fated ruler.

'Seven Remonstrances', 2/9.

Yan, Music-Master (Shi Yan 師延) Music-master under the reign of the wicked Zhow, final ruler of the Shang dynasty, and said to have composed the decadent music that typified his rule. He drowned himself in the Pu 濮 River after the fall of the Shang. See *Shi ji*, 24.1235.
'Nine Threnodies', 2/43.

Yan and Ying 鄢郢 Either an alternative name for Ying itself, or two separate cities of ancient Chu.
'Nine Yearnings', 5/30.

Yan Ying 晏嬰 Wise minister of Qi during Spring and Autumn period.
'Lamenting Time's Fate', 87.

Yang, Lord (Yanghou 陽侯) Water deity.
'Nine Avowals', 3/21; 'Nine Threnodies', 4/31.

Yangcheng 陽城 Site in Henan associated with Yu of Xia, perhaps his capital. Also said to be the name of a gate of Shu (in modern Sichuan).
'Nine Longings', 8/23.

Yao 堯 Benevolent sage king known particularly for passing on the throne not to his own son but to Shun.
'Li sao', 29, 161; 'Nine Phases', 185, 213; 'Heavenly Questions', #48; 'Nine Avowals', 3/53; 'Nine Longings', 8/27, 9/36; 'Seven Remonstrances', 1/17, 2/3, 3/14; 'Lamenting Time's Fate', 48; 'Nine Yearnings', 10/5.

Yaw 姚 Clan of Shun, from which he derived his surname.
'Heavenly Questions', #48.

Yee 夷 A term used for various non-Chinese peoples, especially to the northeast.
'Heavenly Questions', 35; 'Nine Yearnings', 7/20.

Yellow Emperor (Huang Di 黃帝) Mythical sage king and deity. According to the Han euhemerization of ancient myth, he was the first of the Five Highlords/ Emperors (*di*), and was succeeded by Gaoyang (Zhuanxu), Gaoxin (Highlord Ku), Yao, and Shun. See the first chapter of Sima Qian's *Shi ji*: William H. Nienhauser, Jr, ed., *The Grand Scribe's Records*, Vol. 1: *The Basic Annals of Pre-Han China*, 1–20.
'Far Roaming', 53; 'Nine Yearnings', 1/8.

Yi 益 Wise minister of Yu, ruler of the Xia dynasty. He was originally supposed to succeed him but instead was murdered by Yu's heir, Qi.
'Heavenly Questions', #32–3.

Yi 伊, **River** Tributary of the Luo River in modern Henan province.
'Nine Threnodies', 7/14.

Yi Yin 伊尹 Yi Yin, also known as Yi Zhi, was the leading advisor of Tang, founder of the Shang dynasty. He was discovered while working as a butcher. In the pre-Qin era he seems to have been the hero of a greater variety of stories, however, as we can see from the Tsinghua bamboo-slip text discussed in Sarah Allan, '"When Red Pigeons Gathered on Tang's House."'
'Li sao', 288; 'Heavenly Questions', #53–4, #85; 'Nine Avowals', 7/44; 'Nine Threnodies', 7/20.

Yi Zhi 伊摯 See Yi Yin.

Yigou 義鈞 One of Shun's sons.
'Heavenly Questions', #52.

Yih, the Archer (Hou Yi 后羿) A key figure in early mythology and also the legends of the Xia. It is said that there were originally ten suns, of which Yih shot down nine, leaving the world with only one sun. But Archer Yih also appears as an early Xia ruler murdered by his own minister Han Zhuo. Some scholars differentiate multiple figures by the same name in early sources, but these conflations are probably better understood as a natural result of the transmission and elaboration of mythical stories.

'Li sao', 149; 'Heavenly Questions', #29, #35.

Yin 殷 See **Shang**.

Ying 郢 The ancient capital of Chu. Though its location shifted over time, for most of Chu's history it was located at Jiangling, Hubei.

'Nine Avowals', 3/9, 3/43, 4/57; 'Nine Threnodies', 1/51, 2/65, 2/71, 6/14, 6/53, 7/60, 8/19, 8/31, 9/49.

You, King of Zhou (Zhou You wang 周幽王, r. 781–771 BCE): Final ruler of the Western Zhou.

'Heavenly Questions', #71.

Youdi 有狄, **clan** Ancient rival of the Shang ancestors, possibly a graphic variant of **Youyi**.

'Heavenly Questions', #60.

Youshen 有莘 Clan of Tang's consort.

'Heavenly Questions', #62–3.

Yousong 有娀 Ancient clan to which Jian Di, matriarch of the Shang people, belonged.

'Li sao', 236.

Youyi 有易 (also written Youhu 有扈, etc.) Ancient rival clan of the Shang ancestors who murdered Wang Hai and perhaps Wang Heng as well before Wang Hai's son Shangjia Wei took revenge.

'Heavenly Questions', #56–8.

Youyu 有虞 Ancient clan which provided two brides to Shaokang.

'Li sao', 248.

Yu Shun 虞舜 See **Shun**.

Yu 禹 Founding ruler of the Xia dynasty, son of Gun. Among other achievements helped to contain the great flood, and is said to have established the principal territorial divisions, such as the Nine Provinces, of the Xia.

'Li sao', 161, 287; 'Heavenly Questions', #14–18, 30–1; 'Nine Avowals', 5/51; 'Nine Longings', 9/35. 'Lamenting Time's Fate', 50; 'Greater Summons', 204.

Yuan 沅, **River** Key element of the ancient Chu landscape south of the Yangtze River (in modern Hunan province), feeding into Lake Dongting from the west.

'Li sao', 143; 'Nine Songs', 3/5; 'Nine Avowals', 2/19, 5/61, 7/23; 'Seven Remonstrances', 2/77, 6/8; 'Nine Threnodies', 3/51, 8/20, 9/50.

Yue 說 See **Fu Yue**.

Yuweilü 於微閭, **Mount** Obscure, but perhaps equivalent with Mount Yiwulü in Liaoning today; a name for a remote mountain in the northeast.

'Far Roaming', 100.

Zaofu 造父 The distinguished horse expert of King Mu of Zhou, and an ancestor to the ruling house of Zhao.

'Nine Avowals', 6/26.

Zhanghua 章華 An ancient Chu palace.
  'Nine Yearnings', 7/43.

Zhao, King of Zhou (Zhou Zhaowang 周昭王, r. 977/5–957 BCE): Sixth king of Western Zhou, said to have died on a southern expedition.
  'Heavenly Questions', #69.

Zheng, Great Diviner (Zheng zhanyin 鄭詹尹) Qu Yuan's interlocutor in 'Divination'.
  'Divination', 7.

Zhi 摯 See **Yi Yin**.

Zhong Ziqi 鍾子期 See **Bo Ya**.

Zhou 周, **Dynasty** (1045–221 BCE) Though by the Warring States era (5th–3rd c. BCE) its actual power was notional, the Zhou regime, particularly in the ideal form established by its first leaders, King Wu and King Wen, remained a primary moral authority and political inspiration. Its authority was symbolized by Nine Tripods, and their loss in the Si 泗 River represented the decline of Zhou authority.
  'Li sao', 162; 'Heavenly Questions', #66; 'Seven Remonstrances', 2/12, 3/11, 8/14; 'Nine Threnodies', 3/11, 6/47.

Zhou, Duke of (Zhou Gong 周公, a.k.a. Dan 且) Younger brother of King Wu of Zhou and uncle to King Wen, he is often seen as the key figure in establishing the model principles of the Zhou state.
  'Heavenly Questions', #66; 'Nine Threnodies', 7/24; 'Nine Yearnings', 6/6.

Zhow 紂 (r. c.1086–1045 BCE): Wicked final emperor of Shang. A.k.a. Hou Xin 后辛. See 'Li sao', 31, 159; 'Heavenly Questions', #66, #73, #80, #84; 'Seven Remonstrances', 2/11.

Zhurong 祝融 God of the fiery south, and hence patron deity of the state of Chu itself.
  'Far Roaming', 149; 'Nine Longings', 4/23; 'Nine Yearnings', 7/25.

Zhuanxu 顓頊 See **Gaoyang**.

Zou Yan 鄒衍 (3rd c. BCE): Philosopher of correlative cosmology.
  'Nine Yearnings', 6/10.

American Literature

British and Irish Literature

Children's Literature

Classics and Ancient Literature

Colonial Literature

Eastern Literature

European Literature

Gothic Literature

History

Medieval Literature

Oxford English Drama

Philosophy

Poetry

Politics

Religion

The Oxford Shakespeare

A complete list of Oxford World's Classics, including Authors in Context, Oxford English Drama, and the Oxford Shakespeare, is available in the UK from the Marketing Services Department, Oxford University Press, Great Clarendon Street, Oxford OX2 6DP, or visit the website at www.oup.com/uk/worldsclassics.

In the USA, visit www.oup.com/us/owc for a complete title list.

Oxford World's Classics are available from all good bookshops. In case of difficulty, customers in the UK should contact Oxford University Press Bookshop, 116 High Street, Oxford OX1 4BR.